Mass society and political conflict

Mass society and political conflict

Toward a reconstruction of theory

SANDOR HALEBSKY

Associate professor of sociology
Saint Mary's University, Halifax, Nova Scotia

CAMBRIDGE UNIVERSITY PRESS

Cambridge
London · New York · Melbourne

39783

Published by the Syndics of the Cambridge University Press
The Pitt Building, Trumpington Street, Cambridge CB2 1RP
Bentley House, 200 Euston Road, London NW1 2DB
32 East 57th Street, New York, NY 10022, USA
296 Beaconsfield Parade, Middle Park, Melbourne 3206, Australia

First published 1976

Printed in the United States of America
Typeset by Bi-Comp, Inc., York, Pennsylvania
Printed and bound by The Murray Printing Company, Forge Village,
Massachusetts

Library of Congress Cataloging in Publication Data

Halebsky, Sandor.
Mass society and political conflict.

Includes bibliographical references and index.

1. Political sociology. 2. Mass society. 3. Pluralism (Social
sciences). 4. Radicalism. I. Title.
JA76.H34   301.5'92   75-18118
ISBN 0 521 20541 7   hardcovers
ISBN 0 521 09884 4   paperback

Contents

Preface

The author sees the present study as part of what has become in recent years an impressive and growing reanalysis of the character of political dissidence. It attempts to make a modest contribution to such an effort by critically analyzing one of the traditional interpretations of political "extremism" and by suggesting some directions for the formulation of a more adequate theoretical approach. Many of the arguments made here have appeared in some form in the work of other students of mass political theory. However, their integration into and formulation in terms of a moderately comprehensive critique of the political theory of mass society have been lacking. Hopefully, the value of this reanalysis is enhanced by being tied to some suggestions for an altered theoretical model.

The thrust of the analysis in the present volume has moved considerably beyond what was envisioned when it was first initiated several years ago. It should serve to spur further efforts to formulate an adequate theoretical framework for the study of mass society and political conflict.

Most scholarship is a lonely enterprise, and the present effort is no exception. Nevertheless, acknowledgment is due and warmly extended to L. Vaughn Blankenship, Marvin Dicker, David Edelstein, and especially Jan Hajda for their helpful comments on one or more chapters of an early manuscript draft. The continued support of Jan Hajda and Marvin Dicker has also been helpful. In addition, the suggestions made by John Leggett, reader for the Cambridge University Press, were pertinent and useful.

S. H.

July 1976

1. *Introduction*

Confronting a century torn by conflict and societies riven by movements of vigorous dissent, an important body of social and political thought has sought to understand and evaluate our times in terms of the concepts of mass society and mass behavior. The theory of mass society contains cultural, social, psychological, and political themes. The focus of the present study will be confined to analyzing critically the political theory contained in the mass society perspective.

The theoretical perspective implicated in the political theory of mass society is one that has markedly influenced contemporary analysis of political phenomena. This is most particularly true for analyses concerned with the origin and character of various forms of vigorous especially "illegal" protest behavior, mass movements, extremism of the right and left, and other presumed aberrations of the ordered procedures and traditional participants in the political process. Thus the mass political theory perspective is one that has been or can be applied to diverse types of political behavior such as Communist, Fascist, and agrarian movements, as well as instances of right-wing extremism, antidemocratic phenomena such as McCarthyism, and student, radical, and poverty protests. It has been used to help understand popular voting behavior as revealed in the response to local referendums, as well as in the more usual circumstances of voting on candidates for political office.

The popularity of at least some of the elements in the mass politics perspective has been considerable. It is a perspective, however, of which a serious and extensive critical examination is long overdue. The present effort constitutes an attempt at such an analysis. Yet it also goes beyond a criticism of the mass society political framework to suggest the inadequacies of a number of related and influential interpretations of radical behavior.

Mass political theory

The concept of a mass society has been used to refer to an extremely wide variety of phenomena: (1) populations manipulated by and

1

directly exposed to elite elements or vice versa or both; (2) societies characterized by their members' involvement in a centrally integrated society of nationwide institutional and ideological structures;[1] (3) to represent a condition of powerlessness, the inability to communicate opinions and needs effectively and to comprehend the nature and source of one's dilemmas; (4) the deteriorated quality of individual and societal life; (5) a mindless uniformity in behavior, beliefs, and expectations; (6) as a condition in which cultural values and performance have declined; (7) and most loosely and without necessarily any pejorative intent, as merely a condition of widespread popular involvement in societal institutions. In its broadest usage the concerns of a mass society involve social, cultural, political, and personal characteristics and phenomena.

Probably the most effective and clearest statement of the theory of mass society is that developed in William Kornhauser's *The Politics of Mass Society*.[2] While concentrating on the political theory of mass society, Kornhauser has succeeded in bringing together within an integrative framework much of the often quite diverse strains of thought in this area. The greater part of Kornhauser's analysis, particularly on the political dimension of mass society, will be of concern later. Here we merely note the central definition he gives to the concept of the mass society. It serves to integrate reasonably a considerable portion of mass theory into a fairly cohesive concept. For Kornhauser mass society can be understood as a distinctive condition exhibited by elites and the general populace or masses, especially in their relationship to each other. This is a condition in which the elites are directly accessible to the masses, and the masses in turn are available for mobilization or manipulation by the elites. This condition or relationship is understood as arising in many though not in all instances from the decline of what Kornhauser calls intermediate group relationships (or the inoperative character of independent organizational and community relationships). Unmediated elite-mass relationships and the lack of viable intermediate groups also produce those negative qualities of individual and societal life, as well as the decline of cultural levels, that constitute the major focuses in the meaning of the mass society concept for many writers. Thus Kornhauser brings together a number of the major themes in the mass society literature, though he clearly concentrates on the political theory of mass society rather than the broader concerns of mass society theory. Somewhat distinct from such a definition but not in conflict with it is the notion of the mass society as the homogeneous society, in which social and political uniformity, rather than variety and diversity, is the rule.

The political theory of mass society per se can be contrasted with the more diverse and far-ranging concerns of the mass society literature by its focus on the political characteristics and dynamics of the mass society.[3] This essentially refers to the character of political behavior in mass society, the relationship between the political leadership and the broader citizenry, and the consequences for politics and political behavior of the circumstances and feeling tone of this citizenry. A significant feature of the political theory of mass society is its focus on the consequences of the preceding features for democracy and their relationship to antidemocratic behavior and the appearance of totalitarianism. Two major concerns are involved: (1) the character of mass behavior and its consequence for democracy and the appearance of totalitarianism and (2) a theory about the preconditions or circumstances that underlie such behavior. While both are constituent elements of mass political theory, it is possible to express a concern over the nature of mass behavior and its potential antidemocratic consequences in terms similar to those used by mass theorists but without acceptance of the broader political theory of mass society in regard to the preconditions of such behavior. As my later evaluation of mass political theory will treat both dimensions of the theory, part of what I have to say will perforce have a relevance for the work and perspectives of writers who are not mass political theorists in the fullest sense.

The concept of the mass society and mass politics had its origin in the intellectual response to the nature of change and stress apparent since the end of the eighteenth century. It was partly a reaction to the social, cultural, and political changes associated with the increasing industrialization, rationalization, and vertical integration of society. Thus it was also a reaction to the growing strength of previously disenfranchised social and economic groups that assumed an increasing social and political role, at times even a revolutionary one. In a more contemporary vein, mass political theory reflects a response to the tragic disruptions and conflicts of recent history. These have revealed horrors to which ordinary men acquiesed and in which, at times, they even pursued active roles.

Areas of critical assessment

While an increasingly diverse literature has begun to raise reservations about several aspects of the political theory of mass society, no broad and searching critical analysis has yet been undertaken. The present essay initiates such analysis by examining a number of the major features and assumptions of this theory. The criticism developed in the following chapters seriously questions the adequacy of mass political theory's interpretation of the origin, determinants, and nature of vigorous political protest and extremism. In effect, two major dimensions of criticism are developed: First is the adequacy of the theory's description and the interpretation of social and political properties of contemporary society. Second are serious weaknesses in its theory of the roots of political behavior. The latter – involving the interpretations of the bases or origins of support for radical political behavior – is closely related to insufficiencies in the theory's descriptive face.

The present work suggests that a fundamental problem from which many others arise is the inadequacy of social structural analysis. The difficulties here are both descriptive and theoretical. In the former regard serious shortcomings are discussed in mass theory's conceptualization and analysis of the character and consequence of intermediate group personal relationships and social structures. Also, the adequacy of the gross mass–nonmass dichotomy is open to serious question. Further elaborated is the vagueness present in the use of the concept mass and its application to populations that are essentially nonmass in any consistent or reasonable sense of the term. Related is the failure to distinguish among major types of social categories or collectivities. In mass political theory little attention is given to the location of populations within class and broader social structural forms and the consequent character of group interests' needs and their role in determining consciousness and protest. This begins to point to some theoretical insufficiencies in the theory's model of the origin of political behavior.

Within these terms exception is taken to the characteristics imputed to dissident behavior and to the appropriateness of labelling as mass behavior many instances of vigorous political protest. The terms "mass" and "mass behavior" tend to be applied to any class or other social collectivity acting outside the traditional complex of political forms and forces, even when there is not that absence of distinctive group structure or condition of personal estrangement that is presumably the precondition for the appearance of the mass.

There are serious omissions and inadequacies in the analysis of political society. The character of the existing political structure and its functioning is not analyzed by mass political theory. This has meant the absence of attention to the degree to which political responsiveness is present for group needs of significant collectives. Variations in this and other regards would be crucial in evaluating the character, meaning, appropriateness, consequences, and the like, of political behavior or protest. In another direction, the mass theorist's use and assumptions regarding the concept of pluralism are open to serious question. Also, the cohesion and democratic consequences of the nationally integrated homogeneous society are passed over, though little elaboration in these terms is developed in the present essay.

Analysis in broader systemic and historical terms would often suggest, I maintain, the reasonableness of radical protest and at times its contribution – albeit on occasion in terms of long-run consequences – to the strengthening of democratic and humanistic values and social structures. In a related direction, mass political theory lacks an appreciation of the relevance of a more participatory and representative democratic structure and of the positive rather than negative consequences that could develop from such structures and practices. Conversely, in mass theory there is essentially no attention given to the role of established and respectable elite elements in either directly or otherwise bringing about political instability and irrationality and the appearance of mass behavior, political extremism, or mass movements.

An analysis of mass political theory would be seriously incomplete without a consideration of its reliance on pluralist and contemporary democratic theory. In the description of and assumptions concerning contemporary democratic societies, mass political theorists conclude that such polities are pluralist. A preference for a pluralist political order is clearly exhibited in their work. While the writers of pluralist persuasion are not necessarily mass theorists – nor do mass theorists necessarily identify themselves as pluralists – mass political theory clearly evidences not only a pluralist perspective but also pluralist conclusions about stable contemporary democratic regimes. Later analysis in the present volume introduces serious qualifications in these regards, particularly as applied to the United States. Some attention will be given to the character and forms of political representation, community and national power structures, the theory of political balance, current formulations of the meaning of democracy, and the role of the citizen in democratic society.

Models of radical political behavior

An integral part of the present analysis is a criticism of the theory of behavior used to account for radical politics that is implicit in both mass political theory and a set of related explanations of the origins of support for radicalism or extremism. Thus a critical review of mass political theory offers the opportunity of suggesting directions for the reformulation of theory regarding the bases of support for radical politics. Some effort is made, particularly in the case analysis chapter, to suggest some of the bases for a revised political behavioral model. These can be understood in the context of currently conflicting interpretations of radical support.

Mass political theory is merely one variant of a broader set of social psychological theories of radical political behavior. Since the late 1930s these have dominated the social sciences. They have stressed the presumably mass, simplistic, affective, and psychological properties of support for political dissidence. Such prevailing theory has assumed various forms. It includes, of course, the political theory of mass society, as well as various forms of the frustration-aggression hypothesis, related mobility and migration models, the theory of the authoritarian personality, status theory, and theory on political alienation.[4] It is assumed that support for radicalism is found among various elements. Some stress the role of uprooted, anomic, and isolated populations; others, the appeal of radicalism to those with frustrated ambitions or unreachable expectations and those in circumstances of apparent relative deprivation. Support from the socially insecure and from those living in circumstances viewed as productive of authoritarian personal traits is also stressed. The extremist is perceived as often politically untutored, uninterested in politics and impatient. Briefly, "radicalism is viewed by these theories as an abnormal or deviant development constituting, in essence, a simplistic emotional reaction to personal frustrations and solitude."[5]

In what have been the dominant theoretical approaches, social structural analysis and attention to political, cultural, and historical factors have been slighted. Thus the locus of dissidence and its participants within structures of power and representation, class conflict, systems of social hierarchy, patterns of historical loyalties and animosities have been ignored. The circumstances of disparate individuals rather than of collectivities have usually been the focus of attention, though even here a significant element of exteriority has characterized the mode of analysis and interpretation of individual circumstances. Attention has not been given to processes of communication, political socialization, the development of class and interest consciousness, and changing perceptions of the political order and legitimacy. The role of changing political resources and the process of political mobilization in translating grievance and potential radical support into actual behavior are ignored. Certainly on the phenomenological level there has been no recognition of the importance of interactionist and symbolic processes and the individual's effort to develop a meaningful grasp of his political environment.

Since about 1960, but especially in the past few years, however, a vigorous body of research and theory has emerged that has helped initiate a critical reassessment of prevailing perspectives.[6] It is a reassessment that provides a much greater stress on the purposive and cognitive qualities, the social structural and cultural origins, and, in a sense, on the "ordinariness" of support for political dissidence. As a total body of work, these efforts point to the necessity of interpreting radical or dissident political behavior in terms of its roots in social structural, political, cultural, and ideological factors. They focus more on the circumstances, shared experience, common purposes, and behavior of collectivities than on isolated individuals. Dissidence is perceived as part of a broader condition of group and class conflict, struggles over power, and differences over societal policy, among other considerations. Such an approach permits and, in a fuller analysis, requires attention to the role of ideology and group consciousness.[7] It may in fact be suggested that in some circumstances needs and circumstances will not change as much as conditions of consciousness or the spread of new interpretive schemes. Similarly, it may be altered governmental effectiveness, the growth of dissident leadership, declining legitimacy of established leadership and parties, and so on, rather than objectively altered individual and group circumstances that account for radical support, either directly or through their effect on consciousness. These types of considerations, however, do not fall within the framework of prevailing theory.

Some of this work also suggests, either explicitly or implicitly, that the development of radical or dissident political loyalties reflects a process essentially similar to the development of more traditional or moderate political attitudes and commitments. Thus the focus would be on the processes of political socialization, communication, interpersonal associations, individual assessments of the political system, and notions of legitimacy and trust that are usually relied on to interpret more moderate forms of political behavior. Implicit in some of this work and consistent with the analytic framework of most of the other efforts is a stress on the actor's purposive negotiation of his political and social environment, as one important component of a broader causal model.

This type of analysis, which can be deduced from theory and research emerging in the past decade or so, is a distinct advance over the interpretations provided by either mass political theory or other psychological-based models. And given the nature of readily available material these are essentially the terms that have guided the elaboration of the case material in Chapter 5 and my criticism of mass political theory. However, there is little as yet in the way of an overall explanatory model that integrates macrosociological properties with circumstances and experiences on the individual level, that combines structural analysis with a phenomenological analysis of how the individual constructs a meaningful comprehension of his political and social environment, and how he negotiates this environment. I would suggest that the development of an adequate interpretive model of political dissidence must move in such a direction. Its usefulness should be suggested by even the quite partial application of such an approach in my interpretations of instances of radical support (Chapter 5). Thus while the discussion throughout the present work will essentially be of a critical character, it is hoped that it will also provide some direction for a reformulation of sociopolitical analysis.

In brief and in the broadest terms, then, the criticism of mass political theory and other related approaches elaborated in the following pages and conversely the alternative type of analysis suggested stress the following fundamental points. The first is the necessity of systemic analysis, both in regard to examining the social structural basis of individual group membership and the influence on behavior of social, cultural, and political subsystems. Second, attention to the responsiveness of political forms is vital. This relates to the preceding point and to the third criterion, the need for a more phenomenological analysis. How the individual himself experiences and makes sense of his political and social circumstances must be considered. In effect, it is contended that radical or extremist commitments can be interpreted as developing out of the same ordinary or typical processes that account for more traditional loyalties. Lastly, it is necessary to distinguish between potential support for political dissidence and radical behavior itself. The latter cannot be comprehended merely at the level of individual properties but requires a macrolevel analysis, focusing particularly on the changing balance of power and processes of political mobilization. In these different regards serious inadequacies exist in mass political theory and other psychological approaches.

The following two chapters serve to provide an account of both the intellectual origins of mass political theory and a vigorous summary statement of the character of the theory itself. This is followed by three extended analytic chapters that develop the criticisms and perspectives previously suggested. The first criticizes mass political theory for its weakness in social structural analysis. Involved here are issues of descriptive and theoretical adequacy. The second chapter provides a number of case analyses of radical behavior illustrating the inappropriateness of mass political analysis and stressing an approach more attentive to social structural, social organizational, and political institutional factors and, somewhat more implicitly, to the phenomenological world of the individual. These analyses provide a partial illustration of the alternative theoretical approach urged in the present work. The last of the three chapters is a critical assessment of the pluralist perspective. The concluding chapter comments on questions of ideological bias in contemporary political theory and provides some suggestions for further research.

2. *Intellectual origins of and contributions to mass political theory*

Mass society theory is partly derived from and significantly influenced by a number of major elements of Western social and political thought.[1] A comprehension of mass theory, particularly its political dimension, is enhanced by attention to these earlier ideological currents. Political theorists, both of a liberal and a conservative character, have been influential, writing partly as a response to Enlightenment and rationalist thought as well as to the French Revolution. Most significant, perhaps, is the extensive body of sociological analysis on the character of societal change. There is a smaller yet also influential series of sociological writings on the nature of crowds and masses. In addition, the existentialists and other writers in the romantic tradition have contributed to the mass society perspective, though principally to its nonpolitical components. The present discussion, however, will make little reference to the latter tradition.

The major themes developed by these earlier intellectual traditions and upon which mass political thory has drawn include the preservation of the hierarchically ordered organic community, the necessity of maintaining pluralist structures of power, the danger of the unfettered majority in democratic polities, the changing character of community, belonging, and organizational structures, the isolation of the individual and the weakening of normative commitments, and the irrational and emotional nature of crowds and masses.

Response to the thought of the Enlightenment

Mass political theory may be partly understood as a critical response to a body of English and especially French thought that developed principally in the eighteenth century, beginning with the English liberalitarian Enlightenment and later utilitarian thinkers, but finding fuller expression, for our concerns, in the French philosophes or Encyclopedists. The following discussion describes the interpretation given by mass theorists to Rousseau and the concept of general will and to

10

the work of the philosophes, with some attention to the response to the English Enlightenment and utilitarian figures. I am not concerned with evaluating the appropriateness of the interpretations made by mass society theorists; what is important is how they have perceived and responded to this body of thought.

Rousseau and the general will

It is the work of Rousseau that has perhaps evoked the strongest response.[2] A powerful and frequently referred to element in Rousseau's philosophy is his concept of the general will. Albeit not defined in unambiguous terms, it is a key notion of his celebrated treatise, *The Social Contract,* and forms the basis of a good deal of the mass theorists' response not only to Rousseau but more broadly to the development of what has been called totalitarian democracy. Rousseau does not clearly elaborate his concept of the general will, however, and his treatment permits a considerable disparity of interpretation. For the present purposes we are less concerned with what Rousseau may actually have meant than with the reading generally given his work, though more extreme and agitated versions are excluded. Essentially, the general will is that sentiment that embodies the sense of the total community. It refers to the attitudes or purposes that inhere in the community as a unity and not a congeries of disparate elements. It has an existence of its own that exists distinct from the disparate interests and purposes of its individual members. It represents, Rousseau states, "only the common interest."[3] The idea of the general will clearly contains the sense that the community or society is more than merely a sum of its diverse parts. Society represents a collective and moral entity, not merely an aggregation of individuals. The purposes and the interest of society constitute the general will, which is the true will of the individual members. Hence it may differ from individual purpose or interests – the citizen's private interests: "... it has a collective good which is not the same thing as the private interests of its members. In some sense it lives its own life, fulfills its own destiny and suffers its own faith."[4] The general will takes priority over individual interests. Actually, however, there is no difference Rousseau maintained between the will of the community and the true will of the individual. The problem is that the individual may be ignorant of his true will, of what in fact he would desire if he either possessed adequate knowledge or had not been misled by tradition and corrupting institutions and beliefs.

For Rousseau the state or community in which men have joined together by accepting a social contract is preeminent over its individual members, as well as such associations, groups, or organizations of which its citizens may be members. He is suspicious of associations and relationships independent from the state. The individualism of Locke's natural law is replaced by the collectivism of Rousseau's general will, and the sovereignty of the people as a whole, not the individual or his distinct groups, is stressed and paramount.[5] Rousseau perceives the state as the locus of man's hopes and interests. Through it men achieve their purposes and secure their freedom.[6] Man and the state are not in contention; essentially they are one. Rousseau maintains that "the Sovereign, being formed wholly of the individuals who compose it, neither has nor can have any interest contrary to theirs. . . ."[7] The state demands unqualified obedience; because it represents the general will and not merely the prejudicial or private purposes of individuals or groups within the broader society, it cannot err. It is by means of the state that conditions of equality, resolution of conflict, and the freeing of man from the constraints and disabilities of traditional society are achieved. Other commitments impede the sovereignty and functions of the state. Sovereignty, as the exercise of the general will, is inalienable and indivisible. It "can be represented by itself alone"[8] and cannot be general if it is divisible. Commitments to other associations could be interpreted as denying or being contrary to this property of the general will. One has rights within the community represented by the state, but not against it. Yet, at the same time, Rousseau did affirm inalienable individual rights.

Rousseau contended that by participating in the social contract and putting himself under the control of the general will man gains a greater liberty than the rights he loses. But, because of ignorance, perversity, or other reasons, man may be unaware of the benefits of membership in and obedience to the will of the community. Given this circumstance and that without the compliance of all men the social contract and general will are undermined, Rousseau concluded that it may be necessary to compel men to be free:

In order then that the social compact may not be an empty formula, it tacitly includes the undertaking, which alone can give force to the rest, that whoever refuses to obey the general will shall be compelled to do so by the whole body. This means nothing less than that he will be forced to be free; for this is the condition which, by giving each citizen to his country, secures him against all personal dependence.[9]

Sabine has voiced the sentiment of other scholars in his remark that "this kind of argument, in Rousseau and after him Hegel, was a dangerous experiment in juggling with ambiguities."[10] Yet for Rousseau greater freedom and a closer correspondence with man's natural state were attained by submission of the individual to the general will under conditions of equality than by submission to other individuals or groups in circumstances of inequality.

Critical response to Rousseau

The terms in which the mass theorist has critically responded to the thought of Rousseau, and particularly to what is perceived as the logical consequence or development of his ideas, are several. The contention is not that Rousseau and his followers were totalitarian or unconcerned with the well-being of the individual, but rather that while desiring freedom and opportunity for men, they propounded a philosophy in which the "morbid course of development into totalitarian conditions"[11] was laid. The identification of Rousseau's doctrine with freedom[12] has presumably misled men to accept at face value a doctrine that later theorists have taken to be a means toward the servitude of men. To postulate a general will and a common shared interest that it expresses and that can be known has created the condition for a single party to present itself as the embodiment of the general will. Other contending parties then become open not only to the charge of superfluity but, more seriously, to subversion and action counter to the interests of the community.

The practical conclusion drawn from this doctrine, not by Rousseau himself, but by the Jacobins, was the foundation of a single political party to embody the general will. Its logical conclusions were still more far-reaching. The individual, far from enjoying rights against society assured to him by natural law, had no appeal against the deliverances of the general will. The general will was the repository of virtue and justice, the state its instrument for putting them into effect. The individual who dissented from the general will cut himself off from the community and was a self proclaimed traitor to it. Rousseau's doctrine led directly to the Jacobin practice of revolutionary terror.[13]

The mass theorist has further developed his critique of Rousseau in a number of directions. For the mass theorist "Rousseau sees the State as the most exalted of all forms of moral community. For Rousseau there is no morality, no freedom, no community outside the structure of the State."[14] The mass theorist reacts with the greatest aversion to Rousseau's opposition to associations counter to the state. It is suggested that opposition to traditional forms involves a destruction of pluralistic conditions and the first true steps toward the dreaded condition of totalitarianism. "It is in the bearing of Rousseau's general will upon traditional society, however, that the full sweep of its totalitarian significance becomes manifest."[15] Talmon has similarly contended that "the idea of man as an abstraction, independent of the historic groups to which he belongs, is likely to become a powerful vehicle of totalitarianism."[16] Part of the response here is to the "image of the people" imputed to Rousseau's notion of the general will. People were viewed by Rousseau, the mass theorist claims, as an entity apart from "the actual plurality of persons which experience revealed," and disassociated "from existing institutions and beliefs and brought into the single association of the people's State."[17]

A fundamental problem in a concept such as the general will, the mass theorist suggests, is who shall interpret this will and when such an interpretation can be accepted. Usually, whichever group is in power will claim for itself the role of representing and interpreting the general will. The theoretical nature of this concept provides little ground for effectively contesting such a claim. Further, and especially oppressive, "when a regime is by definition regarded as realizing rights and freedoms, the citizen becomes deprived of any right to complain that he is being deprived of his rights and liberties."[18] In effect, the citizen is in a number of ways deprived of the propriety or legitimacy of difference. Present policy and its representatives are to be understood as acting in terms of the individual's interests, a realization of which is only prevented by the ignorance or perversity of the individual. The citizen lacks other acceptable standards or bases for contradicting or presenting contrary opinions. Given that the truth is contained in the person of the general will, to differ is to be in error, and to persist in opposition after being informed of one's error by the state, as an expression of the general will, is to subvert the society. The situation is aggravated by the absence of a concept of natural law and natural rights which if present could be counterposed to the demands of the state. Lacking such rights the citizen is dependent exclusively on the state's interpretation of what his rights are and the knowledge that what the state gives it can take away.

In effect, the mass theorist argues, the logic of Rousseau's philosophy leads to totalitarianism. More particularly, the phenomenon that develops has been referred to as totalitarian democracy because it involves and rests on masses and mass consent. A Rousseau-type argument is seen by the mass theorist as underlying recent totalitarian democratic regimes and as still a potent force in populistic movements and forms of rule.

The philosophes and Enlightenment
and utilitarian thought

Briefer note is made here of mass theory's response to the French rationalists or philosophes to whom Rousseau bears a significant relationship and to other elements in Enlightenment and utilitarian thought. It is to the body of thought of men such as Locke, Adam Smith, Bentham, Voltaire, Diderot, Holbach, Helvetius, and Condorcet, among others, that reference is made. The differences in thought among them are considerable. Some basic common themes, however, that serve as the basis for the mass theorist response can be briefly stated.

The stress on reason is clear. In the words of Crane Brinton's descriptive summary: "Reason will enable us to find human institutions, human relations that are 'natural'; once we find such institutions, we shall conform to them and be happy. Reason will clear up the mess that superstitions, revelation, faith (the devils of the rationalists) have piled up here on earth."[19] The world could be known by the application of reason, and social life and institutions restructured and guided by its application. This rationalist component is joined to an equal attention to the concept that there is a natural man and a natural order of society that have been distorted by human institutions.[20] The Enlightenment, especially the philosophes, marked as they were by rationalism, a scientific spirit, and skepticism, involved both a critique of traditional institutions and whatever kept man in bondage, as well as implied a new conception of man that stressed his inherent goodness. The focus is on the individual and individual rights and freedoms and not on community and ties to traditional beliefs and practices.

An important feature of this philosophy is its conception of the nature of man. Man is seen as naturally good; yet as Rousseau, Condorcet, and Helvetius reasoned, man is a product of circumstances. Thus while they recognized that the mass of men may not appear sensitive, wise, reasonable, or capable of political rule, this was seen as due to the constraints and inadequacies of their environment. Until these are removed, men in fact may act irrationally and intemperately. If man appears other than good, one must change the circumstances – which in the Enlightenment in effect meant traditional institutions, religious constraints, ancient privileges, corrupt rule, and the like. Man is malleable and perfectable. Thus the moral and good man could be created or fashioned.

There are a number of other important elements present in this influential body of thought. An important theme is its belief in both liberty and equality. Freedom was a necessity if man, through his use of reason, is to improve his circumstances. The free and the just society recognizes and is not in conflict with equality among men. In contrast to later thought, equality is not perceived as a constraint upon a meaningful expression of freedom. We have here an optimistic perspective, one oriented to progressive improvement. This is also expressed in the interpretation of history as a progressive development of man's moral and social circumstances. Man could shape his own destiny and the character of society. Not surprisingly, the proper aim of government is to realize the interests of its citizenry, and this required action rather than inaction. An activist stance is further buttressed by the belief in the ability of man and society to achieve an increasing certainty in social and human affairs.

Judith Shklar opens her notable study *After Utopia* with lines appropriately reflective of the critical response that developed to this body of thought.

In the beginning was the Enlightenment. . . . Yet nothing is quite so dead today as the spirit of optimism that the very word Enlightenment evokes. Indeed, we are faced not with the mere end of the Enlightenment but with the prevalence of theories that arose in opposition to it. If the Enlightenment still figures in the realm of ideas it is as a foil for attack, not as an inspiration to new ideas.[21]

The oft cited optimism of the philosophes and the Enlightenment resides in their stress on reason, progress, and the goodness of man. For later theories they provided too limited a conception of the bases of human action and too positive an affirmation of the potential of man and intellect. It was felt that in their optimism they overlooked the possible disparity between public and private purposes, the conflict between the interests of the individual and those of society, and the constraints on freedom that attainment of social purposes might involve. In view of mass political theorists it was by failing to recognize these antinomies that this body of thought lent itself to later ideological developments denying such conflict and stressing the compatibility of individual needs and purposes with state demands and the fulfillment of freedom in acquiescence to state authoritarianism. Thus a potential for repression is perceived in a body of thought that vigorously voiced the freedom and liberation of man.

Further, to the contemporary mass theorist the affirmation by the philosophes and other Enlightenment figures of man's ability to alter and improve his world greatly, when joined with an emphasis on the prerequisite need of releasing man from the bondage of ignorance, tradition, and oppression, has had distressing consequences. It has helped open the door and provide legitimacy for the suppression of dissent and minority belief and for unnecessarily intrusive, violent, and ill-considered political action by an increasingly large proportion of previously inactive masses. To the much agitated mass theorist this has been, in effect, a call to overturn what is, in the delusion that man, freed from traditional restraints, could create the good society. In "The Overpassing of the Bound," a section of his essay "The Decline of the West," Walter Lippman vigorously expressed this typical response of the mass theorist by affirming that

This is the root of the matter, and it is here that the ultimate issue lies. Can men, acting like gods, be appointed to establish heaven on earth? If we believe that they can be, then the rest follows. To fulfill their mission they must assume a godlike omnipotence. They must be jealous gods, monopolizing power, destroying all rivals, compelling exclusive loyalty. The family, the churches, the schools, the corporations, the labor unions and cooperative societies, the voluntary associations and all the arts and sciences, must be their servants. Dissent and deviation are treason and quietism is sacrilege.

. . .

The Jacobins and their successors made a political religion founded upon the reversal of civility. Instead of ruling the elemental impulses, they stimulated and armed them. Instead of treating the pretension of being a god as the mortal sin original, they proclaimed it to be the glory and destiny of man. Upon this gospel they founded a popular religion of the rise of the masses to power. Lenin, Hitler and Stalin, the hard totalitarian Jacobins of the twentieth century, carried this movement and the logical implications of its gospel further and further towards the very bitter end.[22]

In his powerful work, *The Rise of Totalitarian Democracy,* Jacob Talmon discussed the intellectual traditions to which I have referred. He suggested that there are several elements in these traditions that have contributed to the rise of totalitarianism. The idea of a natural order and the stress on the exercise of reason open up the possibility of labeling extant forms as unnatural and help encourage attempts to replace them with planned uniform patterns, with social utility replacing tradition. The denial of the idea of status contains totalitarian potentialities as it suggests the idea of a homogeneous society characterized by a uniform level of existence. He held, of course, that Rousseau's concept of the general will lays the ground for the appearance of a sovereign or state that by definition cannot err or hurt man. The stress is on unity, not diversity. When the regime is defined as realizing rights and freedoms, the citizen cannot very well claim to be deprived. People are to be influenced or educated to understand where their interests lie and how they should act. Those who are unenlightened will not fail to recognize their interests if properly explained. Further, the idea of a people becomes restricted to those who identify themselves with the general will. To Talmon the developments in France at the time of the French Revolution "were the earliest versions of modern political Messianism"[23] or what Talmon has called totalitarian democracy.[24] In his concluding pages Talmon summarized the argument of the mass theorist developed in the preceding discussion.

Totalitarian democracy, far from being a phenomenon of recent growth ... has its roots in the common stock of eighteenth century ideas. It branched out as a separate and identifiable trend in the course of the French Revolution and has had an unbroken continuity ever since. ...

It was the eighteenth century idea of the natural order (or general will) as an attainable, indeed inevitable and all-solving, end, that engendered an attitude of mind unknown hitherto in the sphere of politics, namely the sense of a continuous advance towards a *dénouement* of the historical drama, accompanied by an acute awareness of a structural and incurable crisis in existing society. This state of mind found its expression in the totalitarian democratic tradition. ...

Totalitarian democracy early evolved into a pattern of coercion and centralization not because it rejected the values of eighteenth century liberal individualism, but because it had originally a too perfectionist attitude towards them. It made man the absolute point of reference. Man was not merely to be freed from restraints. All the existing traditions, established institutions, and social arrangements were to be overthrown and remade, with the sole purpose of securing to man the totality of his rights and freedoms, and liberating him from all dependence. ... All the emphasis came to be placed on the destruction of inequalities, on bringing down the privileged to the level of common humanity, and on sweeping away all intermediate centres of power and allegiance, whether social classes, regional communities, professional groups or corporations. Nothing was left to stand between man and the State. The power of the State, unchecked by any intermediate agencies, became unlimited. This exclusive relationship between man and State implied conformity.[25]

Thus while the influential body of Enlightenment thought was developed to free man, to point the way toward a better life and society, to open up opportunities for maximizing human potential, and to strike down the shackles of ignorance and irrelevant custom, the mass political theorist has held that it can lead to quite opposite ends. Man may become increasingly isolated and powerless, an abject subject of a mass "democratic" state on which he depends not only for social, psychic, and political needs but for whatever restricted liberties he may possess and the very security of his person. Even the ideological or philosophic rationale for individual and group freedom becomes undermined.

The liberal tradition of the nineteenth century

Some of the principal perspectives in the contemporary political theory of mass society find support in the writings of some of the major liberal political philosophers of the nineteenth century. While to an extent these writers may be understood in terms of their relationship to the thought of the Enlightenment, in some important respects they also reflect a shift away from the Enlightenment.[26] Regardless of whether nineteenth-century liberalism is interpreted as a disillusioned response to the Enlightenment or as merely reflecting a somewhat altered theoretical emphasis given changes in class, power, and general political circumstances, it is frequently perceived both as providing a perspective partly contributory to mass political theory and as exhibiting a recognition of the desirability of greater constraints on majority action and the need to temper earlier enthusiasms for democratic rule.

This changed emphasis in the developing liberal tradition of the nineteenth century, upon which the mass theorist has drawn, contains several features. These include a commitment to individual freedom and the need to preserve liberties, the necessity of constraining the exercise and concentration of power, a recognition of the fallibility of man, and yet also a tempered trust in the reasonableness and rationality of man. The last point, though, receives less attention in mass theory. Nineteenth-century liberalism is a political philosophy with a more moderate and modified faith in man and a less innovative and radical critique of society. It suggests change but not revolution, opportunity but not complete equality, freedom but not without constraints. It is in the political and historical analyses and theory of Tocqueville, John Mill, and Lord Acton, among others, that the nineteenth-century liberal philosophy of caution, "retrenchment," and disillusionment with the masses finds expression. It is a philosophy that still retains, however, a belief in freedom as a primary value and a secular and worldly emphasis, though on the whole the former hostility to religion is absent. The belief in progress is much tempered. Mill expressed greater hope in this regard than the more conservative French thinker Tocqueville; but even for this son of Enlightenment and utilitarian thought an element of pessimism is present. While accepting change and reform, these nineteenth-century thinkers could, for instance, stress the conserving force of a national constitution and the value of social traditions. There is, therefore, a qualified belief in the ability of man to improve and also in the possibility of achieving the good life, though man's shortcomings posed constraints or limitations in these regards.

They sought to delineate, in famous works such as Tocqueville's *Democracy in America,* the dangers to freedom that inhere in conceptions of mass democracy, majority rule, or sovereignty of the whole people. The feeling expressed in these writings is that in important ways a condition of masses did characterize democratic society in the mid-nineteenth century and that this mass is a "collective mediocrity" that shapes "public opinion (that) now rules the world."[27] Mill spoke elegantly of the "tyranny of the majority" and of "when society is itself the tyrant. . . . Protection . . . against the tyranny of the magistrate is not enough: there needs protection also against the tyranny of society to impose, by other means than civil penalties, its own ideas and practices as rules of conduct on those who dissent from them. . . ."[28] There is a concern with the ability to maintain diversity, difference, and, ultimately, freedom. It is not only public opinion or the majority that is perceived as a threat but public authority or society buttressed by mass opinion or support. In effect, the strain between liberty and democracy is expressed in the work and intellectual heritage of the nineteenth-century liberal. There were increasing doubts concerning the nature and consequences of power, even where it was power possessed by a democratic state. It was Lord Acton who coined the expression that "power corrupts, and absolute power corrupts absolutely." It was in the light of such apprehensions that an important element of liberal concern became the effort to guard against the unfettered exercise of power by the majority of men. Not surprisingly, progress is increasingly understood as manifested by the actions of an intellectual elite rather than those of the greater majority of the society.[29] Mill did not perceive representative government as adequate or effective if it did not contain a place for knowledge and selflessness, properties not likely to be found, he felt, in the ordinary voter or merely in the quantified majority. Shklar has appropriately referred to the liberal philosophy of this period as a "liberalism without self-confidence" and "an intellectualism devoid of optimism."[30]

Tocqueville on democracy and the centralization and diffusion of power

One of the most significant contributions to mass political theory in nineteenth-century political thought was the stress on the importance of voluntary associations and intermediate structures for the preservation of liberty in democratic states. The concern here is a continuation of the attention given by the nineteenth-century liberal to the dangers inhering in the democratic community and to the threat of possible tyranny by the majority. The problem of creating restraints on centralized power as an expression of majority sentiments was scarcely an issue before the eighteenth century and of little practical importance until the nineteenth century. It has been viewed as especially important, however, during the present century. It began to be a phenomenon of possible concern only with the increasing democratization and the growing involvement of the "masses" in the past century and a half, particularly with the increasing extension and growing legitimacy of a role by a centralized state. The seminal discussion in Tocqueville of the role of voluntary associations[31] reflects the concern over majority rule and the preservation of freedom in response to the increasing political involvement of the citizens, the experiences of the French Revolution, and the development of Rousseau's concept of the general will.

In Tocqueville's discussion of the nature and characteristics of democracy and the nature of change in democratic society, the central problems of nineteenth-century liberalism secured some of their profoundest consideration. Tocqueville's treatment of voluntary associations and the distribution of power resident therein stems from some of the major concerns he shared with other liberals of the first half of the century in their "effort to define their attitude toward the Enlightenment and democracy on the one hand and to conservatism on the other."[32] Together with other liberals Tocqueville, while favorably disposed to democracy, argued that the danger of oppression inheres in democratic polities. He reasoned that given the social, economic, and political egalitarian concerns of the democratic society – concerns that he perceived as becoming increasingly dominant – pressure naturally develops upon the state for action to produce equality. This would in turn reduce the prerogatives and ability of private associations to function in areas of policy preempted by state action. Such a possible train of events would further suggest that there will be a stifling of diversity and a movement toward uniformity, as a single agency rather than many varied associations attended to community and personal needs. The dynamics of such a process leads to the assumption of total power in the hands of the state, with which it then controls a population made supine by the abdication of both power and initiative to a state that presumably acts to meet popular needs. Tocqueville's description of the totalitarian state that could evolve out of such a democratic polity is one of the most powerful in the literature and suggests the source of the great influence he has exercised on the contemporary theorist of mass society.

Above this race of men stands an immense and tutelary power, which takes upon itself alone to secure their gratifications and to watch over their fate. That power is absolute, minute, regular, provident and mild. It would be like the authority of a parent if, like that authority, its object was to prepare men for manhood; but it seeks, on the contrary, to keep them in a perpetual state of childhood; it is well content that people should rejoice, provided they think of nothing but rejoicing. For their happiness such a government willingly labors, but it chooses to be the sole agent and the only arbiter of that happiness; it provides for their security, foresees and supplies their necessities, facilitates their pleasures, manages their principal concerns, directs their industry, regulates the descent of property and subdivides their inheritances: what remains, but to spare them all the care of thinking and of all the troubles of living?

. . .

After having thus successively taken each member of the community in its powerful grasp and fashioned him at will, the supreme power then extends its arm over the whole community. It covers the surface of society with a network of small complicated rules, minute and uniform, through which the most original minds and the most energetic characters cannot penetrate, to rise above the crowd. The will of man is not shattered, but softened, bent, and guided; men are seldom forced by it to act, but they are constantly restrained from acting. Such a power does not destroy, but it prevents existence; it does not tyrannize, but it compresses, enervates, extinguishes, and stupefies a people, till each nation is reduced to nothing better than a flock of timid and industrious animals, of which the government is the shepherd.[33]

The potency for mass theory of the line of reasoning developed by Tocqueville is revealed in a comment by a distinguished mass society theorist, Robert Nisbet: ". . . the merit of Tocqueville's analysis is that it points directly to the heart of totalitarianism – the masses. . . . And the genius of his analysis lies in the view of totalitarianism as something not historically 'abnormal' but as closely related to the very trends hailed as progressive in the nineteenth century."[34]

One of the vital elements of a solution to the problems Tocqueville raised was contained in his stress on the necessity of a large number of voluntary associations. In effect, he suggested that such associations serve several functions: They are a means for the expression of the problems, interests, and needs of the diversity of populations within the society; they are also a means of reducing a sense of powerlessness and attendant frustrations. A sense of participation and involvement may also be provided, as such associations offer a means of handling and satisfying at least part of one's needs without recourse to state action. Participation in associations also serves an educative function. Further, he suggests, it advances individual self-interest while furthering the overall common good. Last is the important function of such associations to provide centers of power counter to that of the state. This offers protection not only to minorities and minority interests but also mitigates the possibility of oppression by the state over the broader society. Tocqueville's esteem rests in part on his prescience and his sense of the nature of democratic polities and, more particularly, on his thoughts on the problem of majority tyranny and domination of the citizenry by the democratic state.

Conservative contributions to mass political theory

A portion of mass political theory draws support from conservative as well as liberal theorists. It has found a fruitful ideological heritage in the late eighteenth- and nineteenth-century conservative and Catholic writers. They stressed the necessity for the continuance of traditional forms within the framework of an organic community.

It has been said that in "reaction against the optimistic faith of the eighteenth century in the power of individual reason to fashion and refashion social systems" the conservative Catholic writers Louis de Bonald and Joseph de Maistre "revived all the dead elements of a transcendental philosophy of history – Divine Providence, original sin, final causes, and an infallible Church."[35] Nisbet observed that "it was to the Middle Ages that most of the nineteenth century conservatives looked for inspiration in their revolt against revolutionary secularism, power, and individualism."[36] Thinkers such as Maistre, Bonald, and Burke, among others, evidence in their critical response to Enlightenment thought a number of major themes that carry a significant import for the development of mass theory. They questioned the presumably naïve rationalism of the Enlightenment and the reasonableness that it imputed to man, as well as the Enlightenment contention that man could and should apply his reason to creating the better society. Thus they stressed the positive role of tradition, authority, and religion in maintaining the stable society and averred that human institutions could only be understood as the product of a long-term organic development. They emphasized the need to maintain the integrity and continuance of existing societal institutions, hierarchy, and tradition. A society lacking continuity with its past heritage will lack a sense of direction and suffer the loss of guidelines for wise action, as well as experience the rise of a mass rootless population.

Being that "the objects of society are of the greatest possible complexity"[37] and involve the emotional loyalties of man, it was held that abrupt or extensive change is likely to be unwise and disruptive. It is not change per se, however, that a conservative thinker such as Burke opposed. Yet with his sensitivity to the complexity of society, its organic nature and continuity over time, there was considerable apprehension over the potential disruption concomitant with change, especially radical change. Just as a society, Burke stated, "is an idea of continuity which extends in time,"[38] so it is a slow creation over many ages to which many contribute and which none could usefully change if the transformations are abrupt or extensive. This is an ideology whose potency was enhanced as a consequence of the French Revolution and in later years by the growing disillusionment with the fruits of increasing democratization. The Enlightenment notions of rationalism, secularism, individualism, and progress were perceived as leading to societal disruption, decline of morals, personal confusion and alienation, and even to possible repressive and irresponsible rule. These would undermine societal institutions, traditions, and the social groups crucial to the vitality of the organic timeless unity that constituted society. Bramson has summarized elements of this conservative thought.

It is in the context of small groups, the family, the local community, the occupational associations, the religious groups, that men find the necessary support for their emotional existence. Abstractions, rationality, impersonal relations will not suffice to hold a society together. Here, in fact, among the conservatives of the early nineteenth century, it is not difficult to see the beginnings of a theory of mass society. For in the conservative view the weakening and dislocation of traditional ties results in the creation of a mass of alienated and isolated individual atoms, an easy mark for the demagogue offering political panaceas for salvation in this world.[39]

Sociological analysis of change in Western society

Two major themes in earlier sociological analysis of societal change have significantly contributed to mass political theory. One line of analysis is concerned with the changing character of community in Western society. I refer to the tradition of Tönnies, Maine, Durkheim, and similar scholars. The focus is on the changing bases of societal cohesion, and the decline of community, supportive interpersonal relationships, and of a meaningful and purposive place for the individual within community. A second and related tradition is one that owes much to the profound work of Max Weber on the rationalization of institutional structures and standards. This stresses the changing nature of society in terms of the alteration of organizational structures and the criteria of organizational performance and individual functioning therein. While writers such as Maine, Tönnies, Simmel, Durkheim, and Weber differed in emphasis and certainly in details, as well as in moral and evaluative judgments on societal development, it may be broadly affirmed that they did exhibit at least one common theme: Either explicitly or implicitly they recognized the decline of the organic community marked by intimate, pervasive, and traditionally determined ties, responsibilities, and rights and perceived the development of an increasingly complex, differentiated, segmental, and impersonal modern society.

Change in the nature of community

My discussion is concerned first with analysis of the nature of community change. In this regard we may note a work that influenced the thinking of both Tönnies and Durkeim. This was the sociolegal study *Ancient Law* in 1861 by the conservative English scholar Henry Sumner Maine. Based on a comparative analysis of Western, non-Western, and ancient social structure, law, and legal history, Maine suggested that individual relationships had moved from those of status (in the family) to that of contract in modern society. A legal system based on territoriality and contract has freed man from the constraint of family status. Societal change, viewed in an evolutionary perspective by Maine, has witnessed, he declared, "the gradual dissolution of family dependency and the growth of individual obligation in its place. The individual is steadily substituted for the family, as the unit of which civil laws take account."[40] Obligations are increasingly entered into voluntarily and are formulated and adhered to in terms of a contract. The significance of the group and prescribed relationships of place and status decline in an increasingly individualistic society governed by contractual arrangements.

In his seminal work, *Gemeinschaft und Gesellschaft*,[41] Tönnies developed a distinction among types of society based on the character of community and social relations; it has been very influential, though only years after its initial appearance. The change from a Gemeinschaft to Gesellschaft society is a shift away from a durable organic coherence of persons who share over time a common faith in close consanguinity and are bound together in family and friendship groups,

secular work guilds, local communities, and so on. In the Gemeinschaft a person and his acts are not merely means but ends in their
own right, as the daily course of economic, religious, and personal
activities and responsibilities is an interpersonal exchange reaffirming
the integrity of community and a distinctive way of life and performed and reacted to in particularistic, diffuse, and ascriptive terms.
The Gemeinschaft does not rest on conscious intent, nor is membership partial, or interpersonal relations segmental and impersonal. These
are, rather, some of the distinctive features of Gesellschaft society.
The historical development from the simple Gemeinschaft to the complex and increasingly heterogeneous Gesellschaft society is marked by
a disruption of the traditional closely knit community and the appearance of the impersonal and instrumental relations of the large urban-
ized industrial Gesellschaft society, though this was presaged even
earlier by changes initiated during the Renaissance. This society arises
from the disassociation of individuals and their activities from the
organic community, from community needs and obligations and from
community-based interpersonal patterns. The Gesellschaft society is
the society of choices deliberately arrived at from individualistic criteria of need and gain, relations voluntarily entered into of a narrow
and specifically defined character that are often of limited duration
and involve the individual in segmentary role contacts in an increasingly heterogeneous and impersonal society in which anonymity is
high. We are concerned, of course, with an ideal typology and one
whose sharply contrasting dichotomy has been an object of criticism
and has been modified even by sympathetic theorists. Yet Tönnies'
work has exercised a great influence on social thought generally and
on the concept of the mass society more specifically.

In the same tradition of "German sociological romanticism"[42] are
some features of the work of Georg Simmel. Especially in a major work
such as *Philosophie des Geldes*[43] and his seminal essay, "The Metropolis and Mental Life,"[44] a number of these bearing on some of ·the
more nonpolitical concerns of mass theory are developed with great
insight.[45] The consequences of modern society are traced. It has been
said that Simmel described the movement of modern history "as a
progressive liberation of the individual from the bonds of exclusive
attachment and personal dependencies even as it reveals the increasing domination of man by cultural products of his own creation."[46]
Stressed is the increasing specificity of relationships in the modern
world as individual experience and life are increasingly differentiated,
segmented, and partial. Discussed is the development of a money
economy and the man-made creation of objects that attain their own

autonomy and come to exist independent of man. Attention is also given to increasing dependence, the increase in numbers and associations, heightened specialization, urbanization, the need for punctuality and exactness, and so on. In such a context Simmel has discussed the individualistic emphasis of modern society, as well as the rise of anonymity and emotional detachment. He notes the decline of intimacy and the increased emphasis on rationality, the impersonalness and matter-of-factness in the relationships among men, and the increasingly calculating nature of interpersonal relations, maintained principally in terms of a specific impersonal rational interest end. In effect, in this increasingly secular society traditional social and moral patterns are eviscerated. His work also stresses the increasing estrangement of the individual from his own products and, consequently, the decline of individual capacities. In Simmel's thought in these regards, however, there is a positive strain that is lacking in mass theory, principally in terms of Simmel's recognition of the increasing liberation and freedom of the individual, particularly from any one uniform and comprehensive condition of domination.

Edward Shils has summarized the writings of Simmel, Tönnies, and other theorists of similar theoretical persuasion as depicting

at the very center of its conception of the world, a picture of pre-modern peasant society in which men lived in the harmonious mutual respect of authority and subordinate, in which all felt themselves integral parts of a community which in its turn lived in continuous and inspiring contact with its own past. Traditions were stable, the kinship group was bound together in unquestioned solidarity. No one was alienated from himself or isolated from his territorial community and his kin. Beliefs were firm and were universally shared. . . . This idyll was juxtaposed against a conception of modern urban society which is much like the state of nature described by Hobbes, where no man is bound by ties of sentimental affection or moral obligation or loyalty to any other man. Each man is concerned only with his own interest, which is power over others, their exploitation and manipulation. The family is dissolved, friendship dead, religious belief evaporated. Impersonality and anonymity have taken the place of closer ties.[47]

Writings of an even more profound scope are found in the related efforts of the great French sociologist, Emile Durkheim. The writings of Durkheim powerfully exhibit a number of the theses relevant to our concerns – the change from mechanical to organic solidarity, the condition of anomie, and the bases of individual freedom. Durkheim's treatment of the nature of society and its evolution from mechanical to organic solidarity is a significant contribution to the discussion by Maine and especially Tönnies on the character of change from traditional to modern society. In contrast to Tönnies, however, it is a less evaluative and more balanced and judicious discussion of the nature of contemporary society, lacking the invidious features of the German romantic tradition. It begins to provide a basis for Durkheim's somewhat later work, which because of its treatment of the concept of anomie is at least equally significant for the mass society tradition. Durkheim's discussion of the irreversible historical transition of society from mechanical to organic solidarity is by now a quite familiar theme in recent intellectual history. Essentially, we have a theory of change contingent upon an increasing division of labor or process of role differentiation productive of increasing heterogeneity and functional interdependence, with societal unity dependent upon interdependence or reciprocal fulfillment of obligations and corresponding expectations of responsiveness. This contrasts with the mechanical solidarity of pre-industrial, rural, and more primitive undifferentiated societies based upon a similarity or shared community of beliefs and sentiments, within a common community tradition. Especially significant for the mass theorist is the shift in the character of constraints on personal behavior and the nature of interpersonal relationships. Behavior and interpersonal relationships shift from community-oriented and shared moral sentiments to increasingly individualistic sentiments and consciousness, reflective of segmental role relationships and the stress on individual rights and obligations and a sense of individual purpose, gain, or loss. In an earlier work, *The Division of Labor in Society*, Durkheim has a clearer categorical affirmation of the latter circumstances as present in the society of organic solidarity. A few years later, however, in his work on suicide[48] this is merely a potential condition actualized only in the anomic society, but not in other forms of organic solidarity.

It is in Durkheim's analysis of the anomic society, his consideration of types of social integration and disorganization, and the type of relationships the individual can have with groups and to group norms that we touch even more intimately upon the mass theorist's concerns with the circumstances of modern man. The anomic society is one in which societal norms are weakened, individualism is strong, and the sense of societal obligation, group membership, and a purpose greater than one's own is attenuated. The individual may be extensively involved in society, yet be lacking clarity of standards and expectations, be weakly tied to community, and lack social ties. Man in such circumstances is in a state of anomie. He is uncertain, confused, anxious, and seeking. Nisbet, a profound student of mass society, finds in Durkheim's work an illuminating treatment of "the consequences of moral and economic individualism in modern life. Individualism has resulted in masses of normless, unattached, insecure individuals who lose even the capacity for independence, creative living."[49]

The last major element in Durkheim's work to which reference is made here is his consideration of the prerequisites for the maintenance of freedom. This relates to a theme that runs throughout his work – the concern with the change of community and the disruption of the traditional means of establishing meaningful social ties. It is thus appropriate that Durkheim should stress, the important functions of close personal group associations, or intermediate groups, in providing normative standards, conditions of responsiveness, a sense of meaning, and belonging. Durkheim extended the contributions made by intermediate group structures to include the preservation of individual freedom. In *Professional Ethics and Civic Morals* he saw these as a means of preserving freedom through counterbalancing the strength of the state. While recognizing the importance of the state in freeing the individual from the parochialism and particularistic restraints of local associations he yet affirms "that if that collective force, the State, is to be the liberator of the individual, it has itself need of some counterbalance; it must be restrained by other collective forces, that is, by ... secondary groups ... it is out of this conflict of social forces that individual liberties are born."[50] We have here a theme that is forcefully argued in the pluralist strains of mass theory.

It is not only Durkheim but a considerable portion of the sociological tradition of which he is a part that suggests that both the individual and the broader society have suffered a significant loss in the decline of the ability of intermediate groups to perform their traditional functions. Conditions for personal acceptance, responsiveness, and a sense of appropriateness and meaning have been weakened. These have especial import for mass theory. It is also stressed that community, an effective agency for the exercise of power that both protects the individual and facilitates satisfaction of his needs, has been undermined. The loss of such an agency also means a serious debilitation of a means of mediation and communication between the members of a society and its leaders. In addition, its decline has significantly weakened a pluralistic power structure and the constrains on elite or mass tyranny. It has also heightened accessibility of political leadership to the demands of the multitude.

The rationalization of society

The profound analyses of societal change and modern society by the great German sociologist Max Weber provide the fullest scholarly statement of the second major stream of social thought contributing to a theory of mass society.[51] While related to the perspectives and analyses contributed by the sociological theorists on community already cited, we have in Weber's work on the increasing rationalization of modern society less of a direct discussion of change in community than a treatment of the change of organizational structures and criteria of social role performance. The discussion that follows is brief in view of·the elaboration of rationalization and related processes in the next chapter.

The concept of the rationalization of society has two related referents. One is the stress on maximizing efficiency in the attainment of ends, productive or otherwise, and hence also includes the evaluation of organizational structures and relationships in terms of efficacy or their particular goal attainment qualities. It is an approach related to the increasing use of scientific and technical knowledge, often by specialized or expert personnel, so as to widen control and manipulation of the physical and social world. The following chapter shows how the concept of rationalization involves the differentiation and coordination of activities and roles in order to maximize efficiency. Rationalization also involves the replacement of traditional patterns, custom, and personalized standards by an individualistic self-interest component functioning within universalistic, specific, and achievement terms. Modern rationalized society becomes distinctive in its rational-legal self-interest characteristics. It is the organized society, predictable, planned, and specific. Not only are spontaneity and indeterminancy minimized, but traditional patterns and natural environmental structure are refashioned.

We can see in this "substitution for the unthinking acceptance of ancient custom, of deliberate adaptation to situations in terms of self-interest"[52] the basis for the relationship between the concept of rationalization and the earlier discussion of community. This relationship is again evidenced in the second major referent of the concept of rationalization. This is the increasing "disenchantment of the world" that Weber noted in his pointed use of Scheler's phrase. Weber suggested that rationalization involves more than merely maximizing efficiency. It also involves the sense of an increasing mastery over the world, that man can acquire the knowledge and skills to control and better his surroundings or achieve such goals as he sets himself. This clearly involves an increasing demystification of the world, the loss of a sense of the world as magical or filled with spirits. On the other hand, it has also involved an increased coherence of ideas and the growing scientific character of thought. One has here, as Gerth and Mills have noted, a "change of human attitudes and mentalities."[53] There is a loss of a sense of the world as mysterious or of one's transactions with that world as possessed of distinctive personal or sacred qualities. In Weber's words

the fate of our times is characterized by rationalization and intellectualization and, above all, by the "disenchantment of the world." Precisely the ultimate and most sublime values have retreated from public life either into the transcendental realm of mystic life or into the brotherliness of direct and personal human relations.[54]

The expert becomes of great importance, and reliance is placed on scientific knowledge.[55]

As is well known, it was in bureaucracy and its dominance in all spheres of Western society that Weber perceived the full expression of rationalized society. The bureaucratic structure provides a set of roles and normative standards that accord closely with an impetus toward rationalization:

The development of the modern form of the organization of corporate groups in all fields is nothing less than identical with the development and continual spread of bureaucratic administration. This is true of church and state, of armies, political parties, economic enterprises, organizations to promote all kinds of causes, private associations, clubs, and many others. . . . The whole pattern of everyday life is cut to fit this framework. For bureaucratic administration is, other things being equal, always, from a formal, technical point of view, the most rational type. For the needs of mass administration today, it is completely indispensable. The choice is only that between bureaucracy and dilletantism in the field of administration.[56]

This bureaucratization of all spheres of life has purged the mystery and enchantment of the world from all areas of life.

In his treatment of rationalization Weber suggested a number of possible consequences of this process. These have served as powerful influences upon the formulation of mass theory, though less on its political than cultural aspects. Most relevant, perhaps, is Weber's treatment of bureaucratization to which reference has just been made. Certainly, here the concept of the individual as a heroic actor or romantic figure loses its validity. Wolin has remarked that "nowhere was the anguishing tension between the world of organization and the creative individual more clearly revealed than in the thought of Max Weber. . . ."[57] In still another related direction there is a certain emotional loss that may be perceived as a consequence of the dis-enchantment and rationalization of the world such that human ex-perience is always provisional and no truth final or the ultimate goal of life knowable. The rationalized world is one in which little pro-vision is made for human concerns such as love, passion, or other personal qualities. In fact, it may be argued, following in the tradition of the rationalization of society, that these qualities must be either constricted or manipulated so as to maximize efficiency and maintain rationality. And in Weber's treatment of the concept of rationality an antipathy between rationality and personal freedom is suggested, arising from rationality's demands for conformity to given standards, procedures, and routine. In a related vein, personal freedom is also weakened by decreased recognition and responsiveness to individual difference and uniqueness. Role performance tends to assume a mechanical quality, particularly in bureaucratic structures, with man following a petty, unimaginative routine.

The nature of crowds and masses

There is a moderately extensive sociological literature on the nature of crowds and masses. While the resonance between this material and the formulations of mass political theory may be exaggerated, it does appear to have exercised some influence. Accordingly, a brief summary is offered of some of the major features of this sociological tradition, especially as expressed by Gustave Le Bon, perhaps the most fre-quently referred to source in this regard.

The nineteenth century witnessed a host of derogatory fulminations against the unruly and unreasonable "crowd" caught up in a "con-tagious excitement" that endangered reasonable discourse and tradi-tional societal institutions. The voices of the masses, or of the crowd (they are used interchangeably), are seen as attaining great influence. Yet, as Le Bon states, reflecting the general sentiment of this literature, crowds are effective only for destruction. Civilization depends upon the creativity and leadership of a small intellectual aristocracy.[58] In part, this is a literature responding to the increasing democratization of society, the growth of the working-class movement, radical agita-tion, the French and later revolutions, and the ideas of the counter-Enlightenment.[59] It suggests the increasing presence of crowds in contemporary society, particularly in the major social and political institutions. While referred to in the work of conservative figures such as Maistre, Burke, and especially Taine, it is in the writings of Le Bon, Tarde, Sighele, and MacDougall that there is a distinctive examination and extended formulation of the nature of the crowd and its behavior. In a summary of this work E. V. Walter has suggested that many of the social theorists

used the idea of temporary degeneration from complex and civilized to simple and primitive, to explain the phenomena of crowd behavior. They agreed that degeneration meant psychic regression, although explanations were not uniform. . . . The term "mass," cognate of the German word, could refer either to a psychic state or to a social condition, and tended to be identified with the concept of the crowd, lending a pejorative sense to terms such as "mass behavior," "mass mind," and "mass hysteria." The word had a favorable meaning only in socialist usage, where, in its plural form it referred to the chosen class.[60]

A number of characteristics clearly stand out in the discussion of the crowd. It is stressed that crowds are very credulous and accept as reality the images evoked in the mind. They exaggerate and go to extremes. They do not admit of doubts or uncertainty. They are intolerant. Thus there is frequent and vigorous attention to the loss of individual rationality and reasonableness in the crowd. The member of a crowd does not think. He does not consider the nature of his action but acts directly and responds directly. Not only is he unthinking, but, even worse, he is moved by his basest emotions and prejudices. For Le Bon man's unconscious atavistic substratum finds release. The individual may in fact be found acting in a manner quite the opposite of his usual demeanor, character, and even beliefs. It is frequently stressed that such behavior develops from the anonymity of the individual in the crowd that facilitates a loss of a sense of responsibility. The individual in the crowd is also extremely emotional, impulsive, and suggestible. He is readily carried away by the experience of the moment. "He is no longer himself, but has become an automaton who has ceased to be guided by his will."[61] As this may suggest, the loss of individual distinctiveness is a cardinal property of the crowd. The crowd assumes a general homogeneity wherein all its members respond and act similarly. Clearly, the crowd is distinctly more than the sum of its individual parts. It is the very fact of psychic membership within the crowd that alters the properties and behavior of its individual members while a part of the crowd. Le Bon suggested that homogeneity and similarity were produced by a "contagious excitement" and by suggestion. Tarde spoke of imitation, and

Sighele, like Le Bon, referred to the process of suggestion. Later students, as Roger Brown elaborates, resorted to concepts such as "primitive sympathy," "rapport," and "social facilitation."[62]

Somewhat later, American and European writers elaborated the theory of collective behavior and the meaning of concepts such as mass, crowd, and public. In the United States Park and Blumer and their students have made significant contributions. In Europe the works of Freud, Ortega y Gasset, and Lederer are notable.[63] With the American writers one begins to diverge in part from the irrational and negativist attribution made earlier in regard to collective phenomena. The European writers begin to enter more directly into the corpus of mass society literature itself, rather than with what can more clearly be labeled as antecedents.[64] Park's suggestive writings on collective behavior point to the normal nonpathological constructive character of such phenomena. Crowd behavior is merely the first step, in response to human needs, to the rise of social movements and the establishment of new institutions. Blumer made a significant contribution by distinguishing among public, crowd, and mass. The latter is marked by anonymity, little contact, personal isolation, low affect, and transitoriness. It transcends the local culture or group and tends to be destructive to them. However, its positive feature is that it is a step toward "the formation of a new order of living"[65] and hence the satisfaction of unmet human needs.

The European writers' discussions of the notion of mass or crowd, however, continue to stress merely its negative features. They stress not the temporary but the increasingly permanent character of masses. For Ortega y Gasset, of course, contemporary society exhibited an age of masses. Further, the European theorists suggest the potentially purposive creation of masses, especially with the atomization of society and the breakdown of class structures. A population in such circumstances may then form the very basis for antidemocratic political rule. Both schools of thought tend to stress a certain atomization and isolation in mass populations. In effect, the European theorist has moved from equating a mass with an emotional temporary crowd to viewing it as a durable permanent population that may provide the support of political forms that are destructive of societal institutions and democratic liberties. Yet in the work of American writers the crowd also came to be perceived as a potentially constructive force for reforming social institutions to meet unsatisfied human needs.

The relevance for mass theory of the literature on the crowd and mass, particularly in the European tradition, resides in several elements of this work. One is the critique of the liberal's rationalistic faith in the reasonableness of man.[66] The depiction of the potency and irrationality of large-scale movements, especially when led by the hypnotic leader and enveloping the individual in powerful ritual bonds, has a powerful relevance for the later mass theorist. It points to the danger of providing the broader population greater access to decision-making centers of crucial institutional sectors. There is the stress on the negative consequences of disassociating men from their usual group and institutional ties. While contemporary mass political theory makes few direct allusions to the earlier theorists on the crowd, it writes within this supportive intellectual tradition.

The preceding has suggested the broad variety of intellectual currents and analyses that have provided a perspective reflected in later mass political theory. While it would be difficult to establish a direct linkage between all these earlier ideas and later mass theory, they appear nonetheless to have had a broad general influence. Some mass theorists, of course, acknowledge this ancestry. For the others it seems plausible to suggest that the correspondence of ideas and analysis arises from the mass theorist's awareness and sensitivity to the rich intellectual heritage that has been described, a heritage ingrained in the relatively contemporary history of political and social thought.

3. The political theory
of mass society

The present chapter attempts to provide an overview of the major elements in the political theory of mass society. There is a discussion of the fundamental social processes and structures that are viewed as accounting for mass society and masses and the nature of the political behavior exhibited by such a society and mass populations. There then follows an explicit statement of the major components and perspectives of the mass theory of political behavior. Finally, there is a summary statement of the basic elements of mass political theory. As the stress is on the political theory of mass society, such treatment as there is of the broader theory of mass theory will be limited.

Fundamental social processes and structures

Mass political theory rests on propositions about the nature of change in Western society, the consequent alteration of political values and expectations, the appearance and nature of mass populations, the growing participation of a larger proportion of the society in political institutions, and the increased accessibility of elites. It develops from these a powerful account of the character of our times, the sources of political stress, and the consequences that may develop. Of the latter, its major concern is with the rise and nature of totalitarianism. The present discussion considers the decline of community, the rationalization of society, the origin and nature of masses, increasing democratization, and the loss of elite exclusiveness.

The decline of community

Mass society theory suggests that certain fundamental and related long-run changes have tended to occur in Western society and that a number of sociological and psychological consequences have arisen from these changes, so that we can speak of a mass society.

A basic series of transformations are perceived in terms of the breakdown of organic communities and traditional patterns, with the disruption of intermediate group relationships in forms such as the local community, occupation, the extended family, and the church.

Where, asks Nisbet, are the dislocations and the deprivations that have driven so many men, in this age of economic abundance and political welfare to the quest for community, to narcotic relief from the sense of isolation and anxiety? They lie in the realm of the small, primary, personal relationships of society – the relationships that mediate directly between man and his larger world of economic, moral, and political and religious values.... These are groups that have been morally decisive in the concrete lives of individuals.[1]

It is precisely where, the mass theorist affirms, "intermediate relations of community, occupation, and association are more or less inoperative"[2] that mass society develops. Community declines, Nisbet vigorously maintains, where there is a weakening of function, common and shared tasks, and of authority requisite to their performance, where there is a decline of local as opposed to external or centralized power, and, to some extent, where there is an absence of self-governance.

Intermediate groups have provided not only the historic basis of societal integration but have also defined the individual's place in the community, have helped instill community moral standards, and have constituted the focus of individual participation and the basis for the satisfaction of individual needs. The individual has mediated his relationship to his society and sought the fulfillment of his life needs through comprehensive ascribed participation within organic communities. These are the "social groups which create a sense of belonging, which supply incentive, and which confer upon the individual a sense of status."[3] With the absence of such involvements, a condition productive of the development of a sense of self is lacking. This condition has relevance not only for the psychic but also the political and social person of man. The decline of functionally relevant authoritative associations with which the individual has an intimate relationship has meant the deterioration of a firm base for establishing standards of judgment and behavior, whether political or other. In effect, social structural change has seriously weakened the integrative character of contemporary society and of personal and group life. In fact, only in recent time could one even conceive of any but a small minority of individuals in terms distinctive from their relationship to church, family, geographic community.

The disruption and the decline of intermediate relations and of community are viewed as having had serious consequences. Most succinctly, they are perceived as giving rise to the "atomistic" society, a society in which the individual lacks secure individual and group ties and relates in a tangential and segmental manner to others. It is a society whose members "then, are interconnected only by virtue of this common tie to national centers of communication and organization."[4] It is a bleak picture of man adrift. He is uprooted, displaced, and in a condition of anomie. Social relations are disrupted and atomized. Distinctive identities and membership are greatly weakened. The individual is deprived of a sense of "belongingness." The consequence has been a decline of conditions for personal sustenance and for "moral psychological stability,"[5] isolation from "the major ends and purposes of his culture,"[6] and a heightening of dissatisfaction and restlessness. A major impetus for involvement and commitment has been greatly weakened. The mass political theorist has frequently referred to the absence of community or intermediate group ties as a condition of social isolation.

Mass theorists claim that the decline of community is not, of course, without its consequences for the condition and experience of even noncollective categories, that is, the elites. This will be elaborated later. Essentially, however, three major points are involved. First, the decline of community involves the erosion of the insulation protecting elites and leadership functions from direct mass intrusion. Second, it also means the lack of satisfaction of social and psychic needs by the members of society, with the resulting discomfort leading to efforts to find surcease through demands or attacks upon elite elements. The discussion of the nature of masses and elite accessibility will more fully consider these and related considerations. Third, the weakening of intermediate groups is also perceived as undermining pluralist forms, with a consequent weakening of the diffusion of power and of constraints on concentrated power.

Rationalization of society and associated changes

Some of the principal concerns of the mass theorist – such as the fragmentation and routinization of life, estrangement from self and society, development of conditions of powerlessness, even the decline of social pluralism – have been perceived as having their origins to a significant extent in the processes of rationalization and the dissolution of community. While the phenomenon of rationalization is the more comprehensive conceptualization of the processes involved, with the decline of community and autonomous associations understandable within this broader process of change, there are certain differences between these two major sociological traditions that will receive brief note later.

The process of rationalization has reflected as well as provided an impetus to the process of social differentiation in Western society. Succinctly, the process of social differentiation is, to an extent, an evolutionary phenomenon in which "*one* social role or organization ... differentiates into *two or more roles* or organizations. ..." in which "the new social units are functionally equivalent to the original unit." In effect, it is "the evolution from a multi-functional role structure to several more specialized structures."[7] This signifies that where a complex of functions were initially centered within one role or organization, they have elaborated into a number of more specialized roles and organizations, each performing only one function or a limited number of functions. In effect, each more specialized role or structure performs only a part of what had been the broad range of responsibilities of the original role or institution.[8] This process of social differentiation, the consequent creation of an increasingly elaborated and diversified social structure, and the emphasis on specialized task performance within given organizational or institutional areas create an impetus for the growth over time of large-scale formal organization. In the context of some value structures and goals these may well become bureaucratized structures.

The manifestation of rationalization in terms of bureaucratization evidences the development of an extensively integrated complex functional role network and structure. Under the stress of efficient goal attainment this characteristic of bureaucratic organization places a great stress on regularized expectations and a conformity to given procedures and standards. At the same time, there is an elaboration of role structures, a narrowing of the scope of organizational involvement, and a standardization of any particular role responsibility and work task. Thus there exist pressures for normative conformity and, in effect, for accepting ongoing routine, standards, and directives without interposing a personal or nonorganizational standard of evaluation or criticism. As Mannheim suggested "The average person surrenders part of his own cultural individuality with every new act of integration into a functionally rationalized complex of activities. He becomes increasingly accustomed to being led by others and gradually gives up his own interpretation of events for those which others give him."[9]

Another feature of bureaucratic involvement is that the quality of individual experience is meager. With the increased partial character of tasks the individual has an increasingly distant and fractional connection with the total overall purpose. Yet the number of distant roles experienced increases, not because one's functional responsibilities may or need be any greater but because they are now divided into an increased number of distinct roles. This has also made for an increasingly tenuous relationship among the different spheres of individual involvement. One's life appears fragmented, lacking in unity or even appropriateness among diverse responsibilities and role encounters. The individual performing within such roles experiences an increasingly segmental relationship to others, who are narrowly defined in terms of the nature of each role contact. With work and role performance routinized and scope narrowed, the individual experiences any particular involvement as but distantly and ineffectually related to the overall task, goal, or institutional structure. The responsiveness and potential for personal sustenance in interpersonal relationships under such conditions are thus vitally diminished, and a crucial basis for personal satisfaction is seriously compromised. Further, one relates not to the unique and concrete personal qualities but to the abstract requirements of the segmental role relationship. Given the universalistic and task-oriented quality of interpersonal experiences and orientation, one increasingly perceives others as means to an end, as objects to be manipulated. This developing estrangement from others, and from areas of institutional involvement, is complemented by an estrangement from self, and a clear and satisfying self-image or identity is lacking.[10]

A concomitant of the processes of rationalization and social differentiation, and the societal changes implicit in industrialization and urbanization, has been a diversification and some fragmentation of the social order and an extension of its scale. These have created the necessity of an integrative coordinating structure. Thus an ever-developing network of partial, highly refined, rationalized roles is coordinated and enveloped in increasingly large centralized bureaucratic structures, of both a public and a private character. The members of society become increasingly implicated in nationwide institutional structures and relationships in the economic, political, cultural, and even social and religious spheres of public and private life. This process of vertical integration[11] with its decline of regional and local autonomy and control has meant the centralization of authority and power. The individual has become increasingly implicated in, dependent upon, and controlled by such nationwide structures. Not only are they characterized by their impersonal formal character but also by the concentration of power and decision making beyond the control of the greater mass of individual participants, and even beyond the range of the individual's view: "... the growing scope and complexity of the public realm have made distant decisions and events more decisive for private life and simultaneously less manageable."[12] The individual experiences the policies, decisions, action, and inaction of these organizations in a condition of powerlessness. Thus while the individual in bureaucratized society increasingly confronts large-scale impersonal organizational and social structures whose decisions and functions affect him vitally, these are both beyond his ken and his ability to control or effectively influence.

Much of the meaning of the notion of political alienation and a sense of powerlessness and defenselessness vis-à-vis one's environment exist in such phenomena. This extends not only to relationships with centralized public power but, equally significantly, to the large formal nationwide private bureaucratic structures presumably representative of membership interest. Potency and local autonomy are in many ways no greater in regard to the centralized leadership in these private organizational structures than in public ones. Hence there develops in regard to both bureaucratic organizations and bureaucratic society a sense of estrangement or feeling of apartness, an absence of meaningful relationship or of involvement, and so on. In fact, "Nisbet argues that unless all kinds of large-scale organizations are rooted in partially autonomous subgroups, they intensify rather than counteract the process of atomization."[13] Conjoined with such phenomena, this "centralization of national relations," according to Kornhauser, creates the structures that help account for the increased manipulability of societal populations. "People are more easily manipulated and mobilized when they become directly and exclusively dependent on the national organization for the satisfaction of interests otherwise also met in proximate relations."[14] In his concluding discussion on "Mass Society and Democratic Order," Kornhauser relates a sense of impotence and apathy to both powerlessness and the decline of the ability to communicate and discuss group needs effectively. The latter is an important element of what C. Wright Mills has referred to as publics in his treatment of the decline of publics and the rise of masses.[15] Kornhauser also suggests the differential development of these conditions in terms of social structural position.[16]

Not only, however, have structural change and the centralization of power and decision-making authority produced powerlessness, apathy, atomization, and increased manipulability, but they have weakened social pluralism and individual competence. They have seriously undercut the individual's relationship to intermediate groups and distinct public loyalties and patterns of life and at the same time forced participation within a bureaucratic structure, often in individualistic terms, rather than as a member of a distinctive group. The centralization in the bureaucratic process has reduced the functions and authority of diverse groups, not only thus reducing their vitality but, in its assumption of these properties to itself, increasing dependence upon the impersonal centralized all-powerful bureaucratic structure. Kornhauser in essence makes a similar point as regards the character of property and the entrepreneurial middle class.[17] It is a process that clearly extends, however, beyond the decline of independent property and the atomization of old middle-class elements, though this is a historic theme of considerable importance.[18] A significant and even larger proportion of the population may be atomized. Pluralist structures are destroyed, and this portends an increasing precariousness for freedom and democratic diversity.

Bureaucratization, and the centralization that has been implicated in it, is also a process that has heightened ignorance of the nature of societal events, more particularly the causes of personally experienced strains. Structural change, Mills suggests, has removed the individual from association with those points that are central and crucial to the operation of society and from which one can see an overall view of society or phenomena within it. "Sunk in their routines, they do not transcend, even by discussion, much less by action, their more or less narrow lives. They do not gain a view of the structure of their society and of their role as a public within it. . . . Each is trapped by his confining circle; each is cut off from easily identifiable groups."[19] Mills brings together the phenomenon of the decline of community and the increasingly bureaucratized centralized character of rationalized structures in regard to their consequences for the individual in his observation that "this loss of any structural view of position is the decisive meaning of the lament over the loss of community."[20]

By focusing on rationalization and the circumstances of many in a bureaucratized society rather than on the decline of community, we provide a somewhat different emphasis in regard to the nature of the political consequences of mass society than would be attained from a stress on the decline of community. Most generally, the political consequences of the former circumstances are perceived more in terms of a response to a developing condition of social fragmentation and powerlessness, while the effects of a decline of community are understood more in the light of a loss of ties, a confusion of values, and the appearance of exposed elites. Both recognize the development of an available mass. When the focus is in terms of rationalization, such a result arises out of the fragmentation and narrowing of experience, with its consequent accentuation of powerlessness, meaninglessness, dissatisfaction, and ignorance. When reference is made to the decline of community, there is more of a stress on the efforts of populations that suffer such an experience to replace the associations and meaning that have been lost. Implicit in both approaches – though little or improperly developed as I shall contend later – is the appearance of mass availability as a concomitant of the condition of political alienation, that is, a sense of powerlessness, with a possible consequent attempt to find means of control or resolution to dilemmas by supporting antiestablishment and at times extremist movements and leaders. There is, however, some difference of emphasis. When the focus is on the decline of community, there is a greater emphasis on powerlessness as arising from the undermining of the group basis of power. On the other hand, while this is recognized in the perspective that focuses on bureaucratization, this latter approach provides a very forceful stress on the lack of power as residing in the lack of access to an increasingly unresponsive and distantly centralized point of power and decision making.

This begins to introduce an important difference in emphasis between the two sociological traditions. Rationalization and bureaucratization focus on the circumstances of the individual, the disruption of community on the weakening of collectivities and their constraints. The former more readily permits a stress on the need to reestablish the independence and potency of the individual; the latter highlights community and community normative structures and demands. The bureaucratization approach lends itself more readily to stressing freedom and the need for power by the individual. It is a more radical social perspective that can lead to emphasizing the elite rather than mass threat to viable democratic forms. It suggests the potential for manipulation by the elites of populations that have experienced "the loss of a sense of structure and the submergence into powerless milieux."[21] While it is still true that the danger to democratic political forms and the sources of inadequacies in public policy in bureaucratized society are partly accounted for by the circumstances of the population, this is indirect. The character of these circumstances is relevant not so much in their own terms as in the potential they provide for elite manipulation of the mass community and the difficulty they pose for effective individual and public response to inadequacies in elite functioning. Thus a stress on the bureaucratization of society provides a theoretical rationale for placing a predominant stress on elite failings rather than on mass behavior. Mills was, of course, one of the more vigorous exponents of this view. However, this is a mass theory perspective that receives little elaboration in its political dimension by most theorists. The model of the political theory of mass society that this volume critically evaluates lacks a proper appreciation of these concerns.

It has been suggested that an emphasis on bureaucratization lends itself more to a consideration of powerlessness than is the case with a focus on the decline of community. It is the latter concern, however, that has bulked largest in the political theory of mass society. It is this perspective that has most powerfully induced attention to the condition of anomie and the exposure of elites. When bureaucratization is considered, it tends to be done in terms of isolation and amorphous social relations and populations.

The origins and nature of masses

The mass theorist's concern with masses, the basis of their appearance, their characteristics, and their behavior are fundamental. Actually, as has been noted, the concept of masses has evolved over time. Walter, in his essay "Mass Society: The Late Stages of an Idea,"[22] traces its changing character. Until relatively recently the term "masses" was used essentially as a referent for crowds and crowdlike behavior. It is with Blumer's distinction in the 1930s among "public," "crowd," and "mass" that the sense of the heterogeneous and anonymous population characterized by little interpersonal contact and low affect becomes popular. "Blumer's definition of the 'mass' added anonymity, isolation and atomization."[23] Writers on the Continent provided another ingredient, namely, the understanding that masses were no longer ephemeral but durable and that they need not be spontaneous; but may be constructed by design.[24] Mass theory is concerned with populations distinguished by the nature of group ties and personal existence. Says Selznick,

When we refer to a population as a mass, we are thinking of its members as undifferentiated, as forming an unstructured collectivity withdrawn from the normal, spontaneous commitments of social life. We are also thinking of the consequences which flow from this situation. Mass connotes a "glob of humanity," as against the intricately related, institutionally bound groups that form a healthy social organism.[25]

Or, more succinctly, in the words of Kornhauser, masses are "people who are not integrated into broad social groups, including classes."[26] These are populations whose group relationships and loyalties have been seriously disturbed by either the decline of community or the increasing bureaucratization of life. In the one case their membership in social solidarities has been destroyed or greatly attenuated by the very decline of these groups; in the other instance the bureaucratization of social structures has created isolated and amorphous social relations. The effect of the latter tends, in some respects, to be similar to the decline of organic communities and autonomous associations, and is often so treated. However, it does admit of the possibility of some differences in emphasis.[27]

Hence the masses are those segments of a society that lack a sense of membership in class, religious, occupational, neighborhood, or other major collectivities. Nisbet avers that "what is crucial in the formation of the masses is the atomization of all social and cultural relationships within which human beings gain their moral sense of membership in society."[28] Masses are amorphous populations composed of diverse individuals; absent is a sense of common identity, awareness of shared interest, and group consciousness. Arendt affirms that "masses are not held together by a consciousness of common interest and they lack ... class articulateness. ..."[29] Obviously, it is not denied that individuals possess a particular economic position, religion, occupation, and so on, but the point is that these do not provide the basis of social relationships, conditions of responsiveness, distinctive identity and loyalties, or perceptual schemes with which to understand and interpret the world. Thus masses "cannot be integrated into any organization based on common interest, into political parties or municipal governments or professional organizations or trade unions."[30] Given the absence of a sense of distinctive group membership and interest, as well as the absence of group ties and means of intergroup communication, there is also lacking, as Mills has pointed out, adequate means to express opinions, to respond to elite-generated views, to effectuate opinion into action, or to remain autonomous from institutional authorities.[31] The masses are thus people adrift, confused, disturbed, impotent, ignorant.

The basis and the character of political participation by masses must be perceived as distinctly different than for classes or other structurally defined collectivities. It lacks the distinctive interest-based contention that characterizes, for example, economic, religious, regional, or other sociopolitical groups and that is significant in accounting for their political activities. For such groups the basis of political participation usually inheres in their origins, which significantly defines what are the predominant group interests for which political response and affect are sought. The propositions on the origin of masses are concerned with populations lacking a structurally shared interest group origin in terms of a major social system variable, such as economic role, ethnicity, or religion, and hence they do not exhibit a rational interest basis for political activity as a collectivity. As such, it has been said that "politics meant to them nothing but escape from their petty existence through collective emotionalism."[32]

It should be noted that some uses of the concept of masses by mass theorists do not involve a distinct or consistent definition of masses in terms of the absence of social relationships and group consciousness. Rather, the term is used to refer to populations lacking the qualities requisite for informed participation in political or cultural life. While all usages do in fact tend to share this estimate of the mass, some make it central to their definition of mass man. Thus Ortega y Gasset distinguishes between the "specially qualified" or select minorities and the "essentially unqualified" or masses.

The mass is all that which sets no value on itself – good or ill – based on specific grounds, but which feels itself "just like everybody," and nevertheless is not concerned about it; is, in fact quite happy to feel itself as one with everybody else ... those who demand nothing special of themselves but for whom to live is to be every moment what they already are, without imposing on themselves any effort towards perfection; mere buoys that float on the waves.[33]

Referring to the masses as "a degraded state of the human," Marcel reiterates Ortega y Gasset's usage in his *Man Against Mass Society.*[34] In a similar vein, stressing that mass man is man as an average, Karl Jaspers further contends that a population forms a mass when "the majority ... decides the nature, the actions, the resolves of all members."[35] This usage of mass to refer, in effect, to the broader population of society, the average man undistinguished by any distinctive attributes or qualities and deficient for tasks of leadership or judgment, is also experienced to an extent in Mannheim's and Lippman's uses of the concept. On the whole, however, the treatment throughout the present work is concerned with the preceding conceptualization of masses in terms of the lack of ties.

Mass theory also attempts to account for the appearance of mass man. But this requires little elaboration in light of what has already been discussed. Essentially, as has been noted, masses arise in circumstances in which integral social relationships, the wholeness of experience, and the sense of efficacy are severely undermined and in which the ties that unite men dissolve and "social atomization and extreme individualization" develop. The mass theorist reasons that these tend to be consequences of fundamental long-range change in the social structure of Western society.[36] While this is an important theme in mass literature, it is also vital to recognize that some mass theorists take a more tempered view. While recognizing these tendencies in the evolution of society in recent times, they abjure affirming that all contemporary populations similarly experience such social changes. In other words, the problem is raised as to what populations under what circumstances experience the destruction of intermediate relations and obstacles to the development of new autonomous associations. In his discussion of discontinuities in community and discontinuities in society, Kornhauser has succinctly summarized the kinds of phenomena and their consequences that lead to the production of masses. In regard to discontinuities in community he seeks to show "that the rate and mode of urbanization and industrialization go far toward determining the extent to which the transformation of community is won at the price of creating masses available for mobilization by totalitarian movements."[37] Where urbanization and industrialization occur rapidly, populations are likely to be uprooted, thrust into unfamiliar surroundings and routines, under difficult living conditions, lacking ties, and only over time able to establish new forms of association in the city or on the job that will help in minimizing atomization and in establishing community.[38] Discontinuities in society, such as depression and defeat in war, also weaken community, Kornhauser suggests.[39] Multiple social ties are undermined, social relations to societal institutions and associations are disrupted, integrating experiences of a social and a psychological character may be increasingly lacking, and feelings of uselessness and helplessness tend to develop. Not all groups even within any particular society experience equally the phenomena noted. These are conditions most likely to be found among "unattached intellectuals, marginal members of the middle class, isolated industrial and farm workers."[40]

In its political as well as other dimensions the concept of masses is clearly crucial to mass theory. However, the use of the concept varies. Kornhauser has, in fact, distinguished among mass theorists in these terms. Thus he categorizes mass theorists as either democratic or aristocratic critics of society. Both stress conditions productive for the appearance of mass populations and the characteristics of such populations but differ on the role and responsibility assigned to masses in explaining political phenomena. The democratic theorist, Kornhauser suggests, stresses the availability of masses and their manipulation by marginal elite elements. Thus it is the preservation of viable and independent collectivities that is paramount. The aristocratic theorists, however, emphasize the accessibility of elites, that is, the intrusion of mass populations upon areas and decisions formerly reserved for the more tempered and informed judgments of the elites. The principal need here is to protect the elites, to maintain or reestablish their autonomy and the indirectness of mass access to major elites. It should be clear, however, that for both streams of mass theory the existence of masses – whether they be perceived as agents or as objects of manipulation – is crucial, in that they provide the brute and unreasoning force that typifies mass behavior and disrupts democratic political forms. Even in those writers who presumably stress mass availability, the focus of attention is on the creation, behavior, functioning, and dangers of mass populations, with little attention given to elaborating the nature and specifics of elite functioning and responsibility.

The democratization of political society

For the mass theorist a major societal change has been the increased accessibility of elites. In a historical perspective the phenomenon of elite accessibility is closely tied to the process of democratization that occurred in Western society. Increasing democratization and elite accessibility are closely related to the growing industrialization of Western society and associated economic transformations that have given rise to new or expanded social and economic classes, most particularly a growing working class and lower white-collar population.[41]

In a narrow sense, the process of democratization refers to the increasing participation of the citizenry in the political institutions of society. More broadly, it refers to the changing concept of citizenship itself.[42] Still another possible meaning is increased elite accountability and responsiveness. The principal concern here is with the process of increasing political participation. It should be recognized, however, that the process of democratization in this narrower sense ordinarily depends upon the previous or contemporaneous extension of the concept of citizenship and the guarantee of basic civil rights implicated by such extension. There is little need to elaborate upon the tremendous growth of suffrage during the latter half of the nineteenth century and the beginning of twentieth century in Europe. However, it is not merely the legal fact of being able to vote that is significant. Especially important is the fact that viable political parties have developed based on these previously disenfranchised populations. These changes have produced an altered relationship between ruled and rulers. There has been both a growth of the sense of the propriety or legitimacy of broad citizenry access to elites and an apparent increased dependence of political elites on the approval or at least the neutralization of large segments of the society and their party organizations. A major element in rule or leadership is the need to obtain and to continue to reaffirm public support, frequently in the context of a politically competitive arena. This is a vital basis of legitimizing leadership position. Hence it is important to assess accurately the opinions, grievances, and desires of the public. At the same time, given the growth of the centrally integrated nature of society, the broader community looks increasingly to the central political leadership for action on its needs and alleviation of its discomforts.

The relevance of the long-term process of democratization to the loss of elite exclusiveness arises from a number of factors. Succinctly, three related major consequences seem to arise from this process of democratization, though these are not made explicit in mass political theory. One is the change of values in regard to the relationships between elites and nonelites and their respective roles. There has evolved a value complex that encourages nonelite demands of access to elites and elite recognition of the appropriateness of such claims. An internalization of value change will also have affected the expectations of the actors involved. Most importantly, the consequence of this internalization is likely to be increased discomfort by those population segments that lack access, given the growth of the practice and belief in access. Closely related to these value changes must be some decline in the legitimacy of elite exclusiveness, as it confronts a new altered value complex. The propriety of elite autonomy is thus placed in increasing doubt. Finally, it may be reasonable to suggest that the process of increasing democratization will tend to stimulate its own continued expansion, everything else being equal, though points at which this may be aborted can be visualized. That is, with the change in values, expectations, and the conditions of legitimacy contingent upon democratization, conditions are created for further structural change in response to an altered value complex. Thus the change of both structures and values in the process of the extension of the scope of democratic belief and practice has increased the accessibility of elites to nonelites or the broader population.

Accessibility of elites

There is one fact which, whether for good or ill, is of utmost importance in the public life of Europe at the present moment. This fact is the accession of the masses to complete social power. As the masses, by definition, neither should nor can direct their own personal existence, and still less rule society in general, this fact means that actually Europe is suffering from the greatest crisis that can afflict peoples, nations, and civilizations.[43]

This clarion call of alarm is sounded by Ortega y Gasset in the opening lines of his *The Revolt of the Masses*. Clearly, the nature and the circumstances of what have been called the masses are only one element in the theory of mass society. Another crucial feature of the theory argues that the mass society is that society in which elites have lost their exclusiveness and their authority has been seriously weakened.[44] In other words, traditional authority has been displaced by popular authority, or even pseudoauthority where the masses rule.[45] In his informed account of mass theory Kornhauser has summarized this major element in mass theory:

> What has changed is the structural relationship between the many and the few. In the mass society, there is a marked increase in opportunities for the many to intervene in areas previously reserved to the few. There opportunities invite the determination of social policies and cultural standards by large numbers who are not competent to make such decisions.
>
> Mass society from this standpoint is the society in which there is a loss of *exclusiveness* of elites: it is a social structure possessing high access to governing groups...loss of authority on the part of institutional elites results from widespread opportunities to participate in the formation of major social policies.[46]

The mass theorist offers an extended litany of alarm over the presumably increasing intrusion of untutored, antiliberalitarian, irrational, erratic, incompetent masses upon the reasoned, knowledgeable, and value-preserving functioning of political and cultural elites. There has developed a "democracy of emotions."[47] In addition, echoing the sentiments of conservative thought and the nineteenth-century liberals referred to earlier, we also have in the contemporary mass theorist a reexpression of apprehension over the threat to liberties by the intrusion of the majority into the councils of government.

The growing equalitarianism of contemporary society has encouraged a "sovereignty of the unqualified."[48] Vital to the problem of the loss of elite exclusiveness is the minimization of the necessity of expertise in deciding among political policies or evaluating cultural phenomena. To many mass theorists it appears that, unfortunately, in contemporary society majority opinion is adjudged a sufficient and just basis of decision. The concern of the mass theorist develops because of this reliance on the judgment of man in the mass and not on those equipped to rule. "Mass society is the condition under which rule by the masses – either directly or through the popularly supported demagogue – displaces aristocratic rule."[49] In effect, "the people have acquired power which they are incapable of exercising, and the governments they elect have lost power which they must recover if

they are to govern."[50] The creative political and cultural functions of
the elite and the preservation of associated traditions and principles
are undermined by either denying special expertise and responsibility
in these regards or, correlatively, placing reliance on the broader
populace for the fulfillment of central political and cultural functions.
These require the exclusivity of the elite, tempered if need be by no
more than an indirect and mediated access of the masses. ("Masses"
is used in the present section, unless indicated otherwise, merely as
a referent to nonelites or the general populace. Thus it is not necessarily referring to populations lacking intermediate group membership
and ties.) In effect, the mass theorist maintains that there has been
a derangement of functions between the masses and the elite, or those
who formulate the standards and policies in the political and cultural
realms. In its bolder form the mass theorist in effect affirms the need
for the elite to establish the guidelines and initiatives of policy and
for the general societal population to provide silent support. From a
more tempered perspective the concern over mass access to elites
develops where such access is somehow excessive or direct, lacking
resort to intermediate agencies.

There are a number of considerations involved in the phenomenon
of popular access to elites or the loss of elite exclusiveness. These
include not only who has access but the manner of access, the degree
of directness or mass involvement in access, how much weight is
assigned to popular demands, and the scope or range of elites to
which there is access. Not to attend to these would state the relationship of the populace and elites in a manner too gross to be very
meaningful, since access and the loss of elite exclusiveness may be
found to some extent in almost all modern societies. While not explicitly phrased in terms of these several dimensions of access, a
reading of the mass theory literature does reveal some distinctive
judgments in these regards. Unfortunately, they are quite general,
and there is little analysis of the distinctions or differences that in
reality appear within each of these dimensions, or of the reasons for
or consequences of differences.

The previous discussion has dealt with the mass theorist's treatment of who has access in mass society. The masses are perceived as
having access – the untutored unqualified majority of the community
in contrast to the elites, who presumably have the intellectual, infor-
mational, personal, and psychological qualities essential for wise
decision making. As I have suggested, a concern merely with who has
access would simplify the phenomena involved much too greatly.
For many mass theorists, at least by indirection, the issue is not merely

the necessity to preserve elite rule but the nature of the relationship between elites and the broader community. Several observations may be made in terms of the dimension of access just noted. For instance, the preceding discussion on the loss of elite exclusiveness contains the implication, variously specified in mass literature, of the disruption of institutionalized means of mass access and elite-mass communication. There is, in other words, a disruption or absence of the use of accepted and presumably viable means to express broader community needs and objectives of policy to those in leadership positions. How much weight is given popular demands or opinion refers essentially to the extent to which mass opinion is advisory and suggestive or conclusively determinate. Clearly, the emphasis in mass literature is toward claiming a heavily determinate role of popular opinion in mass society. Finally, the mass society is one in which nearly all elite elements and decision-making centers, cultural, literary, communication media, and the diverse elements of the political system are obeisant to the masses. Unfortunately, there is a tendency to consider each of these relationships in either/or terms. This is in keeping, however, with the broad schematic character of mass theory, which makes it more of a suggestive model of behavior than a clear analytic or predictive scheme.

If the phenomenon of elite accessibility is considered in the terms just noted, it becomes possible to distinguish between what Kornhauser labels as pluralist society and mass society. Both are characterized by mass or popular access to elites, the significant difference being that in the plural political society such access exists in terms of institutionalized structures and procedures. In mass society these are absent. Institutionalization is productive of greater constancy, of more temperate, reasoned, and less emotional pressure of the citizenry on the elites. Ordinarily this is so because such pressure is somewhat indirect and is mediated by the usually more moderate and pragmatic intervening structures and personnel. It also arises from the fact that institutionalization means that to some extent predictability will be greater and constraints on behavior and demands will appear, because of the necessity of functioning in terms of the exigencies of organization and organizational personnel.

The preceding suggests the relationship between the earlier discussion on the origin and nature of masses and the present consideration of the loss of elite exclusiveness. There is a direct correspondence suggested in mass theory between the decline of community, productive of the development of mass populations, and the increasing exposure of elites to the masses. This arises in three fundamental ways: One is the vitiation of structures that can mediate between the two.

Another is that an uprooted and atomized population will be less constrained in seeking to affect elites than a population preoccupied with proximate concerns and a satisfying personal and social milieu. Third, even if they do not receive any greater satisfaction, grievances are more likely to be vented beyond one's personal circle and into the broader community. The mass theorist also stresses that a mass population, bereft of ties, a sense of the integrative character of experience, personal satisfaction, and responsiveness and beset by anxiety, frustration, and a sense of powerlessness, will be more unreasonable and irrational and more insistent and exaggerated in its demands. When combined with the loss of elite exclusiveness and the decline of mediating structures, the consequences for a viable and restrained liberalitarian politics are perceived as grave.

Theory of political behavior

By considering the major processes of change affecting political relationships and behavior, the preceding discussion has provided an introduction to a more explicit treatment in the present section of the perspectives and propositions of mass political theory in regard to political behavior, structures, and forms of governance.

Mass behavior: its characteristics, causes, and forms

The character of mass behavior. The mass political theorist's treatment of mass behavior lends itself to a succinct summarization. Distinct from the behavior itself, and already discussed, are the characteristics of those people involved. The characteristics of the participants help determine the nature of the behavior. It will suffice merely to note again that the participants in mass behavior are the uprooted and atomized segments of society that lack any intimate relationship to class or other intermediate group forms. The behavior itself will reflect little sense of a distinctive interest component and does not bear a realistic relationship to the cause of individual or group strain.[51] Its focus is on remote rather than proximate objects.[52] We may speak of mass behavior when

the mode of response to remote objects is direct.... People act directly when they do not engage in discussion on the matter at hand, and when they do not act through groups in which they are capable of persuading and being persuaded by their fellows.... They may employ various more or less coercive measures against those individuals and groups who resist them.[53]

It is not unreasonable to suggest, from the mass political theorist's perspective, that politics assumes the character of a phobic sector into which individuals inject their own anxieties and anger or from which they seek affective qualities lacking in their nonpolitical involvements. Hence those statements of issues, programs, and attitudes that are evidenced exhibit little rationality or reasonableness of ideology. Aims and purposes are unclear. There is the lack of any realistic socio-political explanation of issues or policy. Heavy reliance is placed on the notion of conspiratorial, external, secret, and mischievous forces controlling and accounting for events.

Mass behavior has little patience with compromise and goes to the extreme in zealous attachment to its own distinctive perspectives. It is also unstable behavior, "readily shifting its focus of attention and intensity of response. Activist responses are likely to alternate with apathetic responses."[54]

Gusfield has summarized its activist, intemperate, and antidemocratic character:

the extremist breaks with the normative patterns of pluralist political behavior: (1) *He attempts to close the political process to opposing forces:* Politics is held to be the legitimate area of conflict for some, but not for all groups. . . . (2) *He attempts to carry on social and economic conflicts outside of political institutions:* The confinement of conflict to politics marks a cardinal principle of democratic politics. Violence, intimidation and fraud are excluded as a means of achieving group ends. (3) *He impairs the culture of democratic discussion:* An emphasis is placed on the value of uniform opinions and behavior. The criteria of rational calculation of interests is replaced by intensive appeals to sentiment and symbolism. . . . The extremist style has little appreciation of dissent and schism in the total society.[55]

Causes of mass behavior. There is little need to elaborate on the causes of mass behavior, given the already extensive discussion on conditions productive of the appearance of masses. For the mass theorist, in the light of such conditions, mass behavior will tend to arise almost as a matter of course. Some theorists do, however, place some stress on the prerequisite of mobilization by marginal elite elements, yet even here the characteristics of mass populations bulk large as determinate of mass behavior. Essentially, these are socially isolated populations, the uprooted and atomized segments of society that lack any intimate relationship to class or other intermediate group forms. Hence they are in a situation that tends to maximize an absence of a sense of purpose, meaning, identity, and efficacy, and one in which conditions of responsiveness and social support are lacking. This makes more difficult engaging in behavior marked by constraint, constancy, consistency, rationality, patience, and so on, that is, nonmass behavior. It also increases a population's mobilizability by extremist movements and leaders. Thus those mass behavioral tendencies that may exist may be exploited and given a means of expression. Without purposive efforts at mobilizing populations or exploiting their behavioral propensities such populations might, however, remain dormant and not evidence any distinctive mass behavioral properties. One could assume that mass behavior proclivities exist to some extent in all populations, though more so in mass populations. It is principally, though, in populations lacking intermediate relations where such behavior is actualized by the appropriate movement or leader. Further, to the extent that there is an impetus toward mass behavior, the decline of community and autonomous social relationships creates a paucity of nonpolitical interpersonal or communal arenas in which to act out mass behavior properties in a nonpolitical manner.

Mass political theory also gives some attention to factors, not resident in the character of the population concerned, that encourage and permit the expression of mass behavior. I am referring to the decline of elite authority and the weakening of intervening structures. When a decline of the authority of elites is experienced, there is likely to be less restraint on behavior. The propriety of direct action, of subverting established procedures and institutions, of seeking new leadership, and other such activities is heightened. This follows from the fact that when one speaks of elite authority, one in effect refers to the legitimacy of certain forms and roles of political expression and representation and the lessened propriety of acting counter to a given leadership and its proclaimed standards of political behavior. In another direction, when the structures intervening between the masses and the central decision-making points of the society are weakened, there is a loss of the moderating qualities possessed by such structures. There are, of course, other nonpopulation-based factors that may influence the appearance of mass behavior, but these receive little or no attention in the greater part of mass literature. Thus only brief attention is given to the nature of mass leadership, and even less note is made of conditions such as the character of political issues and controversy and the lack of political responsiveness experienced by the population in question.

Mass movements. The phenomenon of mass movements is of considerable interest to mass political theory. While discrete instances of mass behavior, both uncoordinated and organized, are of interest to the mass political theorist, it is in the concern with mass movements that the concept of mass behavior is applied most significantly. The same is true for accounts of the nature of the response to conditions of political alienation.[56] And it is with extremist mass movements that the political theory of mass society is most concerned. Essentially, such movements rest on available masses – that is, a population in a mass condition. The support for extremist movements does not come from class groupings. Often the supporters of mass movements are seen as coming from the least organized, the most apathetic, the most indifferent, and least involved members of society: ". . . the masses grew out of the fragments of a highly atomized society whose competitive structure and concomitant loneliness of the individual had been held in check only through membership in a class."[57] Declassed, adrift, and unorganized, lacking ties and commitments that might impede establishing new loyalties, they may well become followers of a demagogic leader and movement that promise both explicitly and implicitly to satisfy personal or material needs, provide protection from a hostile environment, or offer a sense of participation, control, of meaning. "The 'rationalization of the masses' grew out of the extreme loneliness of urban man," Neumann affirmed.[58] In a similar vein Nisbet has argued that

The almost eager acceptance of the fantastic doctrine of the Nazis by millions of otherwise intelligent Germans would be inexplicable were it not for the accompanying proffer of moral community to the disenchanted and alienated German worker, peasant, and intellectual. . . .

Marxism as a mass movement is no different. . . . To a large number of human beings Marxism offers status, belonging, membership, and a coherent moral perspective. . . .

The evidence is strong that the typical convert to communism is a person for whom the processes of ordinary existence are morally empty and spiritually insupportable. His own alienation is translated into the perceived alienation of the many. Consciously or unconsciously he is in quest of secure belief and solid membership in an associative order. . . .[59]

The powerful appeal of mass movements rests on their ability to offer community and also to fill associated needs among the masses. The danger, of course, is that it is an ersatz community whose ends are anathema to the democratic and free society and which in the end leaves unresolved the basic problems of its supporters.

The appeal of mass movements also rests on their being an effective way of striking out at discredited existing political elements and leadership, of giving vent to one's anxieties and lack of political

effectiveness. Naturally, the likelihood of mass participation is heightened where existing elites have lost the authority and respect that
helped mitigate against supporting antiestablishment movements.

A number of elements in the treatment of mass movements may be
described briefly. The character of mass movement behavior has
already been considered in greater part. What can usefully be noted
here, though, is the property of total commitment and loyalty presumably sought by mass movements. The mass theorists further ob-
serve the fanaticism, emotionalism, and blind faith of the movement
and its members. "The vigor of a mass movement," Eric Hoffer affirms,
"stems from the propensity of its followers for united action and self-
sacrifice."[60] Yet another and more general point is that the irrationality,
extremism, and direct quality of mass behavior may be potently and
dangerously intruded into the broadest political arena and into
decision-making centers on the most vital occasions and with great
force: "... the selective apparatus of mass democracy opens the
door to irrationalities in those places where rational direction is
indispensable. Thus, democracy itself produces its own antithesis and
even provides its enemies with their weapons."[61] In addition, one has
here a political force that cannot be integrated into the ongoing
character of the political process and political discourse because it is
likely to deny and reject some of the fundamental procedural and
value elements of the political system.

The mass theorist does not look far to find instances when masses
have presumably been mobilized into extremist movements that have
threatened to destroy or succeeded in destroying existing political
forms and values. The Fascist, Nazi, and Communist movements are
favorite examples, as are some other forms of working-class organization and protest. Various peasant and agrarian movements could be
interpreted in similar terms, and in some respects this appears to be
the case in regard, for instance, to the American Populists and French
Poujadists, among others. It might be argued that some instances of
right-wing extremism in the United States could also be understood
in analogous terms.

Political alienation. Political behavior in response to a condition of
political alienation is another instance of mass politics, and in the
literature on politically alienated behavior one finds some application
of mass political theory concepts.[62] Essentially, the material here deals
with a type of projective politics in which a segment of the population,
lacking a sense of power and of meaningful relationship to existing
political elites and processes, and usually characterized by anxieties,

frustrations, and despair, utilizes political issues and candidates to vent its discomforts. In other words, the discontented and alienated may at times turn politics into a phobic sector into which they inject their own personal discomforts.[63] This is an irrational politics in which political choice is not made in terms either of prior commitments and loyalties or of the specifics of policy or candidate program. Rather, a vote is used as a means of striking out and denying power or support to what are viewed as the established and respectable political forces, the very ones that the alienated have felt to be unresponsive and over which they have felt no control. In this emotional and irrational politics the merits of issues and candidates are ignored as the mass population, cutting across class lines but united by a common alienation, votes out of its insecurities and personal phobias and as a means of lashing out against an increasingly frustrating political environment over which it senses little control.

[W]e are hypothesizing ... Horton and Thompson affirm, that voting down local issues may be in part a type of mass protest, a convergence of the individual assessments and actions of the powerless who have turned politics into a "phobic" sector by projecting into available political symbols the fears and suspicions growing out of the alienated conditions of their existence.[64]

Issues are turned into emotion-laden symbols for something that may have little reality to the issue at hand. This is particularly the case with what are referred to as style or moralistic issues as opposed to position issues. The former are issues of an emotional, moralistic, style-of-life character that lend themselves to a strongly charged irrational approach. The latter issues, concerned as they are with who-gets-what-at-how-much-cost-to-whom, to use Stone's expression,[65] permit of less emotional and non-issue-based response, though even here a politically alienated response may arise.

Analyses of referendum voting, especially in cases of defeat, suggest that referendums lend themselves especially well to alienated voting. Referendums consist of distinctive issues to which the voter can say no rather than merely selecting among proffered candidates. Referendums may have the support of established political forces, which are thus exposed for possible public renunciation by those experiencing powerlessness vis-à-vis politics. They touch at times on distinctive ways of life and belief or can be so construed and hence admit of emotionally charged as well as distorted response and interpretation. Research suggests heavy defeat for such referendums, especially in circumstances of a large voter turnout when the most apathetic and least politically involved, and presumably most alienated, flock to the polls.[66] These are, in effect, instances of negative voting by the "angry voter," in John Horton's phrase.[67]

Not only are the responses to referendums of interest, but perhaps more important is the response to candidates for political office as well. Thus it is argued in the literature of political alienation that the alienated are ready followers of those who present themselves as antiestablishment and populist "men of the people," those who assume the stance of fighting the established, respectable, and aloof political forces that appear beyond the control of the "little man." This may be a demagogic figure who rallies the alienated in a crusade based not on group interests, specific issues, rational policy, or reasoned discourse but on their feelings of powerlessness, anger, and frustration. There may thus be the intrusion, into what are often sensitive political arenas, of unreasoning and emotional masses with little patience or understanding of democratic political forms or process and with little acceptance of the legitimacy of dissent or the complexity of issues.

Totalitarianism. One of the greatest apprehensions of students of mass society is the role played by mass society conditions in facilitating the rise of totalitarianism. Considerable effort has been devoted to elaborating the characteristics of totalitarian movements and rule and their origin in the conditions of mass society. The following briefly notes mass theory's treatment of the conditions requisite to the appearance and continuance of totalitarian rule, the means by which domination is maintained, the character of public support and involvement, and the nature of totalitarian rule.

Fundamental to mass society theory is the proposition that totalitarianism is based on masses. Some of the most distinguished mass theorists have expressed this forcefully. "Totalitarian movements are mass organizations of atomized, isolated individuals."[68] The essence of totalitarianism is "the institutionalization of amorphous masses."[69] In effect, totalitarianism requires a population bereft of any intermediate group ties or autonomous relationships. If atomized and isolated populations are lacking, then totalitarianism creates them. "Totalitarian elites strive to create masses as well as to mobilize existing masses. People cannot be mobilized against the established order until they have been divorced from prevailing codes and relations."[70] Any institutional or organizational structures that could provide a focus for allegiances or loyalties other than to the state or party are rooted out. No autonomous centers of power are permitted to survive. Whatever might provide a sense of alternatives to the cultural, social, and political dogmas of the totalitarian state is destroyed.[71]

Essentially, domination in totalitarian society is maintained through several devices. One is that of demanding and achieving extensive social and psychological involvement of the populace in the state as such, its rituals, symbolism, and purposes, and in the diverse organizations that it controls. This serves to provide a sense of community, belonging, identity, emotional support and response which create loyalty to the totalitarian state and impede the potential development of contrary commitments. "...[T]otalitarian domination of the individual will is not a mysterious process.... It arises and proceeds rationally and relentlessly through the creation of new functions, statuses and allegiances, which, by conferring community, makes the manipulation of the human will scarcely more than an exercise in scientific social psychology."[12] In effect, the totalitarian state demands not passive commitment by its citizens but an unrestricted loyalty and an active participation that take precedence over all other duties. One has here the destruction of any potential countercommitments or any private personal sector of life. Domination is preserved by a network of intermediate organizations controlled by the state in which the citizen is extensively implicated and through which he can be manipulated. They serve as a means of enhancing elite access and control over the populace.[13]

In spite of the oppressive, antilibertarian, and irrational character of totalitarianism, the unusual and especially disturbing feature of such regimes is that they rest on the consent of their people. However heinous these regimes may appear, they do not want for popular support, even where the grotesque qualities or excesses of totalitarian rule are known. Further, such regimes trumpet their mass support and in fact seek substantiation of their claims by evidencing some of the trappings of traditional democratic states (though, of course, little of the actual practices), such as electoral and legislative processes, with an emphasis placed on adhering to legal forms. For the mass theorist it is the mass condition of the population in totalitarian society and the manipulation of this population that accounts for its loyalty to the regime.

The total nature of totalitarian control may need little elaboration. Essentially, the mass theorist argues that such regimes exercise control over all agencies of power, destroying or incorporating any potentially independent power base. Nor are there any limits on the regime's exercise of power or on its ability to carry out its will. In part, however, the potency of the regime rests on its identifying itself with the national will and purpose. It thus presents itself as the embodiment of the nation, not of distinct interests or perspectives therein. As such, difference or organization contrary to the regime, its leadership, or party arm is perceived as being opposed to the nation, to the will of the people. On such grounds, difference then becomes defined as error, and error persisted in thereafter becomes subversive or treasonable. There is no basis provided for accommodating or perceiving difference as merely a representation of distinctive interests within the broader society or as a contrary or different perspective on policy.

The full enormity of totalitarianism thus stands revealed. Either arising out of or creating conditions of dissolution, it attains total control over a loyal population, however repugnant the regime. And in identifying itself with the general will it becomes the depository of truth, any contradiction of which lacks any legitimating basis and becomes defined as subversive.

Conditions for viable democratic polities: autonomous pluralist structures

A major concern of the political mass theorist is the continuance of the viability of liberal democratic forms of governance. Some of the principal issues and considerations in this regard are expressed in the theory's concern with the necessity of autonomous pluralist and intermediate structures and in its partiality to some indirection and minimization of participation in democratic forms of governance.

One of the most significant political aspects of the discussion of the decline of community and the role of autonomous associations is the relationship between democratic polities and autonomous pluralist structures. Freedom, the mass theorist stresses, rests on the autonomy and vitality of diverse social units. This is a crucial condition requisite for the sustenance of conditions preserving the viability and tempered action of both elites and nonelites. It is the destruction or weakness of pluralist structures that undermines democratic freedom.[74]

[F]reedom thrives in cultural diversity, in local and regional differentiation, in associative pluralism, and above all, in the *diversification of power*.

... it is the continued existence of this array of intermediate powers in society, of this plurality of "private sovereignties," that constitutes, above anything else, the greatest single barrier to the conversion of democracy from its liberal form to its totalitarian form.[75]

What is essential are not merely autonomous associations but the decentralization of power, so that effective power and authority will come to reside in such associations. It is the presence of power within these associations that makes possible their exercise of those authoritative functions that are requisite to their vitality. Community and

association persist most effectively only to the extent that they are
the loci for the satisfaction of important needs and the performance
of significant functions for their membership. This rests on a requisite
degree of power and authority.

A structure of viable voluntary private associations and the corresponding network of intermediate relations that diffuse power and
authority perform a number of vital functions. Some of the mass
theorists, especially Nisbet and Kornhauser, address themselves to
these functions, and it is their perspective that is developed here.
(Other writers, however, would appear less concerned with a concentration of power where it resides in the hands of elite elements.) Such
associations limit the centralization of power, and they provide protection from concentrated power. "Where the individual stands alone in
face of the State he is helpless."[76] The power of the state and of
political elites is constrained to the extent that they contain authority
to perform functions necessary for the social and political life of its
membership and the broader society. Direct dependence on the state
for the satisfaction of basic and intimate individual and group needs
not only increases the potential for totalitarianism but may also produce a condition of acceptance and even support for totalitarian rule.
This is facilitated where there is the belief that the satisfaction of
most political, economic, and perhaps even social needs appears possible only by action of the state, which may in fact assume a benign
appearance albeit, nonetheless, a totalitarian one. In addition, the
ability of liberal democratic government to maintain representative
rule rests significantly on the provision of the "social bases of free and
open competition for leadership" and the facilitation of "widespread
participation in the selection of leaders."[77] This is made possible by the
existence of autonomous plural structures. Also, the power of the
broader population, nonelites as Kornhauser labels them, is minimized
by the dispersion of power among a diversity of associations, some of
a contrary and competitive character. In a sense they check each
other. Power does not become cumulative. Related is the proposition
that with multiple affiliations no one association is likely to acquire
hegemony over different aspects of its members' lives. Hence there is
"a separation of the various spheres of society,"[78] and commitment
to any association is qualified and limited to the narrow goals or
purposes of the association. The power it can exercise tends to be
constrained by the particular basis of the members' commitment,
and this may in turn be of a qualified character. The consequences
of these conditions serve to preserve a viable democratic order in that
they prevent the appearance of unlimited power either among the

elite or nonelites, agencies of the state or the mass of the community. Conditions are maintained of moderate access as well as of a heightened possibility of responsiveness.

Mass theory suggests additional consequences of pluralist structures, though in some instances by implication only. Some of these, however, are phrased more in terms of the functions of autonomous intermediate structures than in terms of the results of political pluralism. But these are closely related conditions. In the absence of intermediate groups, Kornhauser affirms, "elites lose their insulation since demands and impulses of large numbers of people that formerly were sublimated and fulfilled by intermediate groups now are focused directly on the national level."[79] Demands and communications are presented less erratically and suddenly and in a less extreme form when done via intermediate groupings, given the more planned and ordered functioning and greater moderation and rational consideration of program and objectives exhibited by association leadership. Intermediate associations also provide a number of social and psychological functions, such as fellowship and interpersonal relationship, involvement in "multiple proximate concerns,"[80] some sense of purposiveness, a sense of self, conditions for personal expression and responsiveness, a sense of meaningfulness for one's life and self, a minimization of a sense of anxiety, and so on. This minimizes availability for some extremist movement or demagogic leader through which one would seek to find the satisfactions and the sense of control lacking in the absence of autonomous associations.

The necessity of social and political pluralism and the vital role of viable autonomous associations are clear. A couple of major questions, however, must be explored. What is the nature, in fact, of the autonomous associations in contemporary democratic society? This is particularly important given the assumption in some strains of mass political theory, and more especially in much of current political commentary, that some of the major Western democratic societies by nature of their associational character are successful pluralist political societies. I will be concerned particularly with evaluating the United States in this respect. A second concern centers on which other conditions must be satisfied if there is to be an effective and equitable pluralist political order. This will receive brief attention in later discussion.

Perspectives on democratic practice and theory

The thoughtful reader may have deduced that implicit in mass theory are two somewhat different theories of a democratic polity, or, in other words, of democracy. While these theories may ostensibly appear to be contradictory, they do in fact contain important compatible elements. One stresses the necessity of the decentralization of power so as to maintain and secure a diversity of autonomous and even contrary units of authority, power, and decision making. The other, making little reference to questions of diversification of power, stresses the importance of elite autonomy and the minimization of nonelite involvement in decision making. The former is intimately associated with the pluralist strain in mass theory and has received the greatest attention in the present account. Essentially, it urges the necessity not only of diversity but also of the nonincorporable properties of the individual and his associations. Thus an irrevocable distinction is drawn between the state and society, and the individual and the state. The state, another form of association, is hence distinct from and cannot subsume in any unitary form the individual and his associations. The obverse is "the collectivist, unitary ideology of democracy," the origin of which is often traced to French rationalist thought of the eighteenth century. The continuance and even the increased credibility of such thought today are viewed as ominous.[81]

Mass theorists do differ on their conceptions of the role and authority of the state. Yet in their concern with elite autonomy and their denigration of nonelite competence and commitment to democratic freedoms, they suggest a revisionist theory of democracy, or what has critically been referred to as either democratic elitism[82] or contemporary democratic theory.[83] This may be contrasted with classical democratic theory in which a greater stress is given citizen participation and the personal benefits that flow from such participation. It is not claimed here that mass political theory attempts to develop a democratic theory in these revisionist terms; rather, an important portion of mass theory accords with contemporary democratic theory and is therefore open to similar critical evaluations. In fact, the arguments of the democratic elitists may be viewed as buttressing the propositions of mass political theory.[84] At the same time, it is not unreasonable to suggest that in fact the theorist of contemporary or elitist democratic theory in turn finds his own theoretical and ideological concerns significantly strengthened and supplemented by the propositions of mass theory.

The conceptualization of democracy developed by contemporary democratic theory, implicit in most of mass political theory, may be described succinctly. Essentially, I am referring to a concept of democracy that stresses the indirect over the direct form of citizen exercise of power, the procedural over the normative content of

democracy, liberty over equality. In contemporary or elitist democratic theory, democracy is defined principally in terms of the opportunity of the citizenry periodically to choose freely among candidates.
A direct exercise of political power in terms of initiating, carrying
out, or deciding public policy is seen as potentially disruptive and a
threat to liberty. Minimal participation and indirect access are virtues,
not disabilities. Even citizen ignorance and apathy can be viewed
positively. The emphasis is on the mass rather than the elite threat
to democracy. The latter is seen as diminished through the existence
of elite diversity and competition and the need to obtain periodic
renewal of public support. The ability to replace elites thus becomes
a significant defining dimension of a democratic polity. Democracy is
perceived in somewhat narrow terms, as a means to maintain orderly
and stable rule under conditions of liberty wherein the possibility of
change in personnel and policy is theoretically available. It is not considered as providing a means for the growth of the political and personal sensibilities and talents of the individual citizen.

In mass political theory, as well as in the more explicit theory of
contemporary democratic forms, there is a shared belief of the
antinomy between equality and liberty. This is true for both the pluralist and the elitist strains in mass theory. The problem contained in
the conflict between the maintenance of individual freedom and the
stress on the equality of men is certainly not a new one. Essentially,
it rests on the proposition that an effort to create equality among
men must inevitably constrain the efforts, fortunes, talents, and opportunities of at least some men. Otherwise, through the exercise of these
properties, inequalities will arise as a matter of course. Yet to impose
constraints is to limit the freedom of those affected, at least in the
use of these personal properties. Hence the theorist reasons that to
proclaim a quest for equality may not only be illusory but, more
significantly, demagogic and also deleterious to human liberty. The
strain between liberty and equality is for most theorists, mass and
otherwise, generally resolved in favor of liberty, at the cost of a
continuing inequality. The vital problem is then perceived to be that
of maintaining a maximization of freedoms while yet seeking as great
a degree of equality as possible under a condition of liberty. Where
the balance is to be drawn is, of course, an important unresolved issue.

It is significant that mass theory's conceptualization of the conditions that underlie a viable liberal democratic order does not include
the role of unmet group needs and the nature of elite responsiveness
to such needs. Their absence arises, in part, from the lack of attention
to the interest origin of conditions of strain and availability that are

exhibited by collectivities. The significance of these omissions will become clearer later.

Basic distinctions, processes, and variables

The preceding elaboration of the political theory of mass society has provided, in effect, an account of the basic distinctions, processes, and variables utilized by the theory. These may be summarized as follows: (1) The distinction between and the characterization of mass and nonmass are crucial. The concept of masses in essence involves a population lacking distinctive group membership or intermediate relationships. It is in effect an uprooted and atomized population. (2) Political behavior is either mass behavior or nonmass behavior. The former is the political behavior of masses. Such behavior is erratic, unrealistic, and even irrational, direct, activist, and coercive in the use of legitimate and nonlegitimate forms of protest and pressure. (3) The availability for mass movements is "due primarily to the strength of social ties, and not to the influence of class, or any other social status."[85] (4) "When mass behavior becomes organized around a program and acquires a certain continuity in purpose and effort, it takes on the character of a mass movement."[86] Mass movements by definition are constituted of masses.[87] (5) The relationship among elites, nonelites, and masses is central. Elites refer to the occupants of positions in the political and other institutional areas of society that are superordinate in those areas – that is, they are positions with significant decision-making power for political, economic, and cultural policy. Such power is usually authoritative.

In regard to the character of elite functions an important perspective in mass political theory stresses the role of elites in the preservation of the major political values and objectives of the society, of acting in tempered terms, utilizing reasoned discourse, and as being knowledgeable and effective in policy formation and in their response to threats to the society. The sources of disruption, irrationality, and the destruction of democratic political standards reside in the actions of the masses. The role of the nonelite population is to choose among competing elites or elite aspirants and leave major decision making itself to the elites. Minimal rather than maximum political participation is stressed. Elites are perceived as acting in accord with the political traditions and standards of the society and as generally moderate and consistent in their politics and political activities. It is the nonelite mass populations that intrude actively, intemperately, and with anti-liberalitarian consequences on either elite responsibilities or, more generally, upon the more reasoned value-preserving functioning of those in authority in the democratic state. (6) It is the processes of democratization and associated value change that are seen as important influences on the decline of elite exclusiveness and authority. These related phenomena are perceived as causal to the increasing intrusion of the broader society into the functioning of elites in crucial decision-making centers. (7) A number of related processes are perceived as both productive of the appearance of mass populations and the development among such populations of a sense of powerlessness, frustration, and anxiety.

First receiving particular stress has been the concept of the decline of community, that is, of a functionally and morally integrated population centering on a major social system dimension such as work, religious belief, and area of residence. These are the focuses of interpersonal relations and of social and psychic support and expression. There is usually a sense of some autonomy from other societal elements, such as other communities and centers of political rule, and particularly the elites in each. An essential element of such autonomy is the maintenance of some degree of independent function and authority. These are thus centers of power and a means of protection and of control over one's political environment. Second, the long-term process in Western civilization of rationalization and the centralization of institutional sectors, including of course the political, has had some consequences similar to the decline of community. These have included an increased sense of powerlessness, particularly with the heightened sense of the inappropriateness of the lack of individual or group control. Other consequences have included the weakening of meaningful extensive intimate interrelationships, the appearance of a sense of dissatisfaction, insecurity, a vague malaise, ignorance of social and political dynamics, and so on. These forces have turned nonmasses or publics into mass populations that may at times provide marginal elite elements with an available population. If writers such as Mills are excluded, however, the political theory of mass society has given little attention to the processes of rationalization and centralization and their associated consequences.

4. Social structural analysis assessed and related comments

The present chapter critically evaluates the deficiencies in social structural analysis that exist in the political theory of mass society. As noted earlier, these concerns touch both descriptive inadequacies in mass political theory and its theoretical shortcomings as a theory of radical political behavior. Three major concerns are discussed. The first focuses on inadequacies in intermediate group analysis. The second extends the dimensions for defining mass society by focusing on sensed integration. The third deals with a fundamental issue – the inability to comprehend all but a very small proportion of political phenomena, extremist or otherwise, in terms of a mass–nonmass distinction. In effect it elaborates, in terms of their structural and interest basis, an extended typology of possible politically active collectivities. The present discussion essentially seeks to advance the conceptual analysis of a number of vital questions.

Intermediate group analysis

Specifications of the intermediate group concept as inadequate and diverse

Fundamental to mass theory is its analysis of intermediate relations and group structure.

We can conceive, states William Kornhauser, of all but the simplest societies as comprising three levels of social relations. The first level consists of highly personal or primary relations, notably the family. The third level contains relations inclusive of the whole population, notably the state. The second level comprises all intermediate relations, notably the local community, voluntary association, and occupational group. These intermediate relations function as links between the individual and his primary relations, on the one hand, and the state and other national relations, on the other hand.[1]

However, neither Kornhauser nor other mass theorists of the concept of intermediate relations and groups provide a clear, unambiguous statement of what constitutes such relations and structure. This is not surprising given the diverse sources that have contributed to mass political theory and their generally discoursive quality. Intermediate groups and relations have been specified as those that exist between the individual and his primary groups on the one hand, and the state or nationwide organizations on the other hand. They have been identified as a buffer between the two, as autonomous centers of power, and as intervening structures for communication and mediation. Yet such general treatments lack specification of the individual's place within the intermediate organizations in question and of his experiences with them, as well as of the nature of the relationships between such structures and other nonintermediate structures. More precisely, there is a lack of an attempt to specify what particulars suffice to represent intermediate group structures, with respect to intimacy of interpersonal relationships, degree of personal affect provided, size of group, degree of individual control and responsiveness of the organization, nature of external group relations, nature of group consciousness, and so on. Not surprisingly, insufficient attention is given to the consequences that would follow from different group properties.[2] Without a paradigm of community or intermediate structures in these terms it is difficult to apply the concept with any broad degree of consensus to actual situations, group structures, and societies. This difficulty partly underlies the disagreement over what constitutes conditions of pluralist and mass society. Thus, for instance, for some scholars America is a pluralist society, whereas for others it appears to be a mass society. Lastly, work within the mass political theory perspective lacks any considerable attempt to examine in detail the extent to which existing intermediate structures in fact fulfill the presumed characteristics and functions of such structures.

There is also some disparity of emphasis in the use of the intermediate group concept by different mass theorists. Nisbet,[3] writing in a more historical vein than Kornhauser, uses the concept to represent a much more intimate and comprehensive set of relationships whose psychic functions for the individual receive considerably greater attention. There is a greater stress on the integrative, functionally diffuse, and ascriptive nature of these relationships in contrast to segmental, functionally specific, and voluntaristic properties. These are relationships that cannot be found within the large-scale secondary organization. On the other hand, Kornhauser's use of voluntary associations as the principal empirical indicator of intermediate structures tends toward an application of the concept to relationships and structures of a less personal character, with more limited individual involvement, and of a more segmental, specific, and voluntaristic nature. The reference in many instances is, in effect, to secondary types of associations, in many ways the usual type of narrow-interest-oriented association. From Nisbet's perspective such a type of association would be unable to fulfill the same functions served by earlier more intimate group structures. In Kornhauser's usage a greater degree of variation in intermediate structures exists among societies, with such associations or intermediate groups abundant and vital in some societies but lacking in others. Thus Nisbet appears readier than Kornhauser to see their decline and inadequacy in contemporary society, whether in democratic polities or not. In an important sense, however, Nisbet is referring to what for Kornhauser is, in effect, communal society.[4]

Intermediate group functions

The relevance of intermediate group structures to mass theory rests on the functions they presumably serve. A number are suggested by mass society writers. The following lists the major ones appearing in the literature. Intermediate group structures have been viewed as providing a sense of personal security and nurturance, partly because of the conditions they provide for personal expression, responsiveness, and control. They make possible the maintenance of a sense of membership within a community. They offer channels of political expression and means of political pressure, as well as a sense of participation in and control over one's political and social environment.[5] In terms of the broader society they provide for conditions of countervailing power, the diffusion of power, and protection against possibly oppressive state power. They perform a socializing function into the norms and procedures of political moderation, help create a diversity of concerns and preoccupations, and, concomitantly, heighten the likelihood of producing a condition of competing commitments. In addition, they are usually viewed as providing centers of power to protect the population and to protect the elite through establishing structured channels of communication and action. The elite is further safeguarded by the restraint, disunion, and preoccupations, produced by group membership and its diversity. In effect, intermediate relationships and structures are perceived as restraining and protecting the population, guarding the elite, limiting the concentration of power, creating a condition of countervailing power, and providing means for ordered political expression.

Functions evaluated

While there is merit in some of these propositions, the theory is both incomplete and in need of qualification in significant respects. Though the present analysis does not attempt a comprehensive evaluation of the concept of intermediate structures and their functions, it will suggest a number of distinct particulars in which the empirical and theoretical adequacy of mass theory formulations are incomplete or open to question. Additional observations of a related nature will be made in Chapter 6 in the assessment of pluralist theory.

Secondary associations as intermediate groups. It may be possible to accept, with some reservations, the historical role of intermediate groups as a viable source of personal nurturance and security. As a contemporary phenomenon, however, this seems much more doubtful. In fact, some mass theorists vigorously maintain that there has been a desiccation of intermediate groups, with a consequent vacuum as regards provision of the functions that such groups offered. In the broader usage of the intermediate group concept, as expressed ·in Nisbet, for example, the significance of local community, church, and so on, is greatly diminished. Individual involvement in intermediate associations is slight and sometimes even lacking. In terms of the more usual types of secondary associations it would appear correct to say, as a broad generalization, that many individuals are not members, and of those who are, frequent attendance is low and active involvement is even less.[6] Studies by the National Opinion Research Center (NORC) have revealed that nearly one-half of the American population are without any voluntary association membership. If trade-union membership were excluded, this proportion would increase by about 10 to 15 percent, leaving only 35 to 40 percent with association memberships. Even for those who are members, only about one-half belong to more than one voluntary association.[7] Similarly, somewhat less than 50 percent of organizational members have ever been officers of their associations, and only a somewhat larger proportion respond affirmatively to the question of whether they are very active in the associations to which they belong.

Even where there is membership and some participation, the individual finds little satisfaction for the greater part of his concerns. Such associations often lack psychological force as a center for the individual. Given the at times large, rationalized, and impersonally organized association, he may not find in it the opportunity for personal expression and responsiveness or the sense of belonging and commitment that presumably the more personal dimension of intermediate group membership would provide. Divested of affect, partial and even alien, and of meager political effectiveness, such associations are not psychologically meaningful.[8] Both the psychic as well as political socialization functions of intermediate groups would partly depend on such groups serving as important reference groups for their members. Maurice Pinard, however, has persuasively questioned whether the intermediate structures in which an individual is implicated do, in fact, act as important reference groups.[9]

Further, as Kariel has noted, "maturing under modern, industrial conditions, associations assumed a scale and an organizational structure making them oligarchical in their actual operations, and likely to smother the individual as effectively as the state."[10] It is likely that the individual will not attain effective control over the secondary association. Certainly, Michel's classic work has made this a not unexceptional observation.[11] In addition, the individual may find existing associations lacking the power or means to alter his situation, resolve his problems, or effectively contend with a threatening and inaccessible environment. Effectiveness in regard to community circumstances, broader economic strain, high prices, shoddy consumer goods, polluted environs, or in regard to societal change, threatening life styles, foreign adventurism, and personal confusion or failure are in most regards beyond even the more viable and potent associations. A related dilemma is posed by Richard Hamilton's recent citation of Almond and Verba's finding that when asked "what citizens would do to try to influence their national government," "only 1 percent said they would work through a political party and only 4 percent said they would work through a formal group such as a union or professional association."[12]

A serious failing in mass theory's treatment of the role of intermediate associations is the absence of attention to the adequacy of substitutes for those instances when such types of relationships have declined. In other words, the individual may actually be variously implicated in relationships or circles that succeed in fulfilling some of the sociopsychic functions usually attributed to intermediate structures. The subject has still not been fully clarified, but there does exist considerable doubt as to whether merely the decline of what have been called intermediate groupings does, in fact, lead to the personal consequences suggested when account is taken of the total individual situation. These functions may be even more effectively fulfilled by a host of what are still strong interpersonal relationships, even in the absence of intermediate group structures. That is, the greater part of society's members appear to be implicated in a personal world and daily commitments of a character that probably does provide a sense of belonging, social membership, conditions for personal expression, and a feeling of satisfaction. One may legitimately question the quality of these experiences and the absence of opportunities for personal growth and recognize the petty anxieties that are created and even the perversion of human sensibilities and talents. Yet if the former conditions or experiences are met – as I suspect they are in this less than adequately conceptualized or researched area – then social and psychological functions presumably fulfilled by intermediate group structures may to a considerable degree actually find satisfaction through other means. To an extent, the perspective developed by social area analysts in their attempt to establish the conditions for integration in large-scale urban life has looked at new forms of involvement and some still continued sources of membership and concern at the local community level.[13]

The following discussion draws on a diverse range of data and research in order to provide some empirical elaboration of the various types of involvements and activities exhibited by Americans in recent years. These include recreational, sport, cultural, and hobby activities, as well as relationships with communal groups, friends, neighbors, and neighborhood. While there are clearly differential rates of participation, the extensive range and quite considerable degree of involvement suggest that for most members of society there are at least a number of experiences and relationships through which a sense of place, personal ties, and conditions of responsiveness may be established. While certainly many meaningful experiences are not included in the present material and the data are of unequal quality, it nonetheless forcefully suggests the rather extensive range of opportunities possessed by many in society.

The most extensively catalogued activities are recreational, leisure, and cultural pursuits. Table 4.1 reports recent levels of participation in a number of diverse areas.

One of the major bases of involvement and experience is that of communal identity. Ethnicity is a potentially significant component of such identity for many. Ethnic populations are considerable in the United States, and many still have strong group ties. There are more than 5 million Americans of Mexican background, and 1.5 million of Puerto Rican heritage.[14] Even using severe standards for establishing ethnic background, we find that distinct German and Italian populations number between 3.5 and 4.25 million each; the Polish population is a little less than 2.3 million; and the Irish people number at

Table 4.1. *Participation in leisure-time activities*

Activity	Number of participants (in millions)	Average days per participant	Number of visitor days (in millions)
National forest recreation use, 1973 total			188.2
Used for fishing	—	—	15.8
Used for camping	—	—	49.8
Selected recreational activities, sport, 1972			
Baseball attendance	26.9	—	—
Collegiate football attendance	30.8	—	—
Outboard motors in use	7.4	—	—
Selected recreational activities, miscellaneous, 1970, except as noted (persons nine years old and over)			
Golf (1972)	7.7	8.2	—
Boating, canoeing, sailing	41.1	10.2	—
Playing outdoor games or sports	60.0	44.6	—
Attending outdoor sports events and concerts	59.4	10.6	—
Hunting	20.9	10.4	—
Fishing (1972)	38.0	7.3	—

Table 4.1 (*continued*)

Activity	Participation rates		
	Number of participants (in millions)	Average days per participant	Number of visitor days (in millions)
Bird watching	7.5	58.0	—
Wildlife and bird photography	4.9	8.2	—
Selected cultural/educational activities			
Average weekly movie attendance (1964)	44.0	—	—
Museum attendance (1962)	184.8	—	—
Adult education participation, (1972)	15.7	—	—
Major orchestra attendance (1971)	10.6	—	—

Source: U.S. Bureau of the Census, *Statistical Abstract of the United States: 1974:* Table Nos. 337, 348, 349; in the 1972 edition, Table No. 323; and in the 1966 edition, Table Nos. 298, 299.

somewhat under 1.5 million. Scotch, Czech, Hungarian, Oriental, and Cuban people range from around 600,000 to a million.[15] Considerable numbers of Yugoslav, Lithuanian, Greek, and other populations can also be counted.[16] These ethnic groups are disproportionately resident in metropolitan areas, which suggests their presence in either relatively distinct ethnic communities or within circumstances permitting fairly close contact or association.

Several other possible means and areas for securing involvement and integration are present. A major one is family ties and relationships. Family visiting and ordinary socializing, group activities, and mutual aid continue for a considerable proportion of Americans, even if in a tempered degree in comparison with earlier periods.[17] Popular dogma notes the destruction of the extended family and the triumph of the isolated nuclear family; it is, however, possible to speak of an intervening form in which family functions have declined and the scope of family relationship narrowed, yet continued contact and assistance persist. Litwak has suggested that what we see today is the "modified extended family."[18] The few findings reported in the following tables from diverse cities such as Los Angeles, Greensboro, San Francisco, and a number of midwestern communities suggest these continued family relationships. The tables also provide a contrast between family contacts and relationships maintained with other social groups.

In Tables 4.2 and 4.3 one sees a fairly high level of family contact even in cities as different as Los Angeles and Greensboro.

Considerable ability to call on family members for help is illustrated by Table 4.4, from the 1950s San Francisco study by Bell and Boat. The table is based on responses to the question of how many persons from each of the groups listed the respondent could call on for assistance if he were sick. It provides a comparative view of the relative importance of a number of different types of social groups and shows the variation among four urban neighborhoods distinguished by economic and life style differences. The findings also suggest the considerable degree to which respondents feel able to rely on nonfamilial social groups.

Even with the decline of local neighborhood communities, such areas still offer limited small-scale networks of association for a significant number of area residents.[19] This is illustrated not only in Table 4.4 but also in Greer's findings (Table 4.5) for local community participation in a couple of neighborhoods in Los Angeles.

A more recent and intensive analysis of local Chicago communities by Hunter perceptively analyzes the changed but still continued

Table 4.2. *Kin visiting in two Los Angeles neighborhoods*

	Neighborhood type*	
Visiting kin (%)	Low urban	High urban
Once a week or more often	49	55
At least once a month, but less than once a week	24	21
A few times a year, but less than once a month	11	8
Never	5	9
No kin in Los Angeles	11	7
No. of respondents	(162)	(150)

Source: Scott Greer, "Urbanism Reconsidered: A Comparative Study of Local Areas in a Metropolis" *American Sociological Review,* 21 (February 1956), 19–25, Table 3.

* Neighborhood types are distinguished by the proportion of house type, women in the labor force, and the number of children in households. Low urban are single-family residential areas with few women in the labor force and a large number of children; high urban areas are the converse of these conditions. Neighborhood is a tract area.

vitality for many people of their attachments to local communities of residence, as well as to "symbolic communities" within an emerging, differentiated, and reorganized hierarchy of communities within the urban environment.[20] He also describes the "proliferation of purposively organized local community voluntary associations which serve to integrate members into the social structure and symbolic culture of the local community."[21]

The findings of other researchers are in a similar direction. Wilensky found in the beginning of the sixties that, in Detroit, 63 percent of his respondents expressed either strong or medium-strong community attachments.[22] Earlier work in Lansing, Michigan, revealed a high degree of neighborhood social intimacy for 37 percent of the respondents; 44 percent had a medium degree of intimacy.[23] In their summary assessment of a part of the Los Angeles research Greer and Kube have affirmed:

that the disappearance of the local community and neighborhood in the city is far from complete. It is most nearly true in the highly urban area,

Table 4.3. *Expression of affection, obligation, and family contacts – Greensboro*

Kin category	No. of respondents	Affectionally close (%)	Obligation impt. (%)	Contact monthly or more (%)	Contact sev. times a yr. or more (%)	Mean no. of contact patterns
Parent(s)	(724)	75	50	94	98	3.8
Age-near sibling	(697)	48	32	61	90	2.1
Best-known cousin	(682)	18	10	27	63	1.0

Source: Bert N. Adams, *Kinship in an Urban Setting* (Chicago: Markham Publishing Co., 1968), Table VI-1.

Table 4.4. Reliance on at least one member of the specified group

Group on which respondent relies	Low family, low income status (Mission) (%)	Low family, high economic status (Pacific Heights) (%)	High family, low economic status (Outer Mission) (%)	High family, high economic status (St. Francis Wood) (%)
Neighbors	34.3	29.3	44.7	39.9
Co-workers	39.9	49.4	23.5	43.6
Relatives	70.9	83.8	81.2	85.1
Friends	59.9	65.3	52.7	73.2

Source: Wendell Bell and Marion Boat, "Urban Neighborhoods and Informal Relationships," *American Journal of Sociology,* 62 (January 1957), 391–398, Table 5. Published by The University of Chicago Press.

Table 4.5. *Local community participation in two Los Angeles neighborhoods*

	Type of neighborhood (%)	
Type of social participation	Low urban	High urban
High neighborhood scores	67	56
Friends in local area	50	29
% of all friends who live in local area	41	25

Source: Scott Greer, "Urbanism Reconsidered: A Comparative Study of Local Areas in a Metropolis," *American Sociological Review,* 21 (February 1956), 19–25, from Table 1.

but in those neighborhoods characterized by familism there is considerable vitality in local associations. This is evident in neighboring, local organization and church participation, readership of the local community press, and ability to name local leaders. It is accompanied by an attitude of commitment to the area as "home" – a place from which one does not want or expect to move. In participation and in felt permanence, the highly urban areas had a much weaker hold on their residents.[24]

Not only neighborhood and family, of course, but also friends, casual cliques, associations existing at the place of work, and contacts in areas of leisure pursuit and elsewhere may offer opportunities for involvement. In the Los Angeles study to which reference has been made, nearly 50 percent of the adult males participated twice a week or more in informal groups, and almost one-fifth participated about once a week.[25] William Key's study of social participation in a number of midwestern rural and urban communities provides further support for the preceding observations.[26] Table 4.6 reveals moderate to heavy participation with a number of different types of groups in various types of communities.

Initial data reflective of life circumstances are generally lacking. The little that is available does not support a contention of a population troubled by a lack of ties. In their 1964 national survey Free and Cantril found very little expression (Table 4.7) of concern over the more personal circumstances of one's life situation.[27] Thus in response to a question on wishes and hopes for the future, imagining the future in the *best* possible light, the responses most relevant to possible

Table 4.6. *Mean scores on social participation scales by place of residence*

| | Maximum scale score | Place of residence | | | | |
		Rural	Village	Small urban	Terre Haute	Indianapolis
Immediate family	10	9.56	7.86	8.10	8.37	8.51
Extended family	10	6.22	5.19	5.50	5.92	5.87
Informal groups	6	3.00	3.60	4.50	4.00	4.00
Work groups	10	4.10	4.27	6.90	8.51	8.65
Formal groups (Chapin Scale)	unlimited	6.14	8.67	13.49	11.08	10.50
Neighboring	10	6.26	5.67	5.40	5.30	4.50

Source: William H. Key, "Rural-Urban Social Participation," in Sylvia F. Fava, ed., *Urbanism in World Perspective* (New York: Thomas Y. Crowell Co., 1968), 305–313, Table 1, p. 309.

Table 4.7. *Personal aspirations and circumstances*

Aspirations in order to be happy	
Emotional stability and maturity – peace of mind	9%
Resolution of one's religious, spiritual, or ethical problems	6%
Life situation – self-rated, from 0 to 10 points	6.85

Source: Lloyd A. Free and Hadley Cantril, *The Political Beliefs of Americans* (New York: Simon and Schuster, 1968), p. 101, Table VII–I.

circumstances of estrangement and lack of community were voiced by very few. And the rating of one's life situation was moderately high.

Unstructured, diffuse, and quite personal in their character, these various relationships may well be supplemented by the social circles and sets to which Charles Kadushin refers when speaking of literary, therapeutic, recreational, media, and other sets and circles that "exhibit the peculiar combination of indirect interaction based on common interest, together with a relatively low degree of institutionalization."[28] As he suggests, these may help fill "the vacuum created by the demise of traditional kinship and neighborhood forms of organization."[29] Even the continuance of at least some sense of community related to the place of work may not be completely displaced in contemporary society, what with the creation of a modest structure of non-production-associated activities within or related to the place of work. Elsewhere, even if one were to assume the decline of occupational community, there may still exist what could be called "status communities" centering on areas of personal commitment, in the usage developed by Joseph Bensman. That is, one can posit non-territorial-specific communities "of shared meanings" in regard to that area in which an "individual chooses to live out his major life interests" and with which he identifies and where he shares certain common perspectives, finds responsiveness, and so forth, with those similarly engaged.[30] In a different yet relevant direction, the social group character of audience systems may result in at least some social and psychological conditions and experiences, even if of a somewhat diminished order, analogous to the personal circumstances and consequences usually associated as characteristic of more typical group membership. In other words, conditions of interaction, involvement, and responsiveness may be developed in group settings lacking some of the more personal, organizational, or community relationships viewed as crucial in the more typical speculations of mass theory.[31]

An important function, in theory, of intermediate structures is the provision of a sense of self, place, and relationship. This may be provided in some instances by elements such as satisfaction in one's work, the nature of one's sacred or secular value scheme, the sense of relationship to – even without involvement in – regional, ethnic, cultural, or other groups, and at least some satisfying personal ties. Similarly, involvement in national structures of culture, politics, entertainment, mass media, and the like, may tend to fulfill such functions. In other words, the bases and means of maintaining ties, involvements, meaning, and personal satisfaction may be much more various than suggested by mass theorists. Much of the preceding data is of a somewhat superficial character. However, if it points in any direction, it is quite clearly away from that suggested by the mass theorists. There is little warrant to suggest a widespread existence of the isolated individual, therefore, at least in a fashion creating political availability.

Independence of sociopsychic and political functions. There is little effort made in mass theory to analyze the distinction between the sociopsychic functions of intermediate relationships and their political functions. There is no theoretical ground upon which to assume that relationships that provide for a satisfaction of sociopsychic needs, either through membership in intermediate structures or in other previously noted terms, will also mean that the political functions of countervailing power and political efficacy will be attained. Or, conversely, even if structures of group relationships exist that do create conditions of countervailing power, it does not follow that those somehow implicated in such structures will either objectively experience a condition of political responsiveness or a sense of political efficacy. Serious question is thus raised as to the political potency of intermediate-type relationships. For example, a not too uncommon phenomenon would be the existence of the geographic-based community of diverse social groups in which the individual is implicated and a member and that successfully provide the sociopsychic functions usually attributed to intermediate associations. Yet neither set of relationships – neither those within the community nor those within other social groups – needs necessarily provide to any adequate degree the political functions usually attributed to such collectivities: political representation, countervailing power, and political mediation. Thus the political consequences and conditions of political pluralism usually understood as arising from the presence of intermediate-group-type relationships may be lacking. Without seriously considering this possibility, mass political theorists will inevitably exhibit a grave bias when evaluating and interpreting contemporary society. Part of my discussion and criticism in later chapters, particularly on pluralism, derives from this discrepancy.

If the preceding distinctions are tenable ones, (1) a population that is implicated in diverse group structures or more diffuse relationships and secures sociopsychic satisfactions, and in these terms is therefore not suggestive of a mass population, may yet in fact be an available population if political efficacy is lacking; and (2) the presence of pluralist political structures need not negate feelings of political estrangement and the possibility of the existence of availability. Whether such populations are to be referred to as mass populations or not is arguable and depends on the usage of the term "mass," but they may well be available collectivities. Presumably, the problem of political unrest and potential support for demagogic leaders among important elements in contemporary American society rests not so much with those who are adrift and isolated but on whether there is a lack of any meaningful sense of a means to control one's environment. The maintenance of involvements, whether by intermediate group relations or otherwise, does not necessarily prevent the population concerned from becoming ardent followers of extremist movements or demagogues, but this is a different question and one with which I am concerned elsewhere. It may be noted in passing, however, that many followers of extremist movements – from Hitler's Fascist supporters to the at times successful and affluent West Coast right-wing extremists[32] – have not in fact been bereft of personal ties and opportunities for personal expression and response. The obverse, of course, is that many groups that are lacking intermediate group ties have not been and do not appear available for mobilization. As suggested previously, it would seem likely that for many among such elements personal ties and a sense of place have been attained through other interpersonal forms. These comments suggest the need for a type of analysis and a consideration of alternative circumstances such as is not being undertaken, certainly not by scholars working in the tradition of mass political theory. The implication of some of these considerations for conceptualization of the mass and nonmass society are very important.

The quality rather than fact of relationship. In his thoughtful summary of Kornhauser's work, W. Alvin Pitcher has pointed to Kornhauser's undue "emphasis on the presence or absence of a certain kind of social relation."[33] As Kornhauser himself suggests at times, and this in a manner somewhat anomalous to his treatment elsewhere, it may not be so much the existence of intermediate group relations as, in Pitcher's words,

the lack of a certain kind of attachment ... the subjective ... "feeling" of being unattached to the larger society which is crucial. The issue thus seems to be social alienation rather than social isolation. Availability is more a matter of a "mental break with the milieux" than of a physical separation from other people in intermediate groups.

In other words, it is not so much the absence of intermediate group membership per se as "the cause and ... the attitude toward the separation" that may be crucial. "Similarly, the significance of participation is to be measured perhaps more by the attitude toward it than by the fact itself."[34] These comments also suggest that it may not be membership in intermediate associations but the quality of such involvement that is crucial.

Some may be alienated because of their participation in a society in which activity is a substitute for meaning. These individuals may be just as latently mass man as are the apathetic. Their availability for mass movements may take a different direction from that of the socially isolated; but in Kornhauser's terms, it will be the same, other directed. . . .
    . . . the crucial issue is not whether the middle-class "belongers" are atomized but whether only atomized persons – that is individuals without relations to the larger society through intermediate organizations – are available for mobilization.[35]

The contention here is twofold: The lack of intermediate group ties need not confirm availability, and their presence does not eliminate it. Crucial may be the development of a significant sense of place, meaning, and responsiveness by the individual. This may be variously achieved. Similarly, it may be lacking in diverse relationships, intermediate associations included.

Indeterminateness of response to estrangement. While mass political theory by its concept of availability recognizes that conditions of estrangement for populations do not automatically lead to mass political behavior, there does appear to be the assumption that at least in contemporary times – if there is a response – it will be a political one, and if political, then in the form of mass political behavior. Yet it may be suggested that estrangement and the lack of intermediate relations or substitutes do not as such lead to any particular distinctive type of political expression. Joseph Gusfield has pointed out that writers on mass society such as David Riesman and C. Wright Mills "have emphasized developing trends toward conformity and passivity rather than toward militance and activism."[36] An important thrust of this essay suggests that the character of behavior that may follow from the social and psychological condition contingent upon the absence of intermediate structures and similar relationships depends on the extent of interest-issue discomfort, the availability of means of political expression, the nature of prevailing ideology, the degree and character of group consciousness, and so on. Generally, it is only with the absence of group consciousness and traditions, the lack of a distinct interest basis for group behavior, and the absence of suitable leadership and organization that one has a heightened potential for the kind of mass behavior and mass movements to which the mass theorist refers. In a related vein, mass theory does not attempt to develop the conditions under which the alienated or estranged would simply indulge in individual deviant behavior, join a nonpolitical expressive social movement, or in fact become a follower of a political mass movement.

Intermediate and heterogeneous structures and societal disunion and disorganization. Gusfield has reasoned that the lack of local intermediate structures and the concomitant participation in and loyalty to more removed impersonal nationwide structures may well be productive of national unity, commitment to common norms, and mediation of differences.[37] This contrasts with the potential for difference, disunion, and lack of common bases of agreement, more likely to inhere in a society marked by a multitude of distinct and different loyalties, membership, and perspectives.

Conditions of mass society develop a homogeneous set of cultural experiences for members. Technological forces have led to an economy and a means of communication which can absorb all the citizens in common. As this has occurred, the autonomy of the local community has given way to a national politics, a national economy and a national culture. . . . the trend toward mass society provides opportunities for strengthening the attachments of the individuals to institutions which accept diversity and support political balance. The conditions of mass society . . . mitigate against political extremism because they operate against the isolation of differentiated subcultures from which strong ideological attachments can develop. At the same time, they provide conditions which promote acceptance of innovations.[38]

It is in the national structure, not in intermediate or local structures, where the greater expressions of the democratic ethnic and the most forceful behavioral commitment to liberty are to be found.

Pitcher raises a somewhat different point. He suggests that the heterogeneous character of pluralist society and widespread mobility have more likely resulted in personal and social disorganization than the autonomous man. A criticism of a quite different nature was found in Durkheim's warning cited earlier, concerning the provincialism and constraints on individual freedom that reside in some intermediate structures. Shils has made a somewhat similar point.[39] It could be argued that part of the estrangement of the individual today arises from the oppressive qualities of intermediate structures.

These points are not, of course, addressed to the maintenance of countervailing power, a presumably positive function of pluralist structures. Nonetheless, they raise concerns very relevant to the issue of conflict and societal disruption of a potentially extremist character. As such they merit consideration by mass political theory and point to the need for a broader interpretative scheme than such theory provides. They also suggest the need for a more profound analysis of the structural properties and conditions of integration and disunion characteristic of mass and plural society than is present in mass theory.

Mobilizing functions of intermediate structures. Not only may the constraining function of intermediate groups be misperceived, but contrary to restraining mass movements Pinard effectively reasons that "the intermediate structure may actually . . . exert *mobilizing* . . . *effects* . . . certain intermediate groups, because of their positive orientations to the means and goals of a social movement, can be a strong force acting to *motivate* and *legitimate* individual as well as group participation in a movement."[40] In other words, it may be the presence and not the absence of intermediate group structures that is productive of mass movement participation.

wherever pre-existing primary and secondary groupings *possess* or *develop* an ideology or simply subjective interests congruent with that of a new movement, they will act as mobilizing rather than restraining agents toward that movement. And their members will be not late joiners, but the early joiners of the movement, much earlier than the atomized masses.[41]

Intermediate structures, given a situation of concern or strain, serve to facilitate mass movements by offering means of mobilization and communication and providing motivation and legitimation. The individuals most likely affected by these factors are the most highly integrated, not the least, as argued by mass theory.[42] This is not an unusual observation and finds support in a very diversified range of phenomena. Community studies in regard to various local issues, research on the Social Credit Party in Quebec, the C.C.F. party in Saskatchewan, Poujadism in France, and Goldwaterism in the U.S. appear to support this contention,[43] as do the beginnings of women's lib[44] and the character of civil rights,[45] desegregation, and student protest.[46] The earliest participants and leaders were *not* those without ties, misfits, or anomic. Rather, the reverse seems to be the case. Factors that help account for this phenomenon, in contrast to mass theory expectations, include the inability of the most estranged to be able to visualize alternatives and the possibility of change. This hopelessness is likely to be combined with a lack of information and organizational channels to facilitate involvement in a new movement. In his assessment of the literature on collective behavior Carl Couch, in a recent essay, devotes particular attention to the difficulty, without stable associations, of "developing consensus on the cause of dissatis-faction, on the solution to the situation, and on plans for coordinate actions."[47]

These observations relate and give added meaning to the possible suggestion that interest group organizations may in fact stimulate those "mass" movements that suggest new reform policies related to the interest of the organized groupings and may serve to revitalize political and social society and overcome the often strong elements of rigidity and constraint of the existing system. Such movements usually owe their effectiveness, and sometimes their origin, to the existence of intermediate group structures. Further, movements of reform and revitalization, some of which I refer to later, do not necessarily exhibit the features of mass behavior proposed by mass theorists as typifying mass movements and movements of protest.

Comments on the problem of specifying social isolation. The lack of social and normative ties with one's community – in other words, a condition of social isolation – is a concept too vague and general to be applied with any precision or clarity. What, for instance, will be defined as one's community? Is face-to-face contact essential? More generally, what kind of relationship is there between social ties and acceptance of normative standards? Without exploring these and other problems, it is necessary to suggest four of the communities to which one may be related or isolated. There may be (1) isolation from societal institutions or society as such, (2) personal isolation, in the sense of an absence of ties to groups within one's immediate environ-ment or community, (3) isolation from non-community- and non-class-defined organizations, in a sense secondary-type organizations, or (4) isolation from the group or class, and its organizational forms, in terms of which one's social structural and interest position is established. Mass theory's failure to distinguish the latter condition from the first three is a crucial defect. In fact, it appears to perceive social isolation only in terms of societal, community, or secondary group relationships. This is a serious shortcoming, given the fact that the different forms of isolation may vary independently from each other. Only at certain historical moments do they correspond, and populations are bereft of ties to both class as well as broader societal or community structures. Only when isolation exists in all these forms can one really speak of mass man in terms of the texture of personal experience that characterizes its use by much of the mass political literature. There may be a condition of isolation from society as such, in terms of both personal ties as well as involvement in normative standards and expectations, but yet the individual may be heavily implicated in strong class ties. The latter condition would not be one of personal isolation or of a mass state. And radical protest behavior of such individuals, where it occurs, would in all probability be some form of interest conflict rather than mass behavior.

Mass society analysis elaborated

The preceding discussion has suggested that the social and psychological integrative functions presumably served by intermediate structures may not always be attained even where such structures exist and, conversely, they may be secured through other forms of personal or organizational ties. Thus mass society cannot be defined merely in social structural terms. In effect, of course, the mass society literature is quite clear on the need to take other elements into account, and the degree of sensed integration by the individual with his society is one of these. The difficulty is that this is often perceived as following as a matter of course from the existence of organizational or community membership. I have noted in the preceding discussion that this should be taken as problematic and hence suggest that it must be considered as a separate dimension or causal variable in the determination of the mass or nonmass nature of society.

The extent to which the individual achieves a sense of integration, in effect a sense of belonging and of place, may be derived, in some circumstances, from organizational and communal memberships. It also seems likely, however, that such a purpose may be accomplished by personal ties, familial and communal identities, community rituals and other symbolic activities, in some cases even the presence of a philosophical or intellectual sense of place, unity, or membership, occupational pursuits, communication media and cultural involvements, some recreational involvements, and some apparently slender organizational participation. At least this is a reasonable contention, though as I have noted this is a crucial area that does require more extensive research. At the same time, with the decline of community, the nature of organizational membership in contemporary society often appears to leave indeterminate in many cases whether a condition of integration and belonging has been attained. This arises from the already mentioned factors of powerlessness and the tangential minimal participation experienced vis-à-vis such organizations. I am concerned here not with the political dimension of mass society theory, that is, with whether structural forms suggest a diffusion of power or its concentration. Our interest for the moment is with whether the personal circumstances of a societal population are such as to create a condition of "masses." Of course, such a condition may have potent consequences for political behavior and the possibility of mobilizing and concentrating political power.

In the barest and simplest of terms, in order to postulate a condition of mass society it is essential to determine the nature of two conditions – the degree of involvement in intermediate associations and, even more crucially, the individual sociopsychic sense of belonging and place, or what may be referred to as sensed integration. As has been noted, the mass theorist, where he does recognize the latter, derives this concept from the condition of intermediate organization. However, these two factors must be kept separate. It has already been suggested that a considerable degree of independent variation is possible among these two dimensions. And, to reiterate, it is reasonable to maintain that where a condition of sensed integration prevails a condition of mass society is absent, regardless of the presence or absence of intermediate group associations. In any case, these must be conceptualized as possibly independent variables. The table on page 91 dichotomizes these two dimensions. While the content of each of the cells is somewhat uncertain, given the absence of research on the issues raised in the previous and present section, they are filled in so as to reflect reasonable estimates of the probabilities. Given the absence of attention to other vitally crucial determinate factors, variously noted in the body of this essay, even these probabilities must be tentative and qualified by the usual expression of all other factors being constant.

What would be observed, I suggest, is that the condition of mass society would be more nearly present in cells C and D, more strongly in the former, while the suggestion of mass theory is that cells B and

	Intermediate group ties	
	High proportion	Low proportion
	A	**B**
High degree	Nonmass society, less likely to be qualified	Nonmass society, possibly qualified
Sensed integration (of individuals)	Vigorous protest possible in both cells, more likely to be of a group interest nature; erratic character less likely.	
	D	**C**
Low degree	Leaning toward mass society	Mass society
	Vigorous protest possible in both cells, less likely to be of a group interest nature; erratic character more likely.	

C would exhibit a condition of mass society.[48] I see vigorous protest behavior as equally possible in all cells, not merely B and C as would be expected from mass theory. Behavior exhibited in the different cells, however, can be distinguished by variations in the degree of manifest interest conflict and the extent to which behavior is erratic. These tend to vary inversely. Mass theory would predict a low interest component and high erratic quality for cells B and C, rather than cells C and D as given in the table. In practice, in fact, mass theory will generally neglect to distinguish between noninterest and interest components within behavior of a vigorous protest nature. The population in cells C and D would, more likely than that in A and B, be what the mass theorists have referred to as an available population, but derived here from the degree of sensed integration rather than group ties. Thus the population in cell B is not equally available for the type of behavior that more usually arises in the lower two cells. As the reader will probably have grasped, the treatment here distinguishes merely in terms of the type of *behavior* that is, mass or not, for which availability does or does not exist. This arises from the contention developed later that availability for protest behavior can also exist among integrated and group-involved populations – where political response is low and group interests are unmet.

One last observation may be of some interest. Having distinguished between societal dimensions that are ordinarily treated as joined, we have raised the possibility of a mix of plural and mass society features. This is evidenced by cells B and D. Thus for the mass theorists the condition of few intermediate group ties, as is the case in cell B, represents the mass society. Yet certain qualities of plural society inhere, given the high degree of sensed integration. Conversely, the high proportion of ties in cell D would represent plural society, but the condition of a low degree of sensed integration also suggests the quality of a mass society. The other two cases, of course, are more clearly instances of plural and mass society – at least as defined by group ties and individually experienced conditions of integration.

I have been concerned here with altering and to some extent extending the terms by which a determination is made of whether a condition of mass society prevails or not. It may be noted that the referent can be either the condition of a society as such or the condition of particular population groups within a given society. The preceding comments apply equally well to either situation.

Inadequacies in the mass–nonmass distinction

Social categories and their determinants

A basic difficulty of mass theory is its failure to develop an analysis of the social or structural position of dissident populations in terms of its possible implications for political behavior. This is a somewhat anomalous situation, in light of the fact that one of the major features of mass theory is a social structural proposition dividing the population into mass and nonmass groupings. Yet uninformed by any adequate conceptual scheme of the nature of the major actual or potential political groups within society, their origin, and their relationship to each other, mass theory lacks the rudimentary framework with which to begin to account for and contrast the diversity of political behavior within society, given the partial basis of such diversity in the fact of group differences. Hence a great deal of the analysis and propositions of mass political theory are reduced to unsatisfactory comparisons of groups and behavior inappropriately labeled as mass and nonmass. The present discussion confronts the failure to distinguish structurally diverse types of interest categories, such as economic, status, regional, and other distinctive collectivities from non-interest-based masses.[49]

Social structural analysis that focuses on the social structural location of collectivities in the terms outlined next facilitates attention to the possible interest component in behavior, as well as raises the probability of focusing on the character of political representation and responsiveness. These two concerns are of great importance in determining the rationality, appropriateness, and nature of any vigorous protest behavior or movement that might arise. Mass theory, however, lacking such an analysis, is burdened with a cumbersome and often misleading mass–nonmass dichotomy. Structural analysis has the further related and not inconsiderable virtue that it facilitates a more accurate location of a society· on a mass-plural continuum and helps clarify the bases of societal cohesion.

The following discussion seeks to make clear mass theory's lack of attention to the major defining dimensions of distinctive and different social categories in society – economic, status, communal, regional, and other bases of distinctive groupings. It also points in very general and speculative terms to some of the potential political behavioral qualities of such collectivities. In effect, the simplistic nature of a mass–nonmass dichotomy is stressed, as well as the relative rarity of a population sector that could be labeled as a mass, if that term is used with precision in regard to structural characteristics now absent in mass theory. The distinctions drawn here are neither original nor exceptional. The implications of their omission, however, will become clearer when later consideration is given topics such as the rationality of protest behavior and its interest basis and objectives.

Dimensions of societal organization

It is important to note the disparity between conceptual formulations on social structure used by the mass theorist and the complex circumstances to which in reality they must be applied. In light of the fact that mass theory rests upon a structural proposition, part of any extensive critique must examine this disparity. Some of the inadequacies in the mass theorist's analysis of social structure can perhaps be suggested by indicating some of the more important factors that would have to be considered in any effort to account for the politically relevant group structure and hence potential interest structure in society. The principal dimensions in terms of which social groupings may develop include those in whose terms society itself becomes structured. These are also the basic dimensions in which a significant portion of political conflict becomes manifest. Being the major, though not exclusive, terms in which contemporary society is organized, they are the bases of distinctive identities, commitment, and purposes. They provide the grounds for difference and conflict. They specify the nature of some of the major conflicted ends or "interests" that inhere in society.

The underlying or implicit thesis here is not that there is any automatic or uniform determinism in social structure or the individual's location therein but that social structural position significantly defines certain shared experiences, life circumstances, types of identity and loyalties, differential social rewards and needs and distinctive response from the broader society. These serve to establish distinctive group interests. They do so in a broadly uniform fashion for those "similarly" circumstanced or situated. As social location differs, so too must the elements of individual experience vary. Collectivities will thus confront their society differently, and with somewhat different needs and potential demands. In a different direction, social structural location is also significantly determinate of political behavior not merely because of the needs or interests implicated in the social position of a collectivity but because it also exposes populations to distinctive patterns of socialization, group experiences, communication, leadership, and political responsiveness. In these terms, then, social location helps establish how the actor defines and responds to his circumstances. This implication of social structural position, however, is not developed in the present analysis.

Some of the most important dimensions that define the social structural shape of society include the character of production and economy, authority and power, status, culture, characteristics of language, race, and ethnicity – or what may more concisely be referred to as a communal dimension, distinctive beliefs, religion, and region.[50] Age, sex, and kinship attributes can also form the basis of distinctive ongoing social categories but are not considered in the following discussion.

Specific social categories, potential common interests, and distinctive political issues and movements may develop around each of the preceding bases of difference and shared concern. Each of these dimensions may also be understood as generating a particular type of conflict, for example, class, status, communal, and so on. In effect, I am essentially reiterating a well-recognized proposition in traditional political and social analysis. The following discussion describes the major collectivities that may appear in society, with some brief attention to the character of associated political contention.

The following account does not include reference to the diversity of more narrow and fleeting interests and associations that characterize the political scene of any society at any particular time and that need not be a reflection of the major societal defining dimensions or of purely belief-based orientations. The diversity of such interest groups is great, including varied purposes such as education reform, increased recreational facilities, protection against crime, and safer automobiles. To some extent, such concerns suggest the concept of belief-based collectivities to be described shortly. Where the interest in question is explicable in terms of individual advantage relating to distinctive individual position and needs, however, such a designation would not be appropriate. Where this is not the case, but such interest groups merely reflect a perspective or set of beliefs not associated with distinctive individual gains or needs, then reference can be made to belief-based collectivities.

The present discussion takes exception to the conceptualizations of value-consensus theory, which establish, I would hold, grounds too limited for analyzing conflict, perceiving it almost as a form of deviance. In such terms conflict is understood as arising out of faulty socialization, strains in role structures, normative dissentience, and administrative failure.[51] Clearly, my approach to conflict is perceived in terms closer to conflict theory. In effect, it is maintained that society is importantly though not exclusively characterized by relations of conflict, which are in Dahrendorf's terms "all relations between sets of individuals that involve an incompatible difference of objective."[52]

Even a brief consideration of the role of each of the basic dimensions that serves to delineate societal social organization may begin to suggest the inadequacies of a crude mass–nonmass dichotomy. While these dimensions of social organization are not finally determinate of the appearance of groups, they do define social categories. Factors crucial in converting these objective social categories to group- or class-conscious collectivities will be briefly referred to later. The following specifies the principal dimensions in terms of which social categories are established. From this basis corresponding collectivities may develop and group purposes may be elaborated, with consequent group differences and bases for conflict and political dissent behavior established. However, whether conflict and dissent do in fact appear, and their character, depends on many other factors.

1. From the structure of access to the means of production are derived the employment market, the credit or money market, and the commodity market. These give rise in turn to groups[53] in the labor, agrarian, and business area and to the conflict associated with the distinctive interests of each of these groups.[54] These groups may appropriately be referred to as classes in the objective sense. Tradi-

tional notions of class conflict find their application in these terms. Many of the labor and peasant movements of the nineteenth and twentieth centuries throughout western Europe, in the United States, and even in the less developed societies of the world offer abundant evidence for the existence of such groups or classes. A great deal of the contention in contemporary society among diverse business interests, labor, financial, and farm groups is constituted of collectivities defined or based upon the dimension stated here.

It is possible to distinguish two broad categories of class conflict and class movements. One may be referred to as traditional class movements and the other populist class movements. The former refers to class movements where there is a history of traditional class organization, ideology, and conflict, as, for example, among the working-class Communists in France and the Chilean left, to which references are made in the following chapter. The members of such movements are likely to have strong ties to class organization, be participants in the organizational and social structures of the class and its political agencies, and have considerable sensitivity to past and current ideological class programs. The reference here is to a movement, sense of membership, and organizational forms that have continued over time. Populist class movements refer to movements whose membership is characterized by their distinctive structural location and some sense of common group membership, though less fully developed than in the former case and which lack much of the class traditions and historical organization of traditional class movements. The appearance of such a class movement will be fairly recent, the class ties less, and the political behavior may tend to be somewhat more erratic and ill tempered. The population in question may have lacked an earlier effective organizational expression before the present movement. There is a greater potential for the charismatic leader. While quite certainly a class movement and not an alienated or mass movement, populist class movements are closer to the latter forms of conflict than is traditional class conflict. This is not a distinction that should be pushed too far. It is intended merely to suggest certain moderate differences in origin, structure, and behavior. The usefulness of the dichotomy is principally as a heuristic analytic framework.

2. Given the existence of power and authority in all social systems and societal institutions and their importance as scarce resources for the attainment of ends within these systems, differences in authority and power may be a basis for group distinctions, and access to power and its legitimation an important source of conflict. The existence of a group and conflict in terms of ends that are principally that of exercis-

ing and seeking authority and power would refer to types of situations in which the group in question is characterized in terms of its authority or power position, not its class, status, communal, or other properties. The desire and possibility of possessing power may stimulate group organization and conflict as a goal valued in its own right. However, a group existing merely in terms of the desire to secure power is unusual. This is not to deny the obvious fact that conflict often arises from the desire to secure or maintain power, but usually this is because other group interests are served thereby.

Three types of groups and conflicts may be sketched in terms of power and power conflict. One type of group refers to administrative or bureaucratic structures and the population involved therein. Here contention would be of an intra- and interadministrative character within bureaucratic structures, among branches of government, among community agencies, and so on. Note, of course, that such administrative structures are also interest groups (e. g., agricultural, commercial, conservationist, etc.) in terms of interadministrative conflict, as well as in the case of intraadministrative conflict in which the contention may be among interagency units such as marketing, personnel, design, and finance. Thus contention is often evidence of no more than a narrow interest group type of conflict. These are not collectivities whose existence can be established in terms of a quest for greater authority. However, contention or conflict may at times be manifest in and among these structures in terms not of distinctive interests or of service to such interests but of prerogatives of authority and the preservation and expansion of authority and power for its own sake. The emphasis here would be principally on conflict over the range of legitimated power or, in other words, authority. However, in contrast to the other types of social categories cited in this section, the preceding comments are not concerned with a particular population group within the society, but rather with conflict among distinctive administrative units. The notion of group conflict is thus present only in the somewhat attenuated form of the conflict of administrative structures and the individuals or groups associated with them.

Related to the preceding is a second type of circumstance. This is when power conflict develops in terms of limiting or extending the scope and depth of individual and group authority and control. This is essentially the thrust for greater self-governance and, more generally, for increasing the extent to which one controls one's environment. Various collectivities may be so engaged. It is an increasing source of conflict. Examples include disparate phenomena such as student or faculty efforts at increased self-governance and control within educational institutions and workers' efforts at self-management in the industrial plant.

The third type of circumstance occurs when a collectivity appears principally to seek authority and power and hence engages in an authority and power conflict. In other words, in some circumstances groups can be recognized primarily in terms of the power that they hold or aspire to, with little distinctive interest of class, status, ideology, or other category that might more precisely identify the group. This is a circumstance in which political conflict is for authority and power for its own sake. Most accurately, however, this can properly be understood more as a tendency or outer limit than an actually experienced phenomenon. Almost invariably some other functional interest will reside in a quest for power. Ordinarily, it is where the usual interest group structure is more rudimentary, as in the underdeveloped nations, that groups and ensuing conflict may take shape principally in terms of power. The palace revolts in some of the Latin American states and the coups d'état in a few of the new African nations would appear to offer examples of groups and behavior that in some instances may be understood principally, though perhaps not exclusively, in terms of power. At times groups struggle for power in these societies for little significant end other than that of possessing and exercising power, with whatever varied and even unique meaning and significance this may hold for the individual or individuals concerned. Even here, though, as Merle Kling[55] suggests in regard to Latin America, other functional interest concerns may be perceived. But one has here some instances that tend toward pure cases of power struggle. This is not to deny that at times a naked power struggle is clothed in purposes of a loftier character. It is for the social analyst, however, to determine the difference between reality and rationalization. This is not to demean the political importance of rationalization, but this importance is principally in terms of its relevance in providing legitimacy to the group in question and to such behavior as it may be engaged in.

3. When conceptualized in terms of prestige or honor, class produces a number of objective status categories that usually assume a hierarchical character. Members of such status categories may engage in political behavior in response to either the appearance of uncertainty in regard to status or competition in regard to status position. Uncertainty may express itself either in terms of status insecurity or, more dramatically, in some sense of status panic or by the felt need to affirm one's status position. An element present in both these circumstances may be a disparity between a group's sense of dignity

and the respect or status recognition it is accorded. Status competition refers to the attempt to improve one's position in a status hierarchy. Status uncertainty and competition prevail most strongly in societies marked by change. Where present, they will be exhibited by groups relatively recently arrived to positions of prominence in terms other than status or by groups whose long-time position of social respect may appear tenuous in light of the advances of other groups or the decline of the cultural, political, or economic supports of a given status position.[56]

Two types of status conflict categories are implicated in these comments.[57] One may be labeled directly as a status category and the other as a status-culture category.[58] In the former category are individuals who feel concerned because they are either not securing what they view as a proper amount prestige or deference or who feel their prestige position is endangered. A frequently cited example of the latter are lower-middle-class whites who presumably feel a status threat from integrated housing. Instances of the former circumstance sometimes cited are high-ranking military personnel or the *nouveaux riche* who feel they are not accorded adequate deference. In both of the preceding situations the reference is to those populations who can be understood or conceptualized solely in terms of a distinctive status position and not a distinctive way of life or value system. However, a second and somewhat different status category is that of status-culture. This concept refers to populations that also exhibit a distinctive status position but one with which a particular way of life, set of values, and forms of behavior are associated. One thinks here, for example, of the categories of small independent businessmen, self-employed professionals, the New England traditionalist, or rural small-town populations. Such populations tend to combine a distinctive status position with a particular way of life and set of beliefs. For these populations a status threat extends beyond merely a jeopardy to a position of deference. The relative emphasis here as between the status and cultural element is variable, both among different status-culture categories and, more especially, in regard to the phenomenon in question to which a presumed status-culture population is responding.

Status conflict finds expression on those issues that provide a means of striking out at those policies or groups presumed to be principally implicated in failing to acknowledge sufficiently the status of the population in question or viewed as a threat to that status position.[59] Controversy over a wide range of issues is often interpreted in status terms, such as the temperance crusade, antifluoridation sentiment, the response to desegregation, support for Sunday blue laws, opposition to deficit financing, criticism of international organizations and cooperation, and the McCarthy witch-hunting phenomenon of the 1950s.[60] It is the presumed importance of the symbolic component of these policies that receives a major stress in status interpretations of politics. In other words, many public policies or issues may be interpreted as affirming or honoring or, conversely, as ignoring or being antithetical to distinctive styles of life, systems of morality, and particular behavioral and cultural patterns. Thus if one assumes that the prestige position of certain populations is associated with particular life styles, moral values. and so forth, then the actions of government supportive of or in accord with them may serve to "symbolize the position of groups in the status structure"[61] of society. The issues themselves may appear trivial, but their import resides more significantly in the extent to which they provide a means for the denial or expression of public support for a given morality and life style. In such terms it is the response of status-culture populations (rather than pure status categories) to issues or policy that is at the heart of the discussion. Yet this distinction is not clearly drawn in present discussions of status politics.

Status populations will probably exhibit less of a sense of distinctive group membership and identity than is the case for most of the other categories to which reference is being made. This is more clearly the case for status categories than status-culture populations, though it is also true for the latter. This quality of status populations develops from the more intangible quality of status and status circumstances, as compared with economic, religious, communal, and other concerns and membership. It is also partly accounted for by the lack of some of the more concrete and even physical evidence, including organizational structures, of group existence and membership that is exhibited by most social categories. The continuance over time of a status-based political movement may thus be made more difficult but also helps account for the more erratic character of such behavior.

While status and status-culture categories can be objectively established, there is a considerable danger that the analyst has imputed a presumably meaningful existence to status categories and phenomena when in fact it may be lacking. In other words, it is frequently not clearly established that the members of any given category perceive their objective status position in subjective terms as a significant element of self and hence an important determinant of behavioral response to broader social, political, or cultural conditions. Even less frequent is the likelihood that status category members develop a sense of a common status identity and shared status concerns. The presumed concern over status and thus its causal potency on political behavior seems, in fact, to be considerably exaggerated.[62] There is a danger here – perhaps to a greater extent than for any of our other interest-based categories – that the status categories established by the social analyst will be more an artifact of his own theoretical schemes than a reflection of any phenomenal reality. Related, especially where a population can be roughly defined in an objective sense as a distinct status category, is the possibility of imputing a status basis to political behavior when another objective interest factor may more appropriately be the explanatory factor. Concomitantly, behavior perceived principally in symbolic terms may at times be understood more appropriately on an instrumental level.[63] Finally, the preceding may have suggested the impropriety of viewing status politics as necessarily of an irrational and unreasonable character. Meyer and Roth remark on "the importance of social status rights as valuable and necessary resources in controlling human action, and thus as quite appropriate objects of 'rational' political action."[64]

4. Racial, ethnic, linguistic, and other cultural traits are a frequent source of group differences and conflict. While components of status are involved, these do not exhaust the distinctive attributes of and response to such categories. The concepts of class or status are clearly not adequate as a referent for the distinctive character of such groups.[65] Essentially, the reference here is to the not unusual phenomenon of communal groups within society and some of the elements that constitute such collectivites. The term "communal" is used quite broadly to refer to narrow-based racial or ethnic groups, as well as to the broader-based collectivities in which distinct cultural, linguistic, and other differences may be combined. A population is communal when it considers itself a community or kindred group – defined in cultural, social, or biological terms such as ethnicity, language, cultural forms, and race. Consciousness of communal membership is crucial in creating a communal population and will usually reflect a group heritage extending over time, certain common traditions, and shared circumstances, partly including a similar situation or experience vis-à-vis the broader society. These serve to induce a sense of common identity and experience and to distinguish a communal population from other populations in terms beyond merely that of objective group differences.[66] The intention here is to exclude identification in terms of the usual functional criteria, such as class or other shared economic interests, or in ideological terms, such as distinct intellectual or religious beliefs. Religious beliefs, however, when combined with

other properties, especially that of geographic concentration with a shared distinctive historical and social heritage, may constitute an important element in influencing the establishment of a communal group. Frequently, religious, communal, and regional elements are all present in an overlapping manner. Regional groups, to be discussed shortly, are in fact most often also communal populations.

Examples of communal groups as used here are naturally very various. Ethnic and racial groups hardly need illustration. In addition there are, for instance, communal collectivities such as the Walloons and Flemish population in Belgium, the French Canadians, the tribal differences in many African states, the Basques in Spain, and the ethnic minorities in the Southeast Asian societies, who are illustrative of collectivities whose distinctive character is based on linguistic, ethnic, cultural, or racial differences and often a combination of two or more of such characteristics. Included under the communal heading would also be nationalist movements in colonial societies.

Communal conflict will center on the attempt by a communal population to maintain, reassert, or reestablish its authority, power, status, social or cultural integrity, and at times even its political independence. It may also arise out of efforts to secure conditions of equity corresponding with those characterizing other major populations. One of the most important reasons for the strength of the communal appeal is the sense of identity and worth it provides. Another important source of communal conflict is the demand for public recognition of that identity and of its importance or its preservation from domination by other identities.[67]

Clearly, communal groups and communal conflict implicate a wide range of populations and types of movements.[68] Millenial and messianic movements would appear to be on the border line between communal and religious movements, given on the one hand their religious, sacred, or supernatural orientation, yet on the other their distinctive communal and cultural character. As is sometimes true of religious movements, and often of communal movements, millenarian and messianic movements may have political aims in addition to their cultural and religious purposes. Communal movements also tend toward the character of religious movements when distinctive religious membership is an important element of a communal focus, for example, in the case of religious collectivities in Belgium and to some extent in Canada and Switzerland. Many, though certainly not all, communal populations and instances of communal conflict when they occur also have a regional character, as they are often more or less located in a specific region within the broader geographic society.

Where the purposes and political behavior of populations appear essentially in terms of securing or maintaining the social, cultural, or political integrity or authority of the social collectivity, then there is an instance of "pure" communal conflict. More likely, however, associated with the communal properties of the population in question there will be one or more other distinctive functional interests importantly implicated in and aggravating the conflict, particularly factors of class or economic interests, blocked social mobility, and, as already suggested, regional and religious interest differences.[69] Black communal conflict in the United States today, the agrarian Flemish-industrial Walloon conflict in Belgium, the conflict between the more economically advanced Catalans with the poorer and economically disadvantaged Castilians in Spain, and the clash between the poorer agrarian French-speaking majority in Quebec and the more affluent English population of Quebec and Canada are several examples of the involvement of other interests in communal conflict. In all these instances economic disparities exist, and, in all but the case of blacks in the United States, regional factors are present. In Belgium and Canada religious differences further confound the situation.

In a related vein, a not infrequent source of communal conflict involves contention between dominant "alien" economic and political elites and a broader population of different tribal, cultural, ethnic, or linguistic properties. Such communal conflict is evidenced, for example, in the colonial societies vis-à-vis elites of the imperial power or in various noncolonial circumstances in which a minority with distinctive communal properties dominate important aspects of political or economic life, as in Nigeria, the Congo, Indonesia, and Malaya.

5. Society is clearly characterized by value and ideological diversity. While such diversity will often be associated with a distinctive social and/or economic category, particular values and beliefs may nonetheless be the sole basis of distinctive politically active social groups and even social movements. However, this develops when they rather than the social or economic characteristics of the occupants of the social category create the grounds for cohesion of the collectivity and for its potential conflict with the broader society. Thus, for example, the intellectual revolutionary or anarchist association, dissident radical organizations among the young, the religious sect as well as the church,[70] and conservationists and antipollution campaigners in some instances – all definable in terms of distinctive beliefs – may each also exhibit distinctive social or economic characteristics. Yet where the basis of contention is, as in the preceding

examples, in the realm of beliefs and has no distinctive relationship to the social structural position of the group involved, then it is necessary to speak of a belief-oriented group and of belief-oriented conflict.[71] Of course, a specific value or belief may frequently be joined to a specific and structurally distinct group. Usually the belief or value held will merely be a means of advancing the purposes distinctive to the group in question, as, for example, when a distinctive economic, communal, status or other group develops an ideology in terms of which it seeks to rationalize the programs or demands it propounds. This, however, would then simply refer to some of the other aforementioned bases of group structure and conflict.

Given the absence of a distinct functional interest character and hence some minimization of competing interest conflict, belief-based collectivities have the potential for appealing to a wide diversity of individuals. Yet in most instances this diversity is lacking because those who are most frequently implicated in belief-based protest are the more highly educated and more affluent segment of society. Religious-oriented movements, treated separately, are an important exception. The absence of the usual functional interest component in belief-based movements may also greatly reduce their attractiveness, particularly given the usually apathetic quality of the citizenry. However, their potential appeal and range of purposes are wider. Functionally based interest collectivities, because of the very attraction they have for certain specific class, regional, and communal populations will also deter elements of a contrary class, regional, communal, or other nature. This kind of deterrent quality is usually diminished in belief-based movements, whatever the potency or inadequacy of their distinctive ideological appeals.

It should be recognized that the circumstances of movement members are various, and so is their relationship to the objective or belief around which they may be rallied. As the categorization of a movement cannot be made apart from the circumstances and purposes of its members, a given movement may be described in more than one fashion depending from what sector of its membership it is perceived. Thus, for instance, the civil rights movement can be seen as a belief-based movement in terms of its white well-to-do middle-class elements but as an example of communal conflict when interpreted in light of the interest needs of its black membership.

An estimate of the occasions when belief-based collectivities are likely to appear most strongly is hazardous. A few hypotheses do, however, seem plausible. Their frequency is likely to be greater at certain points of social and political development. One such occasion is at the stage of advanced industrial and economic achievement when the material benefits of such advance become increasingly diffused and when class conflict has moderated sufficiently for non-class-specific issues – such as conservation, pollution, consumer-directed concerns – to receive some public concern and following. Regardless of levels of societal development, issues and events may arise – either because of broad ideological currents both within and without the particular society or because of the appearance of episodic events – that stimulate the formation of belief-oriented groups and underlie movements of protest. Antiwar and some civil rights movements and participants are examples of such groups, in which a distinct class or other structurally defined interest basis is lacking. Somewhat related is another type of circumstance, in which the appearance of belief-based collectivities increases in response to societal stress or change that disrupts or puts in question the usual career patterns and previous ideological commitments or options of certain segments of the population, for instance, relatively affluent and educated youth in many societies today or youthful revolutionaries in late nineteenth-century Russia. A related condition exists when there is an exhaustion or increasing questioning of the major purposes of a society and of the tasks worthy of individual commitment. While historical analogues can perhaps be found, this is certainly a circumstance that many social commentators have identified in the more advanced portion of the contemporary Western world. It is likely to affect some particular groups, leadership elements, and institutions within a society more than others. Elements of the intelligentsia, educated and prosperous strata, and cultural elites and institutions seem especially likely to nourish political, social, and cultural belief-based movements. Perhaps an intermediate type of circumstance to the preceding ones is when certain group traditions, some degree of societal strain, or group marginality may encourage dissident perspectives not necessarily related to structurally determined interests, as for example, various intellectual protest movements in France in the past 75 years. However, the adequacy of these propositions can only be tested by a historical and comparative examination of belief-based protests and societal and group circumstances.

It is important to recognize that there are occasions when one finds implicated in belief-based conflicts qualities of a more fundamental nature than would be suggested from the mere practice or belief in contention. For example, some ostensible differences of belief in regard to appropriate styles of dress and grooming, use of time, or appropriate personal behavior may more fundamentally involve conflict over competing ways of life. Even more basically involved may be a symbolic issue reflecting questions central to the maintenance or affirmation of conditions upon which self-respect, identity, and personal sustenance may be dependent. In such circumstances the nature of the conflict in question cannot be comprehended merely at the level of the beliefs involved. A more basic social, cultural, and psychological inquiry would appear appropriate. Hence a category of ostensibly belief-based conflicts may on analysis involve circumstances somewhat similar to those discussed in regard to status-culture conflict, though without a clear status condition being involved.

6. As has just been noted, religious groups can be included in the dimension of belief-oriented collectivities. Yet they pose such a distinctive as well as significant group that it is useful to suggest a separate category of group formation – religious-based collectivities. Though often associated with communal and regional categories, it is not uncommon to find religious belief and organizational structures the principal basis for distinctive collectivities and conflict groups. This is not to deny that in some kinds of circumstances communal properties are as important in defining the collectivity as religious beliefs. This is the case with millenarian and messianic movements, cargo cults, and some revivalist movements. Efforts at revitalizing a culture within some religious or sacred framework bridge both communal and religious categories and are not clearly identifiable as predominantly in one or the other category.[12]

While in most instances populations defined in religious terms are not involved in political contention, nor experienced as such by the communicants, in some cases they are clearly in a conflicted relationship arising principally from distinctive religious membership and loyalty. The examples are various – Catholics in the United States as regards public financial support for parochial schools, Jehovah's Witnesses' attempts to attain exemption from certain secular state demands, the Irish and Protestant conflict in Northern Ireland, and the historic experiences of religious groups in Europe. Related, but of a different character, is the historical process during which the supremacy of the state over the church was established and the ongoing conflicts this engendered in respect to areas of secular and sacred authority and jurisdiction and freedom of religious beliefs and practices. Clearly, questions of power and authority were crucial here – but as a means of weakening or maintaining the prerogatives of a distinctive collectivity that is defined in religious terms and is represented in its organizational form by the church.

Not infrequently, commitments to religious movements and the resulting conflict developed in response to conditions of great stress – economic strains, disruptions of community, and societal threat. Where the resulting response, commitments, purposes, and behavior are defined in religious terms, however, and the group involved so defines itself, then the resulting movement can appropriately be labeled as religious. Whether a response to marginality and deprivation is of a religious or secular character is dependent on various factors, such as the nature of existing leadership and organizational influences, historical and cultural traditions, including the interpretive schemes of the society and the population concerned, type of group consciousness that exists initially, freedom available for political expression, and so on.

7. An occasional and now decreasing basis of distinctiveness and contention in society is that of region. A complex of factors, such as historical experiences, patterns of nation building, difference in immigration and settlement patterns, distinctive economic forms and needs, electoral and political structure shifts – usually originating to some extent from one or more of the preceding – have usually produced and then tended to perpetuate regional or territorial categories. The consequence of the kind of factors noted is to lead to disparities among regions (and, of course, populations) in terms of the sources of difference already indicated – economic, status, power, race, ethnicity or language, values and ideology, religion, as well as in the area of sentiment, loyalties, traditions, and attitudes. The basis that functional sources of difference provide for distinctive sentiment and loyalties and the latter's reinforcement of structural differences are major reasons for the difficulty in eliminating regional differences and the societal division that follows from them. Regional areas often have a high cultural distinctiveness, and thus it is appropriate to refer in many instances to a regional culture and to cultural differences and conflict as long as the distinct regional focus is understood.

Conflict may be defined exclusively in regional terms when it is the maintenance or recognition of the integrity of regional properties – minimally, that is, of the prestige, authority, or culture of the region rather than questions of class, status, and beliefs at issue. Of course, frequently the two will be found to appear together, and in most instances all that can be said is that regional factors constitute an element of a broader-based conflict. "Pure" regional conflict seems rare, especially in the more contemporary period. On the whole, region assumes an importance less in its own right than in terms of its serving as the locale of a population distinctive in some respects vis-à-vis the broader society, whether it be in economic, ethnic, religious, or other terms.

Regional identity itself, however, may be heightened by increased consciousness of shared functional interests in circumstances of either disadvantagement or conflict with other regions, as, for example, an economically impoverished region or one significantly characterized by a declining status-culture in contrast to other regions' growing ascendency in these regards. This provides another circumstance in which nonregional functional interests influence the appearance of regional conflict. Where regional difference is joined to other sources of contention – communal, economic, and religious, for instance – then the resulting conflict is likely to be exacerbated.

In a historical perspective an important type of regional conflict has been contention between the political center and local political and cultural authorities. The American South, the southern and western regions of Norway, and Wales vis-à-vis England, as well as urban-rural differences in many societies are diverse examples of regional distinctiveness, commitment, and resulting conflict that cannot be reduced merely to one or more of the bases of group formation and contention to which reference has been made. Another form in which conflict has a certain regional focus is that of contention between two or more different populations that are also located in distinct regions. There is some tendency for a significant communal element to be present in the preceding situations. When this does occur, it seems best to refer to the conflict as communal, albeit with a certain regional dimension.

From a long-run historical perspective, regional conflict is likely to assume an approximately curvilinear relationship over time: low where a unified political state is both lacking and not in the process of formation, high during a period of political consolidation, and low after processes of economic growth and social differentiation weaken regional attachments and distinctiveness. With increasing economic development and social differentiation the likelihood of regional cleavage is diminished, and regional ties and regional bases for conflict are of declining importance. In the ordinary course of events, as there is economic development and increasing social differentiation, isolation from nationwide institutions declines and a more and more diverse population is increasingly implicated in a variety of national associations of a nonregional character. The mobility of the population will increase. Economic growth and developing organizational forms will encourage conditions productive of a consciousness of functional interest group membership. Political democratization is likely to appear and involve the extension of the franchise. Class politics will tend to develop, and nationwide alliances are likely to be made among groups sharing certain common functional interests.

These conditions encourage the appearance of nationwide mass parties. It is where one political party is clearly dominant in a region, with other parties strong in the rest of the country, that regionalism may still be a strong element. However, over time the types of changes noted decrease this possibility. In effect, regional cleavage declines with economic growth, the development of mass nationwide political parties and universal suffrage, and urbanization.[73]

Social structure and politically relevant collectivities cannot be described without attention to that portion of the population that does not assume a distinct character in terms of a major social structural dimension or basis of group identity. In other words, society may also contain what the mass theorist has called masses.[74] Clearly, a mass population is composed of individuals who lack regional, religious, economic status, or other conscious identities that suggest distinctive group membership. It is not possible, of course, for these to be absent as objective facts of individual circumstances. What is lacking in a situation of conflict involving masses, however, is any distinctive sense of identity by those involved. Masses are groups of individuals who exhibit diversity in regard to the major social structural dimensions and who, lacking a distinctive group structure and certainly a sense of group membership in existing collectivities, may yet be identified as forming an ongoing social category by virtue of a similar response to a common experience. Such an experience may be economically induced stress, migration, or some other major social or personal disruption. Such populations, or masses, are seldom likely to occur. Generally, where such a population lacks any distinctive defining dimension, it may be further identified in terms of a common manifestation of political powerlessness, anomie, and personal malaise. However, productive analysis of political conflict will be impeded rather than aided if the existence of the latter properties in a population conscious of a distinctive group identity and acting in terms of that identity is used as the basis for labeling such a collectivity as a mass. To do so, and thus slight interest-based and probably rational determinants of behavior, is to weaken and confuse one's analysis by confounding too diverse a set of factors. This will become clearer in later discussion of the role of interests, political responsiveness, and other determinate elements in behavior.

The relevance of attention to a structurally based typology

There can be little disagreement with the contention that mass theory does not attend to either the potential for or the actual existence of diverse interest groups. The important issues are whether the types of distinctions suggested here qualify the mass theorist's analysis of dissent politics and whether they raise serious reservations regarding the usefulness of the mass–nonmass dichotomy. I feel that they do. A number of advantages are derived from developing and attending to social structural and belief-based social categories in society. These essentially consist of being led to give attention to a number of vital group properties (history, alliances, consciousness, etc.) and political conditions that are determinate of the nature of group behavior.[75] Further, by working in terms of a typology such as that developed here, or some similar one, it would become possible to make some rudimentary distinctions among types of protest and political movements – their organization, character, purposes, and possible development – which is not possible with the analytic scheme of mass political theory or with other common political behavioral models.

The mass theory literature lacks attention to behavior in the political arena as reflecting possible distinctive group grievances, distinctive group purposes, consciousness, organization, or other such areas. The gross mass–nonmass distinction sums up this absence of structural analysis. In effect, I have suggested that it is based on too simplified an analysis of societal structure and actual group forms and hence of consequent behavioral properties. Both the character of political behavior as well as that of group structure, ties, and interests are too diverse to lend themselves effectively to a mass–nonmass distinction. Karl Deutsch has pointed this out with considerable clarity. Reviewing Kornhauser's *The Politics of Mass Society*, he notes that

> Its conceptual division of politics into "mass" and "non-mass" phenomena would become a bed of Procrustes, on which case studies would rest at their peril. Are Nenni's Socialists "extremist" in the same sense as Fascists or Communists are? Is it wise to deal mainly with the similarities among the latter two movements, or should a more rounded treatment not also bring out more fully the difference between these two in ideology and behavior, as well as in recruitment. . . .
>
> Where in this simple dichotomy would Professor Kornhauser put the many nationalist movements in the underdeveloped areas? How are Gandhi's Indian Congress Party, Sun Yat Sen's Kuo Min Tang in the early 1920's, the followers of Mustafa Kemal, of Kwame Nkrumah, of General Nasser, of Fidel Castro all to be fitted into this scheme?[76]

A population bereft of all sense of distinctive group loyalties and membership, distinctive organizational forms, ideologies, and so on, is a mass. In such terms, however, it is a somewhat unique phenomenon.[77] A nonmass population clearly exists when similarly situated populations, experiencing similar inequities and needs, develop, as over time they usually will, a sense of common group membership and awareness of shared interest, and this produces an organized group structure and program related to the needs and disabilities of the group. These may be of a labor, agrarian, nationalist, ethnic, racial, or other character. They are not, however, masses. Nor can the diversity of protests in which they have played a preponderant role be characterized as extremist or mass politics.

Any attempt to retain and still utilize the mass–nonmass distinction can be viable only under certain specific conditions. One, careful account is taken of the varied group and interest structures existing within the social system. And within that context, the concept of mass is used to refer to that population or social category lacking a distinctive social structural or ideological basis, group consciousness, and some sense of reasonable interest purpose. Such a population will usually be lacking a sense of efficacy in regard to the decisions and events in the political arena. Some elements in society do exhibit such traits, but their numbers and frequency are not great. The alienated or angry voter of whom John Horton, Wayne Thompson, and others have written[78] may begin to approach such a category. Yet without knowing their relationship to the political arena more broadly and to a variety of political issues the scope of their mass character is uncertain. Some, but by no means all, of those uprooted by personal and social catastrophes – war, depression, migration, and the like – may also fit into this category, though Leggett, for instance, shows how even here a ready consequence of these disruptions may be the development of a class-conscious group rather than a "mass" population.[79] In fact, it is reasonable to hold that in many instances neither the alienated nor the uprooted will be a mass, though such a likelihood is increased in regard to these types of populations.

Additional determinants of interest collectivities, structural and otherwise

The major dimensions of societal organization provide only the potential for the appearance of groups, whether in terms of economic, status, ethnic, regional, or other dimensions. Whether such collectivities do in fact appear, and their character, depends on various other causal factors. Some of these are well recognized, others less so. They receive, however, little consideration in mass political theory or other types of social psychological theory. Without elaboration some of the principal determining elements of the appearance of subjective group membership (from an objective structural position) and of the purposes and behavior of such a membership are the presence and nature of the following: the type of distinctive experiences, needs, or desires provided by membership in particular collectivities; the historical experience and background of the collectivity; contemporary experiences in regard to representation within and the responsiveness of existing political structures; the nature of political socialization – partly comprehended by the preceding; the belief system or ideology of a society (which partly defines the forms and purposes of possible organizational and interpersonal group loyalties); the availability, character, and abilities of group leadership; patterns of communication; the activities of a major control agency such as the government, and so on. As has been noted, it is social structural location that significantly determines the nature of the potential influence of the factors noted on consciousness, personality, and behavior.

Structural analysis and referents for the mass concept, especially as applied to behavior

The pertinence of the structural analysis suggested here and of the attempt to develop a typology of conflict groups rests partly on the answers to two questions: Can interest-based and motivated collectivities be masses? Where such collectivities are not masses, can they engage nonetheless in mass behavior? Clearly, the first question incorporates two somewhat different conditions. It refers to objective and subjective dimensions of group membership. Where an individual is located within the social structure of society in objective terms of class, status, religion, region, and so forth, but without possessing a sense of identity with or membership in these categories, these properties of group consciousness could not serve as a basis for the support of a nonmass population. Such support would, I agree, have to be sought elsewhere and may or may not exist. If not present, there would be grounds for positing a mass population. However, if such structurally defined categories are in fact interest-motivated collectivities – that is, there exists a sense of membership and shared interest or purpose – then it would be inappropriate to use the appellation mass. The concept of mass cannot be applied accurately where there exists a sense of place, relationship, and perhaps identity, except in one limited though not completely unimportant sense. That is, the conditions specified do not by themselves assure that conditions prevail for the more intimate, responsive, and involved experiences that smaller-scale and organized group structures may provide. The absence of such experiences may be productive of a vague discontent, and in some respects the population affected may exhibit some mass properties. Yet, even as regards this possibility, it has already been suggested that it is by no means established that other types of relationships will not replace such group structures or that even, in their absence, the consequence may not be greater availability but rather heightened apathy or inaccessibility.

The question of whether interest-motivated collectivities can exhibit mass behavior when they act as members of such collectivities remains. In somewhat different but related terms, can nonmass populations exhibit mass behavior? Obviously not, if mass behavior is defined, among its other features, as involving mass populations. While it would clearly not be productive to utilize such a tautological definition, it is nonetheless true that in the actual description or allusion to mass behavior mass theorists generally, and usually explicitly, develop or take as given that the population concerned is in fact a mass. Is this assumption or treatment warranted? In part, the answer again depends on how mass behavior is defined. The usual definition of mass behavior appears to include two major yet different dimensions of behavior that should be distinguished, because they may occur independently of each other. Mass behavior may be described in terms of its aims and political character as activist, intemperate, and antidemocratic or, as is also sometimes the case, analyzed in terms of its more psychic and social properties, that is, its irrational, erratic, noninterest, and projective character. These two sets of behavior may occur together or separately. Actually, it is likely that if the latter qualities are present, there will also be a manifestation of the former characteristics. However, there appears less grounds to argue that the former set of properties – closing of the political arena to others, the lack of civility, and the like – need be associated with irrational, projective, and similar politics. The former characteristics may be features of class, revolutionary, or other political forms of protest where it is not the mass content of support but the depth of grievance and the absence of the means of change, among other properties of the situation, that underlie the behavior. In such instances we are not dealing with mass populations, and, in the terms usually used by the mass theorist, it becomes inappropriate to perceive such phenomena as mass behavior, without some qualification. Where behavior also exhibits the psychic properties noted, however, there is a much greater likelihood that the population involved may exhibit the characteristics of a mass population, one in which the population is not an interest-based collectivity. It seems reasonable to hold that mass behavior as usually conceived by the mass theorist is likely to appear only if one has a mass population, though in some circumstances mass behavior in both its major aspects may appear in nonmass populations.[80] If we distinguish between the two major dimensions or types of mass behavior, however, then nonmass populations may exhibit some of the properties of "mass behavior."

In the meaning usually residing in the concept of mass behavior the referent is to the behavior of mass populations. I have suggested that a possible response to the present stress on the necessity of structural analysis is to accept the existence of distinct interest collectivities yet maintain that such populations as well as masses may engage in mass behavior as it has been qualified previously. In other words, by narrowing the meaning of mass behavior and broadening that of mass theory one could apply it to interest-group-based behavior and not merely to the behavior of mass populations. But even if one were to accept, in some circumstances, the reasonableness of such an approach, it would in effect so generalize the nature of mass political theory as to weaken seriously its distinctive focus and character. Major aspects of the political theory of mass society would be compromised, that is, defined away, in those situations where mass behavior is not understood in terms of mass populations. The properties of mass political theory that would be jeopardized would include the interpretation of mass behavior in terms of the circumstances of populations defined as masses, concern with the creation of masses, the presumed distinctive mass character of contemporary populations, the presumably distinctive nature of extremist political behavior, the analysis of extremist or mass behavior in terms of the search for community or the availability of populations. In other words, the theory would be converted in major respects, implicitly if not otherwise, to more traditional social science perspectives on conflict behavior that perceive it in class or other group interest terms.

Developmental perspectives on political behavior and social movements

The lack of adequate structural analysis contributes to, but by no means completely accounts for, a historical and static character in the mass analysis of political behavior. There is little in the way of a meaningful processional analysis. Because of the lack of attention to the existence of distinctive collectivities that are recognized by their relationship to some major dimension of societal organization, the impetus is removed from recognizing change in political behavior. This, in part, is a reflection of the alteration over time in properties of the dimension that defines a collectivity and hence of the circumstances of the collectivity itself. Thus, for example, a class group such as the working class or a status-culture group such as small-town independent entrepreneurs assumes quite different characteristics at different historical periods. This reflects the partially predictable developmental patterns of the class concerned, such as changing numbers, developing consciousness, growth or organization, and development of traditions. It also reflects changes over time in external factors that affect the societal position and political behavior of the group, such as an altered ideological and cultural acceptability, a shifting status position, a change in the availability of economic opportunities, and development of centralized nation states. Group behavior then is likely to change in a very broadly predictive pattern over time as a group's structure and place in the wider society change during the evolution of the economic, social, cultural, and political forms of that society and of its own properties. One may speak of two broadly predictable patterns of change over time, one that is experienced by distinct collectivities, and the other the developmental pattern characterizing the polity and society. Both, of course, significantly influence the character of group political behavior. The mass theorist, however, can provide little sense of the variability or change in group behavior, the conditions productive of that variation, and the extent to which group behavior may in fact follow a general developmental pattern.

It seems plausible to suggest that by utilizing a limited number of crucial causal variables, such as group consciousness, isolation, and interest needs, plus broader system properties vis-à-vis the group, such as political representation and societal recognition, a typology of group circumstances and political behavior properties could be developed, to some extent in a broadly predictive developmental scheme. And only in very distinctive circumstances such as low political representation, low group consciousness, and high social isolation, for instance, might a given collectivity evidence mass group characteristics or behavior. These may well be group properties present only at a given stage in the development (and decline or diffusion) of a group, whether a working-class, landed, small-business, or other type collectivity. Thus behavior resembling mass behavior in some respects may appear – if at all – only at a certain and limited stage in the historical life and development of a group. Such an analysis begins not only to relate the character of social movement behavior to broad cultural, social, economic, and political changes but to place – though only very approximately – the properties and types of social movements and their societal determinants within a broad historical developmental scheme.

5. Radical political behavior: cognitive negotiation of a sociopolitical environment

Toward an appropriate analytic perspective

While particularly concerned with a critical assessment of mass political theory, my broader though as yet less fully developed purpose is to suggest a perspective for the analysis of radical political behavior. The preceding treatment of the importance of social structural factors is a very partial interpretive scheme. The inadequacy in social structural analysis is merely one difficulty, though a fundamental one, with mass political theory, as well as with prevailing social psychological theories. However, a fuller criticism and more adequate alternative theoretical scheme must move considerably beyond attention to merely social structure or even other systemic properties.

Some areas of theoretical and empirical development[1]

It may be useful to survey first a body of recent research and theory for suggestions of factors and processes relevant to the determination of the bases and nature of radical support. The efforts reviewed essentially treat considerations ignored in mass political theory and other prevailing social psychological theories. This is a growing body of scholarship that has stressed the volitional, cognitive, learned, and interest basis of radical support. It has urged the importance of social and political factors as they are experienced, in effect, from the distinct social position and circumstances of the individual. Some of the recent material that has gone beyond questions of individual motivations and circumstances has stressed the role of macrolevel processes, particularly political ones, in determining the appearance of radical politics and change. In spite of useful theoretical and descriptive advances there is, however, at the microlevel of analysis insufficient interpretation of support for vigorous protests and social movements from the perspective and experiential framework of the individuals and groups involved. While this literature is still incomplete and lacks

116

sufficient theoretical integration, it is a considerable advance over the body of work being criticized and offers a basis for further theoretical and empirical development.

The largest portion of these efforts consists of an impressive array of studies, principally though not exclusively descriptive, dealing with past and current dissident protest. This work examines the bases of support for radical or extremist large-scale political movements and also attempts to account for more episodic protests, radical voting behavior, party preference, and ideological disposition. We find, for instance, that the rational, purposive, and interest-based character of late eighteenth- and early nineteenth-century urban and rural protest in England and western Europe has been revealed in the imaginative analyses of distinguished historians such as Eric Hobsbawm and George Rudé. Similar efforts have been made by the sociologist Charles Tilly and his colleagues.[2] Their work shows that these disturbances reflected real and reasonable grievances where means of redress were limited. For the most part they involved stable and established community members rather than marginal rootless elements. The behavior was, essentially, appropriate to the circumstances that existed and can be viewed in the context of the political processes and distribution of power existing at the time. They also argue vigorously for the preponderant influence in the appearance of dissident behavior of political processes that affect the balance of power and political resources. In another direction the anthropologist Eric Wolf[3] has perceptively reviewed the genesis and character of some of the major peasant revolutions of the twentieth century. His analysis supports the need to focus attention on interest needs, conditions of consciousness, structures of power and lack of responsiveness. Though of a somewhat different character, the burgeoning collective behavior literature on contemporary protests offers a diverse number of studies, including those of Fogelson and Hill, McPhail, Obershall, Paige, Wanderer, and Berk and Aldrich,[4] among others, that provide empirical support for the changing perspectives that have been noted.

Further supportive material is found in the work of some younger historians, such as Pollack, Nugent, Clanton, and Durden.[5] Their refutation of the revisionist interpretations of the Populist movement in the United States in the 1890s shows both the generally tempered democratic, interest-based nature of this movement and its partisans and the necessity to interpret the movement within the context of the political processes and power struggles occurring at the local and national levels. These studies are extended by the reanalysis and interpretation, by the political scientist Michael Rogin,[6] of the support received by McCarthyism in the 1950s. He shows its basis to be principally among conservative, not populist, elements and describes the contribution of political leadership practice to its rise and continuance.

Additional case material has further contributed to critical re-analysis of extremist support. Historian William Allen's[7] illuminating study of growing Nazi support in one German town in the late 1920s and early 1930s shows its basis resting on stable respectable community elements, and as arising from class divisions, existing political antagonisms, party failure, and more or less ordinary political processes. An analysis of a quite different character, the exploration of the nature of Communist party allegiance in France by Richard Hamilton,[8] also points to the importance of factors of class consciousness and political socialization, without finding support for the notions of political primitivism, lack of group ties, and other features usually at the center of recently prevailing theory. Examining a much earlier historical event, Gerald Sorin's[9] study of the New York abolitionists challenges the tension-reduction theory of political radicalism. Critical of the political theory of mass society and other related explanations is Maurice Pinard's[10] theoretically informed and thoughtful analysis of the emergence of the Social Credit Party in Quebec, Canada, as well as his earlier essays on dissident political movements and on mass society.[11] Especially appropriate is Alejandro Portes' recent delineation of some of the properties of the working-class supporters of the radical left coalition in contemporary Chile.[12] He finds no support for the interpretation of leftist radicalism as a "simplistic political response of those who know no better" or as arising from the "lack of integrative bonds."[13] In his work Portes has also initiated a broad-ranging theoretical critique of a number of prevailing social psychological interpretations of radicalism that derive from the frustration-aggression hypothesis.

The works cited place in serious question the psychological models of the nature and genesis of popular support for dissident political movements or events. They show support for radicalism as reflecting political socialization, group membership, historic loyalties, dominant themes in the national political culture, interest consciousness, class divisions, the lack of responsiveness by political elites, the nature of available alternatives, and such other influences that account for most political commitments, radical or otherwise. The case materials cited offer pictures of individuals trying to make a sensible adjustment to their political environment in light of typical social and political influences and constraints. Some of the material also goes beyond analyzing individual motivations and properties to an analysis of the influence of system properties, especially political ones, on the appearance and scope of dissidence and violent behavior. This is sharply at variance with what I have labeled as prevailing theory. Some of the contributions also point to the need for a reassessment of the consequences of many dissident political movements so as to comprehend their positive influence on broadening the range of groups, issues, and policies represented in the political system and in increasing the responsiveness of that system.

The second body of developing research and analysis consists of recent efforts at determining whether certain forms of large-scale social change, particularly urbanization and migration, are in fact productive of volatile and available populations and political instability, as has frequently been claimed. Urban migrants have been perceived as presenting an especially appropriate example of an uprooted mass population and mass politics, as well as a population in which political behavior reflected circumstances of frustration and disappointment. Yet studies of migration, the political role of marginal urban populations, movement from farm to factory labor, and of urban protest refute such notions. Recent research in Latin America and Europe by Cornelius, Portes, and Tilly,[14] among others, as well as some excellent reviews of existing studies are pertinent here.[15] These studies do not find

severe frustration of expectations for socioeconomic improvement or personal and social disorganization; and even where these conditions are present, they do not necessarily lead to political radicalization or disruptive behavior.... With few exceptions these studies find that urban migrants fail in most respects to conform to the usual conception of a highly politicized, disposable mass. On the contrary, the persistent non-politicization or even de-politicization of these sectors over time appears to be one of their most prominent characteristics as political actors.[16]

A third area of research and theory qualifying prevailing theory explores the relationship between various political, social, and cultural factors and the genesis of political loyalties and political dissidence. Portes' work, to which reference has been made, is related to these efforts, especially in his concept of structural blame and concern with political socialization.

A number of research reports have appeared testing the relationship between relative deprivation and orientations toward protest or violence.[17] Suggesting little support for such a relationship, they have stressed the role of social and political conditions such as political trust, sense of legitimacy or support for existing political actors and institutions, isolation, sense of political efficacy, and belief in the effectiveness of violence. Of a somewhat different character is McPhail's[18] empirical and theoretical criticism of the deprivation-frustration-aggression model. He urges, in effect, a phenomenological approach that stresses the need to move away "from continued attention to individual attributes and to 'predispositions to behave' which are inferred therefrom"[19] toward a study of individuals' immediate interactional environments as principally determinate of civil disorder. Other efforts not concerned with relative deprivation or related theories have stressed the role of factors such as communication, political generations, class consciousness, and distinctive subcultural community.[20] Paige provides an especially interesting paper relating protest to conditions of efficacy and trust, suggesting the need to base an explanatory model on "variables tied to the political system"[21] and not to conditions of alienation and isolation.

Framework for a more comprehensive theoretical model

The recent efforts at understanding political dissidence are useful. But they lack an integration between macro- and microlevels of sociological analysis, and their analyses at both levels, especially the latter, are incomplete. While the present student cannot offer a comprehensive theoretical model, some of the elements and the general direction such an effort might take can be suggested. My own sympathy is toward an approach with a greater stress on the significance of social organizational and institutional forms and processes and on the active cognitive role of the individual. It is vital, however, to distinguish between a micro- and macrolevel of analysis, in effect, between the motivations, properties, and circumstances of individuals, on the one hand, and organizational- and societal-level phenomena on the other.

A closer understanding must be sought of the subjective world of the political dissident and of the interpretive construction of meaning in terms of which he negotiates his environmental circumstances. This must include seeking to understand the conscious experience and interpretation by the individual of external systemic properties, as well as of the diverse conditions peculiarly present within the immediate environment. Thus we see an individual's "action (as) constructed or built up instead of being mere release ... behavior, accordingly, is not a result of such things as environmental pressures, stimuli, motives, attitudes, and ideas but arises instead from how he interprets and handles these things in the action which he is constructing."[22] Political support (radical or otherwise) is behavior that arises from the individual's effort to make sense of his circumstances, his past conditions and loyalties, the events he perceives and experiences, current pressures and communication to which he is subject, the political alternatives of which he is aware, the costs, gains and dangers that these appear to carry, and the like. It is not some automatic response to one or more of the diverse social or psychological categories too frequently and easily constructed by the social analyst. This also means that social structural and social organizational forms are, in part, significant in terms of the meaning assigned them or developed in regard to them by the human actor. The social world, even in its presumably concrete social structural forms, is in one sense then created by the actor. In a somewhat different but related direction it also appears necessary to recognize that the explanation of particular behavioral instances will require "more systematic knowledge of individuals' immediate interactional environments,"[23] the sequences of interpersonal exchanges, chance happenings, spread of information, behavioral response of other actors and groups, and so on.

Radical politics hence is generally not an expressive striking out, either in frustration, a search for community, or as a means of acting out hostilities or personal peculiarities. It is, rather, a selection of one of several alternatives, in light of individual needs, that involves an interpretive interaction with the environment and a process of political education or learning over time little different in principle from most types of attitude formation. Thus radical political behavior is frequently not self-evident or a simplistic response to either psychological or social factors. A radical option or response usually constitutes a fairly complex sociopolitical interpretation and alternative.[24] It is an interpretive construction of meaning rooted in social, political, cultural, and ideological conditions, and these assume much of their relevance through a process of political socialization of the members of a collectivity. In these terms, the analytic model accounting for radical behavior is not fundamentally different in most instances from that used to understand traditional political behavior.

At a macrolevel of analysis, but where the focus is still on social psychological properties, attention should be given to properties such as the nature of interest and group consciousness, the legitimacy attributed to the state and major political institutions, perceptions of regime responsiveness, the nature of the attribution of blame, character of political commitments, and attitudes toward dissidence, among others. These should be seen as being shaped by developments at the societal level, directly by social and political organization and processes and indirectly by individual reassessments as other societal-level changes affect both personal circumstances and perceptions. Individual-level properties can be understood only in light of their interrelationship with broader macrolevel phenomena and in terms of the interpretation of meaning developed by the parties concerned as they seek to make sense of their circumstances and establish behavior within it. At the same time, individual consciousness and assessments would to some extent also reflect the cultural and historical uniqueness of a given group and society, that is, group or national character structure, the influence of past historical experience on perceptions, and the nature of available ideologies. Properties of individuals help account for potential support to dissident politics and may to varying degrees be a necessary resource or prerequisite for some forms of protest. However, this factor cannot account for or, in other words, does not produce protest behavior and can only partly explain the "tone" or quality of such behavior.

We may conceive of the major macrolevel determinants of dissidence and violent politics as comprehended by several major dimensions. At the macrolevel the major determinants of dissidence and violent political behavior that would be comprehended by a more adequate theoretical model are several. Attention should be given to the dissident's location within the principal social structural forms in terms of which society is structured – class, status, power, religion, region, communal properties, kinship, sex, and age. These form the major potential bases of individual and group interest and of the conflict that they engender. Dissident politics is also a reflection of social organization. We refer here to interest group organization and the nature of the networks of contact and communication. Social organization would be a major channel through which consciousness and action are generated. It is one source of the perspectives and symbols in terms of which the meaning of social structural categories is established by the actor. Social organization as well as the circumstances of social structurally defined categories are affected by societal processes of change, for example, urbanization, industrialization, and rationalization. Another major consideration is political forms and processes, such as the nature of the concentration and uses of power, regime responsiveness, power relationships, political coalitions and conditions of support and political exchange, and the effectiveness and resources of major political entities. While to some extent these have their own dynamic of change, they do significantly reflect the other societal level properties noted. The significance of the political process is its twofold influence on the nature of individual consciousness, sense of alternatives, and loyalties, as well as on altered resources for action and the mobilization of strategic population elements. Political forms and processes play an especially significant role, particularly in regard to the appearance of violence or revolutionary behavior. They create the timing, opportunity, and spur for action whose potential is principally generated by the preceding factors.

While granting the importance of the phenomenological world of the actor, it is thus essential to recognize the great importance of systemic and external properties. However important be the interpretive and active individual role, much of its character is shaped or generally predictable from the nature of broader system properties.[25] These do have an external reality. While the actor interprets and does not automatically respond to his circumstances and while he in fact partly experiences social structure and social organization in terms of the meanings he has constructed of them, broader institutional and societal properties crucially shape the nature of experiences, alternatives, and resources and, significantly, provide pregiven meanings or interpretive accounts. These are not created out of the thin air or pure unalloyed "experience." Thus the individual's experience and perspective will reflect his location within social, cultural, and political structures. This shared circumstance of many men helps account for the patterned differences among groups and the rough predictability and continuity of behavior. Thus, for example, the nature of stratification and the distribution and exercise of power may crucially determine the individual's initial circumstances of economic need, landlessness, and lack of political responsiveness to which radicalism may be a response in some circumstances. Similarly, other broader system characteristics – for example, the character of communication media and the nature of prevailing ideologies – influence the extent and direction of radical or other commitments. Hence while the individual acts in terms of his creation of a meaningful yet subjective world, the nature of that world and its variation among men, as well as much of the character of possible strains, disabilities, alternatives, and the like, reflect external broader system properties and group experiences. They are reflected, however, only through the consciousness of men – a consciousness not immediately or directly developed. In sum, the "objective" world helps shape both the subjective world of the individual as well as the circumstances that constrain and influence the actor. Human behavior is partly a reflection of both.

The preceding would be incomplete, especially for the understanding of violent behavior, without an examination of the consequences for behavior and violence that follow from the nature of the response of public authorities to protest or potential protest. Such response has historically played a part in shaping, encouraging, or heightening protest through its interactive consequences and its effect on individual assessments. This was exemplified in the urban riots in major American cities. In addition, an interpretive scheme should also recognize the role of chance happenings and evolving interpersonal contacts in the more or less immediate setting of dissidence and violent behavior.

These somewhat sketchy and general comments give little attention to the role of distinctive personal properties – for example, the lack of ties, the quest for community, personality traits, and the like – in dissident political behavior. This reflects our judgment that their importance is usually greatly exaggerated. The role that they may have appears limited to the microlevel of analysis. At this level they may in some circumstances account for differential involvement in dissidence by a population whose members in other respects seem to share more or less equally other causal circumstances. Intensity of involvement will in some situations also reflect differences in the construction of meaning that follows from the influence of distinctive personal properties.

Some elaboration of criticisms of and differences with the approach of mass political theory

While mass theorists and other students of social movements are correct in viewing social movements and the rise of a supportive population as partly a response to conditions of change and stress, a crucial issue, and one of the important differences between the perspective outlined here and the views of mass theory, is in identifying these changes and stresses. The emphasis in mass theory is on the lack of group ties, personal and group isolation, alienation, social and psychic needs, the attempt to find satisfaction of such needs in the political arena, and the like. The reasonable and cognitive quality of vigorous protest receives little attention. There is a general labeling of vigorous protest as violent, mass, irrational, negative and/or anti-democratic. Frequently, the perspective assumed is that of the political and social elements and elites predominant in existing structures of power and that are themselves often the object of large-scale protest. There tends to be a stress, though sometimes implicit, on maintaining social stability, especially as defined by the preservation of existing social structures. The distinguished Italian socialist theoretician

Antonio Gramsci effectively phrased the sentiments nearly 40 years ago:

This is the custom of our time: Instead of studying the origins of a collective event, and the reasons for its spread ... they isolate the protagonist and limit themselves to doing a biography of pathology too often concerning themselves with unascertained motives, or interpreting them in the wrong way; for a social elite the features of subordinate groups always display something barbaric and pathological.[26]

Witness in these different regards the nature of the negative response by the broader public, political and community leadership, and even some social theorists to a diversity of recent protest and social movements – the struggle to broaden civil rights, black militancy, diverse student protests, and antiwar protests. Similarly, reference can be made to the response and distorted interpretations and inappropriate labeling of earlier working-class, trade-union, agrarian, and other social protest.

What is stressed throughout the present essay is that it is not so much social change in terms of social disjunctures of community and society, with a presumed loss of ties, that is usually a vital impetus to dissent and social movements but more probably the threat to group interests, life style, and personal and group identities, of which societal and community change may, of course, be productive. More accurately, it is less a change, in most instances, in these regards than a growth of organization, leadership, consciousness, a sense of new possibilities, altered attributions of legitimacy, and so on, centering on group interests, life style, and similiar needs, that is significant in the appearance of support for protests and social movements. In another direction, some types of social change create conditions that may heighten conflict and stimulate the appearance of dissident movements due to their effect on power relationships and on the expectations, purposes, services, and duties that pertain between a populace, or segments of it, and the political institutions and leadership of society. This is particularly the case in processes of modernization and political development.[27]

Joan Nelson[28] provides a powerful refutation of both mass and deprivation-frustration-aggression theorists. Apropos of the preceding comments are her conclusions in regard to the presumed social disruption, frustration, and political role of urban migrants. Referring to her extensive review of the available literature and to Robert Fried's study "Urbanization and Italian Politics,"[29] she concludes that the migrants' political behavior is not primarily a reflection of the trauma of migration. Rather, it flows from the political attitudes and patterns of behavior migrants bring with them from the country (or the relative absence of clearly formulated attitudes and fixed behavior patterns) and from an active process of political socialization through situations and agents to which they are exposed in the city ... there is little reason to assume an inherent or automatic radicalizing bias to the process.... The appropriate focus of inquiry, then, is not the migrants' autonomous perceptions and emotions, but the active politicizing institutions and influences in individual nations or, better, in specific cities, to which they are exposed.[30]

Clearly, important qualifications on mass theory are suggested by these and earlier comments. Even to recognize in some circumstances a condition of social disjuncture, however, leaves quite undetermined the question of political behavior. Personal disruption, where we assume or discover it to be present, may in a sense be relevant for individual political availability and behavior. The sense of loss and malaise that may thus be created and the need that may arise for meaningful ties and a sense of personal order suggest circumstances that may induce toward a condition of availability. Yet circumstances that encourage withdrawal, helplessness, and apathy that deters mobilization are also suggested. A population's very lack of organizational ties and involvement also make it less likely that people will be "found" by appeals, leaders, and movements or, if accessible, that without group support or encouragement they will as individuals become followers or involved in the new ideas and movement demands. As the reader will recall, this is one of the observations in Tilly's essay where he points out that such populations are less rather than more likely to be involved in protests and new movements. Mention has also been made of the similar findings Pinard reports in his survey of a number of somewhat more contemporary social movements.[31] Thus while in an abstract sense the changes noted may – on occasion – produce an availability, there usually does not appear to be either the psychic, social, or organizational conditions that would effectuate a response and political behavior in accord with that availability. Hence it need not be that the contentions of mass theory in these regards are always irrelevant (though they are exaggerated), but even where personal disturbance and isolation do occur, the social dynamics are more complex than in the mass model and the behavioral results may fall considerably short of expectations. This, of course, is quite apart from the serious reservations already raised as to the extent to which populations do experience the loss of community, whether or not the origin, appeal, and character of social movements are in fact significantly reflective of disruptions of community, and the extent to which the supporters of social movements can be characterized as in quest of community.

In a related vein, mass theorists contend that social movements attract marginal and isolated populations, those less likely to be attentive to the usually prevailing political interest organizations and leadership. Yet where the latter is true because existing mainstream organizations and elites are not responsive to legitimate and reasonable collectivity needs, this would not be a distinctive claim or property of the theoretical framework of mass theory. Many populations defined as isolated would seem to fall appropriately into such a situation. It has already been suggested that the contention of marginality or isolation appears dubious in many instances where protest and social movements appear, if what is meant is a condition other than the lack of political access and a definition of needs and goals at variance with those generally prevailing.

Mass theory's lack of any adequate consideration of political representation and responsiveness is a grave weakness and becomes readily apparent where the rationality and interest basis of social movements and their supporters is stressed. Such a lack has encouraged in mass political theory as well as in much of contemporary political theory an insensitivity to the rigidity and inaccessibility of many political structures and elites.[32] There has been an implicit conclusion that political leadership and forms of representation and interest resolution are adequate to meet specific group needs and the individual's sense of citizenship in a responsive society. Hence the reasonableness and the legitimacy of these movements of protest have generally been denied. Thus mass theorists and

pluralists do not treat mass movements as rational forms of organization of constituencies that lack power. . . . Extraordinary direct-action techniques like marches and demonstrations may be the only ways in which deprived constituencies can exert influence; normal pressure group tactics may not be effective for them. Indeed, these extraordinary techniques may be particularly necessary to force action on a lethargic, decentralized ("pluralist") political system. But since the pluralists stress that power is shared in a pluralist democracy, movements that do not accept the normal political techniques of that society must be dangerous and irrational.[33]

In effect, deficiencies in the analysis of social and political structures have limited the ability to perceive the rationality of a great deal of protest movements, both in the origin of these protests as well as in the character of their goals and the behavior utilized to attain their goals.

Part of the problem in understanding the nature and rationality of many political and social movements arises from the narrow pluralist interest group perspective of mass theory, which in practice generally restricts its recognition of the legitimacy, reasonableness, and rationality of political behavior to only delimited narrow self-interest-based efforts at change and interest satisfaction. That is, it tends to recognize interest conflict only in terms of more functionally specific and delimited collectivities and areas of concern than that connoted by class conflict or the other major structural categories alluded to previously. Thus it fails to incorporate class analysis, among other emphases, into its conceptual and analytical scheme; it is unable to comprehend protest as both nonmass and yet of a character different from the narrow self-interest type of contention that pluralist theory deals with so extensively. Class movements are nonmass movements, yet they are also clearly more than or other than merely a narrow interest group protest. They usually represent a response to much more fundamental and far-reaching conditions of stress and inequity. The failure to perceive class movements as responses to conditions of severe economic and job-related strains and the failure to perceive them as both nonmass and yet distinctively and properly different than pluralist interest group protests have resulted in the frequently unwarranted attribution of irrationality to such movements.

It would be reasonable to suggest that where economic and at times social conditions are severe, where inequities are considerable, demands unmet, and few effective forms of organization, representation, or political action exist within the traditional political organizations or interest representative bodies, working-class support to a Communist party or movement, farmer support for the Populist movement, and earlier black support to CORE, SCLC, and SNCC are quite reasonable responses, as are perhaps many instances of disruptive protest that frequently arise. And it is doubtful how much importance should be placed on rootlessness and atomization. This is especially true when frequently all but some vigorous populist protest movement, Communist party or otherwise, is identified with the prevailing order. Hence workers, peasants, blacks, and similar groups would reasonably seek for a means of redress in a party or movement opposed to the prevailing order. Would it be more rational to expect the worker, for instance, under the kind of conditions noted, to support a party of business or some other interest group that has denied labor demands?

One of the major difficulties here is, of course, the crucial supposition of mass and pluralist theories that elites are responsive and accessible. In fact, it is this presumed accessibility that disturbs the mass society and democratic elitist theorist, and the need to restrict it that motivates many of their propositions and discussions. If in fact elites are accessible, then the character of many mass protests is irrational and unreasonable. The imputation of irrationality is appropriate where behavior flies in the face of reality. But what I suggest is that it is not unreasonable to interpret the situation of much of Latin American labor, the American Populists and various other agrarian movements, the American black, and the situation of some other labor, agrarian, and disadvantaged groups as marked by a considerable lack of accessibility to the elites. It is the *inaccessibility* of elites that would appear to help account for social movements, though, of course, mere inaccessibility does not help define the distinct characteristics and behavior of such movements. In these regards Rogin has stated:

Other factors besides the inaccessibility of elites obviously contribute to the rise of mass movements and determine their character. But whether the movements are democratic or totalitarian, their appearance is related to the inaccessibility of elites. By basing mass movements on the accessibility of elites Kornhauser denies them the possibility of being a rational response to social crises. For if the elites are accessible, mass movements are unnecessary.[34]

The analytical perspective expressed by the preceding comments finds partial expression in the more traditionally oriented theoretical analyses of vigorous protest that eschew the mass theory orientation. Thus, for example, it finds support in the work of Tilly, Rudé, Hobsbawm, Portes, Pollack, and Rogin, among many other scholars to whom reference is made in this chapter. In their application of an analytic framework stressing the cognitive, rational, and interest basis of behavior and its response to deficiencies in political representation and responsiveness, these investigators have provided illuminating analyses of diverse instances of collective behavior and political protest, both violent and peaceful. Their work clearly suggests the need to define the nature of the social structural position and distinct interest basis of the population in question and the importance of establishing the character of the political process and structures of power in which they are implicated. Tilly states in the opening remarks of his insightful theoretical and empirical analysis of urban unrest in eighteenth- and nineteenth-century France that "violent protests seem to grow most directly from the struggle for established places in the structure of power ... instead of constituting a sharp break from 'normal' political life, violent protests tend to accompany, complement, and extend organized, peaceful attempts by the same people to accomplish their objectives."[35] The thrust of such research, as well as the analysis undertaken here and in later chapters, is that in most instances political movements and protests, even when violent, are not pathological nor in need of distinct principles of analysis in order to interpret them.[36] It is fundamentally misleading to view such behavior as some aberration occurring outside of the usual political process or as understood or determined by essentially non-political causal elements.

There is also a misleading quality to the stress by the mass theorist, and pluralist theorists more generally, on the antidemocratic properties and "extremist" qualities of reform movements occurring outside the boundaries of established political and interest organizations and forms. It has already been noted that the assumption about the openness or responsiveness of the political system is often exaggerated. However, also expressed, sometimes implicitly, in preceding and later comments, are the positive consequences for the polity and particular collectivities of many of such dissident movements. Most particularly, of course, is that they may diminish conditions of inequity and strengthened social integration. More broadly, the effects of these movements are often to expand the range of political and social goals and policy, the nature of issues open for serious consideration, the boundaries of the political arena so as to include previously uninvolved and ignored populations, the breadth or diversity of political leadership, the techniques for political negotiation, interest resolution, and the like. They may also strengthen leadership responsiveness and disturb the tendencies toward lethargy among leaders. Many of the major dissident movements in American society, generally outside of the existing pluralist consensus, have made some contribution in these terms.

Radical protest movements: specific cases

The present section turns to the major effort of this chapter. Five brief case studies are presented that attempt to explain the basis of popular support for a number of widely recognized instances of radical or dissident protest. These vary in time, cultural and political setting, and in the type of dissident groups involved. They all provide an opportunity to evaluate the adequacy of applying a mass political theory model to interpret the behavior in question. Such an evaluation also offers the means to suggest a contrary analysis that stresses the apparently purposive, cognitive, and group interest character of dissidence. The vital role of a number of political, cultural, and historical elements, among other more specific factors, is also noted. More broadly, there is a stress on the necessity of viewing political support from the experimental framework of the individuals involved. Such an overall analysis also permits an indirect critical assessment of social psychological theories of radicalism, in addition to mass political theory.

The individual case studies are various. Briefest treatment is given to early peasant and worker protest in western Europe and the agrarian Populist movement in the United States at the end of the past century. In these cases attention is focused principally on conditions of inequity, unresponsiveness to interest needs, and the purposive and reasonable nature of protest. In addition to such factors, the third case, an analysis of working-class support for the radical left-wing movement in Chile, suggests the considerable relevance of past historical events and societal structure in accounting for such support. The analysis of working-class support for the Communist party in France that follows further develops the range of causal determinants by introducing the significant role played by political culture and related societal properties. The fifth case discussion considers the reasons for the support received by the Nazi movement in its rise to power in Germany toward the end of Weimar. In this presumably classic instance of mass political behavior the applicability of aspects of the alternative interpretative model being suggested here is further stressed, and serious reservations are again posed on the appropriateness of mass political theory and, less directly, on related psychological models.

The following analyses, particularly those on Chile, France, and Germany, begin to suggest the inappropriateness of a conception often implicit in mass political theory, that of political primitivism, or the association of radical behavior with ignorance, low education, and low information.[37] However, the case studies also suggest – though less concretely developed and less uniformly treated[38] – that neither are other elements of the expressive and social psychological model necessary to explain the behavior in question. Portes' material on Chile is explicit in these regards, testing and refuting many of the concepts of the social psychological model, various properties of the deprivation-frustration-aggression hypothesis, notions about social mobility and urban migration, and status inconsistency. The diverse material on the Nazi supporters, working-class Communists in France, the Populist movement, and early western European peasant and labor agitation casts doubt on the applicability of the processes and phenomena implicit in these notions, though the explicit treatment that is offered is somewhat limited. Rather, they urge the explanatory importance of systemic properties as they are probably experienced by individuals in a given social structural position.

Early peasant and labor agitation

The analyses of careful scholars like Hobsbawm, Rudé, and Tilly[39] reveal the interest basis and rationality of many instances of the late eighteenth- and nineteenth-century peasant and labor agitation in western Europe, even where these were violent. They also suggest the importance of interpreting protest in terms of the political context within which it arises. Indirectly, they strongly point away from any need to resort to notions of the decline of community or the loss of group ties.

Rudé shows that the disturbances and riots in France and Great Britain during this period arose from real and reasonable grievances in regard to food shortages, high prices, low wages, threats to employment, and so on. In fact, the appearance of protest corresponded closely with those occasions when economic disparities developed and means of redress were lacking, given the unresponsive character of existing political structures. The agitation, in effect, involved a clash between significant segments of a local population suffering distinct and recognized disabilities "against the local elite or the representative of the central power."[40] Recent historical analysis helps support the proposition that the individuals involved essentially perceived their circumstances and behavior in the terms outlined here. The protest behavior was in accord with the cause of grievance and was a utilitarian means to mitigate it. Property, not lives, was destroyed. Destruction was selective, targets and means chosen were appropriate to the circumstances. There was little in the way of indiscriminate pillage. The food riots were in effect "the imposition of an unofficial price control by collective action, or what the French call *taxation populaire*."[41] A somewhat similar practice was also evidenced by industrial labor in England, which Hobsbawm has referred to as "collective bargaining by riot," and Darvall has referred to as "a means of coercing ... employers into granting ... concessions with regard to wages and other matters."[42] Farmer and some labor protests and revolts in eighteenth- and early nineteenth-century America also provide, in a number of respects, some additional instances.

These were rational protests and efforts at interest satisfaction by the established, employed, stable, noncriminal and nonvagrant elements of the countryside and cities for whom no other effective avenues of redress existed. The behavior evidenced in these protests was reasonable to the circumstances that existed. Referring, for instance, to the French rural riots of the eighteenth century, Rudé observed that:

The sole target was the farmer or prosperous peasant, the grain merchant, miller, or baker; and the appeal made, where the King himself did not appear to intervene to protect his people, was to precedent and ancient custom. There was no question of overthrowing the government or established order, of putting forward new solutions, or even of seeking redress of grievances by political action. This is the eighteenth century food riot in its undiluted form.[43]

The protests were primarily efforts to restore rights and conditions that had previously prevailed. They were responses to an unacceptable and illegitimate alteration in economic conditions, not, it would appear, to distinctive personal or psychological properties of the population involved. The thorough and seminal efforts of historical research like Rudé's *The Crowd in History* and *The Crowd in the French Revolution* and Hobsbawm and Rudé's *Captain Swing* suggest neither circumstances of marginality and isolation nor conditions of rising expectations nor relative deprivation. Their work makes clear and explicitly points out the importance and necessity of studying crowd behavior in its social, historical, and political context.

The application of the concepts of mass and mass behavior as used by the mass theorist would be inappropriate here. And one strongly suspects that the same would be true of other interpretations to which exception has been taken. Perhaps the closest one could come to the mass theorist's perspective is where protest, while reflecting a need to which the political order is unresponsive, occurs in a condition of low class organization and consciousness. In such circumstances behavior may be somewhat erratic, with the activist and extrainstitutional qualities of a population lacking class organization and awareness that are also aspects of mass behavior. Yet even this circumstance is increasingly unlikely as we move farther away from conditions of social banditry and preindustrial urban mobs.[44] That is, large-scale interest group organizations develop that are characterized by greater degrees of group consciousness as group interests are increasingly implicated in national structures – concomitants of increasing national dominance, centralization, and coordination.

Tilly extends his study of collective behavior in western Europe beyond the late eighteenth- and early nineteenth-century period of communal protest. He examines collective behavior through the nineteenth-century up to the present, particularly at a time when industrialization, urbanization, and national development were transforming society, encouraging population movement, and leading to the proliferation and increasing prominence of diverse special purpose organizations. While such a change begins to introduce the phenomenon of contemporary class movements to be considered soon, it also permits a test of mass theory's propositions on the association between disruption of community and the appearance of social instability and uprooted populations. These are presumably associated with rapid urbanization and industrialization and the consequent development of available and mass populations engaging in mass behavior. Tilly's analysis, however, including some of the work of Rudé, does not support such a supposition. "The information available points to a slow, collective process of organization and political education – what we may loosely call a development of class consciousness – within the city rather than a process of disruption leading directly to personal malaise and protest."[45] What is evident, Tilly shows, is that protest was greater among the older settled urban and industrial populations, and this protest assumed a class rather than mass character. It is the newer urban immigrants' very lack of the "personal, day-to-day contacts that had given them (the older residents) the incentive and the means for collective action against their enemies" that, among other factors, accounts for the low level of collective behavior.[46] Over time, however, the development of group associations and class organizations, and class consciousness promoted increased collective action. As the following material suggests, though, this does not in most instances manifest a mass character.

In a number of major aspects this historical material is supported by a growing literature on urbanization and urban migration in Latin America and elsewhere. Essentially, this material finds little connection between urbanization and radicalization or degree of disruptive behavior. The comprehensive research reviews by Cornelius and Nelson, to which reference has been made, and the work by Portes, Mangin, and Ray, among others, indicate that theories positing such a relationship are not borne out, regardless of whether they are developed in terms of the personal disruptions attendant upon moving, the frustrations arising from the gap between achievement and expectations, or the increased politicalization wrought by the urban environment.

Agrarian protest: the American Populists

The Populists, adherents of the American agrarian protest movement of the 1890s, have become a synonym for dissident antidemocratic movements appealing to the common man's sense of grievance but without either a realistic assessment of the problems of their supporters or a reasonable and an appropriate program to improve their condition. While rooted in the agrarian unrest of the latter part of the nineteenth century, the Populist movement was formally initiated with the establishment of the People's party in 1892. Eschewing the existing parties as unresponsive to their needs, the farm population of the southern and western states, especially Kansas, Nebraska, the Dakotas in the west, and Alabama, Georgia, and North Carolina in the south, engaged in a historic political movement that won a number of state elections and for a few brief years seriously threatened the political hegemony of the two traditional parties. It then declined precipitously, after the ill-fated association with the Democratic party in 1896, though in later years many of the reforms for which it fought were enacted.

In a shift from the scholarly interpretations of the period prior to World War II, the analyses made by the writers of the 1950s began to interpret the Populists and populism as exhibiting the pathological properties of mass involvement in politics: extremism, irresponsibility, backward-looking utopianism, irrationality.[47] Revisionist interpreters of this agrarian protest movement – Hofstadter, Ferkiss, and Viereck, among others[48] – have minimized the existence of a reasonable response by the Populists to very real economic disabilities and legitimate political grievances. They have, in effect, charged them with responding intemperately to the growth of industrial society and to a presumed consequent status loss and of trying unrealistically to recapture a romanticized image of the yeoman farmer of an earlier preindustrial past. While recognizing – though not incorporating into their explanatory schemes – that the farmers had legitimate grievances, the revisionists have viewed the Populists' interpretations of their problems as unduly simplified, pitched in anti-industrial terms, and hence unrealistic in light of the character of change and the possibilities of redress. It is not only as regards the programmatic aspects of the Populist movement but also in the account of its general tone and behavior that the revisionists exhibit an interpretive model close to the perspective of mass political theory and other related non-interest-based approaches. The movement and its members are perceived as emotional, intemperate, and anxious, acting more in expressive than instrumental terms.

Jingoistic, bigoted, and nativistic, they are ready to deny rights to others and short-circuit democratic practices. These properties are reinforced, it is suggested, by a moral fervor viewed as lending it the air of a crusade.

In recent years, however, the much maligned American Populists have been reassessed in terms peculiarily appropriate to the present argument, and the applicability of the preceding interpretation has been severely questioned. The seminal research and interpretation by scholars (Pollack, Woodward, Nugent, Clanton, and Rogin[49]) make clear that the Populist movement was a rational class response to conditions of great economic distress and a nonresponsive political order. The disabilities that the Populists faced were very real. They included foreclosures, high mortage indebtedness, crop liens, declining crop prices, and adverse marketing arrangements, artificially maintained high prices through monopolistic practices and tariffs, railroad discrimination against the farmer, and domination by these same railroads of state legislatures. Yet the revisionists have interpreted the Populists and their aims in a manner that has minimized and misconstrued their actual historical, economic, and political experiences. This underlies their perception of agrarian protest as unrealistic and rabble-rousing. In fact, however, populism sought "concrete, economic solutions to farmer grievances. . . . They came to see the importance of social relationships rather than individual morality in explaining political attitudes." It was not "irrational obsession" that characterized populism but a program whose "proposed solutions and remedies were economic." The Populists' political proposals were reasonable, practical, and concrete and "concentrated on specific economic grievances rather than vague, unfocused resentment."[50] Its principled response to an inequitous situation was not anti-industrial, but rather was opposed to the forces that profited from industrial expansion.

The People's party was a movement of political and economic protest that sought to displace local elites and secure reasonable reforms in federal and state economic and regulatory policies. It was, in effect, a vigorous thrust at existing local and national power structures, both within government and in the private sector. The movement must be understood in this light of contending economic and power interests, leavened to some extent by social and cultural factors that partly pitted opposing ways of life against each other. The latter fact, however, can by no means serve as the major analytic principle for understanding and interpreting the agrarian protest of the 1890s.

The charges leveled against the Populists, of extremism and of an antidemocratic thrust, appear ill placed. Rather than threatening representative democratic institutions the Populists sought to use both the form and the spirit of these institutions and to invigorate them when they were deficient. It was not the denial of political rights to others that they sought, but rather the attainment of access to centers of political power by the many, which at the time were controlled by and being used for the benefit of the few. Rogin stresses the need to:

measure Populist practice against the claims of its opponents. While many Populists favored the initiative and the referendum, the political reforms most stressed by the Populists were the secret ballot and the direct election of senators. Certainly the Populists sought to challenge the political and economic power of those who dominated American society at the turn of the twentieth century. Certainly the direct election of senators increased the power of the people vis-a-vis the elites. But it is highly dubious that such a Populist reform was a threat to representative democracy. Finally, the Populist attacks on the courts indicate disregard for law and order not so much by the Populists as by the courts themselves ... consistent, narrow partiality in interpreting the laws and the constitution explains Populist attitudes better than deductions concerning "plebiscitory democracy."

... Particularly in contrast to the politics it opposed, Populism was clearly a democratic phenomenon.[51]

Populism was also a distinctly democratic and rational movement in terms of its attempt to expand the political arena to include the people it represented, the character of the political and economic reforms sought, principled adherence to its goal, and commitment to community and society. The Populists were clearly more the objects of unreason and antidemocratic practices than the perpetrators of such deeds.

They had to contend regularly with foreclosure of mortgages, discharge from jobs, eviction as tenants, exclusion from church, withholding of credit, boycott, social ostracism and the endlessly reiterated charge of racial disloyalty and sectional disloyalty.... They contended also against cynical use of fraud comparable with any used against Reconstruction, methods that included stuffed ballot boxes, packed courts, stacked registration and election boards, and open bribery. They saw election after election stolen from them and heard their opponents boast of the theft. They were victims of mobs and lynchers.[52]

Nor can they accurately be labeled as jingoist, nativist, or anti-Semitic, hostile to foreigners, or appealing to prejudice if attention is paid to the character of the movement and to a survey of Populist literature. These properties were no more present, usually in fact less so, than in the broader society at that time.[53]

These characteristics suggest not merely the democratic nature of the movement but its rationality, clear interest character, and reasoned confrontations with its disabilities. Reliance on jingoist, anti-Semitic, antidemocratic, and similar fulminations would have been a way to avoid facing up to their economic disabilities and the problems brought by industrialization.[54] Such behavior, the typical response of social movements in the mass theory framework, was not exhibited by the Populists. In terms of the mass theory model, the irrationalities attributed to populism apply best to non-class, non-interest-based protests of collectivities with little group consciousness or clarity of purpose. This, however, does not fit the Populists.

From recent studies of the Populist movement it is clear that we are dealing with a distinctive social category that can reasonably be referred to as a class in economic terms, that possesses a sense of group or class membership and identity, is neither lacking in group ties nor intermediate group structures nor suffering a condition of estrangement and vague ill-focused malaise. As a political movement populism is based on very reasonable grounds of distress, including the lack of responsiveness and remediable action of ruling political and economic elites. Its major defining dimension is that of a struggle by beleaguered agrarian interests to limit the ruthless exercise of power by local and national industrial, railroad, and financial interests, aided by often corrupt political leadership. It proposed a rational program, as revealed by the objects of its criticism, the quality of that criticism, and the policies of change and reform it sought. The farmer's response to his plight was rational and utilitarian not only in terms of producing a political movement oriented to action on the source of his difficulty but also to a considerable degree in terms of the style of behavior exhibited by this political movement and in its attitudes toward societal change and industrialization. Clearly, these are not the conditions that define either the characteristics or the roots of status conflict, nor of a mass population or political behavior of mass political theory. Nor, it may be added, do they support the possible application of other social psychological explanatory schemes. It is reasonable to conclude that failure to attend to the interest basis, in effect, to the economic and political grievances behind Populist protest, has meant a serious distortion of the nature of populism. Where the interest basis and the political context of legitimate grievances are slighted, it is perhaps not surprising that vigorous protest will be labeled as irrational and expressive. In interpreting populism as irrational, unrealistic, and status-culture protest, the revisionists have failed to perceive the radical and progressive force that inhered in populism, its potential for altering the industrial system and fundamentally extending democratic forms and achieving greater economic and political equality.[55]

Working-class left-wing movements

Radical Communist-inclined working-class movements tend to be viewed as exemplifying mass behavior and noncognitive processes – antidemocratic, extremist, intemperate, and moved more by emotion or psychic-social grievance than rationally responding to class needs and political action choices. While in one sense these are clearly class movements, anomalous as it may appear, they are seen as mass movements! In most instances this is an untenable proposition. Cursory analysis will usually show that the Communist labor population is usually not a mass population. Nor would an analysis of the reasons for supporting such movements, the functions served by such support or membership, the character of involvement, and the actual program of Communist or radical left movements usually support the contention that these are mass movements. Such an analysis, especially where broadened by a more extensive examination of additional historical, social, political, and cultural factors, also suggests the limited utility of an emphasis on the psychological and expressive roots of working-class radicalism.

Working-class support for radical political movements is examined in two quite different circumstances, Chile and France. Neither can be understood in terms of a mass theory model nor, it would appear, in terms of a psychological model, though the present case material confronts the later model less directly and fully. The cases reported here exhibit, among other elements, the very important role of interest grievance and political socialization in determining support for radical movements, the nature of the relationships existing with the broader social system and with the political process, and the individual worker's attempt to negotiate his political environment in a realistic and satisfactory manner.

Chile: radical class movement[56]

Chile provides a classic example of a radical working-class protest movement. Stretching for more than 2600 miles along the southwestern coastline of South America, this mining and moderately industrial nation has for many years contained one of the most vigorous and powerful radical working-class movements in the world.

The explanation for and the basis of working-class support for the Marxist parties in Chile are found neither in mass theory nor the deprivation-frustration-aggression hypothesis. The strength and commitment to the parties of the left are accounted for by a number of considerations, none of which partakes of the mass model, nor do they require resort to various psychological factors to account for their political efficacy. These determinants of support include the severe disabilities and needs of the working class exacerbated by the burden of continuous inflation, the hierarchical, exploitative, and isolated character of Chilean society, the absence of any meaningful representation within the traditional parties, the lack of responsiveness by political and social elites, and a past history of brute repression. Support has also depended on the existence of parties of the left whose programs of reform and vigorous criticism of existing policies and parties have offered a viable alternative to existing political opinions. Implicated in these conditions is the influence exercised by neighborhood and work place – more broadly, processes of political socialization and the development of class consciousness determinate of left-wing sympathy. Conditions of great poverty, denigration, and political unresponsiveness have apparently also played a vital part.

The origin of the Chilean working class is primarily found in the labor force that left the rural countryside for Valparaiso and the desolate northern mine and ports areas of Antofagasta, Iquique, and Arica in the last half of the nineteenth century. In this century it has over time slowly begun to move into the increasingly industrial centers of the country, especially into Santiago and its metropolitan area containing more than one quarter of the nation's population. While there was some economic class organization and protest toward the end of the past century, vigorous and sizable working-class organizations began to develop only by the end of the first decade of the twentieth century, with the establishment in 1909 of the Chilean Labor Federation (FOCH). Shortly thereafter, in 1912, the Socialist Labor party appeared. By 1921 it had evolved into the Communist party. These parties of the left often functioned in close association with the trade-union movement, a significant portion of which early assumed a Marxist orientation. These earlier efforts and their tradition provided the roots of the contemporary Marxist coalitions.

Working-class trade-union and political party organization in the ensuing decade was marked by periods of decline as well as growth and at times faced severe repression. Nonetheless, extensive trade-union and party organization was achieved and became in the past fifteen years or so one of the most imposing and powerful forces in Chilean society. Thus FRAP – the Popular Action Front, a coalition of the forces of the left, principally the Socialist and Communist parties – was nearly victorious in the 1958 presidential elections and ran strongly again in 1964. A reconstituted coalition of left parties with some center support finally won the presidential election of 1970, with Salvador Allende victorious in a three-man contest. Allende's election plurality in his fourth bid for the presidency rested heavily on the copper and nitrate mining and port areas of Chile's desolate northern region, the sprawling urban slums or *callampas* of greater Santiago, the steel and coal area around Concepción some 200 miles south of the capital, and to some extent on the rural peasantry. The working class has had a strong sense of class loyalty and consciousness, a sense of distinct class interest, and extensive class ties and involvements that belie an attribution of social disjunctures and isolation. However, social marginality in regard to the dominant social and political groups and institutions of the society has been severe. While a radical orientation has characterized an important section of the working class, a more moderate political orientation is dominant among the quite considerable remaining portion.

The growth of the lower class as a potent political force with radical sympathies has been significantly furthered by the rapid and extensive urbanization of Chilean society. The capital district has more than doubled in size in the 20 years from 1950 to 1970, to where it contains more than 27 percent of the national population. More broadly, the approximately 56 percent of the population now in communities of 20,000 or more has more than doubled the proportion of 1920.[57] This has contributed to a growing concentration of a lower-class urban-based nonagrarian population increasingly removed from traditional rural patterns of political obeisance and deference. The new circumstances heightened exposure to new contacts and experiences, more radical political communication and organization, and a potential receptivity to more radical political alternatives.

The root condition underlying the circumstances of the lower class of Chilean society can be very succinctly summarized. In its most general terms Chile may be said to have had a two-class system – those who ruled and the masses that were excluded from political and social life – though social and economic distinctions can naturally be drawn among various classes or sectors within the society. This fact is basic to any understanding of the character of Chilean politics. The aristocracy, the upper class, and the middle sectors have been a small and privileged segment of the society that has succeeded in excluding the great majority of the population from national, social, cultural, economic, and political patterns. This is sharply depicted in McBride's authoritative and sensitive analysis of Chilean society:

Here has existed a new World Country with the social organization of old Spain; a twentieth century people still preserving a feudal society; a republic based on the equality of man; yet with a blue blooded aristocracy, a servile class as distinctly separated as in any of the monarchies of the world. Throughout Chile's history this sitution has existed. It is this social heritage that forms the background for the present day problems of the Chilean people.[58]

It is partly within the context of these broad historic and social properties of Chilean society that the interpretation of political loyalties must be initiated. The social divisions and the attitudes associated with it suggest the basis for working-class receptivity to the political appeals of the left, antagonism to traditional political groups, and the roots for a strong class consciousness.

In addition to a sharp invidious exclusion, the lower classes have suffered great disabilities for many years. They have experienced economic distress and wretched living conditions, being ill housed, undernourished, in poor health, afflicted with high infant mortality and other ills. Fifty percent of Chileans suffer from malnutrition. Nearly two-thirds of the urban population lack sewerage systems.[59] As recently as the early 1950s probably one out of every four children born in the lower-class urban slums died before the age of five.[60] The sharp disparities in income between the upper and lower strata have not diminished in recent years. Real income for large sectors of Chilean society declined during significant portions of the postwar years.[61] Fredrick Pike's sketch of a vivid street scene reflects the lower-class life.

The present writer will never forget a 1960 trip to the coal-mining city of Lota. There, as the late-afternoon sun was beginning to set on an unforgettably beautiful scene of tree-covered hills sloping down to a pounding surf, a group of women was seen proceeding down the town's main street. There must have been over a hundred of them, glum expressioned, sallow-complected, their faces lined and distorted by concern, anxiety and, undoubtedly in many cases, by sickness. In the course of the half an hour or more in which they were observed, scarcely a handful so much as smiled. Almost silently, as if in a state of depression and disassociation from their surroundings, they slowly trudged toward their homes. They were dressed in the dark blue uniforms of the Chilean public schools. Their ages must have ranged from twelve to eighteen.[62]

These are conditions that alone, of course, do not generate any particular political sympathies or behavior. Given the presence of the broader system properties and individual experience discussed here, however, they suggest a quite reasonable basis for radical support.

There has in fact been little opportunity for the appearance of effective social policy concerned with improving the conditions of the poor, as the traditional landed aristocracy and the newer business and mining elements have remained closely allied in opposition to the lower classes throughout Chilean history. Many factors contributed to this close relationship. These included intermarriage, investment by affluent aristocratic elements in business, upper-class impoverishment and the consequent availability of some of their land, absence of consistent upper- and middle-class differences on the role of the church, and the character of the educational system, among other factors. These dominant groups formed, in effect, a close alliance excluding the working class and other labor and peasant groups from prevailing political and social patterns. Political power has thus rested in the hands of business, mining, mercantile, landed, and traditional social oligarchic elements. The traditional rightist Conservative and Liberal parties offered no working-class representation and ruled in a completely unresponsive manner. The somewhat more moderate business and middle-class Radical party occasionally gave an appearance of greater responsiveness, especially in the late 1930s when it formed a united Popular Front with the left.[63] In recent years the alliance among dominant interests has been somewhat tempered, most clearly in the activities of the Christian Democratic party under President Eduardo Frei from 1964 to 1970. But in spite of initiating some necessary reforms, efforts at reform by the party met considerable and generally successful congressional opposition quite apart from doubts that one could raise as to the scope and adequacy of the measures envisioned.

On the whole, therefore, except for the recent Christian Democratic party, the major existing non-Marxist parties have essentially not responded to either peasant or worker needs, nor have they concealed their disdain for the lower class.[64] In addition, in earlier years, principally during the first few years of the twentieth century, strikes and protests were suppressed with great force and bloodshed, with many hundreds killed and wounded in some instances. The bloodiest of these repressions occurred in the northern city of Iquique on December 21, 1907, when military forces opened fire upon demonstrating nitrate miners and their families, killing or wounding about 2000 men, women, and children.[65] Later, during the dictatorship of General Ibañez in the

1920s, the trade-union movement again faced severe if less bloody repression.

It is within such a setting of past and present individual circumstances experienced in a bifurcated society that the development and continuance of radical support can be understood. It seems plausible to interpret such support as arising, in effect, from the distinctive historical, structural, and personal experience of the lower-class stratum. These factors created a tradition of Marxist support among some population elements. For most of the lower class it has meant conditions of strain reflective of the stratum's invidious and depressed social and economic position, and an experience of the unresponsiveness or failure of traditional parties. Differential processes of political socialization have also been of crucial importance. While the individual creates or interprets his political environment, he does so in terms provided by his circumstances and experiences. These include not only what has already been sketched but very significantly a situation in which the propriety of Marxist parties and their support has become well established, in which these relatively well organized parties with developed ideologies and programs have increasingly developed their ability to communicate to and voice the grievances and solicit the support of lower-class population elements.

Examination of the growing strength of the working class and its increasing support of the Marxist movement in Chile reveals a traditional pattern of development. It is one that lends further credence to the thesis being illustrated here; such a study would show the development over time of increasing class consciousness. Coming from a rural and traditional background, the early urban working class was not a class-conscious population; it lacked a class ideology and did not evidence consistent political behavior. It is only over time, under conditions of labor concentration and shared industrial experience, penetration by left-wing organizers and communication, the growth of working-class organizations, and the weakening of the semifeudal traditional heritage that a growing class-conscious movement and class organization began to extend beyond its early more limited beginnings into the northern mine and port areas. Petras and Zeitlin have shown that a somewhat similar process holds among depressed labor elements, even in the countryside, when they were exposed to more class-conscious and organized labor centers.[66]

Portes' studies offer support for the argument developed here and in earlier discussion. He casts doubt not only on the mass theory model but also develops a vigorous critique of various explanations that stress the presumably psychological and primitive qualities of radical politics. He explicitly tested various theories of lower-class leftist radicalism among a sample of Chilean slum dwellers in Santiago. His findings show that it was *not* the nonparticipant and socially isolated or the more uneducated and uninformed individuals who were strongest in leftist radical tendencies.[67] Nor did the upwardly or downwardly mobile lower-class individual, the urban migrant, whether recent or not, or those evidencing status inconsistency show any greater leftist proclivity.[68] Similarly, no relationship was found between the frustration of aspirations and radicalism. Correspondence *did* exist, however, between leftist radicalism and the cognitive, social, and political factors comprehended in the individual realization that failure to improve one's circumstances arises from "social structural arrangements rather than in fate, transcendental factors, or themselves."[69] Of course, not all lower-class slum dwellers evidence either similar political perceptions or a leftist orientation. Crucial, Portes suggests, is "differential political socialization as the main determinant of leftist radicalism. . . . Causal explanations of the emergence of leftist radicalism, like other political attitudes, seem thus conditioned by the broader structural circumstances and general political framework in which development of individual orientations takes place."[70] In view of the previously noted circumstances, political exposure, and experiences of the lower classes, and particularly the working class, there is no need to resort to an explanation for support secured by Chile's Marxist movement in terms of the decline of group ties, the need for new commitments and ties, personal malaise, and frustration, nor would it be accurate to label such support as irrational, erratic, or noninstrumental.

The inappropriateness of an explanation in terms of mass political theory is further suggested by a body of research, accumulated during the past 20 years, on neighborhood and migrant settlement in Latin American urban centers. Though variations are introduced by the existence of a number of distinct types of lower-class communities,[71] certain broad generalizations can be made. On the whole these do not support a picture of rootless, disorganized, anomic lower-class urban communities. The role of prior urban experience, regional culture and associations, the strong vitality of the extended family, the continuance of some traditional practices, religious activities, and local community associations and organizations appear to make for a generally cohesive community and personal effectiveness. The evidence does not point to uprooted or demoralized available masses.[72]

Pratt's study of organizational participation and political orientations in two lower-class urban settlements in Santiago offers additional support for some of the conclusions developed in the preceding pages.[73] Pratt compares settlement respondents who identified with the Marxist parties (FRAP), the Christian Democratic party, and with no party in the mid-1960s. The supporters of FRAP were more likely to be involved in local community associations, have greater interest in politics and government, have a greater sense of political efficacy, attach greater significance to politics, discuss politics more, and be more knowledgeable. Thus rather than finding an association between radicalism and the lack of ties, estrangement, a sense of helplessness, and ignorance, Pratt found that the converse appears to be the case. This is revealed in Table 5.1 derived from a number of the tables that appear in his study. These findings cast further doubt on the attempt to account for radical support in terms of mass political theory, political primitivism, nihilism, or estrangement.

It would be unusual and so deserve further attention if working-class support were *not* forthcoming to the left. Would it be more reasonable for the Chilean worker and peasant to support parties that have continually oppressed him? Or to shift after many years of commitment and involvement with the parties of the left to a new distinctly middle-class party such as the Christian Democrats? It is true that the growth of the Christian Democrats in recent years has meant the appearance, as noted previously, of a more liberal, reformist, and responsive political party and leadership. And it has attained a minority, though not inconsiderable, base among some lower-class elements. Yet its failure to secure wider support is not surprising. Developed Marxist party loyalties antedated the Christian Democratic party's assumption of a dominant political position in 1964. In addition, as an essentially middle-class-led, based, and derived party whose control of the presidency from 1964 through 1970 did not produce especially significant structural change or alteration in the circumstances of workers and peasants, it is at some disadvantage in contesting for lower-class support with the older well-established and more distinctly working-class parties of the left.[74] In addition, the political programs and propaganda elaborated over the years by the left have a considerable appeal. They combined a strong nationalistic element characteristic of Latin American radical politics with both practical proposals for improving the circumstances of the lower classes and programs for significant basic economic change.

Now it may, of course, be claimed that the Communist and the Socialist parties will not really benefit the worker but will add still another form of repression while limiting the extensive democratic rights of which Chileans were so justly proud – prior to the brutal

Table 5.1. *Social and political characteristics by party affiliation, lower-class urban settlements, Santiago, Chile, 1965*

Characteristics	3 de Mayo Party affiliation (%)			Santo Domingo Party affiliation (%)		
	None n = 30	Christian Democratic n = 43	FRAP n = 24	None n = 63	Christian Democratic n = 83	FRAP n = 35
Percentage of those identifying with a party who are members of local community association	22	12	42	2	5	17
Political parties perceived as helping people like respondent	17	34	62	31	49	49
Interested in politics	7	10	33	11	17	35
Can detail course of action to influence government	40	28	58	29	29	51
Believes one can act and influence government	38	35	54	27	39	44
Elections have significance	47	53	75	46	66	71
Knows someone who can help respondent to use government programs	17	35	46	19	17	29
Has heard about:						
Local housing program	66	71	79	69	80	54
Recent events in Dominican Republic	63	41	75	69	66	71
Has tried to affect government policy	13	14	46	6	8	17
Engages in political discussions, mean score (max. = 8)	2.8	2.9	3.8	2.5	2.8	3.8

Source: Raymond B. Pratt, *Organizational Participations and Political Orientations: A Comparative Study of Political Consequences of Participation in Community Organizations for Residents of Lower Class Urban Settlements in Chile and Peru*, Ph.D. dissertation, University of Oregon, 1968, from Tables 5.2, 5.3, 5.4, 5.5, 5.6, 5.7, 5.8. For fuller details and original form of these items see original tables.

military seizure of power in 1973. This would be a rather questionable contention, but in any case it is quite irrelevant. The point is whether it is reasonble and rational for the worker and peasant to support the left. A realistic answer must be that it is, given the circumstances of the worker, the past history of repression and denial, the performance of the other parties, his deep grievances to which almost the left alone (except in some respects for the Christian Democrats in recent years) has been responsive, the relevance of the political program of the left, the nature of the perceptions of the political environment that he has most probably developed, and the absence of the specialized "expertise" that the intellectual presumably has about the supposed perfidy of Marxist parties.

It would be quite difficult to put together from the material that presently exists on the politics and support for the left in Chile any fully clear-cut or conclusive affirmation or refutation of one theoretical interpretative scheme compared with another. The present writer is aware of lacunae in the present analysis that could only be filled by further original research (now probably impossible of accomplishment). However, I would contend that from what we do know it has been possible to sketch a case analysis that strongly suggests the interpretative scheme stressed in the present work – the purposive, rational, nonpsychological determination of radical support where both the phenomenological world of the actor and broader systemic properties must be taken into account.

France: the Communist party and working-class support

The Communists have continued since the end of World War II as the leading party in France, with the exception of the Gaullists. In the general election of March 1973 they polled 21 percent of the vote, equal to the unusually high Socialist vote, though falling somewhat behind the U.D.R., the Gaullist party. Throughout this period their support has come preponderantly from the working class.[75] Yet this expression of radical politics cannot be accounted for by mass political theory, nor can its supporters be described as a mass or as engaging in mass behavior. Other social psychological explanations also appear inappropriate. Rather, an understanding of working-class support for the Communist party requires attention to some of the properties of French political culture, national character, and historical traditions and divisions. These have helped shape attitudes and styles of behavior. They have partly determined the functioning and effectiveness of French political and social institutions, which have in turn provided the context and circumstances to which political commitments and purposes are partly a response. This holds for the greater part of the politically involved sectors in France, regardless of the particular ideological or social character of the group in question. Attention to the political culture and national character of France introduces an element not elaborated in the previous case studies. The present analysis will start with their consideration.

Political behavior and attitudes have also been significantly shaped by societal divisions, by openness and responsiveness to the working class of the political system generally and opposing interest collectivities more specifically. Accounting for working-class support also requires recognizing the character of interpersonal experience and communication within the class environment, the nature of class consciousness, and the character of the political alternatives, including the Communist party, experienced by the worker.

Attention to the preceding makes it possible to understand, first, *why* the working class would support a radical party[76] (be it the Communist party or some other far-left party) and, second, why such support is given to the Communists and not to some other dissident party. The circumstances and historical experiences of the working class are relevant to both elements of support, though they play a special role in accounting for the second condition. In the former regard the nature of French society and political culture plays a very significant role and suggests that an important part of the explanation for a disposition to support a radical orientation lies in conditions common to all French people and not merely the working class. Thus the concern of the following discussion must be with both the particular circumstances of the working class and the more general character and influences of French political society.

French political culture and associated political properties. The radicalism of the working class can be understood partly as a phenomenon reflective of the properties of French society and political culture. These find expression in the stance and behavior of many social elements in France. Characteristic features of French political culture, scholars suggest, are a penchant for protest and rebellion, a revolutionary tradition still valued by many, a clash between authoritarian and democratic ideals that severely divided nineteenth-century France and still lingers in some respects, a distrust of authority and governmental leadership, an ideological and a behavioral absolutism, and a rejection of compromise, among other features. For nearly two centuries French political society has been divided by serious disagreements over what would be appropriate structures of governance, and political regimes have tended to suffer from a lack of legitimacy. The constitution adopted in 1958 was the twelfth such document since 1789. In light of such characteristics the political milieu of France lends a reasonableness and propriety to radical political allegiances, though it can only partially be claimed that it creates them. It contains a number of properties that help account for and point to the not untoward character of Communist support by those sympathetic to its class character and strong worker-oriented programs. Merely confronting the character of political and social forms in France and experiencing a typical political socialization often suffice for a political stance that mass theory would ordinarily interpret as a product of unreasoning emotion or a quest for certainty consequent upon a decline of community. Yet the character of French political culture is such that there have been diverse groups in a variety of circumstances that have assumed a stance of vigorous or radical protest.[77]

French political culture reflects, of course, a number of features of French society and personality. Students of French society have noted that French national character is individualistic, anarchistic, rancorous and open to vigorous outbursts. As Raymond Aron remarked:

Americans tend to believe that man fulfills himself when he adjusts to society and cooperates with it as a good citizen who does not challenge its basic values. Frenchmen, on the contrary, think that man is himself only when he rebels and says no to all the conventions or established beliefs that threaten his personality.... In France, protest is the norm.[78]

Part of what is apparently involved here is the presence of a suspicion of authority, a sharp antipathy to its exercise, and an inability to grant authority to others and accept a position within a relationship of hierarchical authority.[79] A related phenomenon is that French society produces an autonomous, independent, and critical individual rather than a participating and responsive one. This quality of *incivisme* has been defined as "a mixture of a diffuse social negativism, a refusal to cooperate with others or to accept responsibility, and a fierce clinging to individual independence – a string of attitudes that might best be characterized as 'privatization.' "[80] Students of French society suggest that the Frenchman is disconcerted by face-to-face associations and the relations of dependency that these could incur. Consequently, a certain barrenness is exhibited in intergroup relationships, and there is a great desire to preserve individual independence and freedom from external pressure or interference. Formal activities are predominant over informal ones, as informal relationships could more likely intrude on and constrain the individual. Brian Crozier's analysis points to the relationship between these social and cultural properties and a style of authority that centralizes decision making, minimizes participation, raises distrust, and produces rebellious and often destructive opposition against the failures and extensions of centralized authority and decision makers.[81] Distrustful of authority, it is not unusual to find working-class support of the Communist party in its critique of the authority of the government and its leaders. More basic consequences, however, are the instability and ineffectiveness of French government and the ridigity and conflicted nature of political groups and political life.

In other ways as well French political culture provides a setting where support for the Communist party is not an atypical type of phenomenon requiring explanation in terms of the sociopsychic situation of its supporters. French politics has remained strongly ideological since the revolution, and solutions to problems are sought within the framework of a broad system of thought, a doctrine, or a faith. The French tradition is that of postulating broad and sweeping models of what society should be and how it should be rebuilt. Thus, for example, "whatever their political or philosophical persuasion, all of the major labor confederations want to rebuild society and the polity on new foundations."[82] It is not peculiar to the Communists to have a far-ranging world view and broad perspective, nor is any distinct explanation required of why some support a party of this character. Regardless of ideological predisposition, such support is typical of the Frenchman. Bargaining and compromise tend to be rejected. Further, regardless of particular political leanings, there is the cultural tendency for discussion to be not for compromise but to show the correctness of one's position.[83] The style of French politics is such as to maintain sharp differences, conflict, and antagonism:

sudden rather than gradual mutation, dramatic conflicts couched in the language of opposing and mutually exclusive, radical ideologies – these are the experiences that excite Frenchmen at historical moments when their minds are particularly malleable ... Frenchmen ... have become accustomed to think that no thorough-going change can ever be brought about except through a major upheaval.[84]

These properties of French character and its political life have been compounded by the immobility of the French political system, in effect, the inability of the system to function effectively to meet national and group needs. Parliament has been an ineffectual and divided body. The government has historically been impotent and unstable. In the 12 years of life granted the Fourth Republic, from 1946 to 1958, there were 20 cabinets. Effective party organization and discipline have been lacking. Communication between political and interest group leaders and their presumed constituency has been poor. The ability of those at the grass-roots level to affect decision making at the center has been severely limited. The system has thus been unable to aggregate interests effectively and has exhibited a lack of responsiveness to various sectors of French society, including the working class.

The combination of the ideological, uncompromising, and conflicted nature of French parties and politicians has fueled vigorous protest movements, by the working class as well as among students, peasants, small businessmen, and others. Thus during the twentieth century frequent protest movements shaped by the historical, cultural, and political traditions of French society, and the failure of its political institutions have shaken the political system and transgressed "legal" bounds. Such events, in fact, have at times acquired a certain romantic flavor. While not an everyday occurrence, extremist protest, at times of a violent nature, has been a not uncommon phenomenon in French political life. It need not, therefore, be surprising or require any special explanation that significant segments of the French population would under some circumstances support a radical antiestablishment movement.

Working-class disabilities, historical experiences, and traditions. There are a number of properties of French politics and the experiences of the working class that help account for receptivity to Communist party appeals. These include past class experiences, the ineffectiveness of French government, and radical ideological traditions.

The history of the working class in France has been one of class struggle in a hostile and oppressive environment within a hierarchically conscious and socially divided society and with an economy slow to change and parsimonious in its rewards. It has experienced repression and armed and bloody conflict with the government and business interests. In the turmoil of 1848 thousands of workers were killed. The Paris Commune of 1871 was brutally crushed, and many thousands of prisoners were shot to death. The government of Premier Reynaud broke the general strike of 1938 and engaged in a mass dismissal of striking workers.

The cooperation between bourgeois elements and the government has been close, and in earlier years they have allied with the military to crush brutally efforts by workingmen to better their situation.

There was little labor or social legislation prior to World War I, with the state, in effect, serving as an arm of the employers. Employers also successfully opposed the appearance of trade unions and collective bargaining. Even as late as the 1930s the trade unions faced problems of recognition and trade-union members the danger of the discharge from employment. When collective-bargaining agreements were finally achieved, employers in many instances did not accept them in practice. Val Lorwin has commented that: "In the national commission that in 1950 drew up a working man's budget preliminary to setting a national minimum wage, some of the employers' comments on workers' needs seemed to echo from the caverns of time supposedly sealed off on the night of August 4, 1789."[85] The record of working-class experience indicates little responsiveness by either government or employer to worker needs or demands. Even today many of the wage and salary employees live on a depressed wage.[86]

Another determining factor in working-class support for radical class movements is the ideological traditions that developed within the trade unions and much of the working class. These arose in response to the abdurance of the established economic, political, and social order and to the divisions and animosities that rent French society. There is a strong tradition of anarchist, revolutionary syndicalist, and Socialist ideology, with a strong sense of distinct working-class membership and of opposition to the state. The need for far-reaching change was stressed. Related are the *communard* traditions in the larger industries and larger communities of "sentiments of civic action, resorting in times of stress to violent self-help and the barricades."[87] An informed reading by students of French politics suggests that many working-class members became inclined to expect improvement only by drastic change of the political and economic system. Given these earlier attitudes and experiences, it is not surprising that the working class might support the Communist party, whose militant antiestablishment and working-class character gave it further positive appeal. Social structural and historical elements, not sociopsychic ones, are basic here.

The conflicted societal context, sources of division, and working-class isolation. The present discussion has suggested that French society is riven by deep conflict and disunion. These take several major forms. French society has exhibited fundamental differences regarding acceptance of the principle of democratic government, the role of traditional elites and of the broader populace. Disunion has also developed from the existence of specific economic and social groupings and their distinctive heritages and sharp interest disparities. A multiple and heterogeneous party system has further exacerbated the fissiparous properties of French society. The preceding partly reflect a basic clash in French society. It is one between the right's commitment to a hierarchical order and the left's stress on liberty and equality. The elitist and hierarchical assumptions of the traditional and conservative forces in French society find their expression not only in the political and social arena but also in the work place between employer and employee and in the former's attitudes toward trade unions and collective bargaining, to which reference has already been made. Nordlinger has said:

In France the common pattern of employer-employee relations is almost simplistically military in nature. The *patron* exercises practically all authority, without even the presence of an American-type foreman through whom authority is mediated. Nor does the *patron* seek advice or approval from his workers, except in those instances in which effective unions force him into this position. It is then no wonder that the worker feels himself to be acted upon, consequently developing an intense desire for liberty.[88]

These qualities of French society have been reflected in the absence of communication across class lines, the lack of shared public and institutional experiences, the extensive differences in life styles among classes, and by the development of a strong sense of working-class membership and solidarity.[89] In 1964 a public-opinion poll showed 6 out of every 10 respondents declaring class membership, with 82 percent of those identifying themselves as workers expressing solidarity with other members of that group. Similar high levels of class solidarity were expressed by other groups.[90] It is not difficult to see here the grounds for vigorous opposition to any parties or movements that smack of the hierarchical, inequitable, and unequal strains inhering in the traditional sectors of French society.

Now it may be said that the economic growth and the modernization of France during recent years have considerably tempered such conditions. There is a degree of truth in such an assertion. Yet the crucible within which class and party loyalties and attitudes toward existing parties and leadership were shaped antedates these more recent developments. There is also considerable doubt that there has been any significant change in the processes of political socialization into left-wing political persuasion.

Clearly, a major feature of French society has been the isolation of the worker and the division of the nation between two different world views. "Society rested on a consensus which included the upper bourgeoisie, the lower middle-classes ... as well as the peasants ... this consensus excluded the individual proletariat and created a major psychological barrier between the workers and the rest of the population."[91] Division in French society has been a source of unresolved class conflict that "has resulted in antagonistic values and beliefs, i.e., a divided political culture with different symbols, flags, and holidays."[92] Upward mobility has been slow and difficult. The education system itself has perpetuated and reinforced existing social divisions. Hence sharp working-class antagonism and a disposition toward a radical stance are not surprising.

The working-class context and its influence. The preceding assumes an increased importance in determining behavior in view of the nature of political communication, group influence, and social pressures to which most French workers are exposed. These conditions stress support of the Communist party, the unacceptability of other parties, the plight and distinctiveness of the working class. In his study of the social bases of French working-class politics, Richard Hamilton has stressed that the working class milieu and the process of working-class political socialization are such as to encourage the continuance of antagonisms, loyalties, and attitudes of an earlier period that serve to induce support for the Communist party. Continued living within a radical working-class environment, he points out, significantly influences individual attitudes and conduct, even if their initial determinants have declined or altered. It is, for instance, in the heavily working-class areas surrounding Paris, where four out of every five voters are from working-class families, that the Communist party regularly secures up to one-half of the vote. "The density of the working-class population," Ehrmann points out, "favors an all-encompassing socialization by the communist subculture."[93] Especially important in this influence process is the radical trade-union orientation and the militancy of Communist party members at the individual plant and worker levels. Hamilton affirms that "the unions constitute the most important influence on working class politics to be discovered in this study ... in their political influence they appear formidable."[94] Even where the economic circumstances of workers differ, the effect of similar exposure to the radical influence of the trade unions and to the broader working-class political, social, and interpersonal environment is such that Hamilton found "in the active union settings.... all workers, from the poorest to the best off, sharing the same political outlooks."[95]

The influences upon working-class members also develop from a broader personal milieu that includes the more radical character of the larger industrial setting, the nature of residence patterns that sharply concentrate the working class in distinct areas and exhibit little residential mobility, and the movement out of the working class of the more conservative and moderate elements.[96] In addition, the working-class milieu and the local working-class community contain a positive appeal for the worker, perhaps even greater than the corresponding community for other class groups.[97] These enhance the possibility of continued support to the Communists even when individual circumstances improve or past instances of repression and unresponsiveness decline. Such a milieu isolates the worker and denigrates other party appeals. It also encourages the development of a feeling of the greater appropriateness of the appeal for support of a working-class party than the exhortations of bourgeois parties. It provides a good opportunity for the conveyance of Communist party appeals. At the same time, the absence of Communist support among working-class elements can generally be attributed to distinctive regional or historical factors and influences, for example, in strong Catholic areas, where a working-class subculture is weakly developed.[98] In these areas the Communist and Socialist vote combined has not exceeded a quarter of the working-class vote.[99]

The Communist party presence and working-class support. The present discussion has pointed to the revolutionary traditions of the working class, past experiences of repression, skepticism regarding bourgeois politicians, and to the failure of government and Parliament to offer any positive response to the working class and its needs. These conditions have weakened the appeal of such a moderate middle-class parliamentary party as the Socialists. They have encouraged reliance on "the efficacy of economic direct action over political action, and reliance on the general strike as the chief weapon of gaining reforms and eventually of seizing power."[100] Such circumstances help account for and accord well with later support for the Communist party – if a couple of conditions are present. One is that the objective condition and experiences of the French working class must be perceived and internalized by individual workers, at least in terms of a strong sense of class membership, distinctiveness, political distrust, and antagonism. The circumstances of working-class members sketched here do suggest that this is the situation that has prevailed. It is also necessary that a distinct antiestablishment working-class-oriented alternative be available. The presence of the Communist party and its appearance as a political force quite different from the usual parliamentary parties meets this need.

Traditional political parties have not been politically responsive. Bourgeois and middle-class elements within these parties and in Parliament have generally been ineffective in securing significant reform. Radical working-class tradition and loyalties, the nature of working-class interpersonal relationships, political socialization, past and present economic disabilities, and occupational career patterns reinforce and expose the worker both to the communication and organization efforts of the Communist party and to the continued influence of a past heritage and prevailing ideological perspectives.[101] The working-class character of the Communist party, in its leadership, appeal, and programs, has contrasted positively with the Socialist party's middle-class leadership and broad-based appeal. Thus, while recognizing the very significant protest vote that it draws, Ehrmann has remarked that: "the P.C. [Communist party] appears to many voters to be the legitimate heir of radical movements and radical causes of the past, the only trust-worthy defender of the small against the government, the church, the powerful, and the rich."[102]

As much, if not more so than is the case of the supporters of any other party, the Communist voter lends his support to what he perceives as a political force closest to expressing his needs and interests. Further confirmation appears in a 1962 population survey that revealed that those who preferred the Communist party were more likely than those with any other party preference to believe that the party they preferred was "the one which best defends people like yourself."[103] This is not inconsistent with other possible facets of voting Communist. Some may possess extensive agreement with its program, objectives, or even its assumption of power. These undoubtedly do hold for some of its supporters. For other voters, however, the Communist party may be perceived as on balance the best of the less than ideal choices available. For some it may be a means to voice discontent or opposition to prevailing unresponsive political policies and parties. In all these regards, however, Communist support can be accounted for by the traditional or ordinary processes of opinion formation and political response and does not require resort to either notions of the decline of community, political primitivism, authoritarian personality types, or variously produced mental states of frustration.

The working class and its nonmass behavior. The nature of the evidence and the analysis sketched would appear sufficient to account for working-class support of the Communists. At the same time, the causal elements upon which mass theory relies are not extensively present. The working-class individual is strongly implicated in a working-class community, and while formal organizational ties may not be great, group involvement and sense of belonging appear high. Taking explicit exception to Kornhauser, as well as other students' contentions on the weakness of intermediate groups Jesse Pitts observes that "it seems that the extensiveness and strength of the informal organizations have been overlooked because they lack the clear references of name, headquarters, formal officers and the like."[104] Duncan MacRae has pointed out that while association membership for Frenchmen is somewhat less than for the United States, it differs only slightly from that of Britain and Germany.[105] He notes that what is lacking in France is not so much intermediate associations "as intermediate decision points, such as local government or local collective bargaining."[106] Thus one finds not so much a mass society as a divided society with energies concentrated, not unreasonably, at central decision points. It is also a society in which in addition to the properties of voluntary associations qualities such as strong family ties, stress on privacy, "institutionalized inaccessibility of the individual," individual freedoms, and strong administrative law suggest that "France was far from the 'ideal type' of the mass society."[107]

In a different but related vein, the Communist voter is usually *most* likely to enjoy political conversations, be politically conscious, attend political meetings, and give money and services to political parties, compared with those of other occupational groups. These properties are most strikingly present when a comparison is made with the working-class voter who supports moderate and presumably non-mass democratic parties such as the Socialists, Radicals, and M.R.P. See Table 5.2 for industrial workers in the early 1950s.

Communist party support does not appear, therefore, to arise from political estrangement or lack or loss of ties and a consequent search for community. Nor need it arise out of irrational and emotional pique or merely reflect a vague *ressentiment*, though this, of course, may be present. While Communist voters may be more disaffected than other groups, this is "based on social realities rather than on character structure."[108] These circumstances provide further support for the "normality" of working-class political behavior. While it may be granted that a Communist vote is a means of venting anger at one's circumstances and existing ruling elements, the analysis employed here has suggested that it is much more than this.

Not only mass theory but explanatory schemes in terms of frustration-aggression or authoritarian personality theories appear to have little support in light of the preceding discussion, though it has applied less directly to these interpretations. Attributions of a "political primitivism" to radical support also seem misplaced. More appropriate

Table 5.2. *Political participation and party identification*

	Industrial male workers (%)	
	Communists[*]	All others
In political matters considers self:		
Well or fairly well informed	65	60
Poorly informed	35	39
Like political conversation?		
Yes	62	16
No	20	52
Depends	18	32
Attended political meetings past year	82	35
Gave money to a party	77	30
Tried to convince others	74	33
Sold newspapers or put up posters	56	13

Source: Richard F. Hamilton, *Affluence and the French Worker in the Fourth Republic* (Princeton, N.J.: Princeton University Press, 1967), published for the Center of International Studies, Princeton University, table, p. 47, footnote 10. Reprinted by permission of Princeton University Press.
[*] Percentages are of those having an opinion. N varies from 41 to 45 for "Communists" and 93 to 138 for "All others."

is a perception of working-class Communist party support as arising out of and explainable in terms of the typical political processes of French society. My discussion has attempted to highlight the rather complex and extensive factors that determine a radical dissident mode of political behavior – the properties of societal political culture, earlier class history and traditions, individual circumstances and experience including political socialization, societal divisions, isolation, and the unresponsiveness of the political order. While the present treatment has provided no direct analysis of how the individual interprets his political and social circumstances and develops a political response, it can be understood as suggesting both what may have been involved here and the usefulness of seeking to perceive political behavior in the terms outlined here.

Accounting for support received by the Nazi movement in Weimar Germany

The mass political theory model finds one of its clearest applications in the rise of nazism to prominence in Germany. Although it is relevant in some regards, I would suggest that reliance on a mass theory interpretive scheme alone would provide a seriously flawed account of the reasons why the National Socialists were able to attain extensive popular support and finally control in Germany.[109] Related difficulties also inhere in other interpretive schemes stressing the non-cognitive, irrational, psychological origins of Nazi support.

The Nazi movement, it will be recalled, had its origins in the years of turmoil immediately following the German defeat in World War I. Many nationalistic and militaristic parties and organizations sprung up during these years stressing betrayal at Versailles, the destruction of Weimar, and nationalistic, *Volkische,* and racist themes. The most successful of these organizations was the Hitler-controlled National Socialist German Workers' Party (NSDAP), which from very modest origins and a vote of less than 3 percent in the elections of 1928 increased its support precipitously to more than one-third of the vote in 1932. When Hitler secured the chancellorship in early 1933, the NSDAP quickly tightened its grip on the government and destroyed not only its opposition but all democratic freedom.

The interpretations of this successful assumption of power by the Nazi movement are various, and the relevant literature is extensive.[110] Several major analytic approaches are stressed in the scholarly literature. The attempt to explain the Nazi phenomenon in terms of cultural and intellectual traditions, including the authoritarian and nationalistic properties of German society, has been influential. The effects of the defeat in World War I and the economic and social strains of the ensuing years have at times received major attention. Often combined with such an emphasis has been a stress on the increasing dissension within contemporary societies generally and the growing unrest and mobilization of mass populations in the nineteenth and twentieth centuries. This, in turn, may be perceived as related to another explanatory dimension, the elaboration by the mass society model of the role of the decline of community, massification, psychic strains and fears, and related themes. Closer to the perspective that has contributed to the present analysis has been the effort to interpret the Nazi success as reflecting a condition of severe class conflict in circumstances of great social and political strain. Crucial has been the response of traditional, Junker, and capitalist elements to the developing social forces, changing class structure, and democratic pressures arising from the emergence of a modern industrial society. The unreconciled split between the Junkers and recent industrial elements, on the one hand, and the working class and developing social and political forms, on the other, had extremely grave consequences.

The failure to accept these changes is fundamental in understanding the circumstances that enabled the Nazis to rise to power. These conditions of course stretch back into the nineteenth century and thus antedate the particular circumstances of World War I and the postwar years. Other elements did play a role, though a less crucial one. Many of these must also be understood as properties of German society prior to Weimar and the Nazi rise to power. And within the perspective of these various circumstances there is need for a more phenomenologically sensitive analysis.

A few features stand out in the mass theory interpretation of the Nazi movement, especially in regard to where it received its support. National socialism is understood as a movement that appealed to the uprooted, declassed, and anomic elements in German society.[111] The nationalization of industry, the growth of bureaucratic organizations, urbanization, depression, and unemployment are interpreted as undermining hope for the future and conditions for personal satisfaction. The existence of social atomization, extreme individualism, social isolation, estrangement from society, the lack of normal social relationships, and other such characteristics are stressed. Even where individual ties among group members are acknowledged, some theorists emphasize a condition of group isolation and alienation from the broader society.[112] The processes, structures, and changes of contemporary society are also interpreted as leading to the "psychological impoverishment" of the lower middle class, as well as to a developing fear of "proletarization." These are viewed as productive of emotional insecurity, fear, and a sense of hopelessness for the future. There was, then, among other conditions in postwar German society a breakdown of bourgeois-dominated class society. This

transformed the slumbering majorities behind all parties into one great unorganized, structureless mass of furious individuals who had nothing in common except their vague apprehension that the hopes of party members were doomed.... The number of this mass of generally dissatisfied and desperate men increased rapidly.... When inflation and unemployment added to the disrupting consequences of military defeat....[113]

It was from these circumstances, it is contended, that a mass movement such as national socialism arose and derived its support.

Those groups found supporting the Nazis were somewhat diverse but were perceived as sharing the kind of conditions and insecurities to which reference is made. The ex-soldiers, the unemployed, the unorganized worker, the young and students, the unsuccessful intellectual or professional, and the lower middle class have all been seen as constituting the population affected by the conditions noted. The populations constituted masses. They were, Arendt has said, "people who . . . cannot be integrated into an organization based on common interest, into political parties or municipal governments or professional organizations or trade unions."[114] They were available for mobilization by new mass movements, in effect new political religions that provided a refuge, a new faith, a sense of esteem, of vitality, and meaning.

The phenomenon of nazism is also of interest to the mass theorist as an example of democratic extremism or mass democracy. In this sense it is understood as deriving from earlier Rousseauistic notions of the general will, with the French Revolution presaging the dangers of the rise of democratic tyranny. Mass theory relates the rise of what it considers democratic tyranny to the appearance of available masses and their direct intrusion on elites, a phenomenon that develops where there is a decline of authority and the disruption of community. In effect, Hitler's success reflected a growing mass movement that willingly, even enthusiastically, albeit emotionally and irrationally, provided a popular mandate for Nazi rule.

While insightful in some respects, such an interpretation is also quite partial and misleading. To assess the mass theory account it is necessary to distinguish why the Nazis came to power from the question of why they secured the support that they did. While the second question cannot be answered without some attention to the first, and vice versa, the reasons the Nazis came to power generally fall beyond the reach of the mass theory explanatory scheme. The mass model distorts an appreciation of the basis of Nazi support. Its use means giving very little attention to the role of military, industrial, landed, and political leadership, class conflict and divisions in Germany, the strains of industrialization in a traditional and autocratic society, the Nazis as an expression of traditional conservative antiliberalism, the behavior of intellectual elements, the nationalist and military traditions of Germany, the defeat in World War I, the question of German national character, and the place of Weimar and democratic forms in German society. Yet these played a significant part in accounting for the successful attainment of power *and* support by the Nazis. However, with some exception, these are not the type of factors to which mass theory (or other social psychological models) directs its attention. Rather, it focuses on the nature of the Nazi appeal, the circumstances of the groups that presumably responded to the appeal, and why they responded as they did. But accounting for the support engendered by the NSDAP cannot be accomplished within such limitations.

Preponderant attention must be given to other forces in the environment, because these often significantly shape how people interpret and experience their environment. Further, to exclude attention to these other factors is to distort the relative importance of the causal elements that are treated in the mass theory model. Nonetheless, the present discussion gives its principal – though not total – attention to concerns corresponding to the major focus of mass theory, as even in the more limited and skewed interpretation contained in mass theory there are difficulties and these will be noted. However, some attempt is made to suggest the necessity and relevance of other factors as they bear on determining why the German people responded as they did to Nazi appeals. In effect, and reflecting the interpretive approach developed previously as well as the circumstances in Germany, I suggest that the mass theory account (and by implication, other social psychological interpretations) gives little weight to nazism as reflecting efforts by traditional, autocratic, Junker, and capitalist elements to preserve industrial, landed, or military interests, as well as to other factors contributing to Nazi support such as derive from historical, political, and social conditions. It is also suggested that scant attention is given to support as coming from class-interest-motivated collectivities or the ongoing character of the Weimar political process and post–World War I events as they were experienced by large sectors of the German population.

The following stresses at the microlevel of analysis the usefulness of interpreting support received by the Nazis up to 1933 in terms of the attempt by individuals and groups to interpret and come to terms with their economic, political, and social environment in light of past experiences and commitments, and contemporary circumstances and knowledge. Implicated here, of course, would also be attention to group interest needs in the context of class conflict and strain. Some of the questions that can guide an inquiry in these terms include: What properties characterized the supporters of the Nazis? To what were they responding? What were they seeking? How did they perceive the Nazis? And, were such ends and perceptions distortions that exceeded the ordinary inadequacies so commonly encountered in most political circumstances and among most political populations? An examination of the German phenomenon in the terms noted here suggests that it differed in a number of important regards from the mass theory model.[115] In a sense the ordinariness or typicality of some of the principal determinants of the Nazi rise to power is revealed. At the same time, the German experience differs from the other political protests and movements already considered. An essential difference is that a much more complex situation and phenomenon are involved, extending beyond questions of class interest and political and social cleavages and reflecting a more complex relationship of historical, cultural, institutional, and psychological factors.

Determinants of Nazi support and some contributions to their rise to power. The following briefly notes some of the circumstances that encouraged a positive response to the Nazi movement by a sizable proportion of the German people. To a considerable degree, these circumstances derived from the failure of a conservative traditional society to adapt to the forces of political and social change engendered by industrialization and a growing and organized working class. A condition of major importance, and a dominant characterisitic of German society, was the deep antagonism and distrust that existed between the working class and middle-class elements such as shop-keepers, artisans, small merchants and farmers, and clerical and minor bureaucratic personnel – in effect, the petite bourgeoisie and white-collar sectors. Class hostility and conflicts can be understood as a significant factor accounting for the paralysis of Weimar, the opposition to democratic forms, and the effort to use the National Socialists as a means of countering and weakening the parties of the left. Equally serious, they lay behind the attempt of elite elements to use Hitler and his movement as a means of eliminating or greatly altering the parliamentary government of Germany.

In Thalburg the politics of crisis had never accepted the SPD as an institution; now with the rise of Nazism it was offered a method of destroying
Social Democracy.... It was hatred for the SPD that drove Thalburgers
into the arms of the Nazis. Few of the conservatives realized that after
the Nazis had destroyed the Social Democrats, they would turn on their erst-
while allies and smash them.[116]

The Nazi victory was to a significant extent based on the middle- and upper-class desire to suppress the working class and debilitate its political strength. Most Germans perceived the Nazis as an anti-Marxist party, and many saw them as an appropriate instrument in a class conflict that preceded their appearance.

The National Socialist protest against liberal democracy voiced the sentiments of the conservative middle and upper classes. In their pro-gram and appeal the NSDAP reflected traditional conservatism and ideological strains dominant in Germany, and conservatism's crucial struggle with the liberal, economic, political, and class forces of modern society. This traditional conservatism to which the Nazis struck a respondent cord was imbedded in German history and social traditions,[117] with their stress on the organic community, the ascendent role of elites, the derogation of democratic institutions, their anti-socialism, blend of myticism and idealism, Pan-Germanism, nationalism and a sense of national purpose and destiny, and racism. Certainly, if read in terms of their protestations of the 1920s, with less attention to the extremity of their policies in the 1930s and 1940s (and we are concerned with the period prior to the assumption of power), they voiced sentiments widespread and deeply rooted in German society.[118] To an important extent the strength of the Nazis came not from the destruction of classes and the decline of class loyalties. Quite the contrary, its support can be accounted for by "class identity, class fears, and the structure of class interests."[119] The defeat in the war, the overthrow of the monarchy, the creation of Weimar, and the severe postwar conditions aggravated ideological, economic, and class differences.

It is often suggested that what was involved here, at least for non-elite, non-upper-class elements, was not so much class conflict as a fear by the middle class of proletarization and a condition of status threat. The latter, however, is better understood as a fear of the decline of a way of life that these middle-class elements valued and with which they had been identified. Apprehension over proletarization and status threat is difficult to establish at least for the broader middle-class German population in contrast to the verbalizations of intellectual elements and political spokesmen. It does seem reasonable to assume, however, that the feudal-estate origins of German society, invidious class distinctions, the strongly hierarchical character of German society, or, more broadly, the social historical and ideological traditions and practices of German society combined with the growth of a vigorous well-organized Socialist and Communist working class could well account for the class antagonism exhibited. It has done so in other societies. And, very probably, middle-class apprehension in regard to the working class increased with the attainment of fully equal suffrage in the revolution of 1918 and with the increased strength of the parties of the left. The fragmented nature of the middle class impeded its ability to organize as a political force with a potency commensurate with labor or large-scale industry. Thus a number of factors quite apart from what could be subsumed under status-culture threat could well account for middle-class antagonism to the working class. Other elements distinctive to proletarization anl status threat may aggravate this antagonism, but sufficient conditions appear to exist without them. In a different vein, it may also be suggested that in some circumstances fear of proletarization and status threat are not unreasonable or irrational concerns or bases for political response.

Intraclass dissension as well as interclass division aided the Nazi rise to power. Within the working class there were deep divisions and conflicting political ideologies that sharply pitted Communist and Social Democratic elements against one another. Not only was the left unable to cooperate, but to a considerable degree the parties of the right and middle would not unite with the Social Democratic party of the left, nor did the left seek cooperation with elements of the right or middle, with the exception of some of the elements with which the SPD maintained a working arrangement.

The period of the Weimar Republic, especially its later years, was a time of great disruption and threat. The uncertainty of the economy, rising unemployment, the growing disabilities arising from the depression, and the growing fears thus engendered affected nearly all groups. Working-class unemployment was on the rise, peasant debts mounted, land was repossessed, and the petite bourgeoisie, while less affected, feared the possible economic plight that might yet afflict it. Yet the principal traditional parties, in addition to being divided and squabbling, were ineffective. They did not develop or suggest the execution of programs commensurate with the needs of the time. The parties of the center lacked relevant programs, and they equivocated. They did not push for reasoned and progressive democracy. Blindly anti-Marxist, they were opportunistically ready to utilize the existing circumstances to try to undermine the parties of the left. The Social Democratic party itself failed to press for reforms sufficient to the crises of German society. Little was offered that was sufficiently attractive to compete with the hopes raised by the NSDAP.

Political rule was ineffective and unstable, especially in the last three years of Weimar. The average life of a government during Weimar was eight months. The various coalition governments were not only short-lived, but they showed very little unity. The state machinery was manned by an officialdom with antidemocratic monarchist sentiments. Senior military leadership viewed Weimar and democracy with antipathy. It is reasonable to contend that considerable blame for prevailing circumstances rested with the counterrevolutionary efforts of the conservative elements in German social and political life.[120]

The Social Democrats, the largest party in Weimar, were not in power during most of this period. In the last couple of years of Weimar confusion was heightened by an increasing number of elections. Not counting regional elections and those called by petition or referendum, there were four national elections in 1932 alone! From 1930 on it was not possible to attain a stable majority in the Reichstag, and increasingly the chancellor ruled by decree. Nor were the laws and policies so proclaimed effective in halting the worsening depression.

In view of these diverse strains in post–World War I German society, therefore, especially by the early 1930s, continuing support of the small center and right regional and special-issue parties must have appeared increasingly unrealistic. The alternatives, however, were limited, as such support could not be expected to move to the working-class parties or to the Catholic party by the Lutherans. The Conservative People's party (DVP) might have been an alternative. However, its ambivalent, shifting, opportunistic performance and the lack of basic ideological difference with the NSDAP, as well as its lack of vigor or an effective program vis-à-vis the pressing problems that confronted the German population, mitigated against holding its own supporters, not to mention attracting the disaffected followers of the smaller regional and splinter parties. In a condition of strain it is not unexpected that the petite bourgeoisie middle-class sector would shift its loyalties away from ineffective and irrelevant center, regional, or special-issue parties. Nor is it surprising, in the light of the sharp class divisions and conflicted relationship in German society, that such a shift would not be toward support of parties of the left but would move toward a movement with a strong antileft stance, especially if it had a patina of respectability marked by vigorous nationalistic and militaristic characteristics. This is reinforced when the ideological predispositions are essentially conservative. For many of those disposed to shift this was a logical direction in which to go.

It seems likely, however, that conditions in addition to economic strain, class animosity, and the ineffectiveness of many of the parties are required to account for the support the Nazis received. At the least, other conditions assured and added to such support, as well as contributed to the Nazi rise to power. These would include the absence of a commitment to the Weimar Republic by many Germans, the unreconcilability of important traditional and business elements with a democratic modern industrial social and political order, the respectability achieved by the National Socialists, and the ineptness, disunion, and weakness of other political groups and leadership.

The Weimar Republic faced class conflict, party division, economic depression, and other causes of threat and disunion without ever having gained the national acceptance necessary to elicit wide support for the governmental forms and political objectives it represented. Many elite and right-wing groups viewed Weimar with aversion and were vigorously opposed to it, and to the radical left it signified the failure to destroy the capitalist order. Weimar had few prestigious supporters. It was thus politically unstable and ineffective and also lacked the legitimacy to secure wide support. While of course new and lacking the commitments that develop over time, more significantly it represented a sharp and widely unacceptable disjuncture with past forms and ideology. A significant element of its difficulty was the clash between traditional conservatism and ideology with a growing modern liberal industrial society and the collectivities and interests of increasing strength found within it. Also debilitating was the fact that Weimar arose from the defeat experienced in World War I and followed upon the November Revolution of 1918. It was identified with national humiliation and economic ruin. It was associated with that defeat and the continued invidious relationship between Germany and the Allies in the years that followed. The German defeat itself and the associated myth of the collapse of the home front provided a major fulcrum for right-wing demagogic propaganda concerning conspiratorial and traitorous elements responsible for Germany's loss and dishonor. The modern sector of German society, the left, and the Jews were the objects of such attacks. The defeat and the loss of the kaiser must have aggravated the sense of political, social, and economic threat increasingly felt by the conservative elements.

A major element and one implicated in much of the preceding was the absence of a democratic sentiment among a great part of the German population and leadership. The middle-class elements were little moved by such sentiments, reflecting the heritage of the authoritarian Prussian spirit, which was antagonistic to expressions of economic and political democracy. The Weimar Republic was a fundamental change in the character of political institutions but without any significant concomitant alteration in social institutions, economic power, or political attitudes. Legal and political forms suggested an enlightened progressive democratic society. Yet, "the army, the bureaucracy, the church, the landowners, and big industrialists emerged from the ordeal of defeat and revolution with their social power unbroken. . . . The Weimar Republic was, in short, the Imperial social order in republic dress."[121] While the political forms had changed, the structure of society remained unaltered. Weimar was opposed by many and was afflicted by the existence of important groups on the right quite ready to use the Nazis to destroy it and the forces of the left and by a middle class with little commitment to Weimar and whose class antagonism and economic fears combined to make it susceptible to the appeal of the Nazi movement. Even under more propitious circumstances than those surrounding the character of Weimar's origin and the difficulties of the 1920s and early 1930s, its viability was questionable.

Not only did Weimar lack legitimacy and commitment from large sectors of German society, but, at the same time, the Nazi movement was marked by a number of features that made it appear respectable, helped define the movement as a positive one and helped make it proper to support NSDAP, even if certain unpleasant characteristics did manifest themselves.

In contrast to existing circumstances and parties the Nazis presented a dynamic image, one of strength, vigor, dedication, unity, a sense of purpose, and the like.[122] Nazi efforts were also furthered by a "persistent, imaginative, and driving effort . . . coupled with a shrewd appreciation of what was specifically suitable for Thalburg, and for each element in the town. . . . The NSDAP succeeded in being all things to all men."[123] It was not too difficult to hope that this dynamic movement might be a way out of the depression, and supporting it may have been a means of stilling the growing economic fears of the middle class. Allen observes that "it was the depression, or more accurately, the fear of its continued effects, that contributed most heavily to the radicalization of Thalburg's people . . . the depression engendered fear. . . . In this situation, the voice of the Nazi began to be heard. Thalburg had previously ignored the NSDAP."[124] Thus a number of factors combined to make the National Socialists' appeal attractive. The Nazis effectively cloaked themselves in a patriotic mantle, vigorously harped on nationalistic and militaristic themes, sought to associate themselves with religious sentiment, and stressed their anti-Socialist and anti-Communist character. These were the sentiments and themes on which were based the organized associations – and there were many – that dominated middle-class life, the sector of German society from which the NSDAP drew its greatest support. Given the contemporary circumstances and the corporate and conservative heritage of the middle class, it is not surprising that these themes evoked middle-class support. However, the respectability and acceptability of the Nazis came not only from the positive themes of German society with which they associated themselves and the traditional conservative orientations they reflected but also from the support they received from the conservative right, Lutheran clergy, and many established and respected community figures.[125] " . . . It was clear that the best people were for the Nazis except where it might affect their money-bags."[126] In his biting assessment of the role of established and respectable elements in German society, which goes beyond merely the provision of respectability to even more direct and positive aid,

Trevor-Roper concludes: "Thus they emerge – the bureaucrats, the aristocratic neuters, the respectable "non-Nazis" who smoothed Hitler's way to power, blurred the ugly features of his rule, masked his intentions, anesthetized his victims."[127]

This begins to introduce a consideration of the most fundamental character in accounting for the creation of those conditions facilitating the Nazis' ability to secure support and weakening the opportunities for the maintenance of effective alternatives. I refer to the nature of elite functioning in German society, that is, the behavior and activities of some of the most important and influential military, landed, governmental, judicial, and political leaders. The strength of the Nazi movement and its appeal, and the weakness of the opposition, was dependent on a situation created and maintained by an inept national leadership, where it was not malevolent or pursuing disastrous and narrow ideological and group interests. Yet the question of the character of elite functioning is ignored in the analytic framework of mass theory.[128] An informed analysis of developments in Germany during Weimar clearly suggests that the ability of the Nazi movement to secure the support and power that it did was vitally dependent upon the attitudes, behavior, and failures of political and other elite or leadership elements in German society. To an important extent such support developed due to the disparagement of democratic forms, the commitment to antiliberal traditions, the absence of effective leadership or the ability to collaborate with other leadership elements, the attempts to destroy working-class political organization, the indulgence of political, religious, and judicial leaders, the aura of respectability and even financial aid provided the Nazis, the ineffectiveness of Weimar, and the attempt in the last year of Weimar to maintain conservative nonrepresentative and nonresponsive authoritarian rule.[129] In all of these regards major elements of the military, industrial, landed, and generally conservative elites of German society were intimately implicated.

[T]he masses of voters would not have been enough; the active collaboration of the government elite – of bankers, industrialists, old time civil servants, and political soldiers – was necessary in the end to undermine Weimar so that Hitler could appear as the last available savior. Not all of these men of little power, frozen in their old fear of socialism and their new horror of Bolshevism, were as cynical or as candid as Kurt von Schleicher, who in 1932 wrote: "If the Nazis did not exist, it would be necessary to invent them."[130]

In effect, important elite elements helped significantly in creating the conditions that facilitated the development of the Nazi movement and furthered its acceptance. To focus on the role of the broader population, as do mass theory and most other interpretive schemes, is to provide an interpretation that is seriously deficient and distorted.

The presumably knowledgeable and detached observer during the rise to power of the NSDAP and certainly present students in retrospective assessment could well perceive the demagogic, oppressive, and strong-arm tactics of the Nazi movement, the absence of a program adequate to the needs of German society and its various elements, and the serious threat that Nazi assumption of power would pose for democratic freedoms. There is little reason, however, to expect that the ordinary German voter, especially where divorced from the parties of the left, would develop a similar perception. This is particularly the case given the usually low degree of political sophistication present within a national citizenry. There were, of course, the additional impediments to a clearer perception of the Nazi party, such as strong anti-working-class hostility, nationalistic and militaristic loyalties, conservative antiliberal bias, and economic fears. Nor are most conditions of this kind among most populations unusual or irrational. The probable absence of a clearer perception of the nature of national socialism is heightened due to the body of information to which many Germans were exposed – most conservative or middle-of-the-road newspapers, for instance, lacked information on the "true" character of the NSDAP. In this context of ignorance, and with the economic, ideological, class strains, and antidemocratic propensities noted, the positive response of many German citizens to the NSDAP is not too unusual, nor does it appear to require, in greater part, an explanation in terms of the disruption of community and the mass character of the population, quest for a communal society in corporate guise, heavy reference to the properties of German national character, or fear of proletarization. This is especially the case when consideration is given to the points made previously concerning the patina of respectability achieved by the Nazis, the inadequacies or irrelevancies of many of the other parties, the lack of options for many middle-class Germans, and the attraction of the vigor and sense of purpose that the Nazis exuded. This is all the more true when the character of the response of the German population is put in proper perspective by viewing it with the same expectations and understandings usually brought to bear on interpreting the behavior of the bulk of democratic and presumably reasonable citizenry that supports the traditional and establishment parties of the various Western democratic societies. In other words, it is now generally recognized that this democratic citizenry is very often poorly informed on the issues, knows little about the candidates or of the stance assumed by the parties, and so on. Yet in most circumstances there is, quite correctly, no imputation that the public's response to candidates and parties is the response to irrational factors or that it must be accounted for by a complex of factors of the kind involved in the mass theory model.

Further interpretations of Nazi support and some qualifications

The preceding has stressed the situational and interest factors that could have led rationally to support of the NSDAP, in effect, the nonmass nonpsychological bases of support for the Nazi movement. The following provides some further elaboration, but principally it briefly assesses and qualifies efforts that rely on different factors to interpret Nazi support. In some respects the discussion extends the preceding treatment, but in other particulars it also suggests some qualifications or, perhaps better, the need to supplement the conditions already noted.

Qualifications in regard to the mass theory perspective on NSDAP support may also be derived from the fact that the greatest support came from the smaller, not the larger, urban centers and from the areas of smaller, not larger, farms.[131] In other words, in just those areas where communal forms, membership, and conditions for personal affect were greatest, support for the Nazis was highest. Just the opposite should have been the case according to mass theory. In addition, much of the Nazis' support, coming as it did from the lower-middle-class population, came from a social collectivity that did not lack group ties but was involved in various associations, clubs, and societies. Allen observes that "the many clubs and societies cemented individual citizens together. Without them, Thalburg would have been an amorphous society."[132] Heberle's study *From Democracy to Nazism*, comparing conditions correlated with high and low support for the NSDAP in a rural farm area, suggests that support was greater where sensitivity to market conditions was greatest, communal solidarity higher, and political experience lower, among other factors. Thus rational grounds of economic interest in a condition of scant political sophistication led to high support for the Nazi movement, not an attempt to satisfy some sociopsychic needs arising from disruption of community. Kornhauser notes, however, that such populations were to a significant extent responding to "*group isolation* and the *alienation* from society which this isolation breeds."[133] Where this represents a lack of strong political loyalties, which might have impeded support of the NSDAP, it is quite unexceptional and certainly need not signify either a mass population or a quest to be part of a movement. Where it reflects a greater responsiveness to a *volksgemeinschaftliche* appeal, it may be unwise to be so moved but not so different than the attraction every group manifests to appeals to its own distinctive *Weltanschauung*. These factors thus supplement the preceding considerations but do not significantly alter their import.

What one may have to recognize as distinctive is a response to a sense of *ressentiment* against the character of change in an increasingly modern and rationalized society. Of course, not only rural elements but, as already noted, also sectors of the middle-class population are perceived as responding in such terms. It is when one acts merely or principally out of hostility and a feeling of *ressentiment* and does so to the detriment of class interest that there is a situation of noncognitive, emotional, and nonrational political behavior. It is the explication of this condition, when it presumably occurs, from a phenomenological perspective that would be essential and illuminating, but this is lacking in mass theory as it is in other interpretive schemes. A condition of alienation or *ressentiment* does add to the appeal of the Nazi movement, and it is a factor that a purely interest-based interpretation would slight, but within the context of the overall interpretation of Nazi support it is a minor factor. It seems unlikely that its absence would have significantly altered support for the Nazis. It is also a condition that the interpretation developed here would suggest is too loosely applied to those elements in German society that supported the Nazi movement, as many responded out of interest group strain and class hostility. And it would in fact appear that the sense of *ressentiment* was often closely related to distinctive class interests, traditions, and ideology and significantly expressed a dimension of class conflict. Class animosity and some consequent emotionalism and unreasonableness are not unusual in other societies, though Germany may have manifested them to a greater degree than most.

A factor to which great weight is often given is that at the root of the petite bourgeoisie middle-class elements' support for the NSDAP was a fear of proletarization, in effect of losing their distinctive economic, social, and cultural position in an increasingly industrialized and bureaucratized society in which the organized power and social forms of industrial labor and capitalist enterprise were becoming increasingly dominant. As indicated, a number of distinct elements reside in this fear. That of *ressentiment* was noted previously. Another element is the not unusual one of economic threat. Economic fears were present, arising principally from the actual or feared effects of the depression, certainly not an unusual cause for concern. Another element is class hostility, to which reference has already been made. Class hostility may tend to dim perception and impede cooperation, but it is a very common political phenomenon and does not fall within the mass theory framework. Related to a fear of proletarization and to class conflict is a condition of sensed status-culture stress. It can be acknowledged that in some circumstances middle-class behavior and unreasonable class hostility are partly accounted for by such a condition – that is, a fear that the way of life and world view of the middle class is threatened. Although reliance on such a causal interpretation may be something of an exaggeration if events are read in terms of the explanatory scheme that has been outlined, it is plausible that status-culture stress is present to some extent and that the petite bourgeoisie is responding to it. However, this is not an unreasonable concern. It is as valid an interest as any other, specifically economic. Though it involves a concern more hopeless of preservation than most, it is no less a legitimate interest and it is scarcely reasonable either to find its pursuit unwarranted and irrational or to expect that a population facing such a loss would not respond to it.

It is likely that the mass critic's reaction to such responsive behavior is probably importantly determined by another characteristic of the support the NSDAP received. This is that, in the face of status-culture threat, economic fears, and class hostility, the concerned population elements responded positively to a party whose program was vague, amorphous, and in many ways irrelevant. While in many respects this cannot be disputed, the party did modulate its appeal and made programmatic statements to particular grievances and needs, and enunciated broad – if ill-defined – plans of action. This was one reason for its success, and a response to such appeals is not very different from the general response and level of awareness exhibited by much of the populace in the much more ordinary politics of the traditional stable democratic societies of western Europe and the United States. It is a sad commentary on the level of awareness and the lack of political interest that characterize the greater part of most citizenries.

It is also suggested that the antiestablishment posture of the Nazi movement attracted not only those with a sense of *ressentiment* but that its stance of vigor, force, regeneration, purity, and national rebirth appealed to those population elements that were characterized by a strain of moral indignation or evidenced authoritarian predispositions.[134] Yet the present discussion suggests that there are conditions, even aside from this element, sufficient to account for Nazi support, though concern with the authoritarian predisposition of the lower middle class does help provide for a fuller account of the phenomenon in question. The role of moral indignation and personality properties would seem more important in accounting for who became active in the Nazi movement and for explaining to some degree, perhaps, the nature of rule after power was secured. We are not dealing here with an element in the mass theory framework but with one of the psychological influences on political behavior, more or less present in all political and social systems. Elaboration of the circumstances in which such a property becomes consequential is the relevant task of analysis, and in most instances it is to these circumstances that we must look in order to account for the political behavior in question.

Other factors presumably underlying support also deserve brief mention. I would suggest that a closer examination of the role of charismatic leadership, dedication to a *Führer,* elaborate ceremony, massed meetings, and the like, would not support the mass theory supposition that these factors played a significant role in Nazi support. These are viewed by mass theory as providing for the sense of personal involvement, relationship to a meaningful cause, and experience of personal affect presumably sought by the man in the mass. From the account delineated here, these were not necessary factors for supporting the NSDAP. Further, it is questionable whether many of those who voted for the Nazis were much more significantly moved by such considerations or involved in such circumstances than the followers of the parties of the left. Allen's study indicates that no major figures among the principal leadership of the Nazi party ever reached Thalburg, nor of course were many of the townspeople who voted NSDAP involved in the party and its activities beyond attending its meetings, meetings somewhat more elaborate perhaps than those of the SDP but otherwise not so significantly different. The value of the many ceremonies, parades, and meetings probably rested more on the suggestion they made of strength, vigor, dedication, and extensive support, as well as in the wide publicity of the movement that they provided. In a related vein, Allen makes clear that in Thalburg – and there is no reason to doubt its occurrence in most of the small or moderate-sized cities of Germany as well as in the rural areas – the success of the Nazis was a locally based phenomenon, as the national leadership rarely entered and the mass meetings involved local functionaries.

There are, of course, additional factors variously considered as accounting for the support nazism was able to generate. Two fall somewhat marginally within the ambience of mass theory. One is the presumed effectiveness of the Nazi appeals to patriotism, nationalism, and militarism. Perceiving this condition as a phenomenon falling within the framework of mass theory rests on the presumed irrelevance of such appeals to the "real" needs of the NSDAP supporters and on the contention that it was the decline of community and the massification of large sectors of German society that underlay the response the Nazis evoked. However, if these appeals are ones positively evaluated by the population concerned, some question could be raised as to whether it is appropriate to label them as irrelevant. In a sense they merely state a different set of group purposes or needs.[135] Presumably, relevance or rationality could be defined in terms of whether these concerns furthered or impeded attention to and action on other group interests – economic or otherwise. It may be recognized that they do in fact have little value in satisfying such other pressing group needs. The fact of these appeals, however, does not mean that they were the principal reason for supporting the NSDAP, nor does this appear to have been the case. Rather, they were one among several appealing elements – and not a completely irrelevant element in its own terms either – and they served as much to give legitimacy, respectability, and propriety to the Nazi movement as to attract support outright because of their innate appeal. Thus while some decline of certain communal forms may have provided the NSDAP with a slightly added fillip of support in light of its stress on nationalistic and other emotional themes, its relative importance and uniqueness seem modest in light of the broader interpretative framework outlined here.[136] In explaining the strength and acceptance of nazism considerable attention is often given to another factor – to elements of German national character and German traditions, such as the stress on duty, order, obedience, loyalty, the subordination of the individual to the well-being of the state, and so forth. Without attempting to explain the role of historical and cultural factors, however, their greatest relevance would appear to be in helping to account for the absence of greater constraints on German support for the Nazis and in accounting for attitudes toward and the acceptance of the Nazi movement once it was in power. Less important, though of some value, would be the support that the Nazis generated – apart from other considerations, due to the correspondence of some of these factors and the terms in which the populace perceived the NSDAP.

A final note

The preceding has stressed the limitations of mass theory, and less directly of other social psychological theories, in determining why the Nazi movement received considerable popular support. In some re-

gards the developments in Germany in the 1920s and early 1930s
suggest mass phenomena. In these respects a certain applicability
resides in mass theory, but it is a strongly qualified one. In some
instances it would appear that the response to the Nazi movement
had an emotional, affect-laden, noninterest character, especially where
support derived predominantly from a sense of alienation or *ressentiment*. In other words, circumstances in accord with the mass theory
perspective are evidenced when supporting the Nazi movement was
principally a means of striking out blindly at the existing order and
the character of change or where support manifested an effort by
uprooted and anomic elements to find community and meaningfulness
through relationship to a dynamic mass movement. For much of the
population that voted National Socialist, however, it is questionable
whether such conditions were either present or accounted to a significant degree for the support provided the Nazi movement.

The present discussion has stressed the need for caution in labeling
as irrational or as mass behavior a positive response to nationalist,
militarist, or other traditional themes. It has also been suggested that
much in the German support for the rising Nazi movement can be
accounted for by emotions, hostilities, needs, and political ignorance
and naïveté that we take for granted in the political dynamics of the
older, more stable, and less strife-torn polities of some of the western
European nations and the United States. In Germany these features
were exaggerated by the immense political and economic disabilities
that existed and were further aggravated by a political framework
that lacked legitimacy in the eyes of many. It is generally recognized,
however, that on the whole such features in the United States and
European societies need not be accounted for by a mass theory
framework. The same in many though not all respects is also true, I
suggest, in regard to the increasing support secured by the Nazi
movement.

In a related vein, note has been made of the greater support provided by the more rather than less communally circumstanced populations, by the already high degree of organizational involvement of
the middle-class population, class hostilities and conservative ideological orientations, the lack of alternative efficacious political parties,
economic fear, political instability and the failure to stem increasing
economic and political dissolution, and so on. These appear crucial, as
does the behavior and attitudes of elite elements in accounting for
Nazi support. The vital role of these last few factors reflects the
conditions basic to understanding Hitler's rise, "the deepening
antagonism between a powerful but increasingly anachronistic author-

itarianism and a growing democratic movement."[137] In effect, one had here the efforts by the conservative traditional forces in German society to suppress the developing class and social forms arising from modern industrial change. The behavior that developed from this circumstance was crucial in shaping many of the distinct conditions noted as accounting for the rising support received by the NSDAP. In a sense the destruction of Weimar was more the result of efforts by conservative elements than of the National Socialists. In addition, the conservative counterrevolution in the early 1930s lay at the root of Hitler's ability to secure power, quite apart from other influences it may have had.

In a different vein, however, attention to many of the distinct concerns noted suggests the pertinence of studying how individual and group circumstances are perceived by the actor. Economic strain, political instability, the absence of apparently effective alternatives, and other conditions help suggest something of the phenomenological world of many Nazi supporters. Attention to these elements and to group circumstances, loyalties, and ideological commitments – however obnoxious the latter may be judged – encourages a stress on the interest and rational component of political behavior. Thus we can perceive political behavior in one important sense as a consequence of the actor attempting to negotiate the political process and environment as he has experienced it, from his distinctive group situation, set of beliefs, and past experiences. The properties of the environment to which the individual is responding and the distinctive orientations brought to this transaction reflect broader systemic properties. Further, whatever the properties of individuals, we have also stressed that support for the Nazis was fundamentally also a result of the properties and processes of societal institutions, particularly political ones, and their change.

Summary comments

The illustrative material in the present chapter has sought to demonstrate that various forms of activist political protest may be understood as other than merely mass, expressive, or psychologically derived behavior when systemic properties and the individual's response to them, among other properties and circumstances, are taken into account. Frequently such collective behavior may be recognized as efforts, for example, to remove unreasonable credit provisions, expand employment opportunities, alter economic or political disabilities, and to preserve the distinctiveness of different cultures, and so forth.

Furthermore, such "sources" of radical behavior are interpreted as creating a potential for behavior or protest movements of a particular character. Other properties of the population in question, of society, and of the political process determine the appearance and form of the behavior. The determination of behavior is thus seen to reside in a broad complex of factors that extends much beyond, and may not even include, the mass theorist's concern with the decline of intermediate groups, social isolation, available populations, and extremist or demagogic counterelites.

For the mass political theorist, mass movements (if defined with any precision and within the context of mass theory) are movements of the uprooted, the powerless, those lacking integrative relationships. Their protest behavior is episodic, abrupt, and erratic in nature, of rudimentary intellectual substance, negativistic in character, simplistic in approach, unrealistic in "program," immediate in its demands, and often of a highly emotionally charged character. Yet this is not the behavior of many vigorous and at times radical movements for agrarian and industrial reform, civil rights, and other political change. These are frequently protest movements for change based on the discrete interests of a particular social category seeking concrete ends that are based on legitimate remediable grievances. In many instances political protest may be understood in traditional terms – as a case of class conflict or as communal, cultural, or other conflict as the case may be, though much of the preceding material principally illustrates class-type conflict. When such protest is perceived as mass behavior, it is because of the failure to attend to the social and political circumstances of the group in question, to the possible interest component in radical, coercive, or "nonlegal" behavior, and to how a collectivity experiences, imputes meaning to, and negotiates the political environment.

It is by failing to distinguish between mass movements and social movements – particularly through a disregard of the interest component or source of strain residing in the latter – that the basis is created for denying legitimacy and rationality to the latter type of movements and their individual supporters. By ignoring the existence of a sense of inequity, the individual's awareness of distinct group membership and needs, and conditions of political unresponsiveness, few grounds other than estrangement, anomie, and psychological disturbance remain to account for support of vigorous protest.[138] It is when attention to social, political, cultural, and distinctive group properties is lacking and when the individual's attempt to make sense of his circumstances is left unexamined that an attribution of irrationality, unreasonableness, and emotionalism can be made. The labeling of such movements and their support as mass behavior can then be accomplished with a minimum of dissonance.

The purposive, instrumental, and interest basis of social movements and the historical, political, and social factors contributing to their rise and properties cannot be understood from mass or psychological analysis. The nature of radical or protest political behavior will be misunderstood in the absence of attention to its possible class or other interest character, and the broader determining circumstances within which it arises. This is not necessarily to affirm that class or other movements based on a discrete social category may not also exhibit mass behavior traits. It does suggest, however, that if in fact the movements are class or group based, the likelihood of mass traits or their derivation from psychological properties is considerably reduced; also, that whatever the behavior exhibited, its origin will be inaccurately accessed without attention to a broad-ranging social, political, and cultural analysis sensitive to the functional and reasonable basis of individual and group strain and the actor's attempt to negotiate his political environment. What is significant about many radical and dissident movements is not merely that the behavior in question is based on class interest and inequity and lack of redress within a broader political and social context but also that the character of the behavior and the demands made are generally not irrational, erratic, or remote from actual disabilities and their cause, not even intolerant in many instances of the just needs of other elements of the society. This is not to say that against some standard of all-knowing wisdom, informed by hindsight, the action undertaken and the objectives and perspectives of the movements were always the wisest, most accurate, or efficient; behavior rarely is. There is a natural fallibility, error, and distortion due to particular interests and prejudices, the difficulties of maintaining support, the precariousness of available resources, and the perversities of particular personnel. But these are conditions that afflict all movements, mass and nonmass, and they lead to behavior that inevitably falls short for protesting populations as well as for elites and other communities of what, especially in retrospect, is seen as the "best" and most reasonable course of action and protest. The concern must be, however, not with the absence of error but with the rationality and appropriateness of the support, participation, or action in question. And in these terms many instances of so-called mass behavior, including those cited previously, suggest that the behavior is not in keeping with that imputed in the analysis of the mass society or in frustration-aggression theory.[139]

It is clear that the present discussion has not given attention to the irrational or psychological elements of political behavior. Partly this reflects the attempt to stress the importance of elements omitted by mass theory. It also arises from the contention that to a considerable extent, even in the types of cases with which mass theory is likely to be concerned, the reasons for political commitments can be significantly accounted for without such factors, though this may be less true for the political activist or leader. To an important degree the discussion of the preceding cases sought to illustrate briefly these contentions. While these accounts did *not* seek to provide an outline of a total explanation of the behavior in question, they did try to point out the most significant causal elements and stressed – though without elaboration – the usefulness of an approach attentive to the individual's construction of meaning within a social structural, historical, and political context.

6. Critical assessment
of the pluralist perspective

An adequate assessment of mass political theory and the bases of dissident politics requires an analysis of pluralist theory and associated political forms. This can contribute to our present interests in a number of ways. It permits an examination of the presumed accessibility of elites to the general public. It makes possible an assessment of the responsiveness of the political system, which, in turn, influences the evaluation of whether dissident politics is rational or reasonable. In a more general vein, an analysis of political forms and functioning can also suggest some of the impetus to protest that may be present in the political system.

Introductory comments

Pluralist theory and the temper of the times

In the past two decades American political scientists have shown an increased interest in interest group theory and its pragmatist forebears and, more generally, in pluralist theory and analysis. This appears to be less a reflection of some intrinsic virtue in these areas than a reflection of a number of contemporary phenomena. These include the increasing behavioral orientation of the political and sociological disciplines, the attempt by liberal theorists to develop a more realistic account of democratic society in the face of conservative and radical criticism, the widespread celebration of American political forms, and heightened sensitivity to extremist politics in the period since the end of World War II. The cold war years had been marked by a period of caution and a time of apprehension about the "masses," and in the "end of ideology" philosophy of recent years there had been a derogation of the relevancy of ideological conflict and of the notion that there exist irreconcilable or far-reaching differences among groups.

Pluralist theory, especially where its interest group component is stressed, suggests the reality of only that which is manifest and directly observable in the activity of individuals and groups. It relegates notions of power, interests, and needs unsupported by explicit group structures and process to the metaphysical realm of Alfred Bentley's "spooks." It offers a defense of liberal democratic society while granting the inadequacies and apathy of the individual citizen. In the face of the totalitarian potential of mass movements and apprehension over extremism it offers a positive evaluation of narrow-based constituencies and a definition of the desirable and stable political order as one constituted of such collectivities. Yet "the defense offered for the narrow constituencies into which American politics is broken . . . is an almost explicitly conservative justification of the power of interest-group elites."[1] Perhaps more grievous than the "preference for selfish and material values"[2] is the presumption that pluralist interest group theory is not merely a hypothesis but in fact an accurate and realistic description of the character of American political structure and process. It is also relevant to suggest that the continued reaffirmation of the presumed pluralist character of American political society serves to maintain a presumption that conditions of equity, responsiveness, and efficacious rule prevail, when in reality these are illusory in a number of very important particulars.[3] Hence pluralist dogma has served the function of aiding in the maintenance of the status quo and current forms of power distribution and its exercise.

Pluralist and contemporary democratic theory in mass political theory

Mass political theory's commitment to a pluralist perspective is revealed in its general perspectives, ideological character, and structural analysis, to which attention has already been given. Its pluralist perspective tends to be joined to a positive evaluation of the role of political elites within the pluralist system. It is particularly essential to assess critically and qualify the pluralist perspective in mass theory. This arises from the foundation provided by the pluralist perspective for mass theory's criticism of dissident politics or of what it considers mass behavior. At least partial implicit justification for such criticism rests on the proposition that the existing political system possesses means of redress, representation, and responsiveness of leadership. Hence to suggest, as pluralism does, that these conditions are strongly present in democratic societies, whether in contemporary America or other nations, would undermine one of the bases supporting the propriety of "mass" or sharply dissident behavior in these societies.

The elitist strain in contemporary democratic theory suggests that elites preserve democracy through their superior commitment to democratic forms and values and by possession of an important degree of freedom for action independent of the vagaries of the broader population, as well as by maintenance of a counterbalance among themselves through a condition of elite competition.[4] Democratic elitist propositions are joined to pluralist theory both organically and pragmatically: organically, because one of the significant propositions of pluralism is that the democratic essence can be retained if there are competing countervailing elites, even where they are not wholly responsible to their followers; pragmatically, because of the need to resolve the ambiguity between the felt commitment of these writers to democratic forms and their fear of the "masses." Reliance on presumably wise and tolerant elites diminishes apprehension in regard to the masses or, more generally, nonelites. The qualification of democracy that resides in stressing the value of an independent and unimpeded elite is mitigated, it is felt, when such a condition is tied to elite pluralism and competition.

A somewhat anomalous situation has developed. While the theorist perceives the plural political society as a guarantor of widened participation and representation, increased diffusion of power, and minimization of coercion, both the reality of contemporary democratic society and the dynamics of a pluralist political system significantly fail to exhibit an achievement of these ends for large sectors of the population.

Perspectives of the present chapter

The present chapter briefly develops a number of major criticisms of pluralist theory as applied to contemporary political society, particularly in the United States. Special though not exclusive stress is given to the interest group character of pluralist theory, one of the elements that bulks large in the American form of the theory. Drawing on the rather extensive literature in this area, I suggest that pluralist assumptions and analysis are partial or inaccurate on empirical grounds. Pluralist theory is also theoretically inadequate as a statement of what constitutes the arena of political contention and decision making. Thus it is inappropriate to exclude the private sector from the pluralist frame. Note is also made of the fact that responsiveness is often not achieved even in the organizational sectors in which one is directly implicated. Deficiencies in the analysis of structures of power are considered. There is a critical assessment of the presumed diversity of choice in "pluralist" society. The concept of the public interest is succinctly elaborated and defended. Brief critical attention is given to pluralist theory's approach to societal change and system stability. With only slight exception the focus throughout is on political pluralism, not social pluralism, and the criticism of pluralist propositions is not meant to imply the existence of mass society structures, as understood by those mass theorists treated here. The present criticism is directed to what has been overlooked in pluralist theory and its application, as well as to inadequacies in propositions integral to the theory itself. Both the empirical and normative faces of the pluralist framework are open to criticism. The following is significantly concerned with confronting pluralist propositions with the reality of American society and with suggesting in light of the resulting disparity a need to reassess political behavior and the adequacy of pluralist forms and functioning for the attainment of public and group needs.

Pluralist theory evaluated

The pluralist tradition in political and social thought is both distinguished and diverse in its concerns. Developed earlier by European theorists,[5] it is now primarily a concern of American scholars. It has dealt with the nature of sovereignty, the nature of the state, the relationship between the individual and the state, the role of government, and the character of law. The conditions necessary for the preservation of freedom, political responsiveness, and effective rule have been discussed. Pluralist theory has also been concerned with the distribution and scope of power, means of access to power, forms of representation, the relationship between masses and elites, and the mediation and minimization of conflict. It has particularly stressed the preservation of freedom for individuals and groups through the maintenance of a diffusion of power and representation among private associations.

It is clearly a doctrine in the liberal tradition, in which the state is regarded as merely one among numerous forms of human association serving some but not all human needs. It has sharply criticized any assertion of unlimited power for the state, which is essentially limited to being an arbiter and an arena of conflict. Grant McConnell has suggested that its defense of private associations "has provided some of the noblest statements on constitutionalism and the limits of state action."[6] Given the apprehension regarding the dangers in concentrated or unified state power, pluralist theory sought the pluralization of power, the creation and preservation of small governmental units, and a diversity of private associations and centers of power. Further, these smaller units were perceived as more likely to engage the interests of men, be more representative, and provide a more certain basis for fellowship and commitment. This diversity of associations maximizes the likelihood that power is significantly decentralized. In terms of such a formulation and the diversification of authority, interests, and commitments, there is a multicentered system of power, one in which the constrictions upon and the limitations of power give it a situational character.[7]

Public purpose is usually perceived as no more than the purposes of diverse associations. The state is, in effect, interpreted as the locus of diverse pressures that its policy reflects, the character of the state changing as there is a change in the strength, character, and purpose of the groups and pressures acting on it.

The pluralist policy is understood as providing not merely for a peaceful, ordered resolution of conflict but as having as well a distinctive capacity to meet social needs and cope with conflict generated by such needs. Change is seen as occurring in a slow incremental fashion. These conditions combined with an assumption by many American theorists of a basic consensus, at least among the most active political participants, appear to underlie the perception of the pluralist system as one maintaining a stable political order in a condition of equilibrium. It does so, it is held, while exercising minimal coercion and preserving liberty and individual rights.

Pluralist theory is often treated as a generally distinct though quite diffuse entity. This is not too unusual, given a high degree of agreement or commonality among diverse strands of pluralist theory in regard to the nature of the state, the structure of power, the basis of freedom, and the character of the political process. It is possible, however, to distinguish a number of somewhat different though related themes or differences in emphasis and concern. These may be variously characterized. I suggest four major orientations. The writings of many pluralists readily indicate that these are not mutually exclusive.

1. The group basis of freedom is stressed, principally through the diffusion of power and the mediation between a citizenry and its political leadership that group structures make possible. More broadly, one deals here with the diverse functions served by autonomous intermediate groups and community in preserving freedom as is also suggested by the political theory of mass society. Some representative theorists would include Kornhauser, Nisbet, Tocqueville, and Madison.

The concern for the preservation of freedom by maintaining a condition of group competition and constraints on power is generally found in the writing of all theorists in the pluralist tradition.

2. The political process and interest representation are stressed and understood as essentially encompassed by groups and group contention in the process of competition, bargaining, and the ongoing elaboration and change of coalitions. However, political leaders are perceived as playing an important and creative role in this process. A behavioral orientation to politics is clear here. Some representative theorists are Madison, Bentley, Truman, Herring, Latham, Lindblom, and Odegard.[8] Some of the concerns and significant contributions of some of those whose work is cited in the next category are relevant here, such as efforts by Dahl and by Wildavsky.[9] I also include in this strain of pluralist thought the pluralist perspective that denies or severely limits the existence of a given "public interest" distinct from the interests of groups or collectivities in the society.

3. Emphasis is given to the character of the distribution of power and of the decision-making processes. Power is seen as diffused rather than concentrated and as being constrained or checked by the existence of countervailing power. Community and national power structures are studied, particularly the former. The nonoverlapping rather than concentrated character of elites or decision makers is stressed. Here, as well as in the preceding perspective, there is also a stress on the moderation of conflict due to crosscutting ties arising from multiple group affiliations. There are multiple points of access into the political system and diverse types of research in terms of which political influence can be created. This further diffuses power and moderates political conflict. The changing rather than the constant, the situational rather than the institutional or structural properties of power and its exercise are stressed. Democracy is conceptualized as polyarchy, and competition and bargaining among elites rather than citizen participation are seen as vital. Major theorists contributing to this area include Dahl, Polsby, Wildavsky, Berle, and Galbraith, among others.[10]

4. Concern is centered on the partial nature of the state and on restrictions of its claims on the citizenry and voluntary associations. The literature here deals with questions of sovereignty and loyalty, which are perceived as limited. The state is but one among several associations, and these legal pluralists, as they have been called, deny a supreme position to the state. Voluntary associations were a means of preserving the freedom of man. Writers such as Laski, Cole, and Duguit[11] have contributed to this area.

Pluralist propositions

The present discussion is addressed to the concept of political pluralism as it has been developed in the work of American students and that finds expression in the writings of theorists such as Kornhauser, Dahl, Polsby, Galbraith, Truman, and Latham, among others. My interests differ somewhat from the concerns of traditional pluralist theorists. Specifically, I am not concerned with the work of the European scholars and legal pluralists. A major thrust of the present criticism is directed toward the interest group theoretical perspective that is such a significant element in contemporary American pluralist theory.

The propositions that are explicitly stated or that may be deduced as implicit in the writings and perspectives of the pluralist model of American political society are quite extensive.[12] A number, though by no means all, of the major tenets of pluralism are considered in the following discussion.[13] Listed succinctly, they are:

Power is dispersed:
- Power does not reside in any one center; political resources are widely distributed throughout the society, and in effect no small limited number of groups are all powerful, nor is there any single elite group.
- Many diverse groups seek power in continuing competition.
- Hence there exists a condition of countervailing power.

Accessibility and representativeness:
- The political elite and political decision-making centers are acessible. This is a proposition with two closely related aspects – that all significant interests secure representation in the political system and that the political leadership will be responsive to group demands.

Ability and availability of choice:
- Individuals know or can come to know their interests; in other words, they have the ability to make relevant choices.
- And there is the implied assumption in several pluralist propositions that choices or alternatives are in fact available.

Allocation of values:
- Not so much a proposition as a narrowing of theoretical perspective, is the implicit assumption that the allocation of values is essentially comprehended by the activities of and the decisions made in the public sector.

Public interest concept minimized:
> Interests are viewed as existing only where recognized by and associated with explicit group structures. This tends to give a metaphysical and nonobjectively specifiable cast to the notion of a public interest apart from group interests.

There is a disparity between the empirical reality of the contemporary American polity and what is postulated in the propositions of pluralist theory. The cumulative effect of such discrepancies restricts the appropriateness of pluralist interpretation and analysis.

Lack of representation and responsiveness and consequent power inequities

Populations and interests lack equitable representation. The proposition that all significant interests secure representation would include in its more complete form the related assumption that no one or two interests bulk disproportionately large, and hence interest representation is not too inequitable. In either case, we have here an untenable proposition. Representation and responsiveness are considerably qualified. Their presence even moderately commensurate with the size of many collectivities and the scope and seriousness of their concerns is often lacking. This becomes particularly clear when contrasted with the considerable influence of a number of small and even narrow interest groups to be detailed shortly.

Deprived minorities, such as blacks, Puerto Ricans, Indians, Mexican Americans, and the one quarter of the nation that live in poverty, receive scant representation in the political system. Nor is there much prospect that this will alter significantly. At best, all one can say is that they are contending for representation, that is, power. This merely suggests that the system is not completely closed. Nor are these, of course, the only groups lacking in anything like equitable representation, responsiveness, or power. Other categories, like the aged of this society and the more general category of the consumer, find only slight representation and responsiveness.[14]

In an examination of distinctive areas of policy or issues of contention, the fact of a lack of anything approaching equitable interest representation finds support. In a myriad of areas, policy reflects the interests and efforts of narrow interest groups and not the resolution of a plurality of diverse and contending groups. This is true even when the policy area is one where a large portion of the society may be very seriously implicated. The result is usually substantial gain for a few, at the cost of many.

The whole area of military spending and related support to business illustrates the absence of pluralist competition as a determinant of policy. Rather, governmental policy and military spending enhance the interests of a few.

Here government not only permits and facilitates the entrenchment of private power, but serves as its fountainhead. Herein the government creates and institutionalizes power concentrations which tend to breed on themselves and to delay public control.... Lacking any viable in-house capabilities, competitive yardsticks, or the potential for institutional competition, the government tends to become subservient to the private and special interests whose entrenched power bears the governmental seal.[15]

Neither in the granting of contracts and contractual modifications, special governmental favors, or in the development of defense spending is there much that could pass for pluralist competition beyond the scope of groups with already shared purposes and perspectives. It is a situation in which "power is coalescing, not countervailing."[16] It is an area rich with government largess in many forms – considerable cost overruns, noncompetitive bidding, costly financing, payment, and contractual procedures, extravagantly expensive weaponry receiving scant review by a generally acquiescent and poorly informed Congress, large governmental funds for research and development, the ceding of patent rights derived from government-financed research to private enterprise, the provision of working capital, and the use of governmental facilities at no cost for commercial work, among a lengthy list of special-interest-serving policies. Even a program such as the stockpiling of presumably strategic goods (which as early as 1961 had cost $8.9 billion[17]) has, in effect, been used to maintain artificially high prices of raw materials. The program itself is unnecessarily costly to the government, though remunerative for the business interests involved. It constitutes, in effect, a government subsidy and protection of privileged economic interests and cannot be explained in terms of a pluralist political model.[18]

Much the greater part of the decision-making process involved in determining defense spending is such as to undermine the working of a representative and responsive pluralist system. Several features characterize this process.[19] One is congressional abdication of responsibility for military policy and disinclination to question seriously defense spending. Related is the general lack of adequate information, uncertainty as to cost estimates, and unavailability of data on contractor-subcontractor arrangements. There is the manipulation of information and the groundless fear campaigns by the Department of

Defense, the executive office, and the military establishment. Intimate ties exist among industry, the military, and government. This can be seen in the considerable crossing over of personnel from the armed services into private industrial employment. In early 1969, 2124 retired high-ranking armed service officers were employed by the 100 largest military contractors. The 10 largest employed 1065 of these retired offers.[20] There exists highly organized and effectively applied pressure by private military associations and business groups. The urgency of such pressure is readily revealed by the fact that 4 of the top 5 and 10 of the top 15 defense contractors have relied for more than 50 percent of their sales on defense contracts.[21] Generally absent are widespread efforts by organized contrary interests. Huge defense budgets and their relative trouble-free support reflect shared perspectives by military, industrial, and government leaders. A role of some importance is also played by the nature of congressional procedures and decision making. Involved here would be the important part played by the armed services and appropriations committees of the House and Senate, the composition of these committees, and the strength of their chairmen.[22] More generally, congressional ignorance on military budget questions and the lack of resources to evaluate the military budget adequately play a part. And not to be dismissed is the "pork barrel" nature of military contracts for congressmen.

A number of significant qualities are revealed by the preceding sketch. One is the paucity of public involvement. There are, of course, a number of actively organized interests and groups that do vigorously press their particular purposes. These, however, comprise only a small segment of the population affected by the military budget and its operation. Essentially, the military establishment shares common perspectives and purposes. There is little competition over ends or means. Where contention and competition are present, it is principally over who will get what and how much of the available largess.

Other policy areas exhibit similar failings of representation and pluralist policy formation. Brief mention will be made of only a few. Existing tax legislation betrays the potency and preponderance of narrow special interests. A host of special deductions and exemptions seriously compromise the concept of a progressive tax system. They disproportionately profit upper-income groups and shift a correspondingly heavy burden on the majority of taxpayers. This is partly implicit in Kolko's calculations (Table 6.1) of taxes paid by different income classes, though it is not concerned with corporate taxes.[23] Not only do the well-to-do profit by tax concessions, but various business areas – natural gas, oil, aluminum, lumber, tobacco, and so on – gain greatly

Tabe 6.1. *Total income paid in federal, state, and local taxes, 1958*

Income class (dollars)	Federal (%)	Share of taxes state and local (%)	Total (%)
0–2,000	9.6	11.3	21.0
2,000–4,000	11.0	9.4	20.4
4,000–6,000	12.1	8.5	20.6
6,000–8,000	13.9	7.7	21.6
8,000–10,000	13.4	7.2	20.6
10,000–15,000	15.1	6.5	21.6
15,000 plus	28.6	5.9	34.4
Average	16.1	7.5	23.7

Source: Gabriel Kolko, *Wealth and Power in America* (New York: Frederick A. Praeger, 1962), p. 37.

from existing tax policy. The notorious oil depletion allowance is only the most familiar illustration. Resource-based industries have, in effect, had their taxes reduced by approximately 50 percent. That times of great stress and loss by many and unconscionable gains by a few do not alter such conditions is evidenced by the failure in the last days of 1973 at restraining windfall profits by the oil industry.

An expensive and thriving health care industry has over the years benefited from the special consideration given to pharmaceutical, physician, hospital, and other health industry interests.[24] Absent has been a response to the much larger community that has had to bear the costs of exorbitant drug prices, spiraling costs for hospital care, equipment, and supplies, rising doctors' fees, and inadequate and expensive insurance plans. A considerable portion of the more than $75 billion spent annually on medical care consists, in effect, of government subsidies to various sectors of the health industry. In a different direction, the potency of the drug industry was revealed in the removal of Dr. Herbert Ley, Jr., as commissioner of the Food and Drug Administration (FDA) at the end of 1969. Ley had initiated a somewhat more consumer-oriented policy at the FDA during his commissionership. The effectiveness of the pharmaceutical industry lobby and their influence in Congress is clearly depicted in Richard Harris' *The Real Voice.*[25]

The rise in raw milk prices approved by Secretary of Agriculture Clifford Hardin on March 25, 1972, is another example of privileged unbalanced access. This administrative decision will cost the consumer approximately one-half billion dollars a year in increased food prices. Given apparent congressional sentiment on the matter, the price increase might have become public policy even without the action of the executive department.[26] In any case, however, the outcome and the process by which it was attained further confirm the inappropriateness of the plural model. More broadly, current programs and expenditures by the Department of Agriculture and the federal government reveal a strong partiality and munificence to the larger and prosperous farmer and to agribusiness. At the same time, the majority of farmers, whose numbers have continually declined, remain with modest means and generally outside the more profitable ministrations of governmental efforts.

Governmental resource policies have historically reflected lumber, mineral, cattle, and agribusiness interests. The input and responsiveness to broader community concerns have been slender. McConnell has written that "the persistent success of demand for private exploitation has become a tradition, conferring a degree of legitimacy on a wide variety of actions that give control of land and land policy to limited groups within the population."[27] Policies and programs in regard to water projects and water management, public grazing lands, and lumbering on public forest land reveal their narrow interest basis. The U.S. Forest Service has permitted overcutting and clear-cutting of public forests and worked to hold down raw lumber prices while market prices rose precipitously. About one-half the lumber exported annually from the United States comes from public forest land.[28] The Forest Service has failed to keep pace with the need to reforest logged lands. Timber mismanagement has profited a few at the expense of the nation. Elsewhere the eroded lands of the West bear mute witness to the callous overgrazing of public lands by private livestock herds. Federal policy has predominantly reflected the purposes of the narrow interest business groups dependent on land resource exploitation. Possibly the present concerns regarding the environment will see policy more responsive to broader community needs. Past experience, however, does not encourage great optimism that the broader population will be served, at least in any equitable fashion.

Actually, the extent and forms of governmental aid to business go far beyond specific policies tailored to particular industrial areas. More than 60 percent of the vast sums spent on research and development are federal funds. Even where such efforts are carried out by industry (and they account for nearly 70 percent of such work), the government still foots most of the bill. The government provides various types of subsidies: aid for the construction of commercial vessels, a strong program of cargo preferences to American ships, support for some airline operations, for nuclear power companies, and subsidization of various exports. The silver-mining industry has made billions by the Treasury Department's practice of purchasing the entire domestic silver output (which is then simply stored at West Point) at prices well above the market price. Severe restrictions on fuel imports have in recent years raised the price for such products in the American market.[29] Robert Sherrill reports an Associated Press study of August 1971, showing that private business obtains approximately $30 billion from the government annually. Summarizing the report he writes:

Tax breaks, incentives, and exemptions may run as high as $15 billion annually; farm subsidies total between $6 billion and $9 billion; loans to business (direct, guaranteed, and insured) come to $250 billion, "six times the outstanding credit advanced by all commercial banks"; the maritime industry gets $450 million a year, the airlines $63 million (including $10.5 million to multi-millionaire Howard Hughes' Air West Airlines), and the railroads $172 milllion over a five-year period; defense contractors get to use $14.6 billion worth of government property for profit-making purposes; United States companies doing business overseas receive over $6 billion in loans and insurance.[30]

This litany of government largess and openness to business interests illustrates the principal contention of the present section – that some interests secure greatly disproportionate access and response from the political system while much larger sectors of the community that are significantly affected by the policies in question have very little successful input. In fact, a study of policy formation and decision making in these areas would reveal the general lack of competition between the business interests seeking favorable governmental action and any significantly organized sectors of the community opposed to their purposes. Thus a vital element of the pluralist model of the polity is lacking. Of course in some areas there may be contention between the representatives of special business interests, but these do not dispute the fundamental nature of the policies in question. Rather, they are concerned with which business interests and programs will receive the governmental largess. As Richard Barnet remarks, "the consensus on premises and ends has been remarkably secure."[31] In effect, what has tended to develop is that particular economic and policy areas become insulated and privileged reserves where policy formation reflects the interaction between the principal economic

parties in the area and those political leaders, congressional committees, and administrators or regulatory agencies that are implicated
in the particular economic or program sphere. Thus in the areas of defense spending, farm programs, tariffs, trade provisions, transport and
highways, fuels, road and housing construction, land use, and mass
media and communication policy becomes almost the distinct province
or enclave of specific interests. The broader public, including some of
those most directly affected by decision making in these areas, frequently has little access or control over them in practice.

This phenomenon stands clearly revealed in the experiences and
functioning of the governmental regulatory agencies. These agencies
had their origin in the establishment of the Interstate Commerce
Commission (ICC) in 1887. It was in the years following the creation
of the Federal Reserve Board in 1913, however, that we witness their
significant emergence. Kolko, in his study of the Progressive period,[32]
has shown that the initiative for government regulation appeared
among business elements that wished to secure the aid of government
in achieving business cartelization. The regulatory agencies exercise
considerable authority. It extends beyond merely administrative responsibilities to include substantial judicial and legislative power.

The analytic literature and case material that have developed on
the regulatory commissions over more than three decades is extensive.[33]
This material clearly shows that responsiveness to the public has been
slight and that the commissions have been heavily weighted toward
narrow and often small but powerful private interest groups profiting
through their intimate involvement in a particular area of trade, communication, transport, and so forth. The responsiveness of these
agencies to client interests and the preservation of client-shaped policy
guidelines, their protection of monopoly practices and already existing
business interests against competition, their "reciprocal solicitude"[34]
and dependence on the interests they are presumed to be controlling,
their failure of action, mutual good fellowship, and exchange of
personnel have been extensively catalogued.[35] The commissions are
revealed in most respects to be captives of the private interests over
which they are ineffective overseers.

Here I illustrate just one area of agency-business intimacy, the
shuffling of personnel from one to the other. Ten of the 12 commissioners who left the ICC in the sixties either secured employment
in the transportation industry or became lobbyists and consultants for
the industry. Senator Gaylord Nelson revealed that in the three-year
period from 1966 through 1968 24 senior officials of the FDA had
left and secured positions with drug firms. In the late 1960s more

than one-half of the commissioners who had retired from the Federal
Communications Commission moved into high executive positions in
the communications industry.[36] A plethora of individual cases could
be cited, such as former ICC chairman William H. Tucker, who
shortly after leaving the commission became vice president for the
New England operations of the Penn Central Railroad, or Carl Bagge,
who left the Federal Power Commission at the end of 1970 to become president of the National Coal Association. While providing
more vivid illustration than summary figures, such citations become
redundant.[37]

Referring to the so-called regulatory agencies, Murray Edelman has
written:

Administrative agencies are to be understood as economic and political
instruments of the parties they regulate and benefit, not of a reified
"society," "general will," or "public interest." At the same time they perform
this instrumental function, they perform an equally important expressive
function for the polity as a whole; to create and sustain an impression that
induces acquiescence of the public in the face of private tactics that might
otherwise be expected to produce resentment, protest, and resistance. The
instrumental function of administrative agencies ... has been observed,
demonstrated, and documented by every careful observer of regulatory
agencies.[38]

In addition to Edelman's observation, it is important to note that the
relevance of the regulatory commissions and their performance to our
present argument is not exhausted by their friendship with industry
and their failure to be an effective voice of the broader community.
In *The End of Liberalism* Theodore Lowi has stressed that the very
nature of how the commissions function – in effect, as policy-making
and value allocation bodies – is not encompassed by pluralist theory.
This vital area of contemporary political society is thus significantly
outside the operation of a pluralist framework.

A corollary to conditions of inadequate representation and responsiveness sketched in the preceding discussion is that policy is formulated and carried out in many vital areas where those who initiate
and effectuate the programs are for most intents and purposes no more
than minimally accountable to any of the broader populations that are
measurably affected.[39] Yet there is little in the way of any distinct
broad-based interest organizations or effective input reflecting citizen
interests. Nor is it likely in most instances that any will appear as
an ongoing phenomenon. The scope of the population involved and
the often nonimmediate, nonspecific, little recognized consequences

of the decisions made in most policy areas pose serious impediments to the appearance of any ongoing and effective countervailing organizations. In contrast, though, there is the continued and effective presence and organization of the narrow-based interests of the military contractor, the armed services, pharmaceutical companies, and oil and resource industries, among others. The presumably pluralist system of the U.S. polity is, then, severely compromised by policy unreflective of the needs and interests of large sectors of society, the lack of counters to strong vested interests, and, in some cases, the nearly autonomous rule of such interests in their particular domains.

Fragmentation and narrow interest domination. Another aspect of the question of group organization and representation, suggested by the material referred to in the preceding discussion, is that the attempt "to implement governmental policy along geographically decentralized, federalistic, and pluralistic lines means to transfer the power to govern to the commanding elements within the most prosperous, entrenched, and unscrupulous groups. Rather than liberating individuals, it reinforces the power already centralized and consolidated under private auspices."[40] This is related to and usually arises from what Schattschneider refers to as the restriction of the scope of conflict, that is, a limitation of the number and breadth of population elements involved. The smaller and narrower this becomes, the greater the opportunity for control by the most purposeful, effectively organized, and powerful elements. The weak or less conscious sectors of the population, whether great or small in numbers, maximize their strength by the extension of the scope of conflict, by in effect involving others like themselves or, in addition, calling upon possibly different elements as allies. In effect, extension of scope weakens local power monopolies. However, the limitation of scope, either functionally or geographically, to particular political units (e.g., states) in specific areas – such as urban renewal and urban affairs, poverty programs, pollution control, conservation, education – will usually find large elements of the community bereft of any significant degree of representation or influence.

Illustrative material of the point made here, though in a somewhat different direction, is provided by the distribution of power within most of the states of the nation.[41] The state level offers an even sharper instance than that provided in the federal sphere of the domination of business interests and select industries. State constitutions often sharply curtail public authority over corporations, while the legislatures have provided few benefits and protection to labor and the consumer. In many instances competitive policies and party structures are weak, and an effective rallying point and a voice for broader public concerns are lacking. Regulatory boards are staffed principally by industry representatives and often possess considerable influence. Not too surprisingly, a number of states exhibit the preponderant influence of particular economic interests. Some examples would include the role of du Pont in Delaware, oil and grazing interests in Texas, the copper industry in Colorado, lumber and pulp interests, paper manufacturers, and the hydroelectric power company in Maine, and Anaconda power and railroad interests in Montana.

Contrary of the notions of pluralist theory, the seeking of diverse interests after their own good in a presumably open political system has led to the creation of privilege, not a system of checks and balances or citizen control and access. Critics have noted that government is, in effect, fragmented by powerfully organized groups, each of which seeks hegemony within its sphere of special concern. In effect, in many instances group interests are not readily contending with each other.

Not only is there a failure for many in the community to attain effective control over both public and private decision makers, but the "competition" among distinct interests and elites may create somewhat special preserves for the privileged pursuit of gain by distinct group interests.[42] This of course represents an important thrust of our previous discussion, which partly illustrates the present point. Whereas the implication in pluralist theory is that competition will be heightened, in actuality competition is frequently lacking, and often when it does occur, it develops only among a limited spectrum of the potentially concerned and affected interests. This need not mean that corporate or other interest groups are omnipotent. They are not, but all that is required is that their basic interests, policies, and functioning are not on the whole significantly impeded or altered by other antagonistic interests.

In the conclusion of his powerful study McConnell, reflecting on the type of argument and empirical circumstances upon which the previous discussion has focused, summarizes the consequences of interest group pluralist theory and appropriately relates this question to the major theme of the present essay – the sources of conflict and threat to democratic forms.

Federalism and the interest group "pluralism" with which it is associated today are instruments of conservatism and particularism. The ideology of "grass roots democracy" and the gradual growth of power in small units by the institutional process of accommodation have probably betrayed us into yielding too much of the republic's essential values of liberty and equality. The dangers to democracy in the United States have been rarely anomic and mass movements. The real threats, often adeptly met by cooptation of group leaders, have come from narrowly constituted interest groups. Yet it is all too apparent that often the leaders of such groups have coopted the United States instead.[43]

The metaphysics of countervailing power. In many areas of policy and action, for example, corporate enterprise, agriculture, trade, and the military, contention and effective counterpower are lacking or weak. Groups that can effectively counterpose contrary or offsetting purposes and policies to such power interests are lacking. Government or the Congress, the regulatory agencies, labor, public interest lobbies, the consumer, or other businesses do not evidence any particular success as effective centers of countervailing power, and frequently they do not even attempt to function in such a capacity. The foregoing discussion has been suggestive in these regards.

There is a growing body of literature that supplements an already extensive series of studies to suggest the serious inadequacies in the notion of countervailing power as developed by pluralists such as Galbraith and Berle.[44] McConnell's conclusion is especially appropriate: " ... the unstated assumption that the thesis of a given force will create its own antithesis is no more than the wishful metaphysics of countervailing power. Many interests are not represented at all."[45] The opposition that some major centers of power and policy confront is principally located within similarly oriented economic or military interests striving for relative advantage or priority for commonly agreed-upon ends of profit or defense. This is conflict *internal* to a given institutional order. Much less potent is preponderant power or even effective constraint by *external* interests with contrary aims and programs, whether these be in the use of resources, the nature of price and subsidy policies, furtherance of consumer needs, or the restriction of armaments.

It may, of course, be contended that a countervailing force to powerfully organized interests or insulated preserves of power may exist in the person of the government. As I have begun to suggest, however, this is frequently a weak counterforce. Rather, government both in its regulatory agencies and often in its policies and perspectives reflects the bulk of organized and effectively applied power. Engler's impressive study, *The Politics of Oil*, directly confronts this contention. Toward the end of his work he notes that "the image of government as a countervailing force fails to meet the empirical test of how legislative policy is made and how government regulation actually works."[46]

In fact, an astute political student such as Lowi would appropriately point out that as long as we continue to recognize the propriety of administrative and enforcement policies that reflect a continuing contention of diverse interests and powers, then even positively intended policy espoused by publicly elected officials may be for naught in face of the exercise of preponderant power of well-organized interest groups in administrative bodies. Such power will frequently reverse the thrust of legislative action. Thus however appropriate the competition of pluralist interests may be in the formulation of policy, its execution should not again be subject to such a competition.[47]

The pluralist theorist might well have responded to the present discussion that it is not the fact or existence of representation and access by all important sectors of society at any moment in time that partly defines a politically pluralist polity but the ability of such collectivities to obtain access in an open system. Such a contention, however, would not do justice to a number of points that have been either directly or implicitly raised. One is a question of emphasis. Pluralist theory pays too little attention to the fact of the present exclusion of important groups and population segments. In fact, this exclusion is at times not even recognized. Not surprisingly, there is thus too easy a presumption that the system is open to all significant groups. Yet even if this openness was granted as a possibility within the pluralist system, if not at the present then at some later point, it would still be the case that such representation is and will be lacking for a long period of time, with the consequent absence of responsive policy and satisfaction of group needs and interests. It is in these terms, of ongoing denial relieved only by some still uncertain future prospect of equal access, that vigorous and radical dissent must be interpreted and evaluated. However, an important thrust of the present argument is that our "pluralist" polity as presently conceived does not appear likely, even over time, to provide for equitable representation and responsiveness, without some far-reaching changes.

Without planned and intensive efforts, and these are usually lacking, the functioning of a pluralist order will in practice establish areas of privilege. Attention has already been drawn to this phenomenon. Further, power is likely to beget power; and administrative procedures become the handmaiden of the most persistently organized entities in specific areas. The pluralist theoretical framework does not itself provide for an effective ongoing resolution of the problems and shortcomings posed by these difficulties. If these and the other defects noted are to be overcome, there would have to be extensive change in the functioning of a pluralist system. Hence it is much too simple – and ultimately quite misleading – for the pluralist to respond to the present critique in terms that not actual representation but the possibility of access is what defines or establishes a pluralist polity. At least it is simple and misleading if the contention is that this possibility exists within the framework of the contemporary pluralist system.

Some determinants of unequal competition and the lack of access or responsiveness. Both the absence and improbability of change toward more equitable representation, responsiveness, and countervailing power rest on a number of circumstances. A major factor is the considerable inequality exhibited by the structure of power in American society. This is most clearly perceived in economic terms. Sharp disparities in wealth exist. Forty-five percent of personal income is secured by one-fifth of the families in America, with the top 5 percent receiving nearly 20 percent of the total personal income in 1962.[48] Robert Lampman estimates that in the 1950s 1 percent of the population possessed nearly $400 billion. This thin segment of the population possessed 26 percent of personal sector equity, 75 to 80 percent of corporate stock, and virtually all state and local government bonds.[49] Even more consequential is the nature of business concentration and control. The 20 largest corporations (out of 420,000 corporations and partnerships) possess approximately one-half of total manufacturing assets and of net capital assets. Their profits after taxes in 1962 equaled 38 percent of total income after taxes secured by all manufacturing corporations.[50] And the increasing growth of conglomerates and mergers points to increasing concentration. More than ten years ago in mining and manufacturing alone annual acquisitions were almost $2.5 billion.[51] More dominant than the corporation is the concentration and control possessed by the larger banking houses. A Patman Committee survey in the mid-1960s of 49 top banks revealed that on the average they held nearly 3 directorships per corporation in more than one-half of the 500 largest industrial corporations. In addition, the top 10 banks held nearly 35 percent of all bank trust assets. Including the next 20 largest banks brought these holdings to almost 52 percent.[52]

In addition to disparities in wealth and control, other significant economic and political properties of American society and of population elements within it make at least an equal contribution to power inequalities and their continuance. Fundamental is the disparity of resources among different collectivities – such as economic resources, variation in the strategic quality of a group's role in the broader social, political, or economic system, with a consequent variation in relative bargaining power, differing ability to reward affirmative behavior and punish negative actions, and variation in the distinctive skills, expertise, and personal contacts of its members. The social standing and personal relationships of a group are significant and may be considered a group resource, as business and medical groups can attest. These are, of course, a reflection of societal values. Groups will also differ on the extent to which alliances can be achieved with other possibly influential collectivities. The possibility of such alliances reflects shared or congruent ideological and political perspectives more than relative group size or even resources. The varying effectiveness of groups also reflects differences in the degree of cohesion and consciousness, as well as leadership talents and organizational effectiveness. To an extent these reflect group circumstances, such as concentration, ease of communication and contact, availability of organizational channels, numbers involved, grounds for division and commonality, and visibility of common interests.[53] Many of these conditions vary directly with class level. They are disproportionately absent at lower class levels and mean a still additional impediment to changing or initiating public policy responsive to broader populace or social needs.

A difficulty of a different character is that pluralist theory, by basing responsiveness and representation on the resolution of competing group structures, does not provide for even a minimal equality for population sectors that lack a distinctive basis for organizational structures, communication, and shared awareness. The poor, the old, the consumer, and so on, are much less able and likely to develop organizational structures than other narrower more interest-specific collectivities. Thus these broad publics are slighted by pluralist theory.

The nature of societal values and ideology are also of considerable importance in determining the distribution of power and the responsiveness of the political system. This is particularly true in terms of the extent of correspondence between the nature and purposes of a collectivity with prevailing societal ethos, values, and goals, which among other qualities defines the priorities and the limits of legitimate public and private efforts. Business interests profit from a dominant materialist, free-enterprise, and individualistic-oriented national ideology, however inconsistent may be certain aspects of reality and governmental performance. Groups urging policy involving change of a progressive character, governmental planning, social welfare initiatives, prolabor legislation, and governmental assumption of public or community-based needs will inherently face greater impediments than those not desirous of such efforts. Competition will thus be unequal; government will be less responsive to those interests requiring an increased governmental initiative of the kind noted, especially if any extensive effort is desired. Thus, for example, the business sector stands at a distinct advantage in comparison with poverty, ethnic, and those other groups that might need forceful and progressive governmental action.

Inequality of competition and conditions of insufficient representation and responsiveness also prevail because of the nature of governmental structure and processes and the characteristics of the men who hold leadership and decision-making positions. With respect to the latter, the background, education, training, and ideological composition of the leaders and members of government are of major importance. There is a significant correspondence between important government personnel in the executive, the legislature, courts, administrative agencies, and civil service bureaucracy and the dominant interests, institutions, and class structure of the society. This circumstance has already been revealed in the earlier discussion of the regulatory agencies. The same situation holds in even more vital decision-making areas. The variety and detail of research material are great, and the reader is referred to the careful research of Barnet, William Domhoff, and Matthews, and the additional works cited there.[54] Only a few highlights can be cited here in regard to the characteristics of senior executive and administrative officials, the federal courts, and Congress.

Barnet studied the background and careers of the 400 individuals who have occupied the top foreign policy and national security positions (Assistant Secretary and higher) from 1940 to 1967 in the Departments of State, Defense, the Army, the Navy, and the Air Force, the Central Intelligence Agency, the Atomic Energy Commission, and the White House staff. Clearly, the range of concerns and policy established or influenced by so extensive and crucial a series of agencies is immense and is not confined to merely circumscribed military questions or defense industries. They affect the greatest proportion of the federal budget and the circumstances and prosperity of large sectors of the society and of special interest groups within it. Some of Barnet's findings, and those of the other scholars he cites, are impressive.

If we take a look at the men who have held the very top positions, the secretaries and under-secretaries of State and Defense, the secretaries of the three services, the chairman of the Atomic Energy Commission, and the director of the CIA, we find that out of ninety-one individuals who held these offices during the period 1940 to 1967, seventy of them came from major corporations and investment houses. This includes eight out of ten secretaries of Defense, ... three out of five directors of the CIA, and three out of five chairmen of the Atomic Energy Commission.

The historian, Gabriel Kolko, investigated 234 top foreign policy decision makers and found that "men who came from big business, investment and law held 59.6 percent of the posts." The Brookings Institution volume *Men Who Govern,* a comprehensive study of the top federal bureaucracy from 1933 to 1965, reveals that before coming to work in the Pentagon eighty-six percent of the secretaries of the Army, Navy, and the Air Force were either businessmen or lawyers (usually with a business practice). In the Kennedy Administration twenty percent of all civilian executives in defense-related agencies came from defense contractors.[55]

Domhoff's study of cabinet department heads and of the National Security Council produced similar results.[56]

Domhoff has also reviewed studies of the composition of the federal courts and of the Committee of the Federal Judiciary of the American Bar Association (which judges and advises on nominations to the federal bench). He concludes "that federal judges come from the higher levels of society, have an elite education, and are politically and professionally acceptable to lawyers and politicians who are members of the power elite."[57]

.The findings in regard to congressmen are perhaps less surprising, though equally revealing. That the great majority of the members of the House and the Senate come from the more substantial strata of American society is readily supported by Matthews' study of the Senate membership from 1947 to 1957. Not surprisingly, occupational background differs sharply from that of the overall population. Nearly two-thirds are professionals, the great majority lawyers, 29 percent proprietors or managers, and 7 percent farmers.[58] The properties of the House of Representatives are basically the same.[59] What is perhaps of greater relevance, however, is that congressmen come from families whose backgrounds and circumstances diverge sharply from those of the broader society. Thus 90 percent of the fathers of senators were either professionals, businessmen, managers, or farmers in roughly equal proportions. Only one out of ten was either a wage laborer, a lower-white-collar worker, or a farm laborer, though these categories represented more than one-half of the American labor force at the time.[60] One has here not merely some distinctive personal experience or set of self-made men but the long-term molding of distinct attitudes and a sense of successful and stable class membership. The generally tempered and conservative attitudes this suggests are reinforced by other personal characteristics. The average senator is in his mid-fifties. Senators come disproportionately from small towns. Of the 13 percent who are second-generation immigrants, three quarters come from northwestern Europe as compared with 28 percent of second generation Americans.[61] While considerable ideological and policy differences may be exhibited by individuals of similar personal properties and experience, on the whole certain distinct predispositions are probably created by the background properties of senators. Thus one would expect a receptivity to business interests and a reluctance to support extensive social legislation or constraints on individual or corporate behavior. Congressional figures are also more likely to perceive business, agricultural, and military interests, rather than labor, consumer, conservation, and other such concerns, as beneficial to their states and districts.

Clearly, the circumstances sketched here strongly favor certain groups, policies, and alternatives, while mitigating against others. Industrial, financial, large-scale agricultural, and military groups are at a distinct advantage. Conversely, governmental social initiative, planning, and constraints for public ends, encouragement for new social and cultural forms, progressive social policy, and significant reordering of national priorities achieve only scant attention of resources.

The general characteristics of senators appear greatly magnified when those of Senate and House committee chairmen are examined. These exceedingly influential figures are predominantly old – most are over 65, rural, Southern, and midwestern conservatives. Two-thirds have been in Congress since before 1946. All are men, white; more than 80 percent are Protestants, and most are lawyers. They come principally from safe electoral districts or states with one-party domination. In fact 8 of the 21 House chairmen in the Ninety-first Congress ran either unopposed or practically so in the most recent election. Twenty-five percent of Senate chairmen ran unopposed in their states.[62] Green and his colleagues estimate that 88 percent of House committee chairmen from 1950 to 1970 came from virtually one-party districts.[63] Jewell and Patterson point out that "one-party states, and to a greater degree, one-party districts are likely to be conservative, insulated from the liberal trends at the polls and immune to pressures from a President who owes his election . . . primarily to the voters in large metropolitan areas."[64] Even more than the rest of the Congress these men reflect and are unusually responsive to conservative, status quo, business-oriented, and anti-social-welfare philosophy and policy.

These comments on congressional committee chairmen serve to introduce another major factor that increases the unresponsive and unrepresentative nature of the political system and works to favor conservative interests. I refer to the structural and procedural characteristics of the American political system. The role of congressional committees is of paramount importance.[65] These very significantly shape all legislation. Without committee action and approval a bill is doomed. As vital as are the committees, however, the role granted their chairmen is at least as crucial.

The chairman of each committee decides when, and if, the committee shall meet, sets the agenda, and controls all hearings and executive sessions. From the perhaps hundreds of bills submitted to his committee each year, he chooses which, if any, will be considered by the full committee. He can shape the list of witnesses at public hearings, control the detailed drafting of the legislation in executive sessions, manage the bill when it is debated on the floor of the House, and represent the House in any later negotiations with the Senate over differences in bills passed by the two houses. In all of these activities, of course, his personal preferences regarding the form and desirability of the legislation play a crucial role.[66]

The importance of these committees and their chairmen lends great significance to the Congress' reliance on the practice of seniority. The absolute dominance of seniority since World War II as the basis of attaining committee chairmenship has thrust the oldest and most conservative elements of the legislature into the centers of immense power. Other properties that have qualified the responsiveness and adequacy of congressional functioning are committee secrecy, including that of House and Senate conference committees, the filibuster, and the absence of adequate congressional means of evaluating defense budgets.[67]

As a general rule, quite apart from congressional characteristics, it is much easier to stand pat in policy, or to retard action and change than to initiate it, especially given the American system of checks and balances, the dispersion of authority among different regions and levels of government, and the elaborate procedures involved in legislative enactment, administrative action, and judicial review. Another obstacle to change already noted is the continuance of a pluralist framework from the legislative to the administrative area in the application of those decisions that have been established.

A different set of conditions than that comprehended by the preceding, yet also influencing access and responsiveness, is the particular organizational properties of interest groups and collectivities and the dynamics of processes of influence in which groups seeking access may be implicated. One major point is that there is a diverse array of factors internal to a collectivity; they "discourage solidarity and initial political organization."[58] This, of course, affects group access to decision makers and consequently political responsiveness. Gamson lists many of these. They

include (1) lack of access to information about the effects of political decisions; (2) lack of politically experienced and skilled leadership; (3) the "culture of subordination," including self-blame ideologies which locate sources of dissatisfaction in the individual's shortcomings or in irremediable states of nature and society rather than in politically remediable features of the social system; (4) low rates of interaction and organizational participation which might encourage the development of solidarity; (5) lack of financial resources; (6) pursuit of personal rather than group interest; (7) lack of personal trust toward each other among members of the solidary groups; and (8) "opiates" which divert energies from political paths.[69]

Another related factor, unmentioned in this listing, is an ideological awareness of the nature of group interests. This includes not only a consciousness of group interest but also knowledge of the character of competing interests and where and who in the political system opposes as well as reflects group or collectivity interests. Gamson also considers a number of actions to which established leaders and dominant groups may resort in order to limit access. These include "attempts to undermine the legitimacy of their interest groups by discrediting them; harassment of leaders;" cooptation of leaders; "appeals to the constituency of unrepresented groups 'over the head' of its leaders ... and incrementalism. ..."[70] Recent research, especially in the area of community and poverty issues and populations, has illustrated the role of such factors and actions, among others, in determining access and reponsiveness.[71] What is important is that the conditions enumerated here are not randomly distributed among population groups. They are found disproportionately among less advantaged, less politically involved, and newly emerging political groups.

While the factors considered in the preceding discussion point toward an explanation for the inadequacies in representation and responsiveness, there is little effort by pluralist theorists to determine their consequences for pluralist theory and to adjust that theory to these empirical realities. Analysis of one or more of these conditions discussed by scholars of a pluralist and an interest group persuasion is generally isolated from any kind of comprehensive assessment of the theoretical and empirical adequacy of pluralism.

An aside on structures of power. It will be clear to the reader, especially as he progresses further through this chapter, that I have no explicit treatment of a "power elite" or "ruling class." To affirm the existence of either of these vigorously debated propositions would clearly compromise pluralist propositions. Though I am not concerned with so simple (though some would say erroneous and most would agree difficult) an approach, I am sympathetic to power elite and ruling class notions.[72] One may grant for the sake of discussion, however, the questionable supposition that elites are fragmentary and not unitary[73] and still leave unimpaired the argument developed here – that is, that unrepresentative concentrations of power do exist; decisions are partisan yet significantly affect a broad sector of the community; a few will greatly influence, with little effective opposition, broad policy areas; policy will reveal distinctive ideological and interest biases; and so on. These do not logically require a power elite or ruling class but only privileged areas of public or private access or control and effectively applied power in specific areas. The broad array of such circumstances in significant areas of political and economic life of the country produces, in effect, conditions of unrepresentative and unresponsive decision making reflecting narrowed ideological and interest concerns.

The role of parties. The existence of political parties mitigates somewhat the conditions described. Parties do not merely aggregate the interests of several groups but also seek to present themselves as representatives of a broad consensus of various population elements, ostensibly, irrespective of the degree or nature of organization among such elements. Thus programs and policies could theoretically be developed and espoused as responsive to either public needs or the interests of collectivities lacking organization commensurate with their numbers or extent of need. To some degree this does occur. But even the few omissions and commissions of public policy that have been noted indicate how limited representation and responsiveness have in fact turned out to be for important segments of the society and in regard to diverse public and group needs. This is not surprising, because in spite of the claims of commitment to the broader good and to principled politics, parties, like government, are most responsive to organized entities. However, it is their need for the vote of individuals (and sometimes also the effect of ideological-based reformist movements within the parties) that does on occasion make political parties partial spokesmen for unorganized and otherwise unrepresented populations. In a different vein, in some instances political parties, especially third parties, may be viewed as the organized form of some distinctive segment of the population and in effect function as one among several contending organized interests within a pluralist framework.

This very third-party phenomenon, nevertheless, serves as a reminder of the severe shortcomings of political parties as aggregating agents, especially of poorly organized and generally ignored interests. In practice, parties become spokesmen for distinct groups and interests and reflect a particular political and cultural ethos that mitigates against an attempt at a wider appeal, attractive though this may appear. In these terms parties may for an extended period of time become congealed into distinctive molds, such as the long-term Republican reflection of and appeal to industrial urban capitalist interests and the Democratic appeal for almost four decades, from 1896 to 1932, to rural agrarian and individualistic perspectives. Thus at a time of vigorous industrial expansion and a growing proletariat, with its attendant strains, the working class was bereft of representation in government and witnessed few appeals on its behalf or directed to it by the major existing parties. In fact, the major political realignment of the 1930s and the critical election of 1932 reflect this circumstance. To an important extent the lack of responsiveness is also reflected by those other critical and realigning elections and political transformations that have marked American history.[74]

Inadequacy of control over and within the private sector

The present analysis need not be limited merely to decision making in the public political arena. Many of the issues raised find expression in the functioning and decision making of private bodies in the ostensibly nonpublic sector. In many ways the policies and activities of large and powerful economic corporate bodies, little checked by public involvement or access, significantly affect broad sectors of the community. They have great influence on the economy generally, on public tastes, on the continued viability of many communities, and, more broadly, even on what could be called the texture of individual life. Just the ten largest American corporations had expenditures in 1968 of $84 billion and assets nearly as great. Their employees numbered more than 2.6 million.[75] In many ways the consequences of either particular actions or the failure to act, as the case may be, by large private corporate entities are no less potent or influential in determining individual circumstances than action by public bodies and officials in the public arena.

Peter Bachrach has remarked that

> it is not an exaggeration to say ... that the large corporation performs a governmental function by sharing with governmental institutions in "authoritatively allocating values for society...." To argue that the giant corporation is not public because it is not officially designated as such is to place an undue reliance on form at the expense of function.[76]

In actual practice these "private" entities in many respects resemble "public" bodies, certainly in terms of the consequences of their behavior and decisions on broad sectors of the society, their considerable political power, their intimate relationship to and use of many members and agencies of government, particularly the regulatory and administrative agencies of state and federal governments, their crucial role in many social and economic areas of individual, group, and societal behavior, their effect on social change, and so on. A life-long student of corporate structure and functioning and its place in society, Adolf B. Berle, Jr., states that the corporation has "*de facto*, at least, invaded the political sphere and has become in fact, if not in theory a quasi-governing agency."[77] Such private power has at times a potency equivalent and as far ranging as public power. Access to private centers of power is markedly less effective than access to power in the public sphere. A weakness in pluralist theory and of American political life is the lack of a redefinition of public power so that some features of private corporate bodies and not only public agencies may be understood as possessed of a public component and, therefore, accountable in a fashion similar to that presumably prevailing for public power.

The difficulty with the pluralist perspective lies perhaps less in the insufficient attention given to private corporate power than in the theoretical framework developed by the pluralists. The latter does not provide a ready means of considering the activities and consequences of such private concentrations of power. It is this that may underlie the inadequate recognition of the public character of private structures and their lack of accountability to a broader public. The failure to redefine private bodies as exercising political power – power equivalent in many ways to public power – has meant that the mass society and pluralist theorist is unable to comprehend within the usual framework of democratic forms and procedures activist protests against "private" corporate bodies. Pluralist theory, and mass theory more broadly, does not incorporate the exercise of significant private power into its theory of representation, interest representation, and responsiveness.[78] The problem of accountability is not only unresolved, it is hardly recognized.

Even further, as Andrew Hacker has observed, in the case of the private corporation one is dealing with an entity that does not even represent any distinct group. There is no collectivity or body of interest represented except the corporation itself, in contrast to the usual referent in interest group theory to the pluralist competition of interests reflecting organized groups or collectivities, not separate individuals, incorporated or otherwise. Drawing on Arthur Miller's discussion, Hacker thus observes "that neither our constitutional law nor our political theory are able to account for the corporate presence in the arena of social power."[79] Further, private corporate power cannot be perceived as counterbalanced in terms of the usual pluralist dogma. Those nonpublic groups or organizations that ordinarily exist to counter the private exercise of power are, as already noted, directly implicated in the economic sphere within which such power is active. Hence such groups respond in terms of the economic market, and these are generally irrelevant to the social, economic, and cultural consequences for the broader community of private corporate decisions and functioning. Public control, while potentially vastly more effective, is usually quite limited, unconcerned, or reflective of the very corporate interests involved.

A perspective somewhat similar to that being applied to private corporate structures can also be utilized in understanding the functioning of many private associations in the areas of health, law, education, and so on. In a diversity of areas state governments have often given over to private organized interest associations public authority and functions of control, regulation, and evaluation. Certainly here the distinction between public and private power disappears to a significant degree. Yet to an important extent such private associations are autonomous, and public control is slight at best.[80] Even from the pluralist perspective that perceives government as either a mediator among diverse interests or as constituting the arena within which they contend for power, greater attention should be given to private intrusion into public spheres. Such intrusion undermines the ability of government to function equitably as a conciliator or arbiter: ". . . the very idea of constitutionalism seems to be placed in question."[81]

The broad framework within which the preceding observations rest is, again, the problem of representation and responsiveness within the political community and its relationship to the nature of organizational structure and process. Thus while nonelectoral public and private structures play an important role in decision making and policy determination, they are quite deficient in elemental democratic principles of representation, responsiveness and equity. This poses two issues: (1) the equity or appropriateness of the considerable role such organizations exercise in the development of political and administrative policy and (2) the question of internal governance. Commenting on the findings of Rokkan[82] and Finer,[83] while developing his own critical assessment of pluralist theory, Paul Conn has related the latter to the former issue.

> This problem arises because of the stress in social pluralism on providing informal arrangements for facilitating entrance into the decision making process. As a result ... many of the important decisions are not made in the formal political arena but rather as a result of the interaction of representatives of various groups and government officials. It therefore becomes increasingly important to question the degree to which such organizations are (in their) decision making processes representative or accurately reflect the demands of their clientele.
>   ... Unfortunately, the entire relationship between social pluralism and representation has not been adequately explored.[84]

Thus a realistic analysis must recognize that a discrepancy exists between democratic representation and the actual functioning of pluralistic structures.[85]

There is little need to consider the problem of maintaining a sense of control and meaningful involvement within private structures by their memberships. This is an increasingly frequently voiced and well-recognized phenomenon. It has in recent years been expressed in the heightened unrest within institutions of higher education, where students, and sometimes faculty, have contended with college or university administrations and boards of trustees for increased voice in influencing decisions.[86] In a different institutional area some efforts at change in industrial structures have been exhibited in Europe in the movement for workers' councils. This has been an effort to secure some form of participation and influence in the management of the enterprise within which they work, particularly in those aspects that most intimately affect them.[87] Various writers have stressed that the importance of participation in decisions affecting the character of the individual's environment resides not merely in the ability to influence the character of events in which one is implicated but, equally significantly, in the possibility of establishing a sense of commitment, a condition for the growth of self-esteem, and the development of individual wisdom, capacities, and self. Such possibilities are lacking where those implicated in a private corporate entity are excluded from an involvement in its decision-making processes, especially where these affect the quality of individual experience within that organization. Even in regard to voluntary interest associations, however, somewhat similar circumstances of estrangement and lack of control are frequently manifest. In fact, as Mills has observed, as interest associations become more effective, they grow increasingly inaccessible.[88]

Structures of power, pluralism, and research strategies

[C]an a sound concept of power be predicted on the assumption that power is totally embodied and fully reflected in "concrete decisions" or in activity bearing directly upon their making?

We think not. Of course power is exercised when A participates in the making of decisions that affect B. But power is also exercised when A devotes his energies to creating or reinforcing social and political values and institutional practices that limit the scope of the political process to public consideration of only those issues which are comparatively innocuous to A. To the extent that A succeeds in doing this, B is prevented, for all practical purposes, from bringing to the fore any issues that might in their resolution be seriously detrimental to A's set of preferences.[89]

Pluralist formulations find a frequent reiteration in decision-making-based studies of community and national power structures. Yet their conclusions concerning the dispersion of leadership and the limitations and weakness of power among the economic, industrial, and socially prestigious have serious inadequacies.[90] Pluralism stresses a descriptive approach to power structure and political process. It is based on a study of more or less observable events and issues. Its weakness rests on the absence of a theoretical framework concerning the nature and sources of power and the determinants of policy, except to the extent that its propositions that issue conflict reveals power structures be conceived as its theoretical scheme. Most simply, it lacks a theory of power.

Its approach arises partly from the pragmatic and behavioralist origins of interest group theory. From this perspective the process of government is studied in terms of concretely observable and measureable phenomena and wholly as group process, that is, organized group interests, and contention is understood as a complete account of the nature of political issues and decisions and more broadly of the character of the political process itself.[91] In other words, there is an avoidance of adequate attention to either social structural or political and cultural factors determining or constraining issues, decisions, and policies. An effort to develop an overall theory of political power would have necessitated taking account of such factors. My earlier discussion on some of the determinations of differential influence and power began to introduce some of the kind of elements envisioned here. Others will be enumerated shortly. These shape the nature of issues and policies and, more broadly, the differential responsiveness of the political system and the varying gains and losses that flow from it. Lastly, the absence of a theory of power in studies of pluralist community power structure is also exhibited by the failure to examine power, decision making, and policy on the local community level in terms of the broader societal structure of power and decision making. These are crucial in the contemporary vertically integrated and highly interdependent society.

The consequence of the pluralist focus on only those issues that become manifest has meant a disregard of the potential range of difference, policy, and issues within the political system. As options for choice, consideration, or contention, any given political system exhibits only some of the issues, problems, and public discussion that are of crucial concern to the community. In effect, there is a decision making that exists through either the absence of action or the lack of issue confrontation or by the uncontested decision. The selectivity – in effect, partiality – exhibited by the issues that are apparent reflects a number of factors. Decision making arises from the influence of ideology, institutional structures and processes, historical patterns, the distribution of power, the ethos of citizen involvement, the individual's sense of efficacy, and the character of public awareness, among other circumstances. All may be understood as contributing either to the recognition and expression of certain questions or, on the other hand, to the failure of certain issues to appear on the political decision-making map. Hence the nature of the exercise and structure of power and the character of decision making in the community are a consequence of much more than merely who is involved, on what issues and with what effect, or of what individuals or elites hold what and how much power as revealed by their actions or reputations.

The type of factors noted determines the character of prevailing consensus and of notions of the desirable and the possible, as well as the nature of elite structures and their functioning. These conditions also set the boundaries within which decisions will be made or, in other words, the scope of objects over which power may be exercised. These are the conditions that will significantly affect the kinds of issues that may develop, the range of permissible action, and the options for action that become manifest. It is in terms of an analysis of such factors, rather than a mere focusing on the individual actor or decision-making-centered analysis, though these are not to be excluded, that a derivation of "structures" of power and conditions of equity can best be determined.

In an important sense what is being urged is an analysis of the elements determinant of the sources of power. This would not be accomplished merely by a study of the exercise of power, unless attempted in much broader and profounder terms than is usually done. Thus, for example, the influence of cultural or value properties – the character of free-enterprise ideology, homage to businessmen and business pursuits, the Lockean liberal tradition, a consensual theory of American experience, and the like – may combine with the relative absence of power among the disadvantaged and with the almost total inattention to any radical, Socialist, or other similar ideological perspective. These would exclude or strongly qualify the appearance in the political decision-making arena of a wide range of issues as well as alternative policies and programs.[92]

Mannheim's notion of "reality level" expresses a part of what is present in the suggestion that power reflects a complex of nonstructural elements.

> By "reality level" we mean that every society develops a mental climate in which certain facts and their interrelations are considered basic and called "real" whereas other ideas fall below the level of "reasonably acceptable" statements and are called fantastic, utopian, or unrealistic. In every society there is a generally acceptable interpretation of reality.[93]

Significant to our concerns is Mannheim's additional point that a reality level is partly shaped by the political elite. Edelman has forcefully noted that "unless an appropriate political setting has been created, legitimizing a set of values and a mode of access, a group interest cannot be expressed in policy no matter how strong or widespread it may be."[94] And this "appropriate political setting" is greatly dependent upon the ideological tenor of society, though, as Edelman points out, various events may alter this tenor and admit of issue confrontations and policies that may formerly have been beyond serious or effective consideration. The authoritative conclusion is clear: Political contention does not occur in a completely open marketplace where any group can press any demand or issue and seek whatever action appears reasonable.

A fruitful area of research would be the attempt to develop a typology of types of value or ideological orientations that categorizes different communities and broader social systems, such as the nation, in terms of the particular options for discussion and policy that are encouraged, hindered, or excluded. Any detailed treatment would involve a specification of the variation introduced in acceptability or opposition to certain ideas and policies as there is an alteration of the probable range of community involvement that is implicated in any given idea or prospective policy, as the circumstances of its introduction or of the community are altered, and as the parties associated with any given idea are varied.

Some work has been done in a related area. Efforts have been made to assess the differential effect on community decision making, community power structure, styles of local government, and community conflict arising from variations in socioeconomic and labor force characteristics, ethnicity, stability and the size of population, homogeneity, community integration and strife, and the degree of "political crystallization."[95] Of course, what the causal relationships and dependent and independent variables are is variously treated, particularly as the relationship of interest to different researchers changes. Also, to a considerable degree this work refers essentially to social and political structural and processional differences among communities and not to the consequences of value or political cultural variation, though clearly there is an overlap. An overlap is present in studies such as that of Williams and Adrian; yet even here the question of values is constricted to a typology of roles envisioned as proper for local government.[96] While there is also a growing and extensive body of literature incorporating in one or more respects the concept of political culture in the study of national political systems, it has not as yet been developed and applied to any significant extent to the interpretation of power and decision making in American society.

I have suggested that the distribution of power will not be depicted accurately through exclusive reliance on pluralist theory. A focus limited to the character of issue confrontation, the character of the actors involved, and other decision-making features is insufficient, even misleading. The location and scope of power are not properly revealed by the apparent effectiveness or ineffectiveness of particular actors or groups on those issues that may become manifest. A given sector or group in society, it can be maintained, could realistically be regarded as powerless where the political arena lacks issues or policies addressed to or commensurate with its needs or problems. Or, as the case may be, a group could be regarded as powerful even where no participation or controversy is apparent, when policies or issues never appear that go beyond what is acceptable to the group in question. In such situations examination of issues would reveal neither the presence of contrary power nor relative disparities in power (given the absence of issues of A vis-à-vis B). Yet the preceding discussion contends that this kind of an examination is the usual strategy and that consequent distortions would not be readily perceived from the perspective of the pluralist or interest group theorist. Pluralist analysis, in effect, "concentrates on the 'intermediate sectors,' e.g., parties, interest groups, formal structures, without attempting to view the underlying system of 'renewable power' independent of any monetary group of actors."[97] Clearly, the preceding suggests that it is misleading to conceptualize power in individual terms. Power partly reflects a position in both a social structure and a system of values, not properties of the individual.[98]

Failure to attend to the institutional and value determinants and constraints on decision making is usually to sketch a "spurious pluralism"[99] and an "illusory decentralization."[100] McFarland and Felser note that pluralism may be found in almost any system – whether it be the Russian industrial administration, the Russian state, the Communist party, or the U.S. Forest Service – if one relies on merely a determination of the existence of diversity, contention, interdependence, disparate interest groups, and fragmented causation for a confirmation of pluralism.[101] As McFarland notes in regard to a specific case analysis with which he deals,

The reader may be startled to note that Soviet industrial administration exhibits incrementalism and bargaining over margins, processes described by Charles Lindblom in American pluralist contexts. Such decentralized bargaining over marginal changes in policy has been observed in American politics by Charles Lindblom, Aaron Wildavsky, Richard Fenno, and Roger Hilsman, and apparently seems to many to be a distinguishing characteristic of pluralist politics.[102]

In sum, in terms of Schattschneider's discussion of the "mobilization of bias,"[103] Bachrach and Baratz' conception of the "two-faces of power" and "key" and "routine" decisions,[104] and their discussion of "nondecision-making,"[105] it can reasonably be maintained that significant power and issues are to an important degree encapsulated within institutional settings and may never reach the arena of overt decision making. The analyses reviewed here suggest that the structure and distribution of power cannot be adequately perceived by relying on an examination of issue participants. The present criticism, of course, applies not only to the local level but is equally applicable to the analysis of power structure and decision making on the national level. Thus the present discussion has a significant bearing on the earlier treatment of representation, responsiveness, and power inequalities. It argues that the elements noted will bend policy and power toward some groups and interests, and away from others. Most directly, in regard to the most immediate purposes of this discussion, studies of community power structure as pursued by the issue or pluralist approach, as well as the reputational techniques, cannot be used as evidence for pluralist forms, except in a significantly qualified fashion.

A closing summary observation may be appropriate. In an important sense the line of reasoning that has been developed does not require the specification of any existent power elite and its exercise of dominant control. This is not to deny the important role of elite elements but merely to focus on the role of other conditions usually ignored, inattention to which prevents an accurate delineation of power structures. Of course, any structure of elite rule or ruling class dominance that may exist will serve to further extend the power inequities implicated in those ideological and cultural constraints that accord with the political bias of the elite elements.

Availability of choice

Where alternative choices are significantly qualified, pluralism itself becomes seriously compromised. The preceding discussion has indirectly suggested deficiencies in the availability of choice. Inadequacies other than those already suggested are several:

1. For choice to be meaningful there must be considerable correspondence between the intention behind the choice – that is, the expectation concerning the policies and behavior of the political leadership chosen – and the actual performance of leaders selected. At times this is lacking. An example of such disparity is offered by Lyndon Johnson's conduct in regard to the Vietnamese War after the election of 1964, in comparison with the stance assumed during his electoral campaign with Barry Goldwater.

2. Existing issues and candidates do not exhaust the significant alternatives that reside in the political and social community. Rather than the American two-party system having served to stimulate effectively a variety of policy options, the attempt of the parties to appeal to the greatest number, capture the uncommitted voter, maintain existing loyalties, secure personal advantage, and maintain control over privilege and office rather than advance particular action

programs has, to use a phrase of Michael Parenti, "generated competition for orthodoxy on most important questions."[106] At a more basic level, of course, the orthodoxy of American politics resides in a number of material, historical, social, and cultural properties of the society.

The lack of range of significant choices is exhibited in both the national and local political arenas, particularly the latter, in regard to parties, candidates, policy alternatives, discussions of issues, and the character of political analysis and news coverage to which the very great majority of the society are exposed. Nationally, on issues of war and peace, foreign diplomacy and relations with other nation-states, disarmament negotiation, utilization of federal powers on questions of economy and civil justice, the degree of governmental control and regulation over the economy, and the character of programs in the area of poverty and economic transformation, only limited options are presented. The range of policies and serious proposals has on many occassions extended from no action to minimal action, no funds to meager financing, no controls to a few ineffective regulations, no disarmament to meager disarmament, heavy interference into the affairs of other nation-states to moderately heavy interference, no rapprochement with Communist states to mild rapprochement, and so on. Pilisuk and Hayden have made a similar point in their hypothesis "that certain 'core beliefs' are continuously unquestioned ... efficacy is preferable to principle in foreign affairs ... private property is preferable to collective property.... Preferred [is] ... limited parliamentary democracy,... with fundamental limitations placed upon the prerogatives of governing."[107] One has but to compare the broad range of governmental initiative, governmental regulations and control, diversity of economic policies, the nature of social welfare schemes, the character of governmental budgetary distributions and allotments, and commitments to social well-being exhibited among many foreign states, Western and Communist, to discover the paucity of alternatives and ideological differences within the United States and hence of the choices available. The narrow range of foreign policy options offered for many years by the major dominant political groups has been one of the gravest failures of the American political system. There is a great deal of apparent competition in ongoing political controversy and contention, a multitude of newspaper and mass media communication, and great heat and energy shed in a specious contest for support. The significance of this is slight, however, as far as the existence of meaningfully different alternatives is concerned.[108]

3. Not only is the range of meaningful choice quite limited, however, but the opportunity to choose even within this very narrow range is lacking for a large portion of the citizenry in American society. Thus in many communities and areas of the society only the candidates of one party stand any chance of being elected. Extreme illustrations of this circumstance are the approximately three score congressional districts in 1970 where the election was not even contested by one of the major parties. In an even larger number of districts the opposition was quite perfunctory.

4. The availability of choice is also limited by the organizational weakness of large sectors of society. Organizational forms are crucial to the ability to give expression to distinctive points of view and programs. Organization helps develop perspective, ideology, candidates, and political objectives and programs. The lack of potent organization among a large proportion of the population and in regard to a number of areas of considerable importance thus contributes to the paucity of choice.

Some comments on the nature and functions of political representation

The concept and the theory of representation are a fundamental concern for any theory on the nature of the polity. While the literature[109] and issues involved are extensive, present attention must perforce be quite limited. Particularly significant to our interest in political volatility and protest is the relationship these bear to the scope of political representation.

The degree of political representation and acceptance achieved by groups within existing governmental, party, and organizational structures influences the character of political behavior. It is reasonable to suggest, on the basis of broad historical evidence, that the degree of political divisiveness associated with the objectives and activities of socioeconomic groups in society varies approximately inversely with the degree of political representation achieved by the group in question. With political representation, and the interest satisfaction and political socialization it usually involves, there is an increased likelihood of the development of a sense of commitment and involvement in the political life of society, though other factors are of course also quite influential in this regard. In contrast, its absence has been productive of estrangement from dominant political forms.[110] The importance of political representation may be exemplified by examining political behavior. Thus, for instance, working-class political behavior has reflected the extent to which the dominant powers or ruling class of a society recognized the legitimacy of protest and was willing to effect a compromise with the working class, and hence permitted the initiation of policy reflective of working-class interests.

Where some flexibility or compromise was possible with the dominant political and class power, and there existed a sense of at least a moderate ability to influence political and labor-related decisions, the working class assumed a fairly moderate position. This appears to have been the case in England and the Scandinavian countries. Where, on the other hand, the dominant ruling groups continued to be intransigent and, in effect, provided no political representation within the decision-making centers of the society, as in Germany, Italy, France, Spain, and Chile, the working class continued to maintain vigorous opposition and even revolutionary movements.

Where inadequacies in political representation for a major collectivity include the absence of a political party at least moderately reflective of its group interests, the likelihood is heightened that, in addition to probable acrimonious behavior, a new and separate political party will arise to reflect such a population and its interests. To an important extent, for instance, the appearance of the British Labor party at the end of the nineteenth century was due to the unwillingness of existing parties to respond to working-class concerns.[111] The appearance of the Social Democrats as a working-class party in Germany in the late 1800s reflected a similar situation.[112] The same holds for the Chilean Communist party in the present century. Parties that develop under such circumstances are likely to be estranged and isolated from other political actors. Class consciousness is likely to be heightened, and conflict will probably be more embittered. Conflict and issue differences are likely to be of a broad class scope. That these may, however, be mitigated by the character of political and ruling class responsiveness, the properties of the prevailing political culture, and the variation in the depth of class division, among other conditions, is suggested by the British case.

Inadequacies of pluralist model for public needs

By its very nature the pluralist model of the political system cannot provide an adequate means of redress and action in regard to society-wide problems and interests. This is so even if one were to assume the presence of what is in fact lacking – that the large majority of the society were implicated in organizational structures concerned with

such problems and, moreover, that such organizations were in fact responsive to their memberships. Kariel has stated that even among some
of the earlier pluralists it appeared necessary:

> to introduce what they had previously banished; a unified purpose above
> and beyond the will of a plurality of groups. . . . Thus both Laski and Cole
> were finally driven to recognize needs more fundamental than a vibrant
> group life. They were to argue for both leadership to give expression to
> these needs and a state equipped to satisfy them. Thus, under the pres-
> sures of modern group life and revolutionary technological and economical
> developments, pluralists' theory began to grow irrelevant.[113]

Nor can there be any assurance that a pluralist competition among
diverse interest groups will have positive results and further either
the well-being and stability of the society or its constituent population
elements. Certainly the results of generally unfettered competition of
groups in the American polity have been seriously deficient in these
regards. This could occur, however, even for a perfectly representative
pluralist structure.

The weight of books like McConnell's *Private Power and American
Democracy* and Lowi's *The End of Liberalism* is to suggest that an
inherent impediment to the social adequacy of pluralist interest group
theory is its failure to recognize the existence of non-group-derived
public interests. In attending only to the claims of organized interests
(e.g., industrial, agricultural, trade union, realty, shipping, etc.), it
gives meager attention to concerns that are not located in the traditional ongoing institutional spheres (e.g., environmental or quality-of-
life concerns – conservation, pollution, or urban preservation, consumer
issues, the problems of the aged, intergroup relations, etc.). The
organized group structures here are usually weak and episodic,
reflecting the extremely broad and poorly organized nature of the
relevant population. In addition, an analysis such as that given in
Lowi's volume extends the critique of pluralist interest group theory
further by exploring the undermining of the formal authoritative
character of law and the consequent aborting of even those public
interest policies that do take shape in the American "pluralist" polity.
Also, in locating the existence of interests in terms of conscious
awareness by distinct groups, the pluralist theorist not only limits
the concept of interest to groups but excludes unrecognized needs,
either of an individual, a group, or a societal nature.[114]

The pluralist interest group perspective principally suggests a polity of amoral, normless, and valueless content, unredeemed in most instances by any worthier aim than the distinctive purposes of competing group interests.[115] The theoretical formulation of the nature and functioning of the polity sharply minimizes, in effect, the recognition of any public interest beyond that established by interest group competition.[116] The role of the state becomes essentially, though not exclusively, one of mediation and the maintenance of the conditions essential for group competition. It is also a vehicle for the attainment of particular group purposes when these are sought through the activities of the public rather than the private sector. However, the statement of any distinct end or purpose of government is sharply minimized. Government may at times be viewed as establishing "normative goals, as custodian of the consensus."[117] Yet when based on little more than a calculus of the purposes of contending interest groups, societal or public purposes are derived from the terms set by those distinctive group structures that are most potent. Where groups are not present or are poorly organized or do not give expression to particular goals, these cannot usually find expression as public interests. Nor can needs or interests be defined as of a public character, other than quite weakly, when public and private purposes are perceived as predominantly and appropriately established in the light of existing interest group structure. As Lowi has pointed out, pluralism denied the separate functioning of government in what was viewed as an "autonomic political society," with government "nothing but an extension of the 'political process.'"[118]

Yet if one denies or sharply restricts the concept of public needs or interests, then a pluralist system will advance private ends, and usually at the expense of certain fundamental concerns of a broader community character. In effect, to assume that a competitive pluralist system works for the best and to avoid the question of government commitment to public ends or purposes is to leave the door open for the achievement of only selfish ends. The system provides insufficient means for the intrusion of other purposes. Thus an untrammeled pursuit of individual gain characterizes both the theory and the practice of pluralism. I have already suggested that in a society in which many are poorly organized, sharp inequities and grossly inadequate attention to those needs that do not lend themselves to effective organization result. Further, as McConnell has pointed out, the denial of the existence of public ends or interests has also meant the absence of clear standards or criteria to be applied by regulatory and administrative agencies. This lack of an appropriate public philosophy in terms of which to guide the exercise of governmental authority means that once public involvement has declined, such administrative agencies have become "vulnerable to the claims and charges of those very interests they had been established to regulate."[119]

Public policy comes to assume a form reflective of those interest group organizations that exist. The more viable of these are frequently narrow-based constituencies. Regardless of their breadth, however, they predominantly manifest a distinctive type of interest – the "hard," material and economic values of price, trade regulation, tax rate, and scope and nature of regulatory requirements.[120]

Both public interest and particular group interests that such interest-group-based public policy represents have a couple of especially distinctive properties. Public interest can be located in some form of group consciousness or awareness. Needs or problems lacking this quality, however serious their character, usually do not come under the purview of the notions of public interest in pluralist interest group theory. Secondly, public interests and more specific group interests are very predominantly those concerns that can find expression in some institutional or structurally defined collectivity united by a mutually recognized common concern distinguishing it from the rest of the population. Excluded are non-group-based concerns, or what may be thought of as community needs that cannot be located in terms of a social collectivity distinctly defined by institutional structures. In sum, unrestrained interest group pluralism perceives only groups as real, interests as existing only where there is group contention. There is very little in the way of a public or inclusive interest.

The foregoing has in a number of ways begun to point to a fundamental reason for the inadequacies of interest group structures, even if conditions now lacking were to exist. Usually, the most effective and prestigious of such interest group structures are discrete interest organizations whose attention is not directed to society-wide issues or problems. They are ill suited, therefore, to focus on fundamental economic, urban, racial, and environmental problems. These are broad society-wide problems. They are public interests not within the province or concern of merely any one group or within the ability of any one limited sphere to cope with adequately. Some of the most highly esteemed values of American society, for instance, civil and political liberties and rights, do not reside solely or even principally within any narrow constituency, no matter how defined, even though the existence of some groups may be principally predicated on an interest in such concerns. The whole of society is their constituency and that of other public interests, and the resolution of inadequacies in any one of these problem or value areas requires a program that touches on many important groups and aspects of societal life. Hence grievances arising from the character of conditions in these areas cannot find resolution through the actions or appeals of any one or two interest groups in which the individual is implicated. In fact, a substantial part of the problem is that there cannot be any interest group or intermediate structure that is concerned to any adequate degree with issues so comprehensive as to implicate the greater part of the institutional sectors of the society. The only suitable structure is the agency of the community, the government itself. In this instance, the function and responsibility of government is to act on those broad society-wide concerns that extend beyond, even while they include, the focus of interest of any particular interest group.

The purposes of government must include community objectives, not only group objectives. In other words, there is a level of representation and action that goes beyond the level of any particular intermediate or interest group structure. It is the government, as representative of the community, that must provide a final definition of society-wide issues and problems, as well as assume responsibility for the initiation of a program for effective action. Not only should government go beyond merely distinct interest groups, but it must define public interests and needs as something more than the definition arrived at by the pluralist's resort to a calculus of diverse contending group forces and interests. With the government, as the voice of the community, rests both final authority as well as the power, resources, and coordination sufficient for the scope of action required. The failure of government to take account of those community-wide needs and problems that can be resolved only by the government's functioning as an agency of the whole of the community, and not of merely distinct groups within the community, means that unmet grievances will arise from the inadequacy of action on community-wide needs or public issues such as the texture of urban life, the quality of our physical environment, underemployment, and racial inequity. Even in a society with a perfectly constructed intermediate or interest group structure, inadequacy in these areas could provide the potential for disaffection and radical protest.

The present discussion does not deny that opposition or contention exists in regard to phenomena and problems that have been considered to be in the realm of public interest and needs. However, such contention does not alter their public interest character. It merely suggests either that the distinctive interests of one or more group structures will be constrained or affected in some manner or that there may be a divergence over strategies and priorities in dealing with public needs. These arise, in part, because whatever the area of concern and the response developed, gains and losses will accrue in other aspects of individual and group life. This fact leaves some room for differences over particular strategies and to some extent over relative resource commitment. The public interest character of an area or policy, however, requires merely that it be defined by a dimension that transcends any narrow group constituency and by its consequences for all or a greater part of the members of a society.[121] The individual is affected regardless of his distinctive group membership. Some may judge the interests of their particular groups prior to their interests as members of a broader constituency. They may prefer to suffer the disabilities that accrue to them as societal members because of the public disability in question rather than forgo their narrower group gain. This does not negate, however, the significant community-wide scope of some interests or needs. It merely suggests that some weigh their narrow group gains superior to public interests, as they or others are implicated in them. The public interest, however, is affirmed not merely by the fact that those groups opposed to a particular public interest are constituted by individuals who share that public interest but also by the perhaps more important fact that for the larger portion of the community there are no distinctive group memberships and interests of any equal magnitude contrary to their shared public interest.

A shared public interest exists in terms of membership in the human community of a given society, not by virtue of membership within any specific groups in that society. It reflects the needs and experiences of all as members of the society, not as members of distinctive interest groups. Some of these may in fact be adversely affected, for instance, by pollution controls, and all may experience some moderate financial cost. The community secures a gain, not a loss, as does the individual, of course, in any overall calculus of effects. Any consequential adverse effect is, in most instances, primarily limited to some particular groups in the community, for example, the industrial polluter of the stream and the air. Of course, not all phenomena relevant to public interests need involve major questions of pecuniary profit or loss. Frequently the issue is the exercise of public authority to limit individual decisions and prerogatives so as to secure a community oriented and beneficial process of change and growth, as for example, in the area of urban physical development.

Deficiencies in the conceptualization
of system change and cohesion

A few brief critical observations on pluralist theory's contentions regarding system change and cohesion, equilibrium, and the preservation of freedom are in order before concluding the present discussion. This also affords an opportunity for some critical remarks on the conceptualization and response to change that inhere in both mass theory and contemporary democratic theory. These related perspectives in pluralist theory suggest that a pluralist political system has a capacity to cope with societal problems and needs and that such a system functions at an equilibrium and maintains conditions of liberty and equity.

The pluralist and contemporary democratic theorist's conception of change is such as to place a premium on minimal and slow alteration of existing forms and relationships. Given a presumed diffusion of power and, therefore, both the presence of countervailing power and the difficulty of concentrating power, as well as the absence of a recognition of the state as a central agent for initiating change, the political and social system is perceived as changing in an incremental fashion.[122]

The pluralist supposition that the previously mentioned condition is desirable is questionable. Where conditions of inequity or need may be great, a slow response may be far from sufficient or humane. Further, the slowness or inadequacy of response in some circumstances of great need may in fact undermine rather than preserve a stable polity due to the mass disaffections and angered vigorous response of large elements of the society.[123] As Kettler points out,[124] this suggests the need, unrecognized within pluralist theory, for developing and utilizing new approaches for securing change rather than relying merely on the slow incremental working of the "pluralist" system. This, in turn, would require both a theoretical reformulation and a readjustment of existing contemporary pluralist forms so as to provide for the legitimate application of such approaches. This is not done in pluralist theory or practice. Nor can pluralist dogma on stability and equilibrium remain unqualified, in view of pluralism's inability to respond sufficiently to pressing needs and the consequent contribution to the growth of volatile conditions of unrest. It also fails to acknowledge that when conditions of equilibrium do prevail, they may well stabilize at a level far short of that needed to satisfy either vital group or societal needs.[125] Pluralist failures as regards satisfaction of community and group needs have already been noted.

There is a failure to recognize sufficiently that in many instances change is achieved by the mobilization of a sector of the community to apply pressure upon a recalcitrant elite to adopt new policies or alter existing ones. Too great a role in the initiation of change is implicitely imputed to the activities, goals, and competition among political leaders or established narrow-based interest groups. Too little attention is given to the importance of social protest movements, vigorous dissent, or, more generally, to the role of popular pressure. At times, this pressure may clearly assume the form of creative disorder[126] or, from a less sympathetic perspective, coercive protest.[127] At other times, it may shade off toward somewhat more traditional forms of pressure and influence, though there are also occasions when the opposite may occur and violent action may be resorted to in order to achieve change.

In effect, pluralist theory and particularly mass theory fail to accommodate a considerable proportion of efforts at change within an adequate conceptual scheme. Thus many such efforts are too loosely condemned as threats to a democratic political order. A factor that aggravates the difficulty of more adequately incorporating and conceptualizing the process of change is the failure to comprehend in a theoretical fashion the fact that political structures and, more particularly, democratic structures are not a fixed system, nor are the boundaries and functioning of decision-making systems closed. Their character evolves over time, and the interchange with the environment may be quite various and changing. Further, without taking into account the circumstances in which diverse pressure or protest tactics are resorted to, the character of the group involved, and the ends sought – whether the purpose is to open rather than close means of access, expression, and protest, to expand or limit individual or group rights, or to extend or constrict humanistic values – the democratic or antidemocratic character and consequences of the behavior in question cannot be adequately determined. As has already been suggested, democratic forms have evolved historically in the pursuit of purposes such as greater access, expansion of rights, satisfaction of reasonable group interest needs, and extension of humanistic values by groups often lacking adequate means to press these ends. Perception of the possibility of such evolution is lacking in mass theory.

Lastly, mass theory's reliance on pluralist assumptions weakens, in some respects, its ability to account for conditions of political and social cohesion and continuance.[128] Pluralist divisions may actually raise problems in regard to integration and stability. To be sustained pluralistic political and social institutions, where they exist, require certain common normative standards, common symbols and rituals, and shared experience, unless we are referring to dual societies characterized by parallel noncomplementary institutional structures. In such cases, the force of preponderant power is a significant element in societal continuance.

A pluralistic system can be maintained only if the conflict of interest groups is balanced to some extent by cohesive elements in the cultural and social system which moderate the intensity of conflicts and which provide loyalties to maintenance of a defined area in which politics is conducted under pluralistic rules.[129]

Along with the pluralists the mass theorist has assumed that the conditions of power dispersion, countervailing interests, and interdependence – presumably present in circumstances of political and social diversity – are the guarantors of an integrated and cohesive society. Yet it is not in conditions of pluralism per se that the basis for cohesion can most effectively be sought.[130] In reality, of course, a socially and politically diversified society does contain structures, symbols, rituals, and normative standards of a unitary national character that help maintain a degree of nationwide unity and integrity, but these are not distinctly pluralist properties. The problem that needs further theoretical elaboration is the extent, manner, and conditions under which such unitary properties are advanced and retarded by pluralist societies, as both results seem to arise.

Conclusion

The preceding discussion has sought to show some of the major empirical and descriptive inadequacies present in the attempt to apply the pluralist model to American politics. A considerable number of points were raised. Some of these are summarized here, and a few additional observations are entered.

Important segments of the community have found that representation within and the responsiveness of the political system are considerably qualified. Even the existence of a meaningful range of alternative policies and personalities is often lacking. In contrast to the usual assumptions, the extent of crosscutting memberships, especially organizational, is not great. There is a degree of rigidity in the political system, particularly as regards societal needs and the concerns of poorly organized social sectors, that receives little recognition by pluralist theorists.

Inadequacies of a more theoretical nature have included pluralism's failure to take account of the public consequences of activities and decisions in the private sector. More narrowly, it has not developed a conceptualization of the status of private corporate entities. These lack the distinct group constituency characteristic of the contending forces in the pluralist frame. Pluralist theory has not adequately confronted the conundrum that the creation of organizations, presumed to be necessary for the exercise of power by groups, has at the same time usually meant an estrangement from and a powerlessness over the policy and actions of such organizations by the individuals constituting their memberships. Nor have pluralist formulations taken into account that both theoretically and in practice a pluralist interest group balance might stabilize at some point considerably short of both politically representative government and parties and of the needs of important sectors of society, and certainly short of what could be called "the good society." It has not recognized the limitations in its approach to the concept of public interests and, in a quite different area, the inadequacies of the failure to develop a theory of power. This is clearly exhibited in pluralist studies of community power structure. In this, as in other regards, pluralist theory's "conceptual and operational decisions have prejudged the outcomes of inquiry ... draw[ing] attention to those features of the system favorable to the pluralist interpretation while shoving unfavorable features to the background."[131]

Theoretically, pluralist theory has not confronted the politicalization of administration or, in other words, the extension of pluralist competition to the arena of administration. Thus it has not adequately explored and resolved the question of which areas of government should be open to pluralist contention and which closed. Frequently, interest group competition is often no more than a managed competition, one in which areas of privilege are created by distinct interests that become immune from serious intrusion by the broader community. Thus pluralist theory has not adequately confronted the problem that untempered pluralist competition has often merely led to the creation of privileged domination by distinct groups and interests within a particular area. Nor has it adequately recognized the phenomenon of "clientelism." More broadly, and encompassing the vital question of the recognition and response to public interests and needs, there is its failure to come to terms with the fact that organized interests, especially corporate ones, frequently emerge triumphant over broader but less organized societal populations. Other phenomena and problems are also left either unrecognized or insufficiently explored. One of these is certainly that of where the "boundaries of conflict" are to be drawn and what consequences follow from restricting (or expanding) the range and depth of parties concerned with particular issues and policies and the arena within which these are confronted and acted upon.

An attempt at theoretical revision and extension to take these diverse empirical and theoretical considerations into account would require considerable though perhaps not unmanageable revisions in pluralist theory. Such a revised formulation, however, would be a theory quite altered from its present character.

It may be clear to the reader that some of the points and criticisms developed earlier, as well as elements of the interpretive scheme previously suggested, find part of their justification in the empirical and theoretical points that have appeared in the present chapter. This analysis has also, though perhaps less directly, pointed to the importance of reassessing the justification and relevancy of heightened citizenship involvement. Already noted to some extent in earlier discussions, this receives brief attention in the addendum to the present chapter.

Addendum: pluralist, mass, and democratic theory

The justification and the relevance of increased citizenship involvement in politics and governance have been implicit at various points in the present volume. These are issues that touch on the character of the democratic society. Perspectives on the nature of democracy are, of course, quite various. However, a familiar and broad, albeit fundamental, distinction is that drawn between classical and contemporary democratic theory.[132]

As will be familiar to most students in this area, contemporary democratic theory stresses the desirability of indirect forms of popular rule. Democracy exists through the opportunity of the citizenry periodically to choose freely among candidates for political office and power. Not only mass man, however, but also the average citizen is perceived as inadequate to the assumption of direct influence on decision making.[133] The populace of a society is perceived as a potential threat to political stability and to wise and equitable decision making. Citizen inaction or apathy rather then being a defect is partly viewed as a condition for societal stability and a higher level of elite performance. Under the illusion of a value-neutral analysis Berelson and his colleagues have made a spirited and well-known defense of the presumably functional character of citizen indifference, inadequate knowledge, and the lack of principled participation in politics.[134] Yet what we have here (and in a few related respects in some of the writings of Burdick and Parsons and to a somewhat lesser extent in Dahl and Plamenatz, among others)[135] is a shift in emphasis from the needs and potentialities of the individual citizen to the requirements of the political or social system, which are assumed to be that of equilibrium or stabilization. Further, Berelson and others suggest that it is in its very concentration on the individual that classic democratic theory is defective.

The contemporary democratic theorist's conceptualization of democracy on essentially narrow procedural terms deprives it of normative ends, except for a general commitment to procedural forms and a stable polity as presumably furthering the greater good. Democracy is not interpreted in terms of the realization of any personal or social values, qualities, or ends, of any purpose broader than that of exercising choice of political leaders under conditions of civil and political liberty.[136] (Obviously, this is neither an inconsequential condition nor one of little moment.) Nor does the theory or related study adequately consider the range and character of available choice, the extent to which the means exist to develop an ability to choose, the extent to which all sectors share in the opportunity to select leaders, exercise power, and secure responsiveness, the extent to which leaders are responsive, and the extent to which group and societal needs can be expressed and action secured on them. Contemporary democratic theory also ignores participation in governance as a means of self-growth and transcendence and as a means of developing informed political sensibilities and skills. It gives scant attention to its possible role in enhancing the dignity of man and furthering individual growth and development.[137] It urges the desirability of a separation between the individual's nonpolitical and private personal realm and the political.

By its restrictive formulation of democratic practice, prevailing theory slights a significant basis for potential disaffection and political protest and, as a corollary, the need to restructure democratic forms. There is an insensitivity to the inability of significant sectors of society to achieve a sense of participation in governance and of a meaningfully responsive political system and leadership. Lacking these conditions a sense of commitment to ongoing political procedures, policies, and leadership will understandably be low. Thus in an important way some of the pluralist and democratic elitist formulations within mass theory may be understood as weakening rather than promoting the stable and integrated society. Citizen involvement is perceived as the danger rather than as a means of reducing estrangement from the ongoing political forms and leadership. Related to the concept of democracy implicit in mass theory is the theory's inadequacies in comprehending the cause of vigorous political protest. Attributing these forms of protest principally to the weakening of group structures, the inadequacy of interpersonal relations, anxiety, and the like, it cannot account for the vigorous protest behavior of those who do not exhibit these conditions.[138]

We are suggesting the need to move beyond a conception of democratic forms and representation as merely the representation of objective interests or of governance and the political as a separate distinct sphere of individual life, as in the pluralist democratic elitist model. Needed is a conception that recognizes the facilitation of individual growth and expression as an important dimension of democracy. In such a formulation the significance of individual involvement is then not merely to be conceived of as a means to a political end, that of maintaining representative forms, but the means themselves are important. Such a conception has special relevance in light of the character of our times. It accords, of course, with the increased emphasis on individual growth and fulfillment that marks the increasing orientation of some portions of contemporary social thought. Even more significant, however, may be its appropriateness to a dilemma of current society: the alienation of important sectors of society and their increased restiveness in the face of unresponsive large-scale formal administrative structures – private and public, political, and other – in which the citizenry is increasingly involved.

7. Concluding comments:
ideological bias and directions for research

The major concern of the present study has been a critical analysis of the political theory of mass society. A subsidiary and related theme has been the general inadequacies of present efforts that attempt to explain support for dissident politics in social psychological terms as noncognitive, unreasonable, irrational behavior. I have stressed the ordinariness of radical politics and explained it in terms essentially similar to those used to interpret more tempered political behavior.

The broad scope of the present analysis has stemmed from both the fundamental nature of some of the principal elements of mass political theory and the relationship some of these bear to significant theoretical orientations in contemporary political theory and analysis. Thus the import of the foregoing has extended beyond merely a critical assessment of mass political theory. It has begun to suggest the basis for a critique of elements of contemporary political theory and to offer directions for research somewhat at variance with those commonly pursued. The present analysis and discussion are in the nature of a prolegomenon to further efforts. While not an in-depth study of each of the concerns considered, it has sought to raise the major issues, marshal some of the relevant arguments, and, hopefully, suggest some fruitful directions for further analysis, research, and theorization.

The present chapter concludes our discussion by briefly noting the ideological bias inhering in elements of contemporary theory and by offering a number of research suggestions reflecting the perspective developed in the preceding analyses.

Ideological perspectives of mass political theory
and related comments

Implicit in the present analysis has been the suggestion that in spite of protestations of value neutrality, objectivity, and the inappropriateness of applying normative criteria to political analysis, mass theory and dominant elements of contemporary political theory do exhibit distinct ideological or value biases.

The character of mass political theory would perhaps be more clearly perceived if its distinctive ideological perspective and bias were recognized. It exhibits a bias quite common to a great deal of social and political analysis and one that underlies the analysis of a diversity of phenomena and processes. It is perhaps most succinctly comprehended by the familiar order–conflict dichotomy.[1] In a broad sense, mass theory, as well as a great deal of contemporary political theory, may be perceived as reflecting the assumptions, concerns, and ideological stance of an order perspective. Conversely, it would not be unfair to suggest that in important respects my criticism of mass theory arises from a sympathy with the theoretical notions implied by a conflict perspective. The ideological perspective and bias of the order theorist are revealed by many of the implicit and explicit assumptions and propositions of mass theory. These may be briefly suggested here.

In some important respects mass theory operates within a consensual framework. This stresses a common obeisance by the general populace to values crucial to the society, acceptance of the basic legitimacy of existing structural forms, and suggests – while recognizing some differences and conflict within society – the compatibility and reconcilability of difference rather than the possibility of noncompatible nonresolvable difference. Its principal concept, as I shall suggest, is anomie rather than alienation. Associated with its consensus character is its greater stress on system needs rather than human needs.[2] The conceptualization of society is principally in terms of an equilibrium model that stresses stability. This is a perspective in which the basis of order is strongly perceived in terms of the role of group and cultural factors and in some degree in terms of group interest satisfaction rather than in terms of the role of force or power. The basis of vigorous conflict is interpreted, as has been noted, in terms of the decline in social ties and in part as reflecting a social psychological condition that may arise from this circumstance. The interest and power basis of apparently inexorable conflict is slighted. Issues, problems, and differences are perceived as resolved by a slow working out of difficulties within a stable balanced system rather than by countenancing disruption in order to achieve the resolution of problems or the satisfaction of needs. It is not only mass theory, Bramson has suggested, but much of the sociological enterprise itself that exhibits this character.

Many of the key concepts of sociology illustrate this concern with the maintenance and conservation of order; ideas such as status, hierarchy, ritual, integration, social function and social control are themselves a part of the history of the reaction to the ideals of the French Revolution: individualism, secularism, scientific rationalism, and egalitarianism.[3]

It is in the differential use of the concepts of anomie and alienation that the disparity of these two conflicting ideological perspectives – that of order and that of conflict – stands further revealed. Alienation has a much more radical thrust than does the concept of anomie. It has been pointed out in the essays by Horton and Thompson and by Horton[4] that the alienation perspective centers on the plight of the individual rather than that of the society. It focuses on the individual's (and one could extend this to the group as the actor) discontent within and with the social order, his powerlessness and estrangement. The perspective implied by the concept of anomie, however, is that of society. One has here attention to the individual (or group) failure to accept and submit to authority and to what society perceives as legitimate forms and norms. In contrasting the use and development of these concepts, Horton and Thompson have suggested that

The theoretical focus is on the conditions of social order which are imposed from outside the individual and are supra-individual; in Marx's works, the focus is on the individual; order emerges spontaneously when individuals are free, when they are authority and not alienated in their submission to external authority.[5]

In a sense, anomie is a condition of the mass society, and alienation that of plural society. The focus in mass society is not so much on the powerlessness of the individual as on his rootlessness, the fluidity of standards, and the confusion of purposes and values. Concern centers on the absence of or jeopardy to prevailing normative commitments. The problem for society is perceived as one of reducing rootlessness and strenghtening normative commitments, thus minimizing the conditions for the availability of masses and the potential irrational demands of masses on elites. This is not to deny that alienation is also present in mass society but merely to point out that the dilemma of powerlessness and its resolution is not the crucial focus of the mass theorist.[6] The very lack of attention to interest distinctions such as were noted earlier illustrates this absence of concern with conditions of powerlessness. To focus on alienation, however, is to initiate a critique of mass political theory.

The dilemma of pluralist society, when it is recognized, is the powerlessness of individuals and groups within the society. The resolution of this condition is to increase political representation and responsiveness and, in some important instances it could also be argued, participatory forms. This is not to say that the mass theorists treat the inadequacies of pluralist society in terms of alienating circumstances. Rather, I suggest, such inadequacies receive too little attention or are perceived as reflecting the appearance of mass properties, hence, conditions of anomie.

These comments point to the related question of the contrasting basis of societal cohesion as between mass and pluralist society. This receives little attention in mass theory and in fact cannot be adequately discussed without a fuller treatment of these two concepts than appears in the mass theory literature.

Some further comments: the bias in
contemporary political theory

Related to the emphasis on order and consensus is the absence of attention in much of postwar political and sociological theory and research to the need for change in current political forms, structures of power, or major political purposes. The importance of failing to consider these topics adequately is substantial and has received some attention in earlier discussion. The seriousness of such failure would be clearly revealed in any extended analysis of properties of the social and political system such as inequitable circumstances, conditions of strain, bases of system disaffection, the failure to meet serious social needs, the inappropriateness of resource allocation, the unreasonableness of major policy decisions, and the ends and groups served and ill served by present functioning and structures. Yet these too receive little consideration, not surprisingly, perhaps, given the limitations of current theoretical formulations and the ideological bias noted. Elsewhere, the conservative thrust of contemporary theory is revealed in the absence of attention to the disparities or contradictions between certain of the theoretical models of the political system on the one hand and its actual functioning on the other. Related is the tendency to define proper or desirable institutional structure and performance more or less in terms of their existing ongoing character, as for instance, the positive face given to citizen apathy and low participation.[1] The inadequacies in society's institutional structures these may reflect are not examined. Certainly, there is little attempt at any evaluative analysis or criticism or even the provision of programmatic models for planned or induced change in terms of any "idealistic" standards or other nonprevailing criteria.

The last point touches closely on the absence in much of contemporary political thought of any effort to apply normative conceptions or assumptions to the issues studied, the problems posed, and the evaluations made, except to the extent that the type of notions on consensus, order, pluralism, leadership virtue, and democratic practice already noted generates or constitutes implicit normative conceptions. One example of the avoidance of normative criteria is the frequent absence of an extensive conception of the public interest or good that would go beyond some calculus or weighting of contending group interests.[8] Similarly, there is the avoidance of positing any "ideal" political standards for the polity or as criteria for evaluative judgments. This has been clearly perceived in regard to the contemporary evaluation of the role of the citizen, political participation, and the presumed virtues of citizen uninvolvement. As Christian Bay notes, there is in effect little more than an "emphasis on prevailing behavior patterns."[9] The absence of an explicit normative standard, however, has not meant value-free research, either in regard to the issues selected for study, the problems posed, or the interpretive perspective utilized. Partly in response to these circumstances and the ideological perspectives of contemporary political research the chapter closes with a number of suggestions of a somewhat different character.

On a number of occasions the present essay has strongly implied the presence of an ideological bias in the mass political theory perspective and in elements of recent political analysis. The present discussion can be appropriately concluded by a few words on three instances when this is evidenced. One is the tendency to see the inadequacies of political policies as arising from unreasonable demands of the populace, public unwillingness to bear the burdens of constructive policy, and the existence of citizen apathy. This is in contrast to locating an important share of the responsibility for such conditions with political leadership and, more basically, the structure of power it reflects. Whatever the determination as to the whole complex of factors accounting for any particular societal condition, in many significant instances political leadership and dominant class elements clearly could have achieved much more salutary policy and social conditions were they not characterized by strong deficiencies of purpose, knowledge, understanding, and distinctive class interest. However, to raise and explore this possibility would mean applying certain normative criteria in the evaluation of policy and societal circumstances. Also involved would be the shift of theoretical and empirical analysis to an assessment of the adequacy of societal leadership and the appropriateness of its ideological perspectives, its ability to respond rationally and to grasp the wider ramifications of policy and of action and inaction, and its ability to free itself from narrow privileged interest group commitments. This would be a shift away from mass and contemporary political theory's overemphasis on the negative role exhibited by the broader public. It would mean the need for contemporary political theory to concern itself with the quality and origin of major political policies. This would require the intrusion of a number of evaluative and normative criteria, now lacking in political analysis. What one has here, in part, is the significant influence of what the theorist chooses to focus upon as a determinant of the nature of the analysis followed and its findings, as well as of what is omitted from consideration.

This is also revealed in my second example, mass theory's approach to the study and interpretation of "mass" movements. There is little recognition here of the fact that social and political movements may have a function of serving to "encourage political and social mobilization, of widening the boundaries of the polity."[10] In important respects this is what has been accomplished by movements such as the trade-union working-class movement, populist, civil rights, and black power movements. Aversion to extensive popular involvement and a disregard of the class component of protest slight this vital and positive democratic function of "mass" movements. Social and political movements have frequently led to a revitalization of social and political society and from a long-run view to the creation and strengthening of a stable and responsive democratic society. The failure, not the success, of many movements for reform will be productive of the very consequences of alienation, irrationality, disruption, and authoritarianism that mass society and contemporary democratic theorists fear. And such failure, where it occurs, will in important respects be due to the obduracy and the inadequate performance and leadership of the political elite and of dominant class elements.

Lastly, and in another direction, is the restriction of the theoretical and analytic scheme in a manner so that it prejudices the research conclusions. Thus in the pluralist analysis of power structures it has been noted that there has been the failure to attend to the fact that the existence of power is not necessarily expressed by the contention surrounding particular community or political issues. In effect, non-group, non-issue-based properties of the social and political system – values, ideologies, and traditions, as well as awareness, knowledge, and apathy, all serving to define acceptable and unacceptable issues, needs, policies, and alternatives – are influential determinants of the structure of power. Or, putting it somewhat differently, they are influential determinants of who gains and who loses, what privileges and advantages accrue to some but are denied others. In this sense power may be perceived as existing regardless of what issues do or do not appear. Of course, this requires that the analyst apply some normative criteria. The pluralists' attempt to shun such an application has not removed a value emphasis in their work, but rather reduced it to an expression of some of the major existing and potent values characterizing the society. Most political scientists, however, have turned away from the examination of that which is not expressed in open contention. Yet the absence of particular demands, issues, and policies may significantly bespeak the preponderant power of certain groups and the weakness of others.

Research and study prospectus

The criticisms and alternative perspectives developed in the present work suggest a number of major areas and problems for research. The following offers a brief statement of a few possible areas for research that could contribute to a reformulation of existing theory and belief.

The study of political movements and protest

Combining a structural and institutional orientation with a phenomenologically sensitive analysis would prove fruitful to the study of particular political movements and protests. This would contribute toward the development of a more appropriate behavioral model. Such a study would have to recognize and apply the concept that the individual constructs his own social and political reality. Yet he does so in terms of the information, experiences, and ideological perspective he possesses. These, however, reflect his social and political position and to some extent his distinctive psychological attributes or needs. Thus while a possible role does exist for psychodynamic elements, they are significantly constrained and mediated by a large number of other factors. Implicated in the reality constructed by the individual is a structure of meaning that makes sense of experiences and fears and of the response to them. From such a perspective political behavior and attitudes would be studied as phenomena that arise out of the ongoing dialectical process encompassed by the elements noted. Attention would be given to the individual as a more rational, purposive, less impressionable, and less emotional actor. Emphasized is the actor's autonomy and ability to respond reasonably to the environment and to make choices. Minimized is the sense of a somewhat mechanical determinance by either external or internal forces or purposes. At the same time, the systemic determination and constraints on behavior would be incorporated as a basic element of the analysis.

The type of theoretical model sketched in the opening section of Chapter 5 suggests the need for analyses of a case, comparative, and historical character. Considerable attention would have to be given to securing and distinguishing between adequately contrasted population groups and societies. Contrasts in terms of differences in institutional properties and processes, the nature of social change, and economic circumstances, among other considerations, seem essential. Clearly, the research design would have to permit an analysis focusing on the interdependent and processional nature of the relevant phenomena. An appropriate research design would recognize the multicausal character of dissidence and allow for the elaboration of presumed relationships when the number of cases or instances permit.

The research design must permit distinguishing between the micro- and macrolevels of social phenomena and provide for an analysis of their interrelationship. At the macrolevel the design must also provide for delineating among social structural, social organizational, and political forms and processes. It would also permit the assessment of the nature and effect of major processes of social change such as industrialization, urbanization, and rationalization. The consequences of these for individual and group circumstances, consciousness, and behavioral possibilities would be determined. A comprehensive research design would permit an assessment, as suggested previously, of the phenomenological world of individuals. Such a microlevel analysis would establish the nature of individual consciousness and the individual's construction of meaning and negotiation of his environment. Evidence would be sought on the nature and change, if any, of group ties and the sense of community and of consciousness regarding the self and its relationship to the political system, political alternatives and leading political actors, and the broader political order and process. Included here would also be information on the individual's attitudes or feelings in regard to dimensions of political trust, political legitimacy, and isolation. The study population's experience and interpretation of change in significant social, economic, and political factors would be determined.

Also important is study of the possible process of political influence and socialization impinging on the individual and of the political information, ideology, and perspectives characterizing the study population, limited as these may be at times.

The historical pattern and current nature of civil disorder

Mass theory and contemporary political theory lack an informed analysis or sensitivity to both the nature and the positive potential of what Arthur Waskow has referred to as "creative disorder" and David Bayley has called "coercive public protest."[11] The reference here is to acts of public nonviolent suasion supplementary to the usual available means of political communication and protest that seek to influence government and in some instances private policy, frequently though not always within "the bounds of democratic permissibility."[12] More particularly, these include activities such as sit-ins, marches, freedom rides, business boycotts, and rent strikes. While indicative of only one dimension or type of creative disorder, a sense of what is at least partly involved is expressed in the "peaceful civic insurrection" lead by Martin Luther King in the South, "non-violent, disciplined, protracted rebellions against irresponsible authority."[13]

The whole area of civil disorder calls for imaginative and concrete analysis in a number of terms. Research could be addressed to the type of behavioral forms such protests take, from the more disruptive sit-ins to the less disturbing yet vital populist forms such as the organization and political activity of welfare recipients and community-based organization tenant unions. Attention should be given to a number of elements. This would include the kind of circumstances associated with the appearance of such protests, the immediate consequences and effectiveness they engender, their influence in the political system and policy, their possible influence on the expansion of the boundaries of political discourse, issues, and policy attitudes, and the degree to which they constitute "an effective signaling device that sensitize[s] the upper classes to the need for social reconstruction."[14] In most instances far-reaching concomitants like these appear probable only when the disorders are, in effect, part of a broader social or political movement. Thus though their study is useful, the consequences and influence of disorder cannot be completely isolated or determined.

The nature and circumstances of contemporary protest might be illumined by the study of the increased acceptance and legitimacy over time of previously impermissible forms of protest expression.

Thus it is possible to trace the development and use of and the response to various forms of protest and political conflict techniques in the economic, political rights, and civil rights areas. Trade-union organization, efforts at collective bargaining, strikes, picketing, boycotts, sit-ins, electoral franchise, political pamphleteering, electioneering, referendums, demonstrations, and marches – at various times illegitimate activities but now acceptable forms of expression – lend themselves to this kind of analysis. Our ability to interpret and judge the appropriateness of current protest could be increased by such analyses.

The performance of political leadership and its consequences

A more balanced account of the qualities and characteristics of political leadership could be partly sought by study of a little explored area – the negative properties of elite leadership. Of special interest would be an examination of the role of elites in producing conditions productive of societal instability and protest, and of the attempts by political leadership to subvert democratic forms and functioning. Research on elite practices and failures could proceed in a number of directions. (1) One would be a study of elite failure to respond to pressing group and societal needs, as well as of elites' initiation of policies that actually quicken the development of social liabilities and conflict. Both foreign as well as domestic policies could well be studied in these regards. (2) Related would be examination of leadership extremism, irrationality, and hysteria. Attention here could be given to the many occasions when the leadership response to events or movements of protest, change, and opposition resembled that attributed to mass behavior – witch hunts, the abrogation of democratic procedures, distortion of truth, misleading the public and turning a deaf ear to what was displeasing, establishing vigilante groups, and, in somewhat different terms, committing astronomical societal resources to senseless and often disastrous ends. The opportunities for study are various. (3) No less pernicious than the preceding, and contrasting sharply with the democratic ethos, are the little recognized attempts of dominant class and leadership elements to destroy efforts at the creation of democratic forms, the establishment of grass-roots participation, and the revitalization of local communities. This could be revealed in a study of elite response to many poverty programs, efforts at urban community organization, rural revitalization, the establishment of poor and minority group enterprises, and efforts in distinctive program areas such as that of education. Here the reality and undemocratic quality of elite power unsheathed would become clearer.

Decentralization and participatory structures and situations

There is a vital need for knowledge of the processes, relevant areas, and consequences of the decentralization of power and increased individual participation in governance. Fortunately, a range of quite different opportunities exists for possible case studies. They extend from marketing and credit cooperatives among blacks in the South to diverse urban neighborhood organizations, to educational decentralization, to community revitalization efforts, to participation in health and other personal and community service institutions, to situations of plant management and workers' councils. Some of the literature on community change and development, particularly though not solely related to efforts in the developing nations, may contribute toward greater theoretical sophistication in regard to participatory democratic practices. It is likely to be less relevant to questions of decentralization.

There are a number of areas central to an understanding or application of participatory democratic forms to decentralized decision making about which we could be better informed. For example, which societal and institutional sectors admit of what degree of decentralization and participation and with what consequences? With what procedures may power be decentralized in hierarchial and centralized institutions, while performance and normative prescriptions crucial to the integrity and functioning of the institution are maintained? How may appropriate conditions of equity and other rights previously evolved within the institution be safeguarded? How may the rights of minority populations be assured, given the narrowed scope of decision making? What should be the scope of rights and liberties, as well as of participation, permitted or guaranteed? Even the means of achieving and maintaining participation and the decentralization of power may be precarious and require elaboration. These questions are compounded by their probable variations in different institutional areas.

In a different direction, research could usefully be initiated on the personal consequences of decentralization and participation for those involved. A number of questions inhere here on what kind of changes and what type of institutions are productive of more positive personal, social, and political conditions. The relevance of these questions in light of contemporary conditions is great.

The nature and adequacy of institutional functioning

Fuller analysis of how well major institutional areas and specific organizational sectors serve their constituency, clients, or presumed public purpose is needed. While some efforts have been made in the medical, educational, and industrial regulation areas, a great deal of work remains to be done if the disparity between the public face or ethos and the functioning reality of many areas of societal life is to be revealed and reduced.

Many elements of an institutional or organizational sphere require study of the type being proposed. Some of these elements include analysis of decision-making processes and participants and of the kind of groups organized – and not organized – to provide ongoing pressure upon or input into the institution in question. Also, attention would have to be given to the type of orientations, commitments, and self-interests that characterize those involved in the daily functioning of the institutional or organizational area being studied, the purposes behind the initial legislation or establishment of a public body; the original "charter" accounting for an organization in the private sphere should be determined. It would be useful to study constraints or pressures by the broader society or major relevant groups within the society upon the given institutional area or, put somewhat differently, the "place" within the overall societal value structure of the purposes, mode of functioning, and alternative approaches of the particular institutional area. Related would be an analysis of the influence on values and resources – who gains and loses – from the types of institutional policies and outcomes. In a different direction, it would be useful to study the organizational constraints – both the internal institutional structure and procedures, as well as the external institutional environment – in terms of which and through which a particular organization and organizational area must function. Research in the overall direction suggested here would also contribute to the analysis of the broader question of the nature of the structure of power in society, the determinants of public and private institutional decision making, and the conditions and roots of powerlessness in contemporary society for large sectors of that society.

A study of community power structure and decision making

Earlier comments on the inadequacies in theory and research on community power structure pointed to some possible research focuses. Two are explicitly reaffirmed here: the necessity of studying the "submerged" face of power and the nature and the use of the power that is concentrated in the private sector, particularly corporate power. Neither the power elite nor pluralist models have been adequate for the former purposes. A major problem is the development of an appropriate research methodology. The use of comparative studies would appear to be vital to such methodology. The study of power in the private sector poses fewer problems. The absence of substantial research efforts here appears indicative of the bias in the major established currents of political and sociological inquiry.

Social-action-oriented research

There is a considerable need for research at a pragmatic action-oriented level. Its dividends are likely to be of both a social and a scholarly nature. Such study could address itself to a number of questions. A major area of effort would be to determine what constitutes an effective means or policy for achieving an important social goal. Some possible social goals or purposes, for instance, and consequent research, include: increasing minority group political effectiveness and public political sophistication and interest, more effectively and extensively controlling private structures of power and channeling them to public ends, improving the provision and utilization of health and medical services, improving the treatment and minimization of delinquency, crime, and recidivism, creating and assuring the continuance of viable and superior communities, and facilitating institutional and individual movement from armament to peace-based production and attitudes. Another area of inquiry could be the determination of how public and institutional support for the preceding purposes could be secured. Research could also be directed to the possible consequences of specific policies. Of a quite different character, attention could be given to helping define appropriate societal purposes. If it is to be most meaningful, at least some of this research will be possessed of a distinctive normative character. As such, it may disturb the perquisites of a few while it serves the needs of the broader community. In some respects this would be a welcome change from many of the present uses of the social scientist.

The fruits of the efforts recommended extend beyond possible social gains. The theoretical elaboration and empirical studies that would of necessity undergird an adequate action program would mean significant advancement in our understanding of many major social and political processes, patterns of change, institutional forms, and the individual experience in many diverse circumstances.

The present effort has considered a number of basic issues in political and social theory and analysis, at times in a rather abstract manner. While the variety of concerns covered has been considerable, a few basic underlying themes run through the discussion. One has been the reaffirmation of the dignity and reasonableness of man as he seeks to come to terms with an often stressful and confusing world. There has also been an emphasis on the broad scope of factors that impinge on individuals and that shape their behavior and in terms of which individuals also create their behavior. Lastly is the need to provide greater recognition of the failure of our institutions to satisfy the economic, social, and personal needs of people. If the present volume helps heighten attention to these concerns, it will have made a useful contribution.

Notes

Chapter 1. Introduction

1. Edward Shils, "The Theory of Mass Society," in Philip Olson, ed., *America as a Mass Society* (New York: Free Press, 1963), pp. 30–47.

2. London: Routledge & Kegan Paul, 1960.

3. There is a considerable literature that has contributed to the relatively recent development of mass theory. Some of the relevant items would include José Ortega y Gasset, *The Revolt of the Masses* (New York: Norton, 1940); Hannah Arendt's work, especially *The Origins of Totalitarianism* (New York: Harcourt Brace Jovanovich, 1951); Jacob L. Talmon, *The Rise of Totalitarian Democracy* (Boston: Beacon, 1952), and *Political Messianism* (New York: Praeger, 1961); Robert Nisbet, *The Quest for Community* (New York: Oxford University Press, 1953); Emil Lederer, *State of the Masses* (New York: Norton, 1940); Walter Lippman, *Essays in the Public Philosophy* (New York: Mentor Library, 1955); and Philip Selznick, "Vulnerability of Institutional Targets," in *The Organizational Weapon* (New York: McGraw-Hill, 1952), Chap. 7. Kornhauser's *The Politics of Mass Society* is perhaps the most comprehensive statement of mass theory. The present study, while clearly critical of many elements in his book, has profited from the stimulation it provided and its usefulness in offering a clear and effective elaboration of the principal propositions of mass theory.

4. See Erich Fromm, *Escape from Freedom* (New York: Holt, Rinehart & Winston, 1941); Sigmund Neumann, *Permanent Revolution* (New York: Harper & Row, 1942); Hannah Arendt, *The Origins of Totalitarianism* (New York: Harcourt Brace Jovanovich, 1951); Kornhauser, *The Politics of Mass Society*; Nisbet, *The Quest for Community*; James C. Davies, "Toward a Theory of Revolution," *American Sociological Review*, 27 (February 1962), 5–19, and "The J-Curve of Rising and Declining Satisfactions as a Cause of Some Great Revolutions and a Contained Rebellion," in Hugh Davis Graham and Ted Robert Gurr, eds., *The History of Violence in America* (New York: Bantam, 1969), pp. 690–730; Ivo K. Feierabend and Rosalind L. Feierabend, "Aggressive Behaviors Within Politics, 1948–1962: A Cross National Study," *Journal of Conflict Resolution*, 10 (September 1966), 249–271; Ivo K. Feierabend, Rosalind L. Feierabend, and Betty A. Nesvold, "Social Change and Political Violence: Cross-National

Comparisons," in Graham and Gurr, eds., pp. 632–687; Ted Robert Gurr with Charles Ruttenberg, *The Conditions of Civil Violence* (Princeton, N.J.: Princeton University, Center for International Studies, 1967); Gurr, "Psychological Factors in Civil Violence," *World Politics*, 20 (January 1968), 245–278, and *Why Men Rebel* (Princeton, N.J.: Princeton University Press, 1970); Seymour Martin Lipset, "Working-Class Authoritarianism," in *Political Man* (Garden City, N.Y.: Doubleday, 1960), pp. 97–130; and Daniel Bell, ed., *The Radical Right* (Garden City, N.Y.: Doubleday, 1963).

5. Alejandro Portes, "Political Primitivism, Differential Socialization, and Lower-Class Leftist Radicalism," *American Sociological Review*, 36 (October 1971), 832.

6. See Chapter 5 for citations and discussion of the material in this area.

7. There are a diverse number of effects that ideology and consciousness may produce that can significantly influence political behavior, including support. For example, they may alter the sense of what can be expected from the prevailing political and social order, including the existing leadership, elites, parties, and so on, and even of the propriety of certain demands, forms of organization, and protest. Thus they may, among other effects, also influence the type of goals developed and the legitimacy accorded established leadership and political forms. Effects such as these are crucial in both defining the nature of one's personal situation and what the response to it may be.

Chapter 2. Intellectual origins of and contributions to mass political theory

1. Tracing the influences upon or origins of a body of social and political thought such as mass theory can be a difficult and precarious undertaking. This has been pointedly observed by Alfred Cobban, a respected Enlightenment scholar, in his commentary upon some of the works of Jacob Talmon, a distinguished mass theorist.

> [I]t must be pointed out that the game of chasing origins can easily lead to very peculiar conclusions, as Voltaire indicated when he wrote that all children have parents but not all possible parents have children. Tracing a line of descent backwards is bound to produce positive results, and then by a simple process of reversion we can create the illusion of a necessary catena of cause and effect. Thus, one could trace a train of influence leading from Stalin back through Lenin, Marx, Hegel, Kant, Rousseau, Locke and Hooker to Aquinas. Each link in the chain is valid, yet it must be confessed that, though there are common features and affinities in the ideas of Aquinas and Stalin, the whole has distinctly less value than the part. (*In Search of Humanity* [New York: Braziller, 1960], p. 183).

It may be reasonable, therefore, to suggest that the present chapter should perhaps not be wholly perceived as tracing the origins of current mass political theory or as establishing a direct determinative influence of earlier thought. It might better be understood as showing the correspondence between an earlier intellectual tradition and more recent analyses by mass theorists. As such, however, the present discussion still suggests possible origins and derivation. Naturally, when these are explicitly recognized by contemporary mass theorists, the tie with or influence of earlier thought is more clearly established. Also, it seems reasonable to note that the continuing vitality of some major intellectual currents of a century or more ago does suggest their likely influence upon such similar elements as do exist in current mass theory. The difficulty stressed here is more in the attribution of influence to a body of thought that in a number of ways differs significantly from the more recent corpus of ideas of which it is presumably a forebear. Thus, for instance, mass theory finds current totalitarian ideology or practice implicated in or arising from earlier liberal and rationalist thought. This proposition is essentially the object of Cobban's criticism.

2. The brief account here of some elements of Rousseau's thought is presented principally in terms of the reading given Rousseau by many contemporary students, including mass theorists. The present writer is not necessarily in accord with such interpretations, which appear to reflect the influence of contemporary historical circumstances and theory while slighting the historical or political context of the period during which Rousseau wrote. On the issue of the adequacy of popular criticisms of Rousseau see Peter Gay's brief review, "The Old New Man," *New York Review of Books,* December 5, 1968, pp. 33–36, and his larger vigorous essay, "Carl Becker's Heavenly City," in Raymond O. Rockwood, ed., *Carl Becker's Heavenly City Revisited* (Ithaca, N.Y.: Cornell University Press, 1958), pp. 27–51, as well as Alfred Cobban's "New Light on the Political Thought of Rousseau," *Political Science Quarterly,* 16 (1951), 272–284.

3. Jean Jacques Rousseau, *The Social Contract* (New York: Dutton, Everyman's Library Edition, 1950), p. 26.

4. George H. Sabine, *A History of Political Theory,* rev. ed. (New York: Holt, Rinehart & Winston, 1950), pp. 588–589.

5. Edward Hallett Carr, *The New Society* (Boston: Beacon, 1957), p. 63.

6. Rousseau held that it is in the movement from a state of nature to a condition of civil society, as represented by the social contract and the effectuation of the general will, that man's freedom is maximized. While man loses his "natural liberty" and must act in terms of duty rather than impulse, in terms of right and reason rather than desire or inclination, in terms of principle rather than personal gain, he gains a civil and moral liberty or, in effect, the ability of self-governance. He is freed from enslavement to appetite and hence attains an enhanced security (Rousseau, *The Social Contract,* Books I and II).

7. Ibid., p. 17.

8. Rousseau, *The Social Contract*, pp. 23–26.

9. Ibid., p. 18.

10. Sabine, *A History of Political Thought*, p. 591.

11. Walter Lippman, *Essays in the Public Philosophy* (New York: Mentor Library, 1955), p. 54.

12. Robert A. Nisbet, *The Quest for Community* (New York: Oxford University Press, 1953), p. 145.

13. Carr, *The New Society*, p. 63.

14. Nisbet, *The Quest for Community*, p. 140.

15. Ibid., p. 146.

16. Talmon, *The Rise of Totalitarian Democracy* (Boston: Beacon, 1952), p. 4.

17. Nisbet, *The Quest for Community*, p. 251.

18. Talmon, *The Rise of Totalitarian Democracy*, p. 35.

19. Crane Brinton, *The Shaping of Modern Thought* (Englewood Cliffs, N.J.: Prentice-Hall, 1963), p. 110.

20. The utilitarians would have to be exempted from the conception of a natural order of society.

21. Judith Shklar, *After Utopia, the Decline of Political Faith* (Princeton, N.J.: Princeton University Press, 1957), p. 3.

22. Lippman, *Essays in the Public Philosophy*, pp. 69–71.

23. Talmon, *The Rise of Totalitarian Democracy*, p. 249.

24. The French Revolution is the *bête noir* of the mass political theorist. Nisbet has written that it "had something of the same impact upon men's minds in Western Europe at the very end of the eighteenth century that the Communist and Nazi revolutions have had in the twentieth century" (*The Quest for Community*, p. 24). Its vital importance resides in several properties of the revolution. Those of greatest significance appear to be its violent exercise of revolutionary power, the considerable societal disruption it produced, and the increasingly absolute nature of power during the revolution arising from the destruction or weakening of old social structures, such as the guild, church, and class structures. In other words, intermediate structures were not only seriously weakened but were in fact viewed as hostile to the "proper" exercise of democratic rule. The mass political theorist argues that one has here the very essence of the conditions productive of totalitarian rule. This is not only because counter- or competing centers of power were undermined, but in addition the individual became "liberated" from earlier ties and loyalties and, in effect, became available for new movements, leaders, and philosophies. These appeared, briefly held sway, and ruled oppressively. The basis for legitimate differences of opinion was increasingly undermined, as difference began to be defined not as honest disagreement but as subversive or treasonable. The revolution became increasingly extreme and more and more removed in practice from the ideals that initially motivated it.

25. Talmon, *The Rise of Totalitarian Democracy*, pp. 249–250. Excerpted

and reprinted by permission of Praeger Publishers, Inc., New York, and Martin Secker & Warburg Ltd., London.

26. Earlier Enlightenment thought and later writings can be interpreted as reflecting a distinct class position and interest. The later philosophic shift is probably, in part, a response to the ascension to power of the bourgeoisie, in contrast to an earlier period when it was still seeking to attain such ascendency and free itself from societal constraints. To some extent, it is also a response to the rising potency of the working class, previously of little relevance.

27. John S. Mill, "On Liberty," in *Utilitarianism, Liberty and Representative Government* (New York: Dutton, 1951), pp. 165, 166, as quoted in Leon Bramson, *The Political Context of Sociology* (Princeton, N.J.: Princeton University Press, 1961), pp. 29–30.

28. John S. Mill, *Utilitarianism, Liberty and Representative Government* (New York: Dutton, 1947), p. 68.

29. Shklar, *After Utopia*, pp. 226–35, especially p. 230.

30. Ibid., p. 226.

31. See Alexis de Tocqueville, *Democracy in America*, Reeve trans., edited by Phillips Bradley (New York: Knopf, 1946), especially Vol. I, Chap. 12; Vol. II, Bk. 2, Chaps. 5, 6, 7. Tocqueville is the strongest influence in these regards, but certainly not the only one. In this regard see E. V. Walter, " 'Mass Society.' The Late Stages of an Idea," *Social Research*, 31 (Winter 1964), 390–410.

32. Shklar, *After Utopia*, p. 226.

33. Tocqueville, *Democracy in America*, II, pp. 318–319. A more extended quote including the portion given here is quoted in Nisbet, *The Quest for Community*, pp. 190–191.

34. Nisbet, *The Quest for Community*, p. 191.

35. Irving M. Zeitlin, *Ideology and the Development of Sociological Theory* (Englewood Cliffs, N.J.: Prentice-Hall, 1968), p. 44.

36. Nisbet, *The Quest for Community*, p. 286, footnote 2.

37. Ross J. S. Hoffman and Paul Levack, eds., *Burke's Politics* (New York: Knopf, 1949), p. 305.

38. Ibid., p. 227.

39. Bramson, *The Political Context of Sociology*, p. 15.

40. Henry Sumner Maine, *Ancient Law*, 5th ed. (New York: Holt, Rinehart & Winston, 1875), p. 163.

41. *Community and Society* (Ferdinand Tönnies, *Gemeinschaft und Gesellschaft*), translated and edited by Charles P. Loomis (New York: Harper Torchbooks, 1963).

42. Edward Shils, "Daydreams and Nightmares: Reflections on the Criticism of Mass Curture," *The Sewanee Review*, 65 (1957), 586–608, especially 598–599.

43. See Howard Becker, "On Simmel's Philosophy of Money," in *The Sociology of Georg Simmel*, translated and edited by Kurt H. Wolff (New York: Free Press, 1964), paperback, pp. 316–336.

44. Reprinted in Wolff, *The Sociology of Georg Simmel*, pp. 409–429.

45. Relevant discussion will be found scattered through Simmel's work; ibid.

46. Louis Coser, ed., *Georg Simmel* (Englewood Cliffs, N.J.: Prentice-Hall, 1965), Introduction, p. 18. For an extended treatment of Simmel's work, see Nicholas Spykman, *The Social Theory of Georg Simmel* (Chicago: University of Chicago Press, 1925). Also see the essays in Kurt H. Wolff, ed., *Essays on Sociology, Philosophy and Aesthetic* (New York: Harper Torchbooks, 1965), and in Coser's book.

47. Shils, "Daydreams and Nightmares," in *The Intellectuals and the Powers and Other Essays* (Chicago: University of Chicago Press, 1972), p. 257.

48. Emile Durkheim, *Suicide,* translated by John A. Spaulding and George Simpson, edited by George Simpson (New York: Free Press, 1951).

49. Nisbet, *The Quest for Community,* p. 14.

50. Emile Durkeim, *Professional Ethics and Civic Morals* (London: Routledge & Kegan Paul, 1957), p. 63.

51. Also see a similar discussion in Joseph A. Schumpeter, *Capitalism, Socialism and Democracy* (New York: Harper Torchbook, 1962), especially Part II.

52. Max Weber, *The Theory of Social and Economic Organization,* translated by A. M. Henderson and Talcott Parsons, edited by Talcott Parsons (New York: Oxford University Press, 1947), p. 123.

53. *From Max Weber,* translated and edited with an introduction by Hans Gerth and C. Wright Mills (New York: Oxford University Press, 1946), p. 51.

54. Max Weber, "Science as a Vocation," in Gerth and Mills, *From Max Weber,* p. 155.

55. Weber does not, however, suggest that this rationalization of the world – its increased efficiency, scientific character, and disenchantment – makes for a better, more satisfying, or enlightened world. Thus rationalization is not synonymous with progress. In fact, one may reason that the loss of mysteries, forebodings, sacred themes, and mystic life as well as the loss of the sublime and the sacred connoted by the disenchantment of the world have made for an increasingly lackluster and emotionally flat world. Weber himself was disturbed at what he felt to be the consequences for individuals in the dehumanizing constraints and demands inhering in rationalized society.

56. Weber, *The Theory of Social and Economic Organization,* p. 337.

57. Sheldon Wolin, *Politics and Vision* (Boston: Little, Brown and Company, 1960), p. 423.

58. Gustave Le Bon, *The Crowd,* 2nd ed., "Sellanraa" (Dunwoody, Ge.: Norman S. Berg, 1968).

59. See Leon Bramson's study *The Political Context of Sociology* for a discussion of the origins of literature and ideas on the mass society, crowd, mass, and other related topics. See Bramson, p. 53, footnote 8, for some

references on crowd theorists and their published works. Roger Brown's essay "Mass Phenomena" in G. Lindzey, ed., *Handbook of Social Psychology*, II (Reading, Mass.: Addison-Wesley, 1954), pp. 833–873, also provides a useful systematic and far-ranging review of the concepts and literature on crowds and crowd behavior.

60. Walter, " 'Mass Society,' " p. 398.

61. Le Bon, *The Crowd*, p. 12.

62. Brown, "Mass Phenomena," p. 843.

63. Sigmund Freud, *Group Psychology and the Analysis of the Ego* (London: Hogarth Press, 1922); José Ortega y Gasset, *The Revolt of the Masses* (New York: Norton, 1940); Emil Lederer, *State of the Masses* (New York: Norton, 1940).

64. See Bramson, *The Political Context of Sociology*, and Walter, " 'Mass Society.' "

65. Herbert Blumer, "Molding of Mass Behavior Through the Motion Pictures," *Publications of the American Sociological Society*, 29 (1935), 117. Quoted in Bramson, ibid., p. 66.

66. Bramson, ibid., p. 54.

Chapter 3. *The political theory of mass society*

1. Robert Nisbet, *The Quest for Community* (New York: Oxford University Press, 1953), pp. 49–50.

2. William Kornhauser, *The Politics of Mass Society* (London: Routledge & Kegan Paul, 1960), pp. 74–75.

3. Nisbet, *The Quest for Community*, p. 71.

4. Kornhauser, *The Politics of Mass Society*, p. 75.

5. Nisbet, *The Quest for Community*, p. 58.

6. Ibid., p. 72.

7. Neil J. Smelser, "Toward a Theory of Modernization," in Amitai and Eva Etzioni, eds., *Social Change* (New York: Basic Books, 1964), p. 261.

8. A number of examples may help make this clearer (see Smelser, ibid., pp. 26–27). For instance, where economic activities were once undifferentiated and all performed within and by the family, they have come over time to be increasingly comprehended in terms of distinct functions of resource accumulation, production, distribution, sales, and so on. These are handled by different roles and organizations, as is of course evidenced by the growth of banking institutions, trade organizations, and production enterprises. Similarly, the distribution of functions once performed by the family unit but now distributed among educational, entertainment, counseling, training, and other institutions evidences another example of the process of the social differentiation of multifunctional role structures. This phenomenon can also be elaborated in terms of the political as well as value sphere of society.

9. Karl Mannheim, *Man and Society in an Age of Reconstruction* (New York: Harcourt Brace Jovanovich, 1950), p. 59.

10. See the discussion on these and related points in Erich Fromm, *The Sane Society* (New York: Holt, Rinehart & Winston, 1955).

11. Edward Shils, "The Theory of Mass Society," in Philip Olson, ed., *America as a Mass Society* (New York: Free Press, 1963), pp. 30–47.

12. Kornhauser, *The Politics of Mass Society*, p. 234.

13. Ibid., p. 98.

14. Ibid., p. 94.

15. C. Wright Mills, *The Power Elite* (New York: Oxford University Press, 1957), especially pp. 302–310.

16. Kornhauser, *The Politics of Mass Society*, p. 235.

17. Ibid., pp. 232–233.

18. See C. Wright Mills' seminal work, *White Collar* (New York: Oxford University Press, 1951).

19. Mills, *The Power Elite*, pp. 320–321.

20. Ibid., p. 322. Both Mannheim (*Man and Society*, p. 59) and Kornhauser (*The Politics of Mass Society*, p. 94) make similar observations, though more briefly. In contrast to the mass political theorists to which reference is made in the present essay, Mills focuses less on the political danger of extremism from the mass population than on its inability to function with political effectiveness. Nor does he suggest, as do the bulk of the mass theorists, an irrational or a noninterest component to vigorous dissent.

21. Mills, *The Power Elite*, p. 321.

22. E. V. Walter, " 'Mass Society.' The Late Stages of an Idea," *Social Research*, 31 (Winter 1964), 391–410. In this essay the author traces the changing character of the concept of masses over time.

23. Ibid., p. 401.

24. Ibid.

25. Philip Selznick, *The Organizational Weapon* (New York: McGraw-Hill, 1952), p. 284.

26. Kornhauser, *The Politics of Mass Society*, p. 14.

27. The claim here need not be so much the lack of group social relationships as the absence in such relations of a distinctive sense of group interest and the means to interpret social phenomena and personal experience, manipulate and control the environment, seek redress of grievances, or even communicate effectively to those in power.

28. Nisbet, *The Quest for Community*, pp. 198–199.

29. Hannah Arendt, *The Origins of Totalitarianism* (New York: Harcourt Brace Jovanovich, 1951), p. 305. For similar treatment, see Emil Lederer, *State of the Masses* (New York: Norton, 1940), and Sigmund Neumann's chapter, "The Amorphous Masses Emerge," in his *Permanent Revolution*, 2nd ed. (New York: Praeger, 1965), pp. 96–117.

30. Arendt, *The Origins of Totalitarianism*, p. 305.

31. See Mills, *The Power Elite*, pp. 302–304. Note that his use of the concept, however, is actually somewhat distinct from the preceding. For Mills, masses represent the opposite of publics. Mass refers to a population lacking a consciousness or structural unity vis-à-vis an object of concern.

It is a population that has little knowledge, efficacy, or means of expression in regard to the debilitating features of its environment. Mills, however, suggests little distinctive behaviorial dynamics. This is not an interpretation of the concept, though, that characterizes the body of thought being evaluated here.

As is suggested later, it is the very failure of most theorists to recognize the generality of Mills' observation—even among group-involved and secure populations—that leads to major difficulties in their analysis of both dissident behavior and the nature of the political process in presumably democratic societies.

32. Neumann, "The Amorphous Masses Emerge," p. 108.

33. José Ortega y Gasset, *The Revolt of the Masses* (New York: Norton, 1940), p. 10.

34. Gabriel Marcel, *Man Against Mass Society* (Chicago: Regnery, 1952), p. 8. For recognition of the usage as in the tradition of Ortega y Gasset, see p. 10.

35. Karl Jaspers, *Man in the Modern Age* (London: Routledge & Kegan Paul, 1951), p. 41.

36. The creation of masses, however, may at times be a conscious and deliberate process. This is in fact one of the main characteristics of totalitarianism in the mass theorist's discussion of this form of rule.

37. Kornhauser, *The Politics of Mass Society,* p. 142.

38. Ibid., Chap. 7, "Discontinuities in Community."

39. Ibid.

40. Ibid., p. 182.

41. Of course, there are additional features to this change. Thus, new industrial, managerial, and military elements increasingly contended for elite status and membership in the ruling classes. At the same time, there was a decline in the potency of landed aristocratic, theocratic, and some mercantile elements. The ensuing economic and political changes led to a change in the composition of elites and an altered distribution of power within and among major strata of society. In effect, this is the vital other side of the coin to the process of democratization elaborated previously.

42. For a useful summary description see Stein Rokkan's essay "Mass Suffrage, Secret Voting and Political Participation," in Lewis A. Coser, ed., *Political Sociology* (New York: Harper Torchbooks, 1966), pp. 101–131. Also see Reinhard Bendix and Stein Rokkan, "The Extension of Citizenship to the Lower Classes," in R. Bendix, *Nation Building and Citizenship* (New York: Wiley, 1964), pp. 74–101. See T. H. Marshall's classic essay "Citizenship and Social Class," in *Class, Citizenship, and Social Development* (Garden City, N.Y.: Doubleday Anchor, 1965), pp. 71–134.

43. Ortega y Gasset, *The Revolt of the Masses,* p. 7.

44. Kornhauser, *The Politics of Mass Society,* "The Loss of Authority in Mass Society," pp. 25–30, and "Accessible Elites," pp. 51–60.

45. Ibid., p. 27.

46. Ibid., p. 28.

47. This is Scheler's phrase, as used by Mannheim, *Man and Society*, p. 45.

48. Selznick, *The Organizational Weapon*, p. 278. The expression is a part of a descriptive summary of mass theory and is not meant necessarily to represent Selznick's own perspective.

49. Kornhauser, p. 27.

50. Walter Lippman, *Essays in the Public Philosophy* (New York: Mentor Library, 1955), p. 19.

51. It may in some instances be granted that a broader (though one might say compromised) interpretation or use of mass theory permits it to attend to certain forms of political behavior in which the characteristics of the population involved do evidence distinct group interests and intermediate group ties; that is, the population does not constitute a mass. Thus in some instances a loose interpretation of the concerns of mass political theory will cause it to be applied to behavior in which the population involved is not a mass, but the behavior does presumably exhibit the mass behavioral characteristics elaborated earlier. Hence the behavior in question may still pose a threat to freedom and be the antithesis of rational reasonable governance and be productive of consequences similar to those produced by mass populations. In other words, even if the population involved does not satisfy the conditions of a mass population–particularly by the absence of a distinct interest component–mass political theory may be perceived as still retaining some relevance. This would then primarily rest on its attention to a certain type of antidemocratic behavior, the necessity of preventing such behavior, and the kind of social and political structures that mitigate the possibility of mass political behavior. This perspective on mass theory will be evaluated in later chapters.

52. Kornhauser distinguishes between these two terms. "Remote objects are national and international issues or events, abstract symbols, and whatever else is known only through the mas media.... The sphere of proximate objects consists of things that directly concern the individual" (*The Politics of Mass Society*, pp. 43–44).

53. Kornhauser, pp. 44–45.

54. Ibid., p. 46.

55. Joseph R. Gusfield, "Mass Society and Extremist Politics," *American Sociological Review*, 27 (February 1962), p. 23.

56. In this regard, however, the extant literature is less mass political literature than writings influenced by mass political theory.

57. Arendt, *The Origins of Totalitarianism*, p. 310.

58. Neumann, "The Amorphous Masses Emerge," p. 108.

59. Nisbet, *The Quest for Community*, p. 34.

60. Eric Hoffer, *The True Believer* (New York: New American Library, 1951), p. 57.

61. Mannheim, *Man and Society*, p. 63.

62. For discussions and studies of politically alienated behavior see, among others, Wayne Thompson and John E. Horton, "Political Alienation

as a Force in Political Action," *Social Forces*, 38 (1960), 190–195; John E. Horton and Wayne E. Thompson, "Powerlessness and Political Negativism: A Study of Defeated Local Referendums"; *American Journal of Sociology*, 67 (March 1962), 482–493; Murray B. Levin, *The Alienated Voter* (New York: Holt, Rinehart & Winston, 1960); Joel D. Aberback, "Alienation and Political Behavior," *American Political Science Review*, 64 (June 1970), 389–410; David C. Schwartz, *Political Alienation and Political Behavior* (Chicago: Aldine, 1973). A critique of the use of the alienation interpretation may be found in the study by Robert L. Crain, Elihu Katz, and Donald B. Rosenthal, *The Politics of Community Conflicts* (Indianapolis, Ind.: Bobbs-Merrill, 1969). Also see the item by Clarence Stone, "Local Referendums: An Alternative to the Alienated Voter Model," *Public Opinion Quarterly*, 29 (1962), 213–222.

63. See David Riesman, *Faces in the Crowd: Individual Studies in Character and Politics* (Garden City, N.Y.: Doubleday, 1955), p. 35; John Horton, "The Angry Voter: A Study of Political Alienation," Ph.D. dissertation (Cornell University, 1960), p. 486; and Horton and Thompson, "Powerlessness and Political Negativism," especially p. 486.

64. Horton and Thompson, ibid., p. 493.

65. Stone, "Local Referendums."

66. See Crain et al., *The Politics of Community Conflicts*, for a critique of this perspective.

67. Horton, "The Angry Voter."

68. Arendt, *The Origins of Totalitarianism*, p. 316.

69. Neumann, "The Amorphous Masses Emerge," p. 115.

70. Kornhauser, *The Politics of Mass Society*, p. 123.

71. See, for instance, Arendt's development of this theme in regard to the rise of totalitarianism in Russia, *The Origins of Totalitarianism*, pp. 312–316.

72. Nisbet, *The Quest for Community*, p. 208.

73. While most mass society writers view totalitarian society as merely a possible form of mass society, Kornhauser distinguishes between the two. Mass society is the society of accessible elites and available masses in which involvement in intermediate relations is not extensive and those intermediate organizations that exist are not effective centers of autonomous power. Totalitarian society, however, lacks elite accessibility but maintains mass availability. Further, while intermediate organizations do involve individuals extensively, they are merely arms of the state and not autonomous centers of power. In a sense these organizations are of a mass character in terms of the individuals' powerlessness within them.

74. See Nisbet, *The Quest for Community*, and also Kornhauser, *The Politics of Mass Society*, especially pp. 76–90.

75. Nisbet, ibid., pp. 265.

76. Ibid., p. 268.

77. Kornhauser, *The Politics of Mass Society*, p. 230.

78. Ibid., p. 78.

79. Ibid., p. 99.

80. Ibid., p. 76.

81. See Nisbet, *The Quest for Community*, p. 251. Quote is from p. 254.

82. See Peter Bachrach, *The Theory of Democratic Elitism* (Boston: Little, Brown, 1967); Carole Pateman, *Participation and Democratic Theory* (London: Cambridge University Press, 1970); and also Jack Walker, "A Critique of the Elitist Theory of Democracy," *American Political Science Review*, 60 (June 1966), 285–295. See also the response by Robert Dahl, "Further Reflections on 'The Elitist Theory of Democracy,'" *American Political Science Review*, 60 (June 1966), 296–305; and Jack Walker, "A Reply to 'Further Reflections on "The Elitist Theory of Democracy,"'" *American Political Science Review*, 60 (June 1966), 391–392.

83. Lane Davis, "The Cost of Realism: Contemporary Restatements of Democracy," *Western Political Quarterly*, 17 (1964), 37–46.

84. There is considerable question of whether a term or category such as democratic elitism or contemporary democratic theory can be applied to any group of writers with any degree of precision. See Dahl "Further Reflections on 'The Elitist Theory of Democracy.'" Yet I would suggest that there does exist a distinct set of ideas that provides support and sometimes finds expression in mass theory writings. And these are ideas that are evidenced to a greater degree in the writing of some in contrast to other political theorists. Works such as the following exhibit some of these ideas: Bernard R. Berelson, Paul F. Lazarsfeld, and William N. McPhee, *Voting* (Chicago: University of Chicago Press, 1956) Chap. 14, "Democratic Practice and Democratic Theory"; Robert Dahl, *A Preface to Democratic Theory* (Chicago: University of Chicago Press, 1956), and *Who Governs?* (New Haven, Conn.: Yale University Press, 1961) particularly the last portion of the book, "Pluralist Democracy: An Explanation," pp. 223–325; Giovanni Sartori, *Democratic Theory* (Detroit, Mich.: Wayne State University Press, 1962); Seymour M. Lipset, *Political Man* (Garden City, N.Y.: Doubleday, 1960); and Joseph A. Schumpeter, *Capitalism, Socialism and Democracy* (New York: Harper Torchbook; 1962); see especially Part IV, "Socialism and Democracy."

85. Kornhauser, *The Politics of Mass Society*, p. 237.

86. Ibid., p. 47.

87. If we were to define mass behavior and mass society exclusively in terms of behavior, as may be useful at times, without any attention to the character of those involved, then of course mass society need not be constituted of masses.

Chapter 4. Social structural analysis assessed and related comments

1. Kornhauser, *The Politics of Mass Society* (London: Routledge & Kegan Paul, 1960), p. 74.

2. For discussions at least partially relevant to present concerns it would

be necessary to turn to sociological writings of a more theoretical and abstract nature, as well as material in the area of audience research and theory in regard to mass media communication and to some slender elements in the small group research literature. Unfortunately, insufficient effort has been made to bring together research and conceptualization in these diverse areas. While one might point to the electoral behavior and personal influence studies as an attempt, these have dealt with concerns somewhat marginal to the kind of political behavioral and personal experiences to which reference is being made here. Further, the analyses of group properties pertinent to our interests are limited in these research areas. Even in mass media and small group research, however, little is attempted in terms of an analysis of the nature of individual experience within broader societal circumstances. See the discussion in Philip H. Ennis, "The Social Structure of Communication Systems: A Theoretical Proposal," *Studies in Public Communication,* No. 3 (Summer 1961), 120–144, and the references cited there.

3. See Nisbet's powerful and sensitive treatise, *The Quest for Community* (New York: Oxford University Press, 1953).

4. The analogue to the different conceptions of intermediate groups that are obtained is that, in effect, the concept of masses also becomes open to somewhat different interpretations. For writers such as Nisbet and Fromm it is the lack of memberships in viable, functional, and authoritative community structures. For Kornhauser, given his operationalization of intermediate groups, the mass conversely becomes, more narrowly, that population that lacks ties to voluntary or other intermediate organizational structures. Yet his overall theoretical stance appears to accord more closely than the preceding suggests with the perspective of Nisbet and Fromm on masses. And so there is an element of ambiguity introduced into his analysis.

5. See the discussion in Frank Parkin, *Middle Class Radicalism* (Manchester: Manchester University Press, 1968), pp. 12–14.

6. This criticism, as well as others similar to some of the observations found in the present discussion, is raised in Charles Perrow's essay "The Sociological Perspective and Political Pluralism," *Social Research,* 31 (Winter 1964), 411–422.

7. See Richard F. Hamilton, *Class and Politics in the United States* (New York: Wiley, 1972), pp. 67, 68, 69, footnotes 25 and 30; Charles R. Wright and Herbert H. Hyman, "Voluntary Association Memberships of American Adults: Evidence from National Sample Surveys," *American Sociological Review,* 23 (June 1958), 284–294, and "Trends in Voluntary Association Memberships of American Adults: Replication Based on Secondary Analysis of National Sample Surveys," *American Sociological Review,* 36 (April 1971), 191–206; and Gabriel A. Almond and Sidney Verba, *The Civic Culture: Political Attitudes and Democracy in Five Nations* (Princeton, N.J.: Princeton University Press, 1963).

A more precise analysis of organizational membership would, of course, have to distinguish among different socioeconomic strata. Thus involvement would vary inversely with class, as would feelings of alienation and anomie. The important question is not so much how much participation there is, but who participates, to what extent, in what type of organizations, and with what effect. See the review and bibliographic essay by Dale R. Marshall, "Who Participates in What?" *Urban Affairs Quarterly*, 4 (December 1968), 201–223; also the review and sources in Russell L. Curtis, Jr., and Louis A. Zurcher, Jr., "Voluntary Associations and the Social Integration of the Poor," *Social Problems*, 18 (Winter 1971), 339–357.

8. See the discussion in C. Wright Mills, *The Power Elite* (New York: Oxford University Press, 1957), pp. 306–309.

9. Referring to David Holden's "Associations as Reference Groups: An Approach to the Problem," *Rural Sociology*, 30 (1965), 63–74, survey of material in this area, Maurice Pinard states:

> ... that a large number of organizations do not actually represent reference points for their members, even in small rural communities. In this regard, a pluralist society with a proliferation of autonomous intermediate groupings could be relatively little more restraining than a mass society. It would seem, in fact, that if restraining effects are to be ascribed to the intermediate structure, primary groups and the social networks of small communities, rather than most associations and organizations, are the groupings to be considered, since they are more likely to act as reference points (*The Rise of a Third Party, A Study in Crisis Politics* [Englewood Cliffs, N.J.: Prentice-Hall, 1971], p. 184).

10. Henry S. Kariel, "Pluralism," *International Encyclopedia of the Social Sciences*, XII (New York: Macmillan, 1968), p. 168.

11. Robert Michels, *Political Parties* (New York: Dover Publications, 1959). English translation first published in 1915.

12. Hamilton, *Class and Politics in the United States*, p. 36.

13. See Scott Greer, *The Emerging City, Myth and Reality* (New York: Free Press, 1962), and "Urbanism Reconsidered: A Comparative Study of Local Areas in a Metropolis," *American Sociological Review*, 211 (February 1956), 19–25; Peter Orleans, "Robert Park and Social Area Analysis: A Convergence in Urban Sociology," *Urban Affairs Quarterly*, 1 (June 1966), 5–19; and Eshref Shevky and Wendell Bell, *Social Area Analysis* (Stanford, Calif.: Stanford University Press, 1955).

14. U.S. Bureau of Census, *Statistical Abstract of the United States: 1972*, 93d ed. (Washington, D.C., 1972), Table 40.

15. The standard of ethnicity used is that of either foreign-born or born of foreign or mixed parents. The figures used are principally derived from Table 42 of the *Statistical Abstract of the United States: 1972*, with some figures also obtained from Table 29 of the *Statistical Abstract of the United States: 1966*. The totals given in the text would be increased several times if they had been given merely in terms of ethnic origin. Even

defining populations by the existence of a foreign mother tongue would give greater numbers for some ethnic populations; see *Statistical Abstract of the United States: 1972,* Table 40.

16. *U.S. Statistical Abstract: 1966,* Table 29.

17. Some relevant studies on family ties in urban society include Michael Young and Peter Willmott, *Family and Kinship in East London* (London: Routledge & Kegan Paul, 1957); Elizabeth Bott, *Family and Social Network* (London: Tavistock Publications, 1957); Bert N. Adams, *Kinship in an Urban Setting* (Chicago: Markham Publishing Co., 1968); Eugene Litwak, "Geographic Mobility and Extended Family Cohesion," *American Sociological Review,* 25 (February 1960), 9–21; and Marvin Sussman, "The Isolated Nuclear Family: Fact or Fiction," *Social Problems,* 24 (1960), 231–240.

18. Eugene Litwak, "Geographic Mobility and Extended Family Cohesion," *American Sociological Review,* 25 (June 1960), 385–394.

19. Scott Greer, *The Emerging City* (New York: Free Press, 1962), Chap. 4.

20. Albert Hunter, *Symbolic Communities* (Chicago: University of Chicago Press, 1974).

21. Ibid., p. 12.

22. Harold L. Wilensky, "Mass Society and Mass Culture," *American Sociological Review,* 29 (April 1964), 173–197, Table 1.

23. Joel Smith, William H. Form, and Gregory P. Stone, "Local Intimacy in a Middle-Sized City," *American Journal of Sociology,* 60 (November 1954), 276–284, Table 4. Low, medium, and high categories are derived by splitting their six-scale categories into three pairs.

24. Scott Greer and Ella Kube, "Urbanism and Social Structure: A Los Angeles Study," in Marvin Sussman, ed., *Community Structure and Analysis* (New York: T. Y. Crowell, 1959), pp. 93–112.

25. Wendell Bell and Marion Boat, "Urban Neighborhoods and Informal Social Relations," *American Journal of Sociology,* 62 (January 1957), 391–398, Table 1.

26. William H. Key, "Rural–Urban Social Participation," in Sylvia F. Fava, ed., *Urbanism in World Perspective* (New York: T. Y. Crowell Co., 1968), pp. 305–312 and Table 1.

27. Lloyd A. Free and Hadley Cantril, *The Political Beliefs of Americans* (New York: Simon & Schuster, 1968), Table VII-I, p. 97, and p. 101.

28. Charles Kadushin. "The Friends and Supporters of Psychotherapy: On Social Circles in Urban Life," *American Sociological Review,* 31 (December 1966), 790.

29. Ibid., p. 801.

30. Joseph Bensman, "Status Communities in an Urban Society: The Musical Community," paper delivered at the annual meeting of the American Sociological Association, August 1967, as reported by Ceclia S. Heller, in C. S. Heller, ed., *Structural Social Inequality* (New York: Macmillan, 1969), pp. 117–118.

31. Ennis' essay suggests the broadened framework within which to examine group-type relationships.

32. See Raymond F. Wolfinger, et al., "America's Radical Right: Politics and Ideology," in David Apter, ed., *Ideology and Discontent* (New York: Free Press, 1964), pp. 262–293. Rudolf Heberle's research suggests that Nazi support in the rural areas of Germany was highest in the areas where the degree of social solidarity was greatest. See his *Social Movements* (New York: Appleton, 1951) pp. 222–236, and for a fuller treatment his *From Democracy to Nazism: A Regional Case Study on Political Parties in Germany* (Baton Rouge, La.: State University Press, 1945). See my discussion in Chap. 5.

33. W. Alvin Pitcher, " 'The Politics of Mass Society': Significance for the Churches," in D. B. Robertson, ed., *Voluntary Associations, A Study of Groups in Free Societies* (Richmond, Va.: John Knox Press, 1966), p. 255.

34. Ibid., pp. 253–254.

35. Ibid., p. 254.

36. Joseph R. Gusfield, "Mass Society and Extremist Politics," *American Sociological Review*, 27 (February 1962), p. 20.

37. Ibid.

38. Ibid., p. 28.

39. Emile Durkheim, *Professional Ethics and Civic Morals*, and Edward Shils, "Daydreams and Nightmares: Reflections on the Criticism of Mass Culture," *The Sewanee Review*, 65 (1957), 586–608.

40. Pinard, *The Rise of a Third Party*, p. 185. Also see Donald Von Eschen, Jerome Kirk, and Maurice Pinard, "The Organizational Substructure of Disorderly Politics," *Social Forces*, 49 (June 1971), 529–544.

41. Ibid., p. 186. Robert L. Crain and Donald B. Rosenthal's discussion of community conflict and decision making suggests that under some conditions citizen participation in voluntary associations provides a more concerned and more readily mobilizable population and a greater likelihood of community dissidence and conflict. See "Community Status as a Dimension of Local Decision Making," *American Sociological Review*, 30 (December 1967), 970–984. James Coleman also finds that community protest initially implicates the organization member and the more highly integrated, not the least. See *Community Conflict* (New York: Free Press, 1957). Though concerned with somewhat different issues, the material in Seymour Lipset's essays "Working-Class Authoritarianism" and especially " 'Fascism' – Left, Right, and Center" (Chaps. 4 and 5 in *Political Man* [Garden City, N.Y.: Doubleday, 1960]) appear to support this contention. Attention should be called to one qualification made by some of the scholars to whom we have referred. A distinction must be made, in Pinard's words, "between *attraction* to a conflict and *intensity of participation* in it. . . ." The least integrated are least attracted to a conflict, contrary to mass society theory, but when attracted they become the most unrestrained in their participation in accord with mass theory. (See Pinard, pp. 188–189.)

42. See Parkin, *Middle Class Radicalism.*

43. See Pinard, *The Rise of a Third Party*, Chap. 8.

44. Jo Freeman, "The Origins of the Women's Liberation Movement," *American Journal of Sociology*, 78 (January 1973), 792–811.

45. Gary T. Marx, *Protest and Prejudice: A Study of Belief in the Black Community*, rev. ed. (New York: Harper & Row, 1969).

46. John M. Orbell, "Protest Participation Among Southern Negro College Students," *American Political Science Review*, 61 (June 1967), 446–456; Peter K. Eisinger, "Racial Differences in Protest Participation," *American Political Science Review*, 68 (June 1974), 592–606. Also see Clark McPhail's review of the literature on urban disturbance in the United States, "Civil Disorder Participation: A Critical Examination of Recent Research," *American Sociological Review*, 36 (December 1971), 1058–1073.

47. Carl J. Couch, "Collective Behavior: An Examination of Some Stereotypes," *Social Problems*, 15 (winter 1968), p. 318.

48. Note that distinctions are made in terms of integration as it is sensed or experienced by individuals within the society. The reference, hence, is not to societal conditions of consensus or dissension.

49. The notion of interest is an important concept in this essay and is referred to with considerable frequency. Principally, it refers to the needs and associated claims propounded by or resident in a group, usually as a reflection of some distinctive position in society, though sometimes reflecting a particular set of beliefs concerning needs and claims not definable in terms of or reducible to the structural or societal location of the individual group members. In the former case the interest basis of group behavior can be specified in terms of one of the major structurally defining dimensions of society. Interest may be defined in terms of economic, regional, communal, religious, or other bases of group cohesion and concern, each of which is a major dimension of social organization. As noted, however, the interest basis may also reflect needs and claims not based on dimensions of societal organization. Though it receives little attention in the present discussion, interest may also be conceptualized in terms of group-related needs, whether consciousness of such needs or "interests" has developed or not. Thus a collectivity may have interests of which it is not yet aware. While the present student would accept such a proposition, and it is a potentially powerful tool of social analysis and criticism, the present emphasis on behavior has involved a concern principally with interest in its subjective form, hence the frequent reference to the importance of class or group consciousness in influencing the probability and character of political behavior. See Isaac D. Balbus, "The Concept of Interest in Pluralist and Marxian Analysis," *Politics and Society*, 1 (February 1971), 151–177.

50. For discussions of the use of somewhat similar dimensions of social organization and distinctions among political groups see Richard Rose and Derek Urwin, "Social Cohesion, Political Parties, and Strains in Re-

gimes," *Comparative Political Studies*, 2 (April 1969), 7–67, and Seymour Lipset and Stein Rokkan, "Cleavage Structures, Party Systems, and Voter Alignments: An Introduction," in Seymour M. Lipset and Stein Rokkan, eds., *Party Systems and Voter Alignments: Cross-National Perspectives* (New York: Free Press, 1967), pp. 1–64.

51. See the discussion in Chalmers Johnson, *Revolutionary Change* (Boston: Little, Brown, 1966), pp. 32 ff., especially p. 33.

52. Ralf Dahrendorf, *Class and Class Conflict in Industrial Society* (Stanford, Calif.: Stanford University Press, 1959), p. 135, as quoted in Johnson, p. 35.

53. Actually, of course, the dimensions of social organization discussed throughout this section do not lead directly to the appearance of groups in a *subjective* sense. They merely provide the potential for such groups to appear.

54. Norbert Wiley, "America's Unique Class Politics: The Interplay of the Labor, Credit, and Commodity Markets," *American Sociological Review*, 32 (August 1967), 529–541, and Max Weber, "Class, Status, Party," in Hans Gerth and C. Wright Mills, eds., *From Max Weber* (New York: Oxford University Press, 1958), pp. 180–195. The classic treatment is, of course, the work of Karl Marx.

55. Merle Kling, "Towards a Theory of Power and Political Instability in Latin America," *Western Political Quarterly*, 9 (1956), 21–35.

56. See the essays in Daniel Bell, ed., *The Radical Right* (Garden City, N.Y.: Doubleday, 1963), especially Richard Hofstadter's "The Pseudo-Conservative Revolt" and Bell's "Interpretations of American Politics." Also see Hofstadter's *The Age of Reform* (New York: Alfred A. Knopf, 1955). For a useful theoretical and case analysis see Joseph R. Gusfield's study of the temperance movement, *Symbolic Crusade* (Urbana, Ill.: University of Illinois Press, 1963).

57. There is a third social category characterized by a status component that could be established. This refers to communal-type populations, which will be described in the text. Because they involve very distinct population groups and frequently distinct economic, political, and social issues, a separate categorization appears advisable.

58. The discussion that follows in the text elaborates on these in the context of a condition of conflict. Naturally, such categories may be present in a nonconflicted circumstance.

59. Everett Hughes, more than two decades ago, pointed to the potential for what he referred to as "status protest" when a considerable disparity exists between a group's sense of dignity and its objective status position or degree of respect accorded to it. See "Social Change and Status Protest: An Essay on the Marginal Man," *Phylon*, 10 (1949), 48–65.

60. Refer to Gusfield, *Symbolic Crusade*, for these and other examples; also, see the essays in Bell, *The Radical Right*. Also see Hofstadter's treatment of the Progressive movement (in *The Age of Reform*) and Lipset's

discussion on the basis for the liberal orientation of intellectuals in America (in *Political Man*).

61. Gusfield, *Symbolic Crusade*, p. 11.

62. In a related vein see the interesting discussion in John Meyer and James Roth, "A Reinterpretation of American Status Politics," *Pacific Sociological Review*, 13 (Spring 1970), 95–103.

63. In regard to these last two points see the discussion and analysis in Gerard A. Brandmeyer and R. Serge Denisoff, "Status Politics: An Appraisal of the Application of a Concept," *Pacific Sociological Review*, 12 (Spring 1969), 5–11.

64. Meyer and Roth, "A Reinterpretation of American Status Politics," p. 96.

65. This is because racial or ethnic categories possess a much more profound cultural content than is usually present in the concept of status, particularly in terms of the responses of society to a given status and of the status occupant to the society. There is also the absence especially on the matter of race, of the presence or sense of a hierarchy with permeable strata.

66. On communal ties see Karl W. Deutsch, *Nationalism and Social Communication*, 2nd ed. (Cambridge, Mass.: M.I.T. Press, 1966), and Leonard Dobb, *Patriotism and Nationalism* (New Haven, Conn.: Yale University Press, 1964).

67. See Clifford Geertz, "The Integrative Revolution, Primordial Sentiments and Civil Politics in the New States," in Clifford Geertz, ed., *Old Societies and New States* (New York: Free Press, 1963), pp. 105–157, for a discussion of the problem of communal identity (or, as he phrases it following Shils' usage, of "primordial sentiments") and integral civil community in the newly independent underdeveloped states. The exclusive nature of communal identity and conflict vis-à-vis the state poses a much more serious challenge to the new states than conflicts of an economic or narrow interest group nature, as the ties and issues implicated in the latter range of conflicts do not exclude loyalty to or membership within the broader unit of the nation. These are not, as is the case with communal membership, "maximal social units," in Geertz's phrase. "Economic or class or intellectual disaffection threatens revolution, but disaffection based on race, language, or culture threatens partition, irredentism, or merger, a redrawing of the very limits of the state, a new definition of its domain. Civil discontent finds its natural outlet in the seizing, legally or illegally, of the state apparatus. Primordial discontent strives more deeply and is satisfied less easily." (p. 111).

68. Discussions of communal-type conflict are many. Note may be made of a few somewhat more theoretical treatments, such as those of Geertz, Deutsch, and Dobb, already mentioned (notes 66 and 67), and Ronald Inglehart and Margaret Woodward, "Language Conflicts and Political Community," *Comparative Studies in Society and History*, 10 (1968), 27–45.

69. Inglehart and Woodward's survey, ibid., provides an interesting

discussion of a number of instances of the relationship between communal contention and economic and blocked social mobility factors.

70. Religious-based groupings, however, will be considered as a separate category.

71. Vladimir C. Nahirny's "Some Observations on Ideological Groups," *American Journal of Sociology*, 67 (January 1962), 397–405, contains an elaboration of a number of points, some of which are related to the present concept.

72. For some pertinent discussions see such fundamental theoretical and empirical essays and studies as Ralph Linten, "Nativistic Movements," *American Anthropologist*, 58 (February 1943), 230–240; Anthony F. C. Wallace, "Revitalization Movements," *American Anthropologist*, 58 (April 1956), 264–281; Norman Cohn, *The Pursuit of the Millennium*, rev. ed. (New York: Oxford University Press, 1970); Vittorio Lanternari, *The Religions of the Oppressed* (New York: Knopf, 1963); Peter Worsley, *The Trumpet Shall Sound*, rev. ed. (New York: Schocken Books, 1968); and Sylvia A. Thrupp, ed., *Millennial Dreams in Action* (The Hague: Mouton and Co., 1962).

73. Stein Rokkan has, for example, traced this process for Norway in an interesting essay, "Electoral Mobilization, Party Competition, and National Integration," in Joseph La Palombara and Myron Weiner, eds., *Political Parties and Political Development* (Princeton, N.J.: Princeton University Press, 1966), pp. 241–265. These are plausible and probable expectations. Yet it is possible to imagine in the context of changing contemporary ideology and concerns a counterprocess in which increasing stress on local autonomy, control, and distinctiveness might in some circumstances be productive of some regional conflict.

74. As the reader will recall from the discussion in Chapter 3, however, the concept of masses has actually been variously defined by different mass theorists.

75. Attention would more readily be drawn, for instance, to the fact of a group's existence over time and hence to its historical past. Once consideration is given to this circumstance and the nature of past experiences, study could be initiated of the cleavages, loyalties, alliances, grievances, and traditions established or accumulated from the past that have shaped present expectations, policy, and behavioral objectives. This would contribute to a heightening of awareness and attention to the content and nature of group identification and consciousness and consequent behavior, and it would further an assessment of their character. In turn, analysis of class identity and consciousness is crucial to any conclusion as to the mass or nonmass character of the population in question and to the nature of its political behavior. In another direction, attending to structurally and interest-defined collectivities increases the likelihood that a broad analysis of political structures and processes (lacking in mass theory) will be initiated and that consideration will be given to questions of political access, representation, and responsiveness, to questions of unmet grievances, to the

denial of petitions and demands, to inadequacies in elite functioning, the nature of changing political alliances, and processes of political resource mobilization. Attention to factors such as these is crucial in understanding the purposes, developments, and consequences of political behavior, and the extent to which such behavior may be adjudged of a reasonable or rational character.

76. The review by Karl Deutsch appears in the *American Political Science Review*, 55 (March 1961), 149.

77. Michael Harrington, *Accidental Century* (New York: Macmillan, 1965); Chap. 7, "The Masses," makes a similar point.

78. See particularly Wayne Thompson and John Horton, "Political Alienation as a Force in Political Action," *Social Forces*, 38 (1960), 190–195; John Horton, "The Angry Voter: A Study of Political Alienation," Ph.D. dissertation (Cornell University, 1960); and Murray B. Levin, *The Alienated Voter* (New York: Holt, Rinehart & Winston, 1960).

79. See John C. Leggett, *Class, Race, and Labor* (New York: Oxford University Press, 1968), and his "Uprootedness and Working-Class Consiousness," *American Journal of Sociology*, 68 (1963), 682–692.

80. It does appear possible that in some circumstances groups acting in terms of a conscious awareness of being an interest-based collectivity may tend to manifest both dimensions of mass behavior delineated here. This will principally be a tendency, however, not a fully achieved expression, and certain distinct properties will very probably be found in the particular situation. Thus the behavior is likely to exhibit a greater rational interest character than implied by the usual meaning of mass behavior. The situation is also likely to exhibit a past history of highly emotionally charged experiences, devisive events, considerable interest or other group-based threats, and an irresponsible and demagogic leadership elite. It is also more likely to appear among collectivities whose interest basis tends toward a character such as religious, regional, or status identity, rather than quantifiable and negotiable issues of partial gain or loss, as in the economic arenas. (In this regard see the comments of Lipset and Rokkan.) Thus, for instance, communal conflicts would seem to offer not infrequent examples.

Chapter 5. Radical political behavior: cognitive negotiation of a sociopolitical environment

1. Portions of the present sections first appeared in the author's "New Perspectives of Political Radicalism," *Journal of Political and Military Sociology*, 2 (Spring 1974), 113–124.

2. See Charles Tilly, "Collective Violence in European Perspective," in Hugh Davis Graham and Ted Robert Gurr, eds., *The History of Violence in America* (New York: Bantam, 1969), pp. 4–45; "The Changing Place of Collective Violence," in Melvin Richter, ed., *Essays in Social and Political History* (Cambridge, Mass.: Harvard University Press, 1970), pp.

139–164; "Does Modernization Breed Revolution," *Comparative Politics,* 5 (April 1973), 425–447; Edward Shorter and Charles Tilly, *Strikes in France, 1830–1960* (London: Cambridge University Press, 1974); and David Snyder and Charles Tilly, "Hardship and Collective Violence in France, 1830 to 1960," *American Sociological Review,* 37 (October 1972), 520–532.

3. Eric Wolf, *Peasant Wars of the Twentieth Century* (New York: Harper & Row, 1969).

4. Robert M. Fogelson and Robert B. Hill, *Who Riots? A Study of Participation in the 1967 Riots,* Supplemental Studies for the National Advisory Commission on Civil Disorders (Washington, D.C.: GPO, 1968); Clark McPhail, "Civil Disorder Participation: A Critical Examination of Recent Research," *American Sociological Review,* 36 (December 1971), 1058–1073; Anthony Oberschall, "The Los Angeles Riot," *Social Problems,* 15 (Spring 1968), 322–342; Jeffrey M. Paige, "Political Orientation and Riot Participation," *American Sociological Review,* 36 (October 1971), 810–820; Jules J. Wanderer, "1967 Riots: A Test of the Congruity of Events," *Social Problems,* 16 (Fall 1968), 193–198; and Richard A. Berk and Howard E. Aldrich, "Patterns of Vandalism During Civil Disorders as an Indicator of Selection of Targets," *American Sociological Review,* 37 (October 1972), 533–547.

5. Norman Pollack, *The Populist Response to Industrial America* (Cambridge, Mass.: Harvard University Press, 1962); Walter T. K. Nugent, *The Tolerant Populists, Kansas Populism and Nativism* (Lawrence, Kans.: The University of Kansas Press, 1969); Gene O. Clanton, *Kansas Populism* (Lawrence, Kansas: The University of Kansas Press, 1969); Robert F. Durden, *The Climax of Populism: The Election of 1896* (Lexington, Ky.: University Press of Kentucky, 1965).

6. Michael Rogin, *The Intellectuals and McCarthy: The Radical Spector* (Cambridge, Mass.: M.I.T. Press, 1967).

7. William Allen, *The Nazi Seizure of Power* (Chicago: Quadrangle Books, 1965).

8. Richard Hamilton, *Affluence and the French Worker in the Fourth Republic* (Princeton, N.J.: Princeton University Press, 1967).

9. Gerald Sorin, *The New York Abolitionists: A Case Study of Political Radicalism* (Conn.: Greenwood Publishing Corp., 1971).

10. Maurice Pinard, *The Rise of a Third Party: The Social Credit Party in Quebec in the 1962 Federal Election* (Englewood Cliffs, N.J.: Prentice-Hall, 1971).

11. Maurice Pinard, "Poverty and Political Movements," *Social Problems* 15 (Fall 1967), 250–263, and "Mass Society and Political Movements," *American Journal of Sociology,* 73 (May 1968), 682–690.

12. See Alejandro Portes' "Leftist Radicalism in Chile: A Test of Three Hypotheses," *Comparative Politics,* 2 (January 1970), 251–274; "On the Logic of Post-Factum Explanations: The Hypothesis of Lower-Class Frustration as the Cause of Leftist Radicalism," *Social Forces,* 50 (September 1971), 26–44; "Political Primitivism, Differential Socialization, and Lower-

Class Leftist Radicalism," *American Sociological Review,* 36 (October 1971), 820–835; and "Urbanization and Politics in Latin America," *Social Science Quarterly,* 52 (December 1971), 697–720.

13. Portes, "Political Primitivism," ibid., p. 821.

14. Wayne A. Cornelius, Jr., "Urbanization as an Agent in Latin American Political Instability: The Case of Mexico," *American Political Science Review,* 63 (September 1969), 697–720; Portes, "On the Logic of Post-Factum Explanations"; Tilly, "Collective Violence in European Perspective."

15. Wayne A. Cornelius, Jr., "The Political Sociology of Cityward Migration in Latin America: Toward Empirical Theory," in Francine F. Rabinovitz and Felicity M. Trueblood, eds., *Latin American Urban Research,* I (Beverly Hills, Calif.: Sage Publication, 1971), and Joan Nelson, *Migrants, Urban Poverty, and Instability in Developing Nations* (Cambridge, Mass.: Center for International Affairs, Harvard University, 1969).

16. Ibid., p. 103.

17. Joel L. Aberbach and Jack L. Walker, "Political Trust and Racial Ideology," *American Political Science Review,* 64 (December 1970), 1199–1219; Edward N. Muller, "A Test of a Partial Theory of Potential for Violence," *American Political Science Review,* 64 (September 1972), 928–959; and Edward H. Ransford, "Isolation, Powerlessness, and Violence: A Study of Attitudes and Participation in the Watts Riot," *American Journal of Sociology,* 73 (March 1968), 581–720.

18. McPhail, "Civil Disorder Participation."

19. Ibid., p. 1071.

20. Maurice Zeitlin, *Revolutionary Politics and the Cuban Working Class* (Princeton, N.J.: Princeton University Press, 1967); James Petras and Maurice Zeitlin, "Miners and Agrarian Radicalism," *American Sociological Review* 32 (August 1967), 568–587; John C. Leggett, *Class, Race, and Labor* (New York: Oxford University Press, 1968); and Anthony M. Oram and Roberta S. Cohen, "The Development of Political Orientations Among Black and White Children," *American Sociological Review,* 38 (February 1973), 62–74.

21. Paige, "Political Orientation and Riot Participation," p. 818.

22. Herbert Blumer, "Society as Symbolic Interaction," in Arnold M. Rose, ed., *Human Society and Social Processes* (Boston: Houghton Mifflin Co., 1962), pp. 182–183.

23. McPhail, "Civil Disorder Participation," p. 1071. Also see Clark McPhail and David Miller, "The Assembling Process: A Theoretical and Empirical Examination," *American Sociological Review,* 38 (December 1973), 721–735, and Margaret J. Abudu Stark et al., "Some Empirical Patterns in a Riot Process," *American Sociological Review,* 39 (December 1974), 865–876.

24. Portes, "Political Primitivism."

25. Of course, broad systemic properties are also crucial in determining, at a level partially removed from individual determination, the nature of available political alternatives, the effectiveness of opposing political groups,

the possibility of coalitions and opportunities for mobilization, and so on –
all of which influence the likelihood of radical support and, more broadly,
the pattern of developing protest and change.

26. Antonio Gramsci, *Il Risorgimento*, 3rd. ed. (Torine: Einaudi, 1950),
pp. 199–200, quoted by Tilly in "Collective Violence in European Perspective," p. 12.

27. While the focus of Lucien Pye's discussion differs from the present
concerns and does not consider resulting conflicts and movements, his
treatment of six crises in political development – identity, legitimacy, penetration, participation, integration, and distribution – tends to imply these
concerns. See "Crises in Political Development" in his *Aspects of Political
Development* (Boston: Little, Brown, 1966), pp. 62–67.

28. Nelson, *Migrants, Urban Poverty*.

29. Robert Fried, "Urbanization and Italian Politics," *Journal of Politics*,
29 (1967), 505–534.

30. Nelson, *Migrants, Urban Poverty*, pp. 25–26.

31. Pinard, "Poverty and Political Movements."

32. See the discussion in Jack Walker, "A Critique of the Elitist Theory
of Democracy," *American Political Science Review*, 60 (June 1966), 285–
295; Theodore J. Lowi, "The Public Philosophy: Interest Group Liberalism," *American Political Science Review*, 61 (February 1967), 5–24, and
his "American Business, Public Policy, Case Studies and Political Theory,"
World Politics, 16 (1964), 677–715, and also the references cited in the
two Lowi essays.

33. Reprinted from *The Intellectuals and McCarthy* by Michael Paul
Rogin by permission of the MIT Press, Cambridge, Mass., pp. 272–273.

34. Ibid., pp. 185–186.

35. Tilly, "Collective Violence in European Perspective," p. 10.

36. Carl Couch has pointed out in his discussion of crowd behavior, and
more broadly of collective behavior, that the behavior of such populations
is not significantly different from that of other more institutionalized social
systems or of acceptable population elements. Nor can it be understood
"in terms of characteristics of the individual members." Instead, it is
necessary to direct "attention to social processes and social relationships."
(Collective Behavior: An Examination of Some Stereotypes," *Social Problems*, 15 (Winter 1968), 361.) Also see Richard A. Berk, *Collective
Behavior* (Dubuque, Iowa: Brown, 1974).

37. See Seymour M. Lipset, "Working-Class Authoritarianism," in *Political Man* (Garden City, N.Y.: Doubleday, 1960); Portes, "Political Primitivism"; and Walter Korpi, "Working Class Communism in Western
Europe: Rational and Non-Rational," (*American Sociological Review*, 36
(December 1971), 971–984.)

38. The case material is principally framed in terms of a test of mass
political theory. Additional types of data would be needed for a firmer
evaluation or test of other theories. In many instances, however, it is not
readily available. Yet, the case material does show the broad range of non-

psychological factors and conditions implicated in accounting for the behavior in question and points to the ability to explain such behavior as rational, volitional, and interest-based efforts. While the presence of some psychological factors cannot thereby be disproved, considerable question would seem to be raised as to their importance.

39. See earlier citations. Additional relevant work by the distinguished British historian Eric Hobsbawm includes his "The Machine Breakers," *Past and Present*, 1 (1952), 56–67; *The Age of Revolution* (London: Weidenfeld and Nicolson, 1962); and several of his essays in *Labouring Men* (London: Weidenfeld and Nicolson, 1964), which includes "The Machine Breakers." Also see E. P. Thompson, the *Making of the English Working Class* (New York: Vintage Books, 1966).

40. Tilly, "Collective Violence in European Perspective," p. 18.

41. George Rudé, The *Crowd in History, 1730–1848* (New York: Wiley, 1964), p. 23. Tilly similarly affirms the preceding points in his "Collective Violence in European Perspective."

42. Hobsbawm considers this phenomenon in "The Machine Breakers." The second quote appears in Hobsbawm's essay (p. 9 in *Labouring Men* ed.) and is taken from F. O. Darvall, *Popular Disturbance and Public Order in Regency England* (London, 1934).

43. Rudé, *The Crowd in History*, p. 31.

44. In fact, a part of this movement is encompassed in Tilly's model of major behavioral shifts. He refers here to a change from primitive to reactionary to modern forms of collective violence as the nation-state and national economy are increasingly superordinate over local particularisms. See Eric J. Hobsbawm, *Social Bandits and Primitive Rebels* (New York: Free Press, 1960), for elaboration on social banditry.

45. Tilly, "Collective Violence in European Perspective," p. 34.

46. Ibid., pp. 34–37; quote appears on p. 35.

47. See, for instance, works such as the following: Victor C. Ferkiss, "Populist Influences on American Fascism," *Western Political Quarterly*, 10 (June 1957), and his earlier "Ezra Pound and American Fascism," *Journal of Politics* 17 (May 1955), 173–197; Edward A. Shils, *The Torment of Secrecy: The Background and Consequences of American Security Politics* (New York: Free Press, 1956); Peter Viereck, "The Revolt Against the Elite," in Daniel Bell, ed., *The Radical Right* (New York: Criterion Books, 1955), pp. 10–16, and parts of his *The Unadjusted Man* (Boston: Beacon, 1956); Richard Hofstadter, *The Age of Reform* (New York: Knopf, 1955) and several of the essays in the Bell volume, especially those by Hofstadter, Riesman and Glazer, and Parsons, though these generally deal indirectly with the Populists. For a review of this literature see Nugent, "The Populist as a Monster," the opening chapter in his study *The Tolerant Populists, Kansas Populism and Nativism*, pp. 3–27.

48. Ibid.

49. The references made to Pollack, Nugent, Clanton, Durden, and Rogin in notes 5 and 6 also apply here. Also see Norman Pollack, ed.,

The Populist Mind (Indianapolis, Ind.: Bobbs-Merrill, 1967); C. Vann Woodward, *Tom Watson, Agrarian Rebel* (New York: Holt, Rinehart & Winston, 1963), and his noted essay, "The Populist Heritage and the Intellectual," in *The Burden of Southern History*, rev. ed. (Baton Rouge: Louisiana State University Press, 1968), pp. 141–166. Paul S. Holbo, "Wheat or What? Populism and American Fascism," *Western Political Quarterly*, 14 (September 1961), 727–736. Further references are cited in Nugent, Durden, Pollack (ed.) and in the brief collection of items edited by Irwin Unger, *Populism: Nostalgic or Progressive?* (Skokie, Ill.: Rand McNally, 1964), pp. 59–60. The present discussion has especially relied on the fine summary and analytic interpretation by Rogin.

50. All the quotes in the paragraph are from Rogin, *The Intellectuals and McCarthy*, p. 171.

51. Ibid., p. 182.

52. Woodward, "The Populist Heritage and the Intellectual," pp. 150–1.

53. See Rogin, *The Intellectuals and McCarthy*, pp. 168–191, and also the study by Nugent, *The Tolerant Populists*, and work by Woodward cited in note 49.

54. Rogin, *The Intellectuals and McCarthy*, p. 171.

55. See the incisive analysis in Rogin, ibid., and also Pollack's study, *The Populist Response to Industrial America*.

56. There is quite an extensive literature on Chilean political life, working-class circumstances, and the character of Chilean society. A few useful items include Robert Alexander, *Labor Relations in Argentina, Brazil and Chile* (New York: McGraw-Hill, 1962); Ben G. Burnett, *Political Groups in Chile, The Dialogue between Order and Change* (Austin, Tex.: University of Texas Press, 1970); Gilbert J. Butland, *Chile: An Outline of Its Geography, Economics and Politics*, rev. ed. (London: Royal Institute of International Affairs, 1956); Ricardo Cruz Coke, *Geografía electonal de Chile* (Santiago, Chile: Editorial del Pacifico, 1952); Luis Galdames, *A History of Chile*, translated and edited by I. J. Cox (Chapel Hill, N.C.: University of North Carolina Press, 1941); Federico G. Gil, *The Political System of Chile* (Boston: Houghton Mifflin, 1966); Ernest Halperin, *Nationalism and Communism in Chile* (Cambridge, Mass.: M.I.T. Press, 1965); Dale L. Johnson, ed., *The Chilean Road to Socialism* (Garden City, N.Y.: Doubleday Anchor, 1973); Julio César Jobet, *Ensayo crítico del desarrollo económico-social de Chile* (Santiago, Chile: Editorial Universitaria, 1955); James O. Morris, *Elites, Intellectuals and Consensus: A Study of the Social Question and the Industrial Relations System in Chile* (Ithaca, N.Y.: Cornell University Press, 1966); George McBride, *Chile: Land and Society* (New York: American Geographical Society, 1936); James Petras, *Politics and Social Forces in Chilean Development* (Berkeley and Los Angeles, Calif.: University of California Press, 1969); Frederick B. Pike, *Chile and the United States, 1880–1962* (Notre Dame, Ind.: University of Notre Dame Press, 1963); the essays of Portes referred to earlier (note 12); and Hernán Ramírez Necochea, *Historia del movimento obrero*

en Chile – Antecedents – Siglo XIX (Santiago, Chile: Talleres Graficos Lautaro, 1956).

57. See Kingsley Davis, *World Urbanization 1950–1970; Volume I: Basic Data for Cities, Countries, and Regions* (Berkeley, Calif.: Institute of International Studies, 1969), Table C, and Bruce H. Herrick, *Urban Migration and Economic Development in Chile* (Cambridge, Mass.: M.I.T. Press, 1965), Table 3.3.

58. McBride, *Chile: Land and Society*, p. 14. More recently, 25 years later, Joseph Fichter has made a similar observation in his *Cambio Social en Chile* (*Social Change in Chile*) (Santiago, Chile: Editorial Universidad Catolica, 1962): "... there is a phenomenon that remains relatively immutable in Chile. It is the rigid class structure that centers power and privilege in the small and narrow self-perpetuating upper class, and that institutionalize the denial of opportunities to the masses" (p. 10). Sharing this view is the respected Hispanic scholar Frederico Gil, who made this comment on p. 49 in his *Genesis and Modernization of Political Parties in Chile* (Gainesville, Fla.: University of Florida Press, 1962): "There is a greater distance today between classes in Chile than ever before in its modern history. It would seem that Chilean society is not sufficiently open to accomplish democratically the radical alterations now demanded. The question is whether this society is likely to become sufficiently pressed so as to undertake such changes along different channels."

59. Luis Alberto Mansilla, "The Contaminated City," in Dale L. Johnson, pp. 498–502 and p. 499.

60. See Pike, *Chile and the United States, 1880–1962*, p. 279, and p. 436, footnote 38. More recent figures for 1965 still show one of the highest infant mortality rates in the world – 102.8 per 1000 live births. If deaths between ages one through four are included, the rate would be approximately 15 percent (United Nations, *Demographic Yearbook*, 1970, Tables 16 and 18). These average national figures would be appreciably higher if the lower-class urban component ware separately stated.

61. Herrick, *Urban Migration*, pp. 1–9.

62. Pike, *Chile and the United States, 1880–1962*, p. 280.

63. This was essentially acquiesced to by the Radicals as a means for securing political power and patronage, and it did not reflect any real coalition of social and political interests. See Halperin, pp. 48–50. A more positive assessment of the Popular Front is provided by John Reese Stevenson, *The Chilean Populist Front* (Philadelphia: University of Pennsylvania Press, 1942).

64. Several decades ago, before the working-class movement assumed any considerable strength, the Democratic Party exhibited a reformist sentiment. Founded in 1887, it failed to move beyond reformism or to question seriously the status quo. This led to the loss of its left-wing elements before World War I. The effectiveness of the party was slight till its dissolution in the thirties.

65. Pike, *Chile and the United States, 1880–1962*, p. 109.

66. Petras and Zeitlin, "Miners and Agrarian Radicalism."

67. Portes, "Political Primitivism."

68. Portes, "On the Logic of Post-Factum Explanations" and "Leftist Radicalism in Chile."

69. Portes, "On the Logic of Post-Factum Explanations," p. 40.

70. Portes, "Political Primitivism," p. 833.

71. See the summary treatment in Richard M. Morse, "Recent Research on Latin American Urbanization: A Selective Survey with Commentary," in Gerald Breese, ed., *The City in Newly Developing Countries* (Englewood Cliffs, N.J.: Prentice-Hall, 1969), pp. 474–606.

72. A number of works that provide comprehensive reviews and reports on research regarding urban settlements include William Mangin, "Latin American Squatter Settlements: A Problem and a Solution," *Latin American Research Review*, 2 (1967), 65–98; Richard M. Morse, "Trends and Issues in Latin American Urban Research, 1965–1970, Part I & II," *Latin American Research Review*, 6 (Spring and Summer 1971), 3–52, 19–75; Morse, ibid.; William Mangin, ed., *Peasants in Cities, Readings in the Anthropology of Urbanization* (Boston: Houghton Mifflin, 1970); and a number of essays in Dwight B. Heath and Richard N. Adams, eds., *Contemporary Cultures and Societies of Latin America* (New York: Random House, 1965.)

73. Raymond B. Pratt, "Organizational Participation and Political Orientations: A Comparative Study of Political Consequences of Participation in Community Organizations for Residents of Lower Class Urban Settlements in Chile and Peru," Ph.D. dissertation, University of Oregon, 1968. Pratt's study derives from a body of research data reported upon in several publications by Daniel Goldrich and his students. See Daniel Goldrich, Raymond B. Pratt, and C. R. Schuller, "The Political Integration of Lower-Class Urban Settlements in Chile and Peru," *Studies in Comparative International Development*, 3 (1967–1968), 1–22, and Karen Lindenberg, "The Effect of Negative Sanctions on Politicization Among Lower Class Sectors in Santiago, Chile and Lima, Peru," Ph.D. dissertation, University of Oregon, 1969.

74. In spite of apparent advantages of the more radical left parties over the Christian Democratic Party, however, the latter has secured somewhat substantial lower-class support, though less extensive than the parties in FRAP or the more recent Popular Unity coalition. Interestingly, in terms of the present stress on the role of political socialization elements, this support is found more among the diversely employed, unskilled, possibly little unionized, and less politicized populations of the *callampas* than from the more clearly proletarian populations of the older and strongly organized port and mine areas, the historic bases of Chilean radicalism.

75. The present discussion considers only working-class support for the Communist party, which constitutes about 70 percent of its support. Support provided by other sectors of French society is not discussed.

76. The present discussion follows the usual practice of referring to the Communist party as a radical political force or a radical political alterna-

tive. Actually, in some respects this is not a fully satisfying description, especially in regard to contemporary developments and ideology. Thus the events of May 1968 in France reveal the growing conservatism and parliamentary focus of the party. However, there is little question that for much of the postwar period the Communist party was considered the principal radical political party on the French political scene. Its support now and earlier can certainly be considered as the selection of an antiestablishment political force.

77. Referring to a diverse array of right, center, and left business, agrarian, labor, and intellectual protest movements, Stanley Hoffman states that "it seems that whatever the social milieu in which they originated, whatever the channels they used or created, and whatever the issues involved, those movements have acted in a common style," one marked by three closely related features, a fundamentally destructive character, totalism, and defeatism. See his "Protest in Modern France," in Morton A. Kaplan, ed., *The Revolution in World Politics* (New York: Wiley, 1962), pp. 69–74; quote is from p. 71. Hence to focus on the working class and Communist party – in an effort to determine the appropriateness of the mass political theory model or any other scheme – is merely to select one out of a number of possible collectivities in relatively recent French history whose behavior has manifested a distinctly dissident character.

78. Quoted in Hoffman, ibid., p. 69.

79. See the discussion by Eric A. Nordlinger, "Democratic Stability and Instability: The French Case," *World Politics,* 18 (1965–1966), 127–157, which elaborates on the central role of attitudes toward authority in determining political institutions and behavior. Nordlinger's essay is based on Michel Crozier's seminal *The Bureaucratic Phenomenon: An Examination of Bureaucracy in Modern Organizations and Its Cultural Setting in France* (Chicago: University of Chicago Press, 1964).

80. Nordlinger, pp. 149, 151.

81. See Crozier, *The Bureaucratic Phenomenon,* and also the work by Lawrence Wylie, *Village in the Vaucluse,* rev. ed. (New York: Harper & Row, 1964); Jesse R. Pitts, "Continuity and Change in Bourgeois France," in Stanley Hoffman, ed., *In Search of France* (Cambridge, Mass.: Harvard University Press, 1963); and the discussions in Hoffman, pp. 77–79, and Henry W. Ehrmann, *Politics in France,* 2nd ed. (Boston: Little, Brown, 1968), pp. 10–13.

82. Ehrmann, ibid., p. 168.

83. Ibid., p. 79, and Duncan MacRae, Jr., *Parliament, Parties, and Society in France 1946–1958* (New York: St. Martin, 1967), p. 24.

84. Ehrmann, ibid., p. 14.

85. Val Lorwin, "Reflections on the History of French and American Labor Movements," *Journal of Economic History,* 17 (1957), 31. Also see the discussion in Roy Lewis and Rosemary Stewart, *The Managers: A New Examination of the English, German, and American Executives* (New York: Mentor, 1961).

86. Part of the reason for the economic strain suffered by the French proletariat has been the absence of effective modernization in agriculture and industry in the country. This has begun to change significantly in recent years, though some rather anomalous conditions in this regard still persist.

87. David Thompson, *Democracy in France,* 2nd ed. (London: Oxford University Press, 1952), p. 46.

88. "Democratic Stability and Instability, the French Case," by Eric A. Nordlinger, *World Politics,* vol. XVIII, no. 1 (copyright © 1965 by Princeton University Press), pp. 128–129. Reprinted by permission of Princeton University Press.

89. Ehrmann, *Politics in France,* pp. 58–59.

90. See Ehrmann's citation of public-opinion poll data for 1964 in these regards, ibid., p. 57.

91. Hoffman, "Protest in Modern France," pp. 74–75.

92. MacRae, *Parliament, Parties, and Society in France 1946–1958,* p. 23.

93. Ehrmann, *Politics in France,* p. 211.

94. Hamilton, *Affluence and the French Worker in the Fourth Republic,* pp. 278–279.

95. Ibid., p. 279.

96. Ibid., p. 280.

97. Ibid., pp. 99–100.

98. Ibid.

99. Ehrmann, *Politics in France,* p. 211.

100. Thompson, *Democracy in France,* p. 48.

101. Hamilton's study of the French Communist voter shows the significance of earlier individual experiences in determining contemporary political behavior and loyalties even when current circumstances are altered. He stresses the rural and agrarian origins of older working-class members and their "preradicalization" by the experiences and outlook acquired prior to movement to more urban industrial settings. (See *Affluence and the French Worker in the Fourth Republic,* pp. 128–130, 276–278.) He also notes that earlier unemployment experience, regardless of later periods of full employment, will increase radical attitudes and observes that while "the economic effects of cycles can be overcome in a short time, the political impact, however, can easily last an entire generation" (p. 201).

102. Ehrmann, *Politics in France,* p. 209.

103. Roy Pierce, *French Politics and Political Institutions* (New York: Harper & Row, 1968), p. 106, cited from *Sondages* (1962), No. 2, p. 69.

104. Pitts, "Continuity and Change in Bourgeois France," p. 262.

105. See the thoughtful and useful discussion in MacRae, "Voluntary Groups: Was France a Mass Society?" in his *Parliament, Parties and Society in France 1946–1958,* pp. 28–32. Nordlinger makes a similar point, "Democratic Stability and Instability," pp. 145, 147. MacRae notes that the important difference in membership between France and the United States lies in the nature of the organizations in which the individual is implicated.

In France organizations with heterogeneous memberships are fewer. Thus "the types of groups prevalent in France tended to combine like minded persons, rather than to promote communication across political divisions" (p. 29). Hence "... organizations that reinforced existing social divisions were more typical in France, while those that cut across other divisions and made decisions at the community level were more characteristic of the United States" (pp. 29–30).

106. Ibid., p. 30.

107. Ibid., p. 32.

108. Hamilton, *Affluence and the French Worker in the Fourth Republic*, p. 67.

109. The present discussion is principally concerned with why the Nazi movement secured considerable popular support. This is a different question, of course, from why it attained power, even though some of the factors that determine each circumstance are the same.

110. A number of especially useful works include Allen, *The Nazi Seizure of Power;* Geoffrey Barraclough, "New Nazi History," *New York Review of Books* (October 19, 1972), 37–43; (November 2, 1972), 32–38; (November 16, 1972), 25–31. Maurice Baumont et al., *The Third Reich* (New York: Praeger, 1955); Karl Dietrich Bracher, *The German Dictatorship* (New York: Praeger, 1970); Gordon Craig, *The Politics of the Prussian Army* (New York: Oxford University Press, 1955); Milton Mayer, *They Thought They Were Free: The Germans, 1933–1945* (Chicago: University of Chicago Press, 1955); George L. Mosse, *The Crisis of German Ideology: Intellectual Origins of the Third Reich* (New York: Grosset & Dunlap, Universal Library, 1964); Fritz Stern, *The Failure of Illiberalism* (New York: Knopf, 1972); and A. J. P. Taylor, *The Course of German History* (New York: Putnam, 1962).

111. See Hannah Arendt, *Origins of Totalitarianism* (New York: Harcourt Brace Jovanovich, 1951), Chap. 10, "The Classless Society"; Emil Lederer, *State of the Masses* (New York: Norton, 1940); Sigmund Neumann, *The Permanent Revolution* (New York: Praeger, 1965); Gerhard Ritter, "The Historical Foundations of the Rise of National Socialism," in Baumont et al., *The Third Reich*, pp. 381–416; and William Kornhauser, *The Politics of Mass Society* (London: Routledge & Kegan Paul, 1960).

112. Kornhauser, ibid.

113. Ibid., pp. 308–309.

114. Arendt, *Origins of Totalitarianism*, p. 306.

115. Particularly helpful in terms of its empirical material and interpretation and in facilitating an application of the type of analytic approach noted earlier is Allen's previously mentioned excellent case study, *The Nazi Seizure of Power*. It is subtitled: *The Experience of a Single German Town, 1930–1935*. Avoiding resort to notions of the decline of community and the disaffection of the uprooted, the appearance of masses, the irrationality of behavior, the charisma of mass leadership and the appeal of mass movements, and psychological impoverishment, Allen traces the rise to

power of the Nazis from 1930 to 1935 in a moderate-size town (given the fictitious name of Thalburg) of 10,000 in the state of Hanover. From a vote of slightly more than 4 percent in 1929 the National Socialist German Workers' Party vote jumped to nearly two-thirds of the votes in 1933. If the mass model is inappropriate in this case where there has been so heavy a shift to the Nazis, its wider applicability is especially challenged. Also see Mayer's analysis of Nazi supporters, for a treatment that reveals the rather unexceptional circumstances accounting for Nazi support and the similarities between such support and the behavior of citizens in the traditional Western democracies.

116. Allen, *The Nazi Seizure of Power*, p. 133.

117. Mosse, *The Crisis of German Ideology;* Taylor, *The Course of German History.*

118. Mosse, ibid. Also see the brief discussion, "The Ideology of the Radical Right," in John Weiss, *The Fascist Tradition: Radical Right Wing Extremism in Modern Europe* (New York: Harper & Row, 1967), pp. 9–30.

119. Weiss, ibid., p. 134.

120. Barraclough, "New Nazi History"; Stern, *The Failure of Illiberalism.*

121. Carl F. Schorske, "Weimar and the Intellectuals," *New York Review of Books,* May 7, 1970, pp. 22–27, especially p. 24.

122. Allen puts it simply, "To the average Thalburger the Nazi appeared vigorous, dedicated and young" (*The Nazi Seizure of Power*, p. 25).

123. Ibid., p. 136.

124. Ibid., pp. 23–24.

125. Ibid., pp. 133–134.

126. *Ibid.*, p. 134. Allen is referring to the fictional town of Thalburg.

127. H. R. Trevor-Roper, "The Germans Reappraise the War," *Foreign Affairs* (1953), p. 234, as quoted in Andrew Whiteside, "The Nature and Origins of National Socialism," *Journal of Central European Affairs,* 17 (April 1957) 48–73, p. 63.

128. Where attention is given to the behavior of elites, it is limited to elite manipulation of masses, with elite elements often perceived as counterelites.

129. In these regards specific treatments will be found in Craig, *The Politics of the Prussian Army;* J. W. Wheeler-Bennett, *The Nemesis of Power: The German Army in Politics, 1918–1945* (New York: Viking, 1967); Gerhard R. Dramer, "The Influence of National Socialism on the Courts of Justice and on the Police," in Baumont et al., *The Third Reich* pp. 595–632; Carl Schorske on Herbert von Dirksen, in "Two German Ambassadors," in Gordon Craig and Felix Gilbert, eds., *The Diplomats, 1919–1939* (Princeton, N.J.: Princeton University Press, 1953), pp. 479 ff.; and George W. F. Hall Garten, "Hitler and German Heavy Industry, 1931–1933," *Journal of Economic History,* 12 (1952), 222–246. These and other items are cited in Whiteside, "The Nature and Origins of National Socialism," pp. 62–63, and are briefly discussed there. Also see both Stern,

The Failure of Illiberalism, and Barraclough, "New Nazi History," among other general discussions.

130. Fritz Stern, ed., *The Path to Dictatorship, 1918–1933* (Garden City, N.Y.: Doubleday Anchor Books, 1966), Introduction, xv.

131. See Rudolf Heberle, *From Democracy to Nazism* (Baton Rouge, La.: Louisiana State University Press, 1945); and Charles P. Loomis and J. Allen Beegle, "The Spread of German Nazism in Rural Areas," *American Sociological Review,* 11 (1946), 724–734.

132. Allen, *The Nazi Seizure of Power,* p. 19. The quote continues, significantly, "yet few of them cut across class lines."

133. Kornhauser, *The Politics of Mass Society,* p. 208. In his discussion (p. 207) Kornhauser characterizes this isolation, in effect, as referring in a significant degree to the lack of ties to the larger society in the form of commitments to already existing political parties or farmer organizations. Little evidence is presented for the German case in these regards, but even if we assume it is true, a different interpretation is quite possible. Kornhauser suggests that without external ties there is a mass population available for mobilization by an extremist emotional movement. However, such a formulation seems to abandon a great deal of the mass theory interpretive scheme, as it is no longer the absence of the sociopsychic functions of groups membership and the attempt to replace them with new relationships in the form of commitment to a mass movement that are involved here. Rather, it can be interpreted as a situation characterized by the absence of commitments to those national interest organizations that could be perceived as effective political spokesmen. Lacking such commitments, or organizations, and when faced with severe economic strains, it is not surprising or unreasonable that the German farmer would support a new social movement, especially when it suggests a resolution of his difficulties and appeals as well to his ideological sentiments, strong nationalism, and the virtues of rural life. While this presents Kornhauser's explanation in terms somewhat different than he himself might use, it does, in effect, represent the situation he describes. Phrased in these terms, though, the small rural farmer's attraction to the Nazi movement can be seen as a rational and reasonable response of a population under economic strain, lacking a sense of political representation and a responsive political order and thus giving support to an attractive and vigorous movement. This does not dispute the importance of strong party or organizational commitments but interprets their presence or absence from a different perspective. It might even be contended that when there are ties to national, political, or other interest organizations, and when such organizations are ineffectual, their continued support may be a more unreasonable act than shifting loyalties to an "antiestablishment" movement and giving it a try, so to speak.

134. Svend Ranulf, *Moral Indignation and Middle Class Psychology* (New York: Schocken Books, 1964), paperback. First published in 1938.

135. The feudal-estate origin of twentieth-century German society was

a stronger heritage for middle-class elements than for the modern industrialized sector of society in which the class-conscious working class was implicated. Schorske ("Weimar and the Intellectuals") points out how this induced a response toward supporting political action directed toward securing a corporate or communally based society rather than stressing a reestablishment of the conditions of individualistic and open forms – as was the case for the declining American farmer and small businessman. In effect, the corporate and ideologically conservative heritage of the middle class heightened the appeal of nazism and facilitated its acceptance. The German case reasserts the vital importance of examining the historical background of a group if response to strain is to be understood.

136. As noted earlier, perhaps as significant as their communal appeal, a stress on these themes also provided the ability to emphasize even more Germany's defeat in World War I and the consequent further derogation of those elements – the left, Jews, materialists, Weimar – that the Nazis castigated so vigorously.

137. Barraclough, "New Nazi History," Part III, p. 30.

138. Accounting for active political involvement has not been a concern of the present volume. A range of quite different factors seems relevant here, including a greater focus on the psychological properties of the individual and on the character of his social milieu and experiences.

139. See the author's paper "A Critical Assessment of Frustration Based Theories of Political Dissidence," paper delivered at the annual meeting of the Eastern Sociological Society, April 19, 1975, in New York City.

Chapter 6. Critical assessment of the pluralist perspective

1. Grant McConnell, *Private Power and American Democracy* (New York: Knopf, 1966), p. 355.

2. Ibid., p. 385.

3. See Murray Edelman's illuminating discussion, in *The Symbolic Uses of Politics* (Urbana, Ill.: University of Illinois Press, 1964), of a number of related concerns, particularly his suggestion that the functions served by administrative structures and associated democratic ideology are in important ways contrary to the publicly formulated objectives.

4. See Peter Bachrach, *The Theory of Democratic Elitism: A Critique* (Boston: Little, Brown, 1967) for his comment on the shift from pluralist group competition to elite competition as preserving of democracy.

5. The earlier European pluralist literature is extensive. References to many of the earlier writings may be found in Henry S. Kariel, "Pluralism," *International Encyclopedia of the Social Sciences*, XII (New York: Macmillan, 1968), pp. 164–169. This essay also provides a brief summary of pluralist doctrine. Chap. 10, "The Case for Devolution" in his *The Decline of American Pluralism* (Stanford: Stanford University Press, 1961) offers a more extended discussion. For a fuller treatment see the early work by Kung-Chuan Hsiao, *Political Pluralism* (New York: Macmillan, 1928),

Parts 1–3; the study by Henry M. Magid, *English Political Pluralism* (New York: Columbia University Press, 1941); Walter Milnes-Bailey's *Trade Unions and the State* (London: G. Allen, 1934); and some portions of Adam B. Ulam, *The Philosophical Foundations of English Socialism* (Cambridge, Mass.: Harvard University Press, 1951). French pluralists are more directly discussed in Stanley Hoffman, "The Dual Division of Powers in the Writing of French Political Thinkers," in Arthur Moass, ed., *Area and Power: A Theory of Local Government* (New York: Free Press, 1959), pp. 113–149.

6. McConnell, *Private Power and American Democracy*, p. 120.

7. In effect, power is perceived as diffused, fragmented, and competitive. The political process is understood as one within which many groups engage in a political give and take, bargaining, competing, and forming coalitions in terms of common interests or a temporary sharing of objectives.

8. See James Madison, "Federalist No. 10," in Alexander Hamilton, John Jay, and James Madison, *The Federalist: A Commentary on the Constitution of the United States* (New York: Modern Library, 1937); Arthur Bentley, *The Process of Government* (Bloomington, Ind.: Principal Press, 1949); David Truman, *The Governmental Process* (New York: Knopf, 1951); Pendleton Herring, *Group Representation Before Congress* (Baltimore, Md.: Johns Hopkins Press, 1929), and *The Politics of Democracy* (New York: Norton, 1940); Earl Latham, *The Group Basis of Politics* (Ithaca, N. Y.: Cornell University Press, 1952); Charles Lindblom, *The Intelligence of Democracy* (New York: Macmillan, 1965); Peter Odegard, *Pressure Politics* (New York: Columbia University Press, 1929); Bertram D. Gross, *The Legislative Struggle* (New York: McGraw-Hill, 1953).

9. Robert Dahl, *Preface to Democratic Theory* (Chicago: University of Chicago Press, 1956); and with Charles Lindblom, *Politics, Economics and Welfare* (New York: Harper & Row, 1953), paperback; and Aaron Wildavsky, *Dixon-Yates: A Study in Power Politics* (New Haven, Conn.: Yale University Press, 1962).

10. Robert Dahl, *Who Governs?* (New Haven, Conn.: Yale University Press, 1961); Nelson Polsby, *Community Power and Political Theory* (New Haven, Conn.: Yale University Press, 1963); Aaron Wildavsky, *Leadership in a Small Town* (Totowa, N.J.: Bedminister Press, 1964); Adolf A. Berle, *The Twentieth Century Capitalist Revolution* (New York: Harcourt Brace Jovanovich, 1954); John K. Galbraith, *American Capitalism* (Boston: Houghton Mifflin, 1952); Alexis de Tocqueville, *Democracy in America*, Reeve trans., edited by Phillips Bradley (New York: Alfred A. Knopf, 1946).

11. Harold Laski, *Authority in the Modern State* (New Haven, Conn.: Yale University Press); G. D. H. Cole, *Guild Socialism Re-stated* (London: Parsons, 1920); and Leon Duguit, *Law in the Modern State*, English translation by Freida and Harold Laski (New York: Ben Huebsch, 1919).

12. The pluralist perspective in American political theory is reflected in a diversity of writings, particularly in the area of interest group theory. A

number have already been noted in earlier references, especially in note 8. Critical essays include Stanley Rothman, "Systematic Political Theory: Observations on the Group Approach," *American Political Science Review,* 54 (March 1960), 15–33; Peter H. Odegard, "A Group Basis of Politics: A New Name for an Old Myth," *Western Political Quarterly,* 11 (September 1958), 698–702; and Bernard Crick, *The American Science of Politics* (Berkeley, Calif.: University of California Press, 1959), pp. 118–130. Other critical items that give more direct attention to pluralism per se in contrast to the closely related interest group theory include Todd Gitlan, "Local Pluralism as Theory and Ideology," *Studies on the Left,* 5 (1965), 21–45; a companion piece by Shin'ya Ono, "The Limits of Bourgeois Pluralism," *Studies on the Left,* 5 (1965), 46–72; and Theodore Lowi, "American Business, Public Policy, Case Studies and Political Theory, *World Politics,* 16 (1964), 677–715, "Public Philosophy: Interest Group Liberalism," *American Political Science Review,* 61 (1967), 5–24, and *The End of Liberalism* (New York: Norton, 1968), which also contains a reprint of his "Public Philosophy."

13. The principal concerns dealt with by the pluralist propositions not considered in the text are several. These suggest that the pluralist polity is one in which interest organizations represent membership interest and can effectively press member's demands through established political mechanisms; that crosscutting memberships and the difficulty of concentrating power minimize the existence of antidemocratic movements; and that the features of a pluralist system are such as to enhance its stability.

14. See notes for Chapter 4. The existence of representation for and responsiveness to group needs may be particularly problematic for newly developing interest groups or social collectivities. The inadequacies of political structures are compounded by the fact that existing structures have taken shape prior to the appearance of new groups. (Lewis Coser briefly develops this point in his "Internal Violence as a Mechanism for Conflict Resolution," in *Continuities in the Study of Social Conflict* [New York: Free Press, 1967], pp. 96–97. Also see the useful discussion by Seymour M. Lipset and Stein Rokkan, eds., *Party Systems and Voter Alignments: Cross-National Perspectives* [New York: Free Press, 1967], pp. 30–31.) Thus organized interest structures, coalitions, channels of communication, and, perhaps most important, electoral forms and group alliances related to electoral systems will already have been established and may effectively limit the openness of systems of electoral and interest representation. Working-class movements in western Europe, for instance, confronted this dilemma, particularly as "the early electoral systems set a high threshold for rising parties" (Lipset and Rokkan, p. 30).

15. Edgar Litt, *Democracy's Ordeal in America: A Guide to Political Theory and Action* (New York: Holt, Rinehart & Winston, 1973), pp. 87–88, and see the discussion on pp. 87–93 and the references cited by Litt in footnotes 6 and 7 on p. 98; also see Julius Duscha, *Arms, Money and Politics* (New York: Ives Washburn, 1964).

16. Litt, ibid., p. 88.

17. Ibid., p. 91.

18. Ibid., pp. 90–92.

19. See the items just cited in note 15; also see Kenneth M. Dolbeare and Murray J. Edelman, "National Security Through Military Superiority," in *American Politics* (Lexington, Mass.: Heath, 1971), pp. 81–110.

20. Dolbeare and Edelman, ibid., p. 95, from figures released by Senator William Proxmire.

21. Ibid., pp. 96–97, from Ralph E. Lapp, *The Weapons Culture* (New York: Norton, 1968), pp. 186–187.

22. Dolbeare and Edelman, ibid., pp. 95, 98.

23. For a more detailed set of figures revealing even less disparity among income levels in regard to the effect of taxes, see R. A. Musgrave's calculations in Edward C. Budd's "Inequality in Income and Taxes," in Maurice Zeitlin, ed., *American Society, Inc.* (Chicago: Markham Publishing Co., 1970), pp. 143–150.

24. Litt, "Providing Health Care as a Public Right," *Democracy's Ordeal in America,* pp. 192–209; Health Policy Advisory Center, *The American Health Empire: Power, Profits, and Politics* (New York: Random House, 1971); Roul Tunley, *The American Health Scandal* (New York: Dell, 1966); Ed Cray, *In Failing Health: The Medical Crisis and the A.M.A.* (Indianapolis, Ind.: Bobbs-Merrill Co., 1970); and William Michelfelder, *It's Cheaper to Die: Doctors, Drugs, and the A.M.A.* (New York: Braziller, 1960).

25. Richard Harris, *The Real Voice* (New York: Macmillan, 1964).

26. Mark Green, James M. Fallows, David R. Zwick, *Who Runs Congress?* (New York: Bantam Books, 1972), pp. 25–28.

27. McConnell, *Private Power and American Democracy,* p. 196; also Grant McConnell, *The Decline of American Democracy* (Berkeley, Calif.: University of California Press, 1953).

28. Dolbeare and Edelman, *American Politics,* pp. 308–309, from Richard J. Barber, *The American Corporation* (New York: Dutton, 1970), p. 125.

29. For these and other examples see Dolbeare and Edelman, *American Politics,* pp. 308–313; also see Clair Wilcox, *Public Policies Toward Business* (Homewood, Ill.: Irwin, 1968), pp. 429–452.

30. Robert Sherrill, *Why They Call It Politics: A Guide to America's Government* (New York: Harcourt Brace Jovanovich, 1972), p. 97.

31. Richard J. Barnet, "The National Security Managers and the National Interest," *Politics and Society,* 1 (February 1971), p. 266.

32. Gabriel Kolko, *The Triumph of Conservatism* (New York: Free Press, 1963).

33. See Edward F. Cox, Robert C. Fellmeth, and John E. Schultz, *On the Federal Trade Commission* (New York: Richard W. Baron, 1969). The report on the ICC was issued in March 1970 under the aegis of the Center for the Study of Responsive Law. For material in this area see Samuel P.

Huntington, "The Marasmus of the ICC: The Commission, the Railroads and the Public Interest," *Yale Law Review*, 61 (April 1952), 447–509; Marver H. Bernstein, *Regulating Business in Independent Commission*, (Princeton, N.J.: Princeton University Press, 1955); Avery Leiserson, *Administrative Regulation: A Study in Representation of Interests* (Chicago: University of Chicago Press, 1955); McConnell, "Self-Regulation," in *Private Power and American Democracy*, pp. 246–297; Henry J. Friendly, *The Federal Administrative Agencies* (Cambridge, Mass.: Harvard University Press, 1962); Bernard Schwartz, *The Professor and the Commissions* (New York: Knopf, 1959); Robert Engler, *Politics of Oil* (New York: Macmillan, 1961); Philip Foss, *Politics and Grass* (Seattle, Wash.: University of Washington Press, 1960); Harris, *The Real Voice;* Gabriel Kolko, *Railroads and Regulation 1877–1916,* (Princeton, N.J.: Princeton University Press, 1965); Louis M. Kohlmeier, Jr., *The Regulators* (New York: Harper & Row, 1969); Morton Mintz and Jerry S. Cohen, *America Inc.: Who Owns and Operates the United States* (New York: Dial, 1971).

34. Kariel, *The Decline of American Pluralism.*

35. See note 33.

36. Data come from Sherrill, *Why They Call It Politics*, p. 175.

37. For individual cases see ibid., p. 175; Mintz and Cohen, *America Inc.*, pp. 246–247; and Kohlmeier, *The Regulators*, pp. 73 ff.

38. Edelman, *The Symbolic Uses of Politics*, p. 56.

39. Marc Pilisuk points succinctly to the phenomenon involved here. Noting that it is not necessary to understand the lack of power and representation in terms of postulating a ruling group or ruling institutional order, he points out that there may nonetheless be:

> a social structure which is organized to create and protect power centers with only partial accountability. . . . We are describing the current system as one of over-all "minimal accountability . . . and minimal consent." We mean that the role of democratic review, based on genuine popular consent, is made marginal and reactive. Elite groups are minimally accountable to publics and have a substantial, though by no means maximum freedom to shape popular attitudes.

Marc Pilisuk, "Is There a Military-Industrial Complex Which Prevents Peace?" *International Conflict and Social Policy* (Englewood Cliffs, N.J.: Prentice-Hall, 1972), p. 126.

40. Kariel, "Pluralism," pp. 167–168; also see McConnell, *Private Power and American Democracy*. See E. E. Schattschneider, *The Semisovereign People* (New York: Holt, Rinehart and Winston, 1960), for an illuminating discussion of the whole question of the extension of the scope of issue confrontations and conditions of representation and responsiveness. For a sensitive discussion of the inadequacies in pluralist interest group theory, see Lowi's two essays referred to in note 12.

41. See the discussion in McConnell's chapter "The States" in his *Private Power and American Democracy*, pp. 166–195. In addition to the

references cited by McConnell, also see John Burns, *The Sometime Governments* (New York: Bantam, 1971).

42. Among other works, see Lowi, *The End of Liberalism.*

43. McConnell, *Private Power and American Democracy,* p. 359.

44. The relevant books are *American Capitalism* by Galbraith and *Twentieth Century Capitalist Revolution* by Berle (note 10). A similar interpretation on the dispersed nature of power can be found in a number of items discussing the competitive countervailing framework within which business power exists and functions. See David E. Lilenthal, *Big Business: A New Era* (New York: Harper & Row, 1953); A. D. H. Kaplan, *Big Enterprise in a Competitive System* (Washington, D.C.: The Brookings Institute, 1964); also see Joseph A. Schumpeter, *Capitalism, Socialism and Democracy* (New York: Harper Torchbooks, 1962), Chaps. 7 and 8. Some of the works that seek to qualify seriously the notion of countervailing power include the interpretive essay by Marc Pilisuk, "Is There a Military-Industrial Complex Which Prevents Peace?"; Theodore Lowi, "Public Philosophy: Interest Group Liberalism"; G. William Domhoff, *Who Rules America?* (Englewood Cliffs, N.J.: Prentice-Hall, 1967), and his coedited work with H. Ballard, *C. Wright Mills and the Power Elite* (Boston: Beacon, 1967); C. Wright Mills, *The Power Elite* (New York: Oxford University Press, 1957); Victor Perlo's study *Militarism and Industry* (New York: International Publishers, 1963), and his *Empire of High Finance* (New York: International Publishers, 1957); and Bernard Nossiter, *The Mythmakers: An Essay on Wealth* (Boston: Houghton Mifflin, 1964).

45. McConnell, *Private Power and American Democracy,* p. 350.

46. Quoted in Domhoff, *Who Rules America?* p. 114; appears on p. 492 of Engler's book, *Politics of Oil.* See Chap. 16 in Engler for fuller treatment.

47. Lowi has observed in *The End of Liberalism,* pp. 96–97, that

> This may be the most debilitative of all features of interest-group liberalism, for it tends to derange almost all established relations and expectations in the democratic system. It renders formalism impossible. It impairs the self-correctiveness of positive law by the bargaining, cooptation, and incrementalism of its implementing processes. It impairs the very process of administration itself by delegating to administration alien materials – policies that are not laws.

See Lowi's treatment in Part I, ibid., for extended evidence for the point raised here and for other references.

48. Budd, "Inequality in Income and Taxes," Table 1.

49. Robert J. Lampman, "The Share of Top Wealth-Holders in National Wealth, 1922–1956," in Zeitlin, ed., *American Society,* pp. 87–104.

50. See Gardiner C. Means, "Economic Concentration," and Willard F. Mueller, "Recent Changes in Industrial Concentration, and the Current Merger Movement," in Zeitlin, ibid., pp. 3–16, 19–42.

51. Mueller, ibid., pp. 32–33.

52. The Patman Committee, "Investments and Interlocks Between Major

Banks and Major Corporations," in Zeitlin, ibid., pp. 70–77. In the same volume also see other Patman Committee reports, "Concentration of Banks," "Bank Stock Ownership and Control," and "Banks as the Dominant Institutional Investor," pp. 48–76.

53. The greater resources of business groups have been evidenced in a number of the items cited on the regulatory agencies. It is more particularly revealed in E. E. Schattschneider's study, *Politics, Pressure Groups and the Tariff* (Englewood Cliffs, N.J.: Prentice-Hall, 1935). For a general discussion see Chap. 2, "Who Influences Congress?" in Green et al., *Who Runs Congress?* pp. 29–52.

54. Barnet, "The National Security Managers and the National Interest"; G. William Domhoff, *The Higher Circles: The Governing Class in America* (New York: Random House, 1970), and *Who Rules America?;* Donald R. Matthews, *The Social Background of Political Decision-Makers* (Garden City, N.Y.: Doubleday, 1954), and *U.S. Senators and Their World* (New York: Vintage Books, 1960). Many citations appearing in the previous works will be of considerable relevance. Also see the review by Dolbeare and Edelman, *American Politics*, pp. 218–223 and the volume by Ralph Miliband, *The State in Capitalist Society* (New York: Basic Books, 1969).

55. Barnet, ibid., pp. 260–261.

56. See Domhoff, *Who Rules America?* pp. 99–103, and Chap. 5, "How the Power Elite Make Foreign Policy," in *The Higher Circles*, pp. 111–155.

57. Domhoff, *Who Rules America?*, p. 111, and see pp. 109–111.

58. Matthews, *U.S. Senators and Their World*, Figure 4, p. 32.

59. Matthews, *The Social Background of Political Decision-Makers*, Table 7, p. 30.

60. Matthews, *U.S. Senators and Their World*, Table 2, p. 20.

61. Ibid., Tables 4 and 5, pp. 22, 23.

62. See information on congressional committee chairmanship provided in Dolbeare and Edelman, *American Politics*, pp. 281–283.

63. Green, et al., *Who Runs Congress?* p. 60.

64. Malcolm F. Jewell and Samuel C. Patterson, *The Legislative Process in the United States* (New York: Random House, 1966), p. 221, quoted in Litt, *Democracy's Ordeal in America*, p. 135.

65. See Green, et al., "Who Rules Congress?" in *Who Runs Congress?*, pp. 53–92; Matthews, "The Committees," in *U.S. Senators and Their World*, pp. 147–175; Charles L. Clapp, "The Committee System," in his *The Congressman: His Work as He Sees It* (Washington, D.C.: The Brookings Institute, 1963), pp. 213–279; Dolbeare and Edelman, *American Politics*, pp. 268–284; and Joseph S. Clark et al., *The Senate Establishment* (New York: Hill & Wang, 1963).

66. Dolbeare and Edelman, *American Politics*, p. 270.

67. The latest Congress has begun to make some modest changes in the congressional committee system that have affected the selection and authority of committee chairmen. However, the major thrust of the present section is little altered by these recent changes.

68. William A. Gamson, "Stable Unrepresentation in American Society," in Lewis Lipsitz, ed., *The Confused Eagle* (Boston: Allyn & Bacon, 1973), p. 73.

69. William A. Gamson, "Stable Unpresentation in American Society," *American Behavioral Scientist,* Vol. XII, No. 2 (Nov.-Dec. 1968), pp. 15–21. Reprinted by permission of the publisher, Sage Publications, Inc.

70. Ibid., p. 73.

71. See Harry Brill, *Why Organizers Fail: The Story of a Rent Strike* (Berkeley, Calif.: University of California Press, 1971); Michael Lipsky, *Protest in City Politics* (Skokie, Ill.: Rand McNally, 1970); Dale Rogers Marshall, *The Politics of Participation in Poverty* (Berkeley, Calif.: University of California Press, 1971); Jon Van Til, "Becoming Participants: Dynamics of Access Among the Welfare Poor," *Social Science Quarterly,* 54 (September 1973), 345–358; and Louis Zurcher, *Poverty Warriors: The Human Experience of Planned Social Intervention* (Austin, Tex.: University of Texas Press, 1970).

72. The concepts of "power elite" or "governing elite" and "ruling class" refer to somewhat different phenomena. The former notion

> contrasts the organized, ruling minority with the unorganized majority, or masses, while the concept of a "ruling class" contrasts the dominant classes with subject classes, which may themselves be organized, or be creating organizations. From these different conceptions arise differences in the way of conceiving the relations beteween rulers and rules. (See the discussion in T. B. Bottomore, *Elites and Society* [Baltimore, Md.: Penguin, 1966], Chap. 2, "From the Ruling Class to the Power Elite," pp. 24–47; quote from p. 36.)

As a concept or theory of forms of dominance or rule, the notion of "power elite" requires additional elaboration to account for the origin, interrelationships and cohesion of the elite. This is less true for the concept of "ruling class," implicated as it is to some extent in class theory.

73. This is, of course, the supposition that characterizes pluralist analysis. Examination of some of the leading efforts in this vein will readily bear this out. In this regard, for instance, see Dahl, *Who Governs?* pp. 311–315; Wildavsky, *Leadership in a Small Town,* pp. 320–351; Polsby, *Community Power and Political Theory,* pp. 112–138, 320–351; Tocqueville, *Democracy in America,* I, pp. 181–205, 281–342; II, pp. 114–135; John K. Galbraith, *American Capitalism,* pp. 108–153, and more generally Truman, *The Governmental Process,* Wildavsky, *Dixon-Yates,* and Latham, *The Group Basis of Politics,* among others.

74. See Walter Dean Burnham, *Critical Elections and the Mainsprings of American Politics* (New York: Norton, 1970), which contains an illuminating discussion on these and other regards. Burnham also contends that contemporary American party and electorate politics is witnessing a declining electoral aggregation and growing breakdown of party loyalty, with an increasing erosion of the linkage between the broader public and political leadership.

75. Richard J. Barber, *The American Corporation* (New York: Dutton, 1970), p. 259.

76. Peter Bachrach, "Corporate Authority and Democratic Theory," in David Spitz, ed., *Political Theory and Social Change* (New York: Atherton, 1967), pp. 257–258. Also see his *The Theory of Democratic Elitism,* particularly pp. 72–82; and Morton S. Baratz, "Corporate Giants and the Power Structure," *Western Political Quarterly,* 9 (1956), 406–415.

77. Berle, *The Twentieth Century Capitalist Revolution,* p. 105, as quoted by Kariel, *The Decline of American Pluralism,* p. 165. Also see Wolfgang Friedman, "Corporate Power, Government by Private Groups, and the Power Structure," *Columbia Law Review* 57 (1957), 155–186.

78. This need not mean, of course, that a presumably "pluralist" polity cannot secure control over private centers of power. It would do so, however, by the authority and actions of central government. The point, though, is that pluralist theory, focusing as it does on a competition of organized interest groups, does not develop in its analytic framework the nature of the relationship or "balance" between entities such as corporations and government. The role of government is, in fact, insufficiently explicated in American pluralist theory.

79. Andrew Hacker, "Introduction: Corporate America," in A. Hacker, ed., *The Corporation Take-Over* (Garden City, N.Y.: Doubleday Anchor Book, 1964), pp. 1–14; see pp. 6–9; quote is from p. 8. In *The Corporation Take-Over,* pp. 117–144, Hacker refers to Arthur S. Miller's contribution, "Private Governments and the Constitution."

80. A discussion on the exercise of public authority by private associations that generally lack accountability occurs in Kariel's "The States and Captives," *The Decline of Pluralism,* pp. 103–112. A large number of pertinent references can be found cited in footnotes to that chapter, particularly footnote 6, p. 313.

81. McConnell, *Private Power and American Democracy,* p. 362, see especially pp. 361–363. Also see Hacker, *The Corporation Take-Over;* Lowi, *The End of Liberalism;* Miller, "Private Governments and the Constitution"; and Kariel's lengthy study, *The Decline of American Pluralism.*

82. Stein Rokkan, "Norway: Numerical Democracy and Corporate Pluralism," in Robert Dahl, ed., *Political Opposition in Western Democracies* (New Haven, Conn.: Yale University Press, 1966).

83. Samuel Finer, *Anonymous Empire* (London: Pall Mall Publishers, 1966).

84. Paul Conn, "Social Pluralism and Democratic Representation," paper delivered at the 1969 annual meeting of the American Political Science Association, Washington, D. C., September 2–7, 1968, mimeo, p. 12.

85. Lowi, *The End of Liberalism,* elaborates a similar point.

86. In fact, as regards elite-mass relationships, one has the rather anomalous situation – from the mass political theory point of view – that the sometime obdurate individuals who have ultimate authority over important university policies are distinctly less qualified or appropriate for their roles than the "masses" over whom they exercise suzerainty. See the

nationwide study by the Educational Testing Service, Rodney T. Harnett, *College and University Trustees: Their Backgrounds, Roles and Educational Attitudes* (Princeton, N.J.: Educational Testing Service, 1969). Other relevant material includes the analysis by Hubert Beck, *Men Who Control Our Universities* (New York: King's Crown, 1947), and the broad historical discussion by Merle Curtis and Roderick Nash, *Philanthropy in the Shaping of American Higher Education* (New Brunswick, N.J.: Rutgers University Press, 1965).

87. For discussions of workers' influence in industrial management and on workers' councils, see Adolf Sturmthal, *Workers' Councils* (Cambridge, Mass.: Harvard University Press, 1964); J. T. Kolaja, *Workers' Councils: The Yugoslav Experience* (London: Tavistock, 1965); Frederich Singleton and Anthon Topham, *Worker's Control in Yugoslavia* (London: 1959); Fabian Research Series 233 and their "Yugoslav Workers' Control: The Latest Phase," *New Left Review*, No. 18 (January–February 1963), 73–84; Dennis Butt, "Worker's Control," *New Left Review*, No. 10 (July–August 1961); Jaroslav Vanek, "Decentralization Under Workers' Management: A Theoretical Approach," *American Economic Review*, 59 (December 1969), 1006–1014; H. A. Clegg, *Industrial Democracy and Nationalization* (Oxford: Blackwell, 1951); and Carole Pateman, *Participation and Democratic Theory* (London: Cambridge University Press, 1970).

88. Mills, *The Power Elite*, p. 307.

89. Peter Bachrach and Morton S. Baratz, "Two Faces of Power," *American Political Science Review*, 66 (December 1962), 948.

90. There are a number of edited collections that contain many of the major studies and commentaries in this area. Useful are Michael Aiken and Paul E. Mott, eds., *The Structure of Community Power* (New York: Random House, 1970); Terry N. Clark, ed., *Community Structure and Decision Making: Comparative Analysis* (San Francisco: Chandler, 1968); and Willis D. Hawley and Frederick M. Wirt, eds., *The Search for Community Power* (Englewood Cliffs, N.J.: Prentice-Hall, 1968). Several of the major book- or monograph-length studies and commentaries include Robert E. Agger, Daniel Goldrich, and Bert E. Swanson, *The Rulers and the Ruled* (New York: Wiley, 1964); Dahl, *Who Governs?*; Linton G. Freeman, et al., *Metropolitan Decision-Making* (Syracuse, N.Y.: University College of Syracuse University, 1962); Floyd Hunter, *Community Power Structure* (Chapel Hill, N.C.: University of North Carolina Press, 1953); Polsby, *Community Power and Political Theory*; and Robert Presthus, *Men at the Top* (New York: Oxford University Press, 1946).

91. See the interesting discussion of interest group theory by David Smith, "Pragmatism and the Group Theory of Politics," *American Political Science Review*, 58 (September 1964), 600–610, and Rothman, "Systematic Political Theory."

92. Implied in these comments is the somewhat different yet related observation developed by Agger, et al., *The Rulers and the Ruled*. They urge the necessity of defining community power structure in terms of two

dimensions, the distribution of power and leadership ideology. In other words, whether power is broadly or narrowly distributed is only a partial element of an account of community power structure. It is also vital to know whether the ideological perspectives of leaders are convergent or divergent. Thus, for instance, even if power appears widely distributed, similar ideological perspectives will constrain some options, issues, and groups, and promote others.

93. Hans Gerth and Ernest Branstadt, eds., *Freedom, Power, and Democratic Planning* (London: Routledge & Kegan Paul, 1950), p. 138. The quote from Mannheim and a somewhat similar use of the concept appear in William Connolly, *Political Science and Ideology* (New York: Atherton, 1967), p. 45.

94. Edelman, *The Symbolic Uses of Politics*, p. 105.

95. See Terry N. Clark, "Community Structure, Decision-Making, Budget Expenditures and Urban Renewal in 51 American Communities," *American Sociological Review*, 33 (August 1968), 576–593; Robert Crain and Donald Rosenthal, "Community Status as a Dimension of Local Decision Making," *American Sociological Review*, 32 (December 1967), 970–984; William Gamson, "Rancorous Conflict in Community Politics," *American Sociological Review*, 31 (February 1966), 71–81; John Kessel, "Government Structure and Political Environment," *American Political Science Review*, 56 (September 1962), 615–620; David Minar, "The Community Basis of Conflict in School System Politics," *American Sociology Review*, 31 (December 1966), 822–835; and Peter Rossi, "Power and Community Structure," *Midwest Journal of Political Science*, 4 (November 1960), 390–401, among others. Also see the theoretical review essays by Michael Aiken, "The Distribution of Community Power: Structural Bases and Social Consequences," in Michael Aiken and Paul E. Mott, eds., *The Structure of Community Power*, pp. 487–525; Terry N. Clark, "Community Structure and Decision-Making," in Clark, *Community Structure and Decision-Making;* Peter Friedman, "Community Decision-Making in the United States: A Review of Recent Research," *The New Atlantis*, 1 (Winter 1970), 133–142; Claire W. Gilbert, "Community Power and Decision-Making: A Quantitative Examination of Previous Research," also in Clark, pp. 139–156; and John Walton, "A Systematic Survey of Community Power Research," also in Aiken and Mott, pp. 443–469.

96. Oliver P. Williams and Charles R. Adrian, *Four Cities: A Study in Comparative Policy Making* (Philadelphia: University of Pennsylvania Press, 1963). Also see Raymond Wolfinger and John Field, "Political Ethos and the Structure of City Government," *American Political Science Review*, 60 (June 1966), 306–326, and Edward Banfield and James Wilson, *City Politics* (Cambridge, Mass.: Harvard University and M.I.T. Press, 1963). See Friedman for citations to issues raised in the last two items.

97. Pilisuk, "Is There a Military-Industrial Complex Which Prevents Peace?" p. 122, utilizes in part a quote from Bell.

98. See Thomas J. Anton, "Power Pluralism and Local Politics," *Ad-*

ministrative Science Quarterly, 7 (March 1963), 425–457. In a somewhat related yet distinctive vein, power also represents the ability of a social system and, more narrowly, particular groups therein to achieve particular ends and purposes. Power, however, as the property of a social system or its major collectivities, rather than of individual actors or roles, is not the sense in which the concept is used in studies of community power structure or decision making. This appears true for pluralist as well as unitary conceptions and studies of power structure.

99. See Andrew S. McFarland, *Power and Leadership in Pluralist Systems* (Stanford, Calif.: Stanford University Press, 1969), Chap. 4, "Spurious Pluralism," and Chap. 5, "Critical and Routine Decisions."

100. Ibid; James W. Fesler, "Approaches to the Understanding of Decentralization, *Journal of Politics,* 27 (August 1965), 536–566, especially 555–557.

101. Ibid; see also Herbert Kaufman's study, *The Forest Ranger* (Baltimore, Md.: Johns Hopkins Press, 1960). In this regard, the reader, if not already familiar with this material, may find some good summary analyses in McFarland and in Felser and more extended treatment in the references cited there.

102. McFarland, ibid., p. 55.

103. Schattschneider, *The Semi-Sovereign State.* He writes: "All forms of political organization have a bias in favor of the exploitation of some kinds of conflict and the suppression of others because *organization is the mobilization of bias.* Some issues are organized into politics while others are organized out" (p. 71).

See especially Chap. 3, "Whose Game Do We Play?" and Chap. 4, "Displacement of Conflicts" in Schattschneider for pertinent discussion. Peter Bachrach and Morton S. Baratz have defined a "mobilization of bias" as "a set of predominant values, beliefs, rituals and institutional procedures ("rules of the game") that operate systematically and consistently to the benefit of certain persons and groups at the expense of others. Those who benefit are placed in a preferred position to defend and promote their vested interests." *Power and Poverty* (New York: Oxford University Press, 1970), p. 43.

104. Bachrach and Baratz, "Two Faces of Power."

105. Peter Bachrach and Morton S. Baratz, "Decisions and Non-Decisions: An Analytic Framework," *American Political Science Review,* 5 (September 1963), 632–642. The authors state in *Power and Poverty:*

> The primary method for sustaining a given mobilization of bias is nondecision-making. A nondecision as we define it is a decision that results in suppression or thwarting of a latent or manifest challenge to the values or interest of the decision-maker. To be more nearly explicit, nondecision-making is a means by which demands for change in existing allocation of benefits and privileges in the community can be suffocated before they are even voiced; or kept covert; or killed

before they gain access to the relevant decision-making arena; or failing all these things, maimed or destroyed in the decision-implementing stage of the policy process. (p. 44)

For some discussion and criticism of the concepts introduced by Bachrach and Baratz see Richard M. Merelman, "On the Neo-Elitist Critique of Community Power," *American Political Science Review*, 62 (June 1968), 451–461; Raymond E. Wolfinger, "Nondecisions and the Study of Local Politics," *American Political Science Review*, 65 (December 1971), 1063–1080; Frederick W. Frey, "Comment: On Issues and Nonissues in the Study of Power," *American Political Science Review*, 65 (December 1971), 1081–1101 and, Wolfinger's rejoinder, pp. 1102–1104.

106. Michael Parenti, *The Anti-Communist Impulse* (New York: Random House, 1969), p. 101.

107. Pilisuk, "Is There a Military-Industrial Complex Which Prevents Peace?" pp. 125–126.

108. In his *The State in Capitalist Society* Miliband has forcefully made the closely related point that the range of difference over issues among major political leaders in the advanced capitalist countries is seldom fundamental, while their agreement on vital issues is great. See especially Chap. 4, "The Purposes and Role of Governments."

109. See citation in Hanna F. Pitkin, ed., *Representation* (New York: Atherton, 1969), p. 198, for a succinct bibliography of relevant discussions. Pitkin's collection of representative classical statements provides a number of diverse views by leading political theorists. Also see the study by Heinz Eulau and Kenneth Prewitt, "Political Matrix and Political Representation," *The American Political Science Review*, 63 (June 1969), 427–441, and an earlier item by Heinz Eulau, et al., "The Role of the Representative: Some Empirical Observations on the Theory of Edmund Burke," *American Political Science Review*, 53 (September 1959), 742–756.

110. Various students in a diversity of contexts have provided effective illustration of how political behavior has varied with the degree of political representation. See Stein Rokkan's fine essay, "Mass Suffrage and Secret Voting and Political Participation," *European Journal of Sociology*, 11 (1961), 132–152; Bruce Miller, *The Political Role of Labor in Developing Countries* (Washington, D.C.: The Brookings Institute, 1963); Joseph Raffaele, *Labor Leadership in Italy and Denmark* (Madison, Wis.: University of Wisconsin Press, 1962); Gaston Rimlinger, "The Legitimation of Protest: A Comparative Study," *Comparative Studies in Society and History*, 2 (1960), 329–343, and "International Differences in the Strike Propensity of Coal Miners: Experience in Four Countries," *Industrial Labor Relations Review*, 12 (1959), 389–405. The absence of representation has been perceived in a number of additional ways as exacerbating conflict and protest. James Coleman's analysis of community conflict, *Community Conflict* (New York: Free Press, 1957), has noted the effect of the lack of representation on community controversy and behavior. Numerous observa-

tions on student unrest in the United States have pointed to the relationship between the absence of representation and access to decision-making centers and consequent vigorous protest. Following the contribution of Simmel, Lewis Coser has elaborated upon a number of points related to the correspondence suggested here between representation and the characteristics of protest or conflict behavior. See his *Functions of Social Conflict* (Glencoe, Ill.: Free Press, 1957).

111. See Henry Pelling, *Origins of the Labour Party, 1880–1900,* 2nd ed. (Oxford: Clarendon Press, 1965).

112. See Guenther Roth, *The Social Democrats in Imperial Germany, a Study in Working Class Isolation and National Integration* (Totowa, N.J.: Bedminister Press, 1963).

113. Kariel, "Pluralism," p. 167.

114. See the discussion in Isaac Balbus "The Concept of Interest in Pluralist and Marxian Analysis," *Politics and Society* (February 1971), 151–177. In pluralist analysis, interest assumes a subjective character, and where it is unrecognized by the individual or the larger group of which he may be a part, it is not a legitimate object for action or policy. This has mitigated against a conceptualization of interest in terms of the broader community as an objective public need. Thus there is little sense of the propriety or distinctive quality of what could be called "public interests." We have already noted the serious consequences involved in such a conceptualization, when the ends of well-organized yet narrow entities are well served in theory and practice while the recognition and action on the broader and often more basic needs of the society receive little support in either policy or theoretical justification for state activism. Balbus has pointed to related consequences of the subjective criteria of interest.

115. While the pluralist formulation has the specious appearance of excluding any bias or value judgments, these are nonetheless present. They reside in a conceptualization that in effect postulates certain given ends and concerns – those that constitute a condition requisite for the achievement of organized interest group purposes – but it excludes any statement of purpose directed toward "a more humane and more rationally organized society" (Christian Bay, "Politics and Pseudo-Politics, A Critical Evaluation of Some Behavioral Literature," *American Political Science Review,* 59 [March 1965], 39–51, especially p. 44).

116. See Truman, *The Governmental Process,* pp. 50–51; Bentley, *The Process of Government;* Wilfred Binkley and Malcom Moos, *A Grammar of American Politics* (New York: Knopf, 1950), pp. 8–9; Herring, *The Politics of Democracy,* pp. 424–425; and Norton Long, "The Community as an Ecology of Games," *American Journal of Sociology,* 69 (November 1958), 251–261. For a more general treatment denying the viability of a notion such as the public interest, see Frank Sarauf, "Public Interest Reconsidered," *Journal of Politics,* 19 (November 1957), 616–639; also see Gordon A. Schubert, *The Public Interest: A Critique of the Theory of a Political Concept* (New York: Free Press, 1961), and John D. B. Miller,

The Nature of Politics (London: Duckworth, 1962), especially Chap. 3 and 4.

117. Latham, p. 14.

118. Lowi, *The End of Liberalism*, pp. 48–49; see his discussion, pp. 46–54. Lowi stresses that there is absent in the practice of pluralist politics a condition in which government serves to carry out public will through a nonpoliticized administrative process. By making government merely an extension of the political process, this possibility is denied. Thus even the carrying out of whatever can at times become defined as public policy becomes open to political pressures, manipulation, and a give and take among organized interest constituencies. In effect, the process of administration itself becomes an arena of contending groups similar to the condition prevailing in the political legislative arena.

119. McConnell, *Private Power and American Democracy*, p. 360.

120. Ibid., pp. 365–366.

121. In a sense, almost any area can be defined in such a manner and be perceived, therefore, as partaking of the character of public interest. However, for practical purposes and without requiring too sharp a change in prevailing perceptions of the role of government, the application of the concept of public interest may be established if a sense of quantitative difference – leading in effect to qualitative difference – is used. Thus reference is to a significant transcendence of a particular group constituency and to the presence of significant consequences for the members of society. Certainly, the type of public interests noted partake of these qualities.

122. See Lindblom, *The Intelligence of Democracy*, and David Braybrooke and Charles Lindblom, *A Strategy of Decision* (New York: Free Press, 1963). However, for the view that at certain distinct historical periods and elections especially wide-ranging and significant political change has occurred, in the form of electoral realignment greater than that encompassed in the notion of incrementalism, see W. O. Key's noted essay, "A Theory of Critical Elections," *Journal of Politics*, 17 (February 1955), 3–18, and Burnham, *Critical Elections and the Mainsprings of American Politics*.

123. See Lowi, *The End of Liberalism*, pp. 50–51, for some relevant discussion.

124. David Kettler, "The Politics of Social Change: The Relevance of Democratic Approaches," in Connolly, pp. 213–249.

125. Lowi, *The End of Liberalism*, p. 51.

126. See Arthur I. Waskow, *From Race Riot to Sit-in* (Garden City, N.Y.: Anchor-Doubleday, 1967), paperback.

127. See David H. Bayley, "The Pedagogy of Democracy: Coercive Public Protest in India," *American Political Science Review*, 58 (September 1962), 663–672.

128. It may be reasonable to maintain that under some circumstances when pluralist diversity is of a crosscutting character, the possible retardation of unrestricted concentrations of great power minimizes some dis-

ruptive phenomena. Yet this is far from contributing significantly to a cohesive society. It may also be true that overlapping loyalties potentially mitigate the development of unrestrained protest or the strength of commitment to or involvement in particular issues. However, this would appear to hold principally only under certain particular conditions of political responsiveness, the nature of interest need, the character of group loyalties, and the nature of some of the properties of the broader political culture. Lacking these, conflict may still be extremely vigorous.

129. Gusfield, "Mass Society and Extremist Politics," *American Sociological Review,* 27 (February 1962), 19–30.

130. Ibid.

131. Connolly, "The Challenge to Pluralist Theory," p. 21.

132. A number of different expressions other than "contemporary democratic theory" have been used: "democratic elitism" by Peter Bachrach, *The Theory of Democratic Elitism: A Critique* (Boston: Little, Brown, 1967), and by Jack Walker, "A Critique of the Elitist Theory of Democracy," *American Political Science Review* 60 (June 1966), 285–295; "the new democracy" by Graeme Duncan and Steven Lukes, "The New Democracy," *Political Studies,* 2 (June 1963), 156–177; and the "the contemporary theory of democracy" by Carole Pateman, *Participation and Democratic Theory* (Cambridge University Press, 1970). The present text uses the terms "contemporary democratic theory" and "democratic elitism," principally the former. There is a variety of relatively recent writings expressing either sympathy to classical democratic theory or criticism of elements in contemporary democratic theory. See Peter Bachrach, "Elite Consensus and Democracy," *Journal of Politics,* 24 (1962), 439–442, "Corporate Authority and Democratic Theory" and *The Theory of Democratic Elitism;* Pateman, *Participation and Democratic Theory;* Lane Davis, "The Costs of Realism: Contemporary Restatements of Democracy," *Western Political Quarterly,* 17 (March 1964), 37–46; Duncan and Lukes, "The New Democracy"; George H. Sabine, "The Two Democratic Traditions," *The Philosophical Review,* 61 (1952), 441–474; Christian Bay, *The Structure of Freedom* (Stanford: Stanford University Press, 1958), and "Politics and Pseudopolitics"; T. B. Bottomore, "Democracy and the Plurality of Elites," Chap. 6 in *Elites and Society* (Harmondsworth, Middlesex: Penguin Books, 1966); John Dewey, *The Public and Its Problems* (Chicago: Gateway Press, 1946); Henry S. Kariel, *The Decline of American Pluralism;* Sheldon Wolin, *Politics and Vision* (Boston: Little, Brown, 1960). Also see the selection of essays compiled by Henry S. Kariel, ed., *Frontiers of Democratic Theory* (New York: Random House, 1970).

133. The reader may recognize that the perspectives on democratic theory in some mass theorists are not clearly a statement of either classical or contemporary democratic theory. A certain ambiguity is introduced in that the theoretical persuasion of the theorists would rest on the degree and nature of citizen involvement. Though this is generally not explored, the probable commitment appears to be to contemporary democratic

theory. Mass theory writings convey a sense of caution in regard to citizen political involvement and offer little stimulus for participatory forms.

134. Bernard Berelson, "Democratic Theory and Public Opinion," *Public Opinion Quarterly*, 16 (Fall 1952), 313–330; also see Bernard Berelson, Paul Lazarsfeld, William McPhee, "Democratic Practice and Voting," Chap. 14 in *Voting* (Chicago: University of Chicago Press, 1954).

135. See Eugene Burdick, Chap. 6, "Political Theory and the Voting Studies," in Eugene Burdick and Arthur J. Brodbeck, eds., *American Voting Behavior* (New York: Free Press, 1960), and Talcott Parsons, Chap. 4, "'Voting' and the Equilibrium of the American Political System," ibid.; Robert Dahl, "Hierarchy, Democracy and Bargaining in Politics and Economics," in Heinz Eulau, Samuel J. Eldersveld, and Morris Janowitz, eds., *Political Behavior* (Glencoe, Ill.: Free Press, 1956), 83–90; and John Plamenatz, "Electoral Studies and Democratic Theory," *Political Studies* 6 (1958), 1–9.

136. The presumed objectivity or neutrality of the scholarship cited here is questionable. In effect, a standard of adequacy is being applied to the functioning of the political system. This presumes some value criteria; and clearly, whether one's evaluation is a positive or negative one will depend on these criteria. (For an insightful critique of Berelson, Lazarsfeld, and McPhee see Walter Berns, "A Critique of Berelson, Lazersfeld, and McPhee *Voting*," in Herbert J. Storing, ed., *Essays on the Scientific Study of Politics* [New York: Holt, Rinehart and Winston, 1962], 1–62.) Further, the criteria do not include any reference to individual or group needs or even societal needs other than ones related to a condition of equilibrium and stability. Yet, as Bachrach has pointed out, the democratic political system cannot be taken as an end in itself. (See Bachrach, *The Theory of Democratic Elitism*, pp. 33–35.) Nor is it necessarily true that a stable democratic government will even provide a wide degree of liberty for its members.

137. See the citations in note 132.

138. Disaffection is not, of course, avoided only by participatory forms. Also, where effective and responsive political leadership exists, the need for participatory structures to minimize disaffection is considerably reduced. Actually, the extent and circumstances in which participatory forms assume greater or lesser importance have yet to be worked out. However, one function of such structures and practice would reasonably appear to be greater personal and political satisfaction, especially where adequate leadership is lacking and a sense of powerlessness is high.

Chapter 7. Concluding comments: ideological bias and directions for research

1. John Horton's fine essay, "Order and Conflict Theories of Social Problems," *American Journal of Sociology*, 71 (May 1966), 701–713, provides a clear outline of some of the contrasting perspectives comprehended

by the order–conflict dichotomy. Also note Leon Bramson's "distinction between sociologies of conservation and equilibrium on the one hand and sociologies of change on the other" (*The Political Context of Sociology* [Princeton, N.J.: Princeton University Press, 1961], pp. 17–18), and Barrington Moore's discussion of theories of equilibrium and process, "Strategy in Social Science," in *Political Theory and Social Theory* (Cambridge, Mass.: Harvard University Press, 1958), pp. 11–51.

2. Bramson has related this perspective to the early European conservative origins of sociology generally and suggests that there is here a "kind of bias that may be intrinsic to the sociological enterprise" (ibid., p. 11). Robert Nisbet, an eminent theorist of mass society, helps confirm the line of reasoning developed here by locating the foundation of sociology in "the concept of the social group and the problem of social disorganization." The quote is from "The French Revolution and the Rise of Sociology," *American Journal of Sociology*, 49 (September 1943), p. 160, as quoted in Bramson, 12n. In addition, note Nisbet's own work, *The Quest of Community* (New York: Oxford University Press, 1953).

3. Bramson, *The Political Context of Sociology*, pp. 13–14.

4. See John Horton and Wayne Thompson, "Powerlessness and Political Negativism: A Study of Defeated Local Referendums," *American Journal of Sociology*, 67 (March 1962), pp. 482–493 (published by University of Chicago Press); and John Horton, "The Dehumanization of Anomie and Alienation," 15 *British Journal of Sociology* (December 1964), pp. 283–300.

5. Horton and Thompson, ibid., p. 486n.

6. Of course, alienation in the sense of estrangement from existing political groups and institutions is recognized by the mass theorist, certainly in mass society and, to an extent, in pluralist society. But this is often seen as an anomic problem, of the need to reestablish relationships or to "cool off" discontent. Passing allusion to increasing power or altered authority relationships may be made, but little analytical treatment or elaboration is provided.

7. See Bernard Berelson, Paul Lazarsfeld, William McPhee, *Voting* (Chicago: University of Chicago Press, 1954), Chap. 14, "Democratic Practice and Voting."

8. See the related discussion in Isaac D. Balbus, "The Concept of Interest in Pluralist and Marxian Analysis," *Politics and Society*, 1 (February 1971), 151–177.

9. Christian Bay, "Politics and Pseudopolitics: A Critical Evaluation of Some Behavioral Literature," *American Political Science Review*, 59 (March 1965), pp. 39–51.

10. Walker, p. 293.

11. See Arthur I. Waskow's discussion in Chaps. 7, 15, and 16 of his *From Race Riot to Sit-in* (Garden City, N.Y.: Anchor-Doubleday, 1967), paperback. Also note David H. Bayley's essay "The Pedagogy of Democracy: Coercive Public Protest in India," *American Political Science Review*,

58 (September 1962), 663–672. Bayley notes three attributes of coercive public protest: "(1) it is aggregative; (2) it is public, as opposed to conspiratorial or clandestine; and (3) it imposes a constraint upon government by its presence and actions" (p. 663).

12. Bayley, ibid., p. 663.

13. The quoted phrase comes from Joseph Lyford's description in *The Airtight Cage* (New York: Harper & Row, 1966), p. 338. Creative disorder or coercive public protest may usually be understood as a means of achieving some interest-based goal, usually in circumstances in which present political forms or leadership has been perceived as inadequately responsive. In some instances, it has appeared as a means of moral protest against immoral policies or leadership. At times, of course, behavior in response to moral concerns may also exhibit an important element of suasion and hence be related in character to the former circumstances. It may also appear as an unreasonable or ill-conceived response to grievances – real or imagined – in regard to which it lacks any possible effectiveness.

14. Lewis Coser, *Continuities in the Study of Social Conflict* (New York: Free Press, 1967), p. 86.

Index

mechanical to organic solidarity,
27–8
sociological analysis of, 24–35
urbanization, 26–7
Spain, 102, 103, 221
specialization, 27
Southeast Asia, 102
Stalin, J., 17
state, 13, 18, 29, 62, 185, 186, 187
distinguished from society, 64
status, 94, 97, 104, 107, 111, 112,
115, 122
conflict, 98–101
consistency, 138
insecurity, 98
panic, 98
status-culture, 99–101, 115
theory, 6
student protest, 1, 97, 125
suffrage, growth of, 48; *see also*
democratization
symbolic politics, 100, 106
system stability, *see* pluralist theory
Switzerland, 102

Taine, H., 33
Talmon, J., 14, 17–18
Tarde, G., 33
temperance crusade, 99
Thompson, W., 58, 111, 236
Tilly, C., 117, 119, 126, 129, 132,
134
Tocqueville, A. de, 19, 20, 22, 186
on centralization and diffusion of
power, 20–3
on dangers to freedom, 20–3
on democracy, 20–3
on functions of voluntary associations, 22–3
Tönnies, F., 24, 25, 26, 27, 28
totalitarian democracy, 11, 14, 17;
see also authoritarianism; repression; totalitarianism
totalitarianism, 1, 4, 21–2, 36, 59–61;
see also authoritarianism;
mass behavior; repression;

totalitarian democracy
basis of domination, 59–60
conditions for appearance, 59
nature of control, 60–1
support of, 60
trade union movement, 239
Trevor-Roper, H., 170
Truman, D., 187, 188
Tucker, W., 196
tyranny of the majority, 20, 21

United States, 5, 57, 63, 103, 106,
108, 117, 131, 132, 158, 174,
177, 199
pluralist theory in, 182–231
uprooted populations, 6, 38, 53, 54;
see also isolation, social
urban unrest, 129
urbanization, 27, 40, 47, 119, 122,
134, 241
utilitarianism, 10, 11, 15, 19; *see
also* enlightenment; philosophes

value-consensus theory, 95
Verba, S., 72
vertical integration, 3, 40; *see also*
scale, extension of
Viereck, P., 135
Voltaire, F., 15

Wales, 108
Walloons, 102
Walter, E., 33, 44
Wanderer, J., 117
Waskow, A., 242
Weber, M., 25, 30–2
white-collar population, 48
Wildavsky, A., 187, 217
Wilensky, H., 77
Williams, O., 216
Wolf, E., 117
Wolin, S., 31
Woodward, C. V., 136
working class, 48, 115, 125, 128,
139, 221, 239; *see also* Chile,
France, Germany

Zeitlan, M., 144